Jane's

THE BEAT OFFICER'S COMPANION

13th Edition

Gordon Wilson

BA (Law), MSc

Contents

Preface 11

Chapter 1: Crime 13
Criminal attempts 14
Theft 15
Removal of articles from places open to the public 19
Taking a conveyance without authority 20
Vehicle interference 21
Abstracting electricity 22
Robbery 23
Burglary 24
Aggravated burglary 24
Fraud 25
Retaining a wrongful credit 33
False Accounting 34
Blackmail 36
Suppression etc of documents 37
Making off without paying 38
Handling stolen goods 39
Going equipped 40
Assault 41
Female genital mutilation 47
Homicide 48
Causing death of a child or vulnerable adult 49
Damage 50
Drugs 53

Chapter 2: Sexual Offences 63
Rape 64
Assault by penetration 65
Sexual assault 66
Engaging in sexual activity without consent 67
Exposure 67
Offences against children under 13 68
Child sex offences 69
Abuse of position of trust 71
Familial child sex offences 73

Contents

Offences against persons with a mental disorder	75
Inducements etc to persons with a mental disorder	76
Care workers for persons with a mental disorder	77
Abuse of children through prostitution or pornography	78
Indecent photographs	79
Indecent displays	80
Obscene publications	81
Harmful publications	82
Prostitution	83
Kerb-crawling	84
Advertising prostitution	85
Brothels	86
Premises used for the purposes of sex	87
Exploitation of prostitution	88
Trafficking for sexual exploitation	89
Preparatory offences	90
Sex with an adult relative	91
Voyeurism	92
Intercourse with an animal	93
Sexual penetration of a corpse	94
Sexual activity in a public lavatory	94
Offences outside the United Kingdom	94
Presumptions about consent	96
Sexual offences – interpretation	97
Notification requirements for sex offenders	98
Chapter 3: Firearms and explosives	101
Firearms – definitions	102
Firearms certificates	106
Shotguns	109
Criminal use of firearms	110
Firearms dealers	112
Possession of firearms	113
Miscellaneous offences	114
Firearms – ages	115
Police powers	116

Contents

Chapter 4: Licensing	117
Gambling Act – principles	118
Gambling licences	119
Gaming	125
Betting	133
Lotteries	135
Cross-category activities	138
Gaming machines	139
Temporary use of premises	143
General Offences	144
Children and young persons, gambling	145
Children and young persons, employment	147
Gambling – enforcement and powers	149
Licensable activities	157
The premises licence	159
The Club premises certificate	161
Permitted temporary activities	163
Personal licences	165
Unauthorised licensable activities	167
Drunkenness and disorderly conduct	168
Children and alcohol	170
Closure orders	177
Exemptions	179
Police powers and definitions	180
Drunks in public places	181
Alcohol consumption in designated public places	182
Public charitable collections	183
Street and house-to-house collections	184
Chapter 5: Animals	185
Animal welfare	186
Unnecessary suffering	187
Mutilation	188
Docking of Dogs' tails	189
Administration of poisons, etc.	190
Animal fights	191

Contents

Welfare of animals	193
Sale of animals to children	194
Animals in distress	195
Police powers	197
Cruelty to wild mammals	199
Protection of wild animals	200
Protection of plants	202
Sale of dogs	203
Dogs	204
Dangerous wild animals	211
Animals on highways	212
Diseases of animals	213
Importation of animals	216
Pet travel scheme	217
Game licences	218
Poaching	220
Deer	224
Badgers	229
Birds	231
Fish	238
Seals	242
Hunting	243
Chapter 6: People	247
Children and young persons	248
Armed forces	257
Immigration	259
Mental health	262
Pedlars	263
Scrap metal dealers	264
Motor salvage operators	265
Vagrancy	266
Police	268
Chapter 7: Public order	269
Litter	270
Abandoning vehicles etc	271

Contents

Noise	272
Trade disputes	273
Peaceful picketing	274
Fear or provocation of violence	275
Harassment, alarm or distress	276
Harassment intended to deter lawful activities	278
Prevention of harassment in the home	279
Animal research organisations	281
Dispersal of groups	283
Seizure of vehicles causing annoyance etc	284
Football offences	285
Banning orders	286
Sporting events – control	287
Football ticket touts	289
Offensive weapons	290
Marketing of knives	293
Stop and search for knives or offensive weapons	295
Removal of disguises	296
Crossbows	297
Fireworks	298
Racially or religiously aggravated offences	299
Racial hatred	300
Trespassers on land	301
Aggravated trespass	302
Trespassory Assemblies	304
Trespassing on protected site	305
Demonstrating in designated area	306
Power to direct a person to leave a place	306
Raves	308
Violent entry to premises	310
Squatters	311
Trespassing with an offensive weapon	312
Affray	313
Riot/violent disorder	314
Public meetings	315
Uniforms	316
Organisations	317

Contents

Chemical weapons 318
Biological weapons 319
Terrorism – interpretation 320
Terrorism – offences 321
Terrorism – disclosure of information 334
Terrorism – investigations 335
Terrorism – police powers 336
Terrorism – stop and search 337
Terrorism – restrictions on parking 338
Terrorism – proscribed organisations 339
Terrorism – nuclear weapons 340
Terrorism – use of noxious substances 341
Terrorism – hoaxes involving noxious substances 342
Terrorism – control orders 343
Fraudulent use of telecommunications system 344
Postal offences 346
Malicious communications 347
Improper use of public telecommunication system 348
Bomb hoaxes 349
Contamination of goods 350
Taxi touts 351
Computer misuse 352
Intimidation of witnesses, jurors and others 353

Chapter 8: Procedure 355
Cautions 356
Adverse inferences 357
Interviews 359
Written statements under caution 363
Interpreters 365
Powers of arrest 367
Bail elsewhere than at a police station 372
Conduct of a search 374
Records of searches 380
Recording of encounters 381
Summary of main stop and search powers 383
Stop and search 385

Contents

Entry and search of premises	387
Seizure to prevent loss etc	389
Powers of seizure	390
Search upon arrest	393
Search warrants	394
Road checks	395
Stop and search (serious violence)	396
Stop and search at aerodromes	397
Identification methods	398
Identification by witnesses	399
Identification by witnesses – videos	401
Identification by witnesses – identification parades	402
Identification by witnesses – group identification	403
Identification by witnesses – confrontation	404
Identification by witnesses – photographs	404
Identification by other methods	405
Chapter 9: Detention and treatment of persons	409
Custody officers – qualification	410
Custody records	411
Responsibility for detained persons	412
Custody officers – initial action	413
Legal advice	415
Notification of arrest	417
Delays to legal advice or notification of arrest	418
Treatment of detained persons	419
Conditions of detention	421
Fingerprinting	422
Photographing of suspects	423
Intimate searches	424
X-rays and ultrasound scans for drugs	428
Searches to ascertain identity	429
Intimate samples	430
Non-intimate samples	431
Testing for drugs	432
Limits on detention	435
Reviews of detention	436

Contents

Limits on periods of detention without charge	437
Continued detention	438
Warrant of further detention	439
Duties before charge	440
Charging	441
Duties after charge	443
Extradition – treatment of arrested persons	444
Chronological table of legislation	450
Index	469

Further titles available:

- Part I Promotion Crammer for Sergeants and Inspectors
- Part II Pass for Promotion for Sergeants and Inspectors
- The Traffic Officer's Companion
- The Scottish Beat Officer's Companion

To order or for further details phone +44 (0) 20 8700 3700 or fax +44 (0) 20 8763 1006

By the same author
The Traffic Officer's Companion

1st edition 1983
2nd edition 1986
3rd edition 1988
4th edition 1992
5th edition 1994
reprinted 1996
reprinted 1997
6th edition 1998
7th edition 2000
8th edition 2002
9th edition 2003
10th edition 2004
11th edition 2005
12th edition 2006
13th edition 2007

ISBN 978-0-7106-2822-0

Jane's Information Group
Sentinel House
163 Brighton Road
Coulsdon
Surrey CR5 2YH

Printed and bound in Great Britain by
Cambridge University Press

Cover image courtesy of West Mercia Constabulary

Preface

This book is presented in a manner similar to that adopted by The Traffic Officer's Companion. The diagrammatic and pictorial format provides an easily read and understandable interpretation of those aspects of legislation, other than traffic laws, likely to be of practical value to the patrolling police officer. Readers wishing to avail themselves of a similar presentation of traffic legislation are referred to the Traffic Officer's Companion.

The problems encountered by the present-day officer in memorising, interpreting, recalling and making decisions upon an ever-increasing field of legislation are not underestimated. The intention of this book has therefore been to provide a practical and speedy reference to those aspects likely to be of operational value.

Because the book is intended to serve merely as a guide to the operational police officer, the relevant legislation has been subjected to a practical interpretation. It has been necessary to be selective in the material used and the book should not, therefore, be regarded as a definitive work of reference. Specific technical details may require further research.

In this edition the main changes have been brought about by:

1. **The Proscribed Organisations (Name Changes) Order 2006 (S.I. 2006/1919)** which added new names under which certain proscribed organisations are known.
2. **The Terrorism Act 2000 (Proscribed Organisations) (Amendment) Order 2006 (S.I. 2006/2016)** which added a number of new organisations to the list of those proscribed.
3. **Code of practice – Code H** which deals with the detention of terrorist suspects. Code C is also amended to remove reference to such persons.
4. **The Gambling Act 2005** which substantially changes the laws of betting, gaming and lotteries, and introduces the concepts of operating, premises and personal licences.
5. **The Gambling Act (Mandatory and Default Conditions) (England and Wales) Regulations 2007** which attaches various conditions to premises licensed under the Act.
6. **The Fraud Act 2006** which repealed a number of the 'deception' offences in the Theft Acts 1968 (Ss 15, 15A, 16 and 20(2) and 1978 (Ss 1 and 2), and introduced new offences of committing fraud by false representation, by failing to disclose information, and by abuse of position. It also created new offences of obtaining services dishonestly, possessing, making and supplying articles for use in fraud, and fraudulent trading by non-corporate traders.

Preface

7. **The Animal Welfare Act 2006** which repeals most of the cruelty to animals provisions contained in the Protection of Animals Act 1911, together with other provisions e.g. cockfighting. These offences are replaced by a number of provisions which include unnecessary suffering, mutilation, docking of dogs' tails, administering poisons, fighting, welfare, and sale to children.
8. **The Sexual Offences Act 2003 (Amendment of Schedules 3 and 5) Order 2007** which added offences for which, under certain conditions, an offender may be subject to the notification requirements.
9. **The Police and Justice Act 2006** which gives custody officers a power to detain pending the DPP's decision to charge. It introduces a new power to stop and search at aerodromes. It also amends the provisions of PACE relating to bail granted elsewhere than at a police station.
10. **The Violent Crime Reduction Act 2006** which introduced various offences relating to alcohol, weapons, firearms and ammunition, football ticket touts, and the re-programming of mobile telephones.
11. **The Children and Young Persons (Sale of Tobacco, etc.) Order 2007** which increases the age for the sale of tobacco to 18.
12. **The Ticket Touting (Designation of Football Matches) Order 2007** which designated matches in connection with the offence of ticket touting under the Criminal Justice and Public Order Act 1994.
13. **The Serious Organised Crime and Police Act 2005 (Designated Sites under Section 128) Order 2007** which added to the list of designated sites.

Gordon Wilson
Former Superintendent, Warwickshire Constabulary

Chapter 1

Crime

Criminal Attempts

S 1 CRIMINAL ATTEMPTS ACT 1981

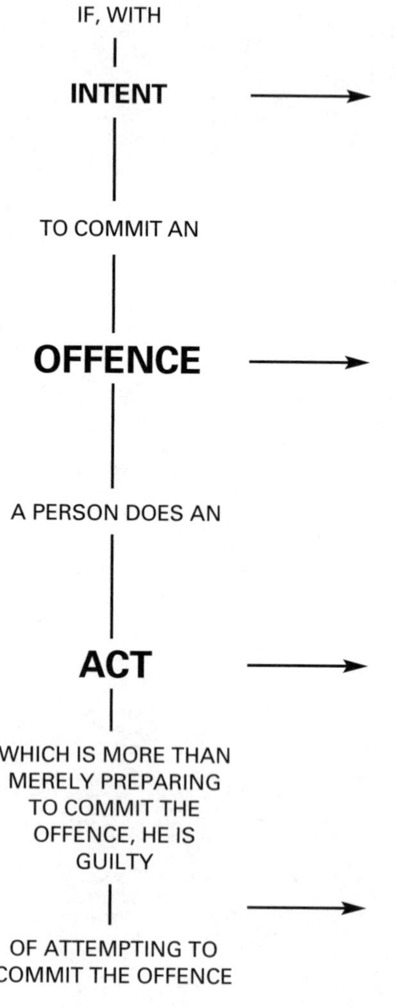

Even though the facts are such that the commission of the offence is impossible

Any offence which, if it were completed, would be triable as an indictable offence in England and Wales, except:

- conspiracy
- aiding, abetting, counselling or procuring or suborning an offence
- assisting offenders or agreeing not to disclose information about arrestable offences

Where a person carries out acts in the *mistaken* belief that he is committing an offence, he will be guilty of an attempt to commit that offence

The powers to arrest and search are the same as they would have been for the full offence

Theft

S 1 THEFT ACT 1968

The essential ingredients of the offence of theft are outlined below and discussed in a little more depth in the following pages

A person will be guilty of theft if he:

- **DISHONESTLY**
- **APPROPRIATES**
- **PROPERTY**
- **BELONGING TO ANOTHER**
- **WITH THE INTENTION TO PERMANENTLY DEPRIVE**

It is immaterial whether the appropriation is made with a view to gain, or is made for the thief's own benefit.

ADVERTISING REWARDS for the return of stolen goods and using words like "no questions will be asked", "safe from apprehension or enquiry" or "money paid for their purchase will be repaid" constitutes an offence (S 23)

Dishonestly

S 2 THEFT ACT 1968

The appropriation of property will not be regarded as 'dishonest' if:

- he believed he had the right in law to take it, or
- he believed he would have had the owner's consent, had the owner known about it, or
- the owner cannot be discovered by taking reasonable steps (except where the property came to him as trustee or personal representative)

but even if he intended to pay for it, it could amount to dishonesty.

Appropriates

S 3 THEFT ACT 1968

An appropriation is any assumption of the rights of an owner.

This includes the case where he comes by the property without stealing it (even if he does so innocently) and later treats it as his own.

But where he gives value for the property in good faith, any later assumption by him of the rights he believed he was acquiring shall not, because of any defect in the vendor's title to the property, amount to theft.

Property

S 4 THEFT ACT 1968

The term 'property' includes money and all other property, real or personal (including things in action and other intangible property)
– but special provisions relate to the following:

Personal property includes the printed paper on which a cheque is written or upon which an examination or other confidential information is written; and other intangible property such as debts and shares in a company.

Land and things forming part of land and severed from it cannot be stolen except:

- by a trustee, personal representative, etc by dealing with it in breach of the confidence reposed in him
- by a person not in possession of it who appropriates something forming part of the land by severing it
- by a person in possession under a tenancy who takes fixtures or structures let with the land

Mushrooms or flowers, fruit or foliage from a plant (but not the plant itself) growing wild cannot be stolen unless for reward, sale or commercial use.

Electricity cannot be stolen but see S 13 later.

Wild creatures or the carcass of wild creatures cannot be stolen if not tamed and not ordinarily kept in captivity unless they have been caught and not since lost or abandoned.

Belonging to Another S 5 THEFT ACT 1968

In normal situations it is obvious who is the owner of the property but sometimes there are complications. The law has therefore defined certain categories of people from whom property may be stolen: **Property belongs to any person who has possession or control of it, or who has in it any proprietary right or interest.**

Control
e.g. *The garage proprietor*

Proprietary right or interest
e.g. *The owner of a vehicle being repaired*

Possession
e.g. *The person repairing the vehicle*

Particular types of property will be regarded as belonging to:	
Type of property	**Belongs to**
Subject to a trust	Any person having a right to enforce the trust
Person receiving is under an obligation to retain and deal with it in a particular way	The person he received it from
Obtained by mistake and obliged to make restoration	Person entitled to restoration
Property of corporation sole	The corporation, not withstanding any vacancy in it

Intention to Permanently Deprive S 6 THEFT ACT 1968

If a person takes property belonging to another, but does not mean the other to be permanently deprived of it, he will still be regarded in law as having such an intention if he means to treat the property as his own to dispose of regardless of the other's rights – such as:

- borrowing or lending in such a way that it is equivalent to an outright taking or disposal
- parting with the property (obtained legally or not) under a condition as to its return which he may not be able to perform, e.g. pawning
- the 'other' to whom the property belongs need not be an individual, but may be a registered company or other legal entity

Removal of Articles from Places Open to the Public

S 11 THEFT ACT 1968

Where the public have access to a building (or part of a building) in order to view the building or a collection housed in it, any person who without lawful authority removes from the building or its grounds any article kept for display to the public, shall be guilty of an offence.

Collection
Includes a temporary collection, but not one intended to promote sales or commercial dealings.

Public access
May be limited to a particular period or occasion but anything removed which is not part of a permanent exhibition must be done on a day when the public have access (but may be guilty of theft).

Unlike theft, it is not necessary to prove an intention permanently to deprive.

Taking a Conveyance without Authority

S 12(1) THEFT ACT 1968

This offence is committed by a person:

without having the consent of the owner or other lawful authority, **taking** a conveyance for his own or another's use	or	knowing that a conveyance has been taken without the consent of the owner or other lawful authority, **drives** it or allows himself to be **carried** in or on it

The conveyance must be moved, however short the distance may be; merely trying to start an engine will not suffice. Also, it must be taken for use as a conveyance, merely pushing it around the corner for a prank will not satisfy this offence.

CONVEYANCE

Constructed or adapted for the carriage of a person by land, water or air.

A similar offence exists in relation to pedal cycles but it is not an arrestable offence. S 12(5)

AGGRAVATED VEHICLE-TAKING ACT 1992 adds S 12A to the Theft Act 1968. Provides for obligatory disqualification and endorsement where the above offence under S 12(1) has been committed and, before the vehicle was recovered, the vehicle was driven dangerously or was damaged or was driven in a way which led to personal injury or damage to other property.

Vehicle Interference

S 9 CRIMINAL ATTEMPTS ACT 1981

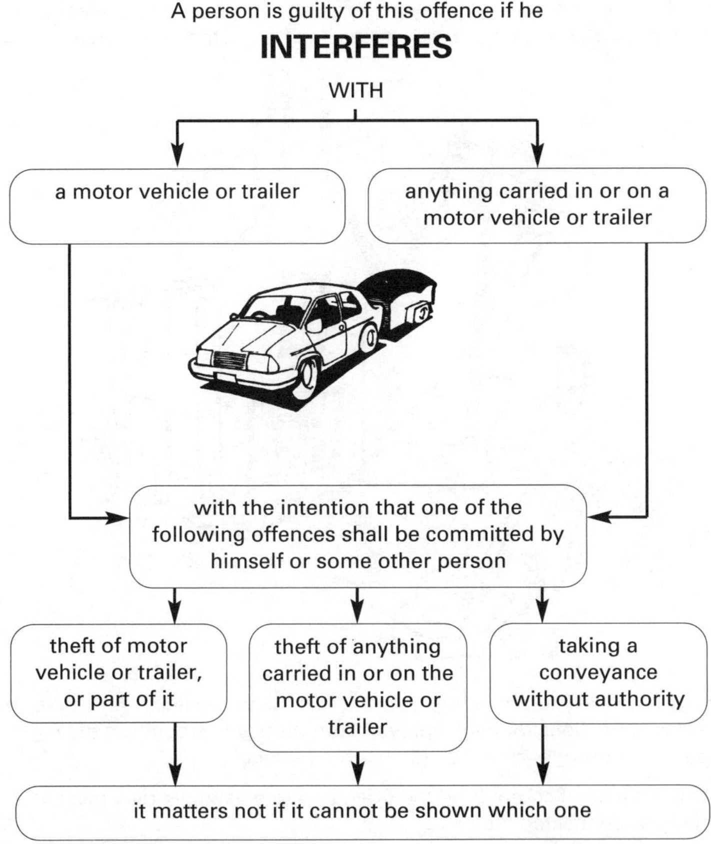

Note: A person may still be guilty of an offence under S 25 of the Road Traffic Act 1988, if, while a motor vehicle is on a road or local authority parking place, he gets onto the vehicle or tampers with the brakes or other parts of its mechanism.

Abstracting Electricity

S 13 THEFT ACT 1968

This offence is committed by any person who dishonestly uses electricity without authority, or dishonestly causes it to be wasted or diverted.

It is not necessary to prove that personal benefit was gained. An employee who leaves the lights of his employer's premises on throughout the night because of a grudge, would be guilty of the offence.

A common way of committing the offence is to unlawfully reconnect an officially disconnected meter.

See also 'fraudulent use of telecommunications system' later.

Robbery

S 8 THEFT ACT 1968

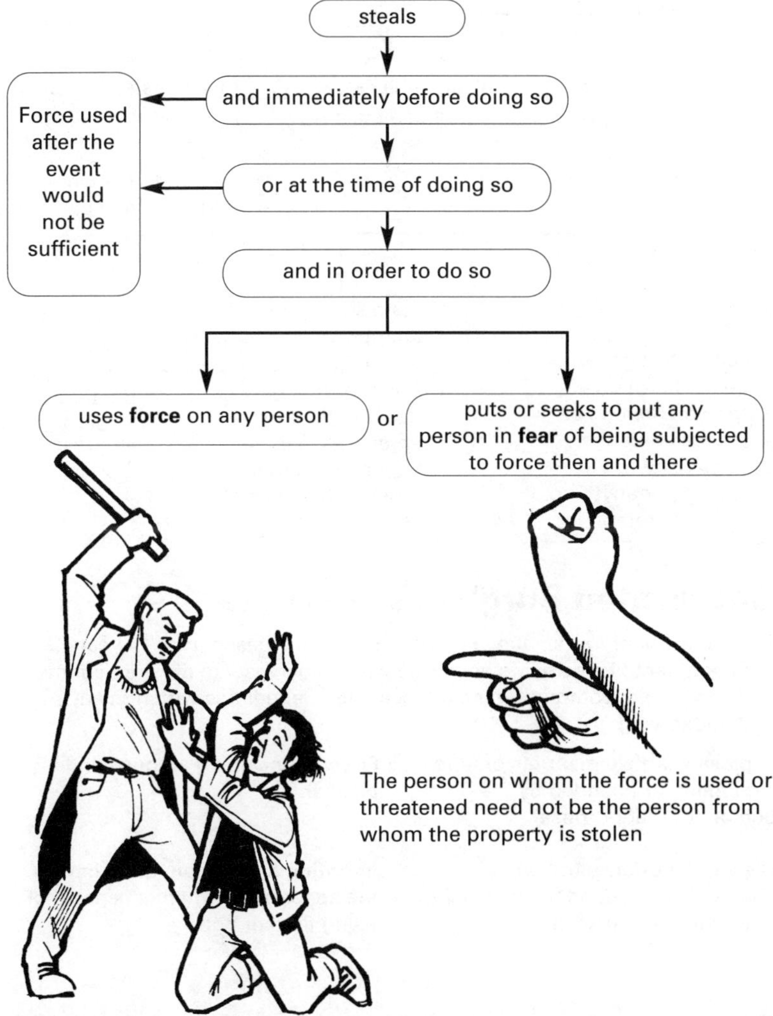

The person on whom the force is used or threatened need not be the person from whom the property is stolen

Burglary

S 9 THEFT ACT 1968

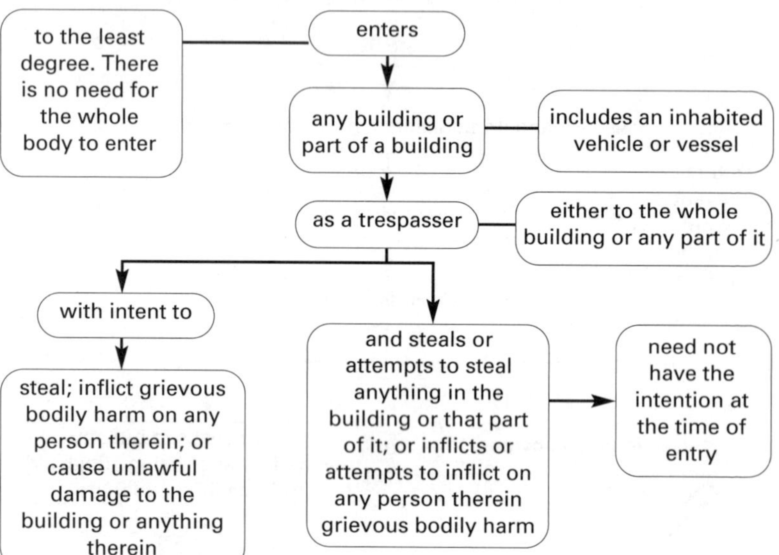

Aggravated Burglary S 10 THEFT ACT 1968

The punishment for the above offence may be increased from 14 years imprisonment (if a dwelling house, 10 years otherwise) to life imprisonment if, at the time of committing the offence, the offender has with him any of the following:

Explosive (article manufactured for exploding, or intended by the person for that purpose)

Firearm (including air guns and air pistols)

Weapon of offence (made or adapted, or intended by the person, to injure or incapacitate)

Imitation firearm (anything having the appearance whether capable of being fired or not)

Fraud

FRAUD ACT 2006

Introduction

This Act provides for criminal liability for fraud and obtaining services dishonestly.

There is a general offence of fraud and three ways of committing it:
1. by false representation,
2. by failing to disclose information and
3. by abuse of position.

This offence is punishable on indictment with 10 years' imprisonment.

The Act creates new offences of obtaining services dishonestly (5 years), possessing articles for use in fraud (5 years), making and supplying articles for use in fraud (10 years), and fraudulent trading by non-corporate traders (10 years). All of these offences are discussed in the following pages.

The Act repeals the deception offences in Ss 15, 15A, 16, and 20(2) of the Theft Act 1968, and Ss 1 and 2 of the Theft Act 1978.

Fraud by false representation (S2)
A person is guilty of this offence if he;
(a) dishonestly makes a false representation, and
(b) intends, by making the representation;
  (i) to make a gain for himself or another, or
  (ii) to cause loss to another or to expose another to a risk of loss.

'Gain' and 'loss' (S5)
(a) extend only to gain or loss in money or other property;
(b) include any such gain or loss whether temporary or permanent.

Further details, explanations and examples may be found on the next page.

Fraud by False Representation

S 2 FRAUD ACT 2006

Element	Meaning	Further explanation
Makes	Includes a representation (or anything implying it) which is submitted in any form to any system or device designed to receive, convey or respond to communications (with or without human intervention).	The offence can be committed where a person makes a representation to a machine and a response can be produced without the need for human involvement e.g. where a person enters a number into a chip and pin machine.
False	(a) It is untrue or misleading, and (b) the person making it knows that it is, or might be, untrue or misleading.	
Representation	As to fact or law, including a representation as to the state of mind of the person making the representation, or any other person. Such representation may be express or implied.	It can be stated in words or communicated by conduct. There is no limitation on the way it must be expressed. So it could be written, spoken or posted on a website. It may also be implied by conduct e.g. by dishonestly using a credit card. It may be by way of phishing where information is disseminated by email to large groups of people falsely representing that it has been sent by a legitimate financial institution. It prompts the reader to provide private information e.g. a credit card number.

Gain	Includes a gain by keeping what one has as well as a gain by getting what one does not have.	
Loss	Includes a loss by not getting what one might get, as well as a loss by parting with what one has.	
Property	Any property whether real or personal (including things in action and other intangible property).	This is based on S 4(1) and S 34(1) of the Theft Act 1968.

Fraud by Failing to Disclose Information

S 3 FRAUD ACT 2006

The offence
A person commits this offence if he;

(a) dishonestly fails to disclose to another person information which he is under a legal duty to disclose, and

(b) intends, by failing to disclose the information;

  (i) to make a gain for himself or another, or

  (ii) to cause loss to another or to expose another to a risk of loss.

'Gain' and 'loss'
See earlier.

Legal duty to disclose information
This may include duties under oral contracts as well as written contracts. In particular such a duty may derive from;

(a) statute (such as the provisions governing company prospectuses),

(b) the fact that the transaction is one of the utmost good faith (such as an insurance contract),

(c) express or implied terms of a contract,

(d) the custom of a particular trade or market, or

(e) the existence of a fiduciary relationship between the parties (such as that of agent and principal).

It would also include instances where the law gives the victim a right to set aside any change in the person's legal position brought about by the non-disclosure.

Examples may include the failure of a solicitor to share vital information with a client, in order to perpetuate a fraud against the client. An offence would similarly be committed if a person intentionally failed to disclose information relating to his heart condition when applying for insurance.

Fraud by Abuse of Position

S 4 FRAUD ACT 2006

The offence
A person commits this offence if he;

(a) occupies a position in which he is expected to safeguard, or not to act against, the financial interests of another person,

(b) dishonestly abuses that position, and

(c) intends, by means of the abuse of that position;

(i) to make a gain for himself or another, or

(ii) to cause loss to another or expose another to a risk of loss.

'Gain' and 'loss'
See previous page.

'Abuse' may include conduct consisting of an omission rather than an act, e.g. an employee of a company who fails to take up a crucial contract in order that a rival company can take it up at the expense of his employer; an employee of a software company who clones software products with the intention of selling them; or where a person employed to care for elderly or disabled persons, having access to that person's bank account uses funds to invest in a venture of his own.

It applies in situations where a person has been put in a privileged position and, by virtue of this position, is expected to safeguard the financial interests of another or not to act against those interests.

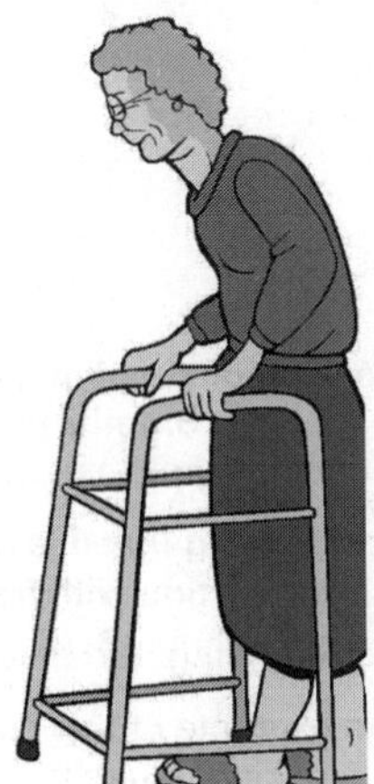

'Position' will include a relationship e.g. between trustee and beneficiary, director and company, professional person and client, agent and principal, employer and employee, and between partners. It may also exist within a family, or in voluntary work, or any other context where it is recognised as having financial duties.

Articles for use in Frauds

Ss 6 & 7 FRAUD ACT 2006

Possession etc of articles (S 6)
A person commits this offence if he has in his possession or under his control any article for use in the course of or in connection with any fraud.

'Article' includes any program or data held in electronic form, e.g. a program which is capable of generating credit card numbers; templates used for producing blank utility bills; and files containing lists of other people's credit card details or draft letters in connection with 'advanced fee' frauds.

'Intention'
Proof is required that the defendant had the article for the purpose or with the intention that it be used in the course of, or in connection with, the offence. However, it is not necessary to prove that there was a specific fraud in mind. A general intention to commit fraud will suffice. Nor is it necessary to prove that he intended to use the article himself. It is sufficient that he intended someone else to do so.

Making or supplying articles (S 7)
A person commits this offence if he makes, adapts, supplies or offers to supply any article-

(a) knowing that it is designed or adapted for use in the course of or in connection with fraud, or

(b) intending it to be used to commit, or assist in the commission of, fraud.

An example of this offence is where a person makes devices which cause electricity meters to malfunction, causing the electricity provider to suffer a loss.

'Article' see above.

Fraudulent Businesses

S 9 FRAUD ACT 2006

A person commits an offence if he is knowingly a party to the carrying on of a business which-

(a) is carried on by a person who is outside S 458 of the Companies Act 1985 (fraudulent trading), and

(b) is carried on with intention to defraud creditors of any person or for any other fraudulent purpose.

S 458 of the Companies Act 1985

This creates the civil offence of fraudulent trading. The following are within reach of S 458-

(a) a company;

(b) a person to whom this section applies as if that person were a company; and

(c) a person exempted from this section.

Explanation

Whilst the above may sound confusing it is really quite straightforward. S 458 of the Companies Act 1985 contains a civil offence of carrying on a fraudulent business by companies and corporate bodies. S 9 of the Fraud Act 2006 creates a parallel criminal offence where the business is not carried on by such a company or corporate body, and therefore it can be committed by sole traders, partnerships, trusts, companies registered overseas, etc.

The offence applies to persons knowingly party to the carrying on of non-corporate businesses to defraud creditors, or for any other fraudulent purposes.

It is intended that the case law appertaining to S 458 will also apply to S 9. Case law has established that

(a) dishonesty is an essential ingredient to the offence;

(b) it constitutes fraudulent trading generally, and not just affecting creditors;

(c) it is aimed at carrying on a business but can be constituted by a single transaction; and

(d) it can be committed only by persons who exercise some form of controlling or managerial function within the company.

Obtaining Services Dishonestly

S 11 FRAUD ACT 2006

A person commits an offence if he obtains services for himself or another-

(a) by a dishonest act,

(b) the services are made available on the basis that payment has been, is being or will be made for or in respect of them,

(c) he obtains them without any payment having been made for or in respect of them or without payment having been made in full, and

(d) when he obtains them he knows that they are being, or that they might be, made available on the basis of (b) above, but intends that payment will not be made, or will not be made in full.

Obtains
There must be an actual obtaining of a service, e.g. dishonestly using false credit card details or false personal details on the internet to obtain software or other information which would normally have to be paid for.

Dishonest act
The offence can not be committed by an omission. There must be a dishonest act with intent not to pay.

Knowledge
The person must know that the services are chargeable, or might be. Attaching a decoder to a television to enable the viewing of cable or satellite television channels, without any intention of paying, would be an offence.

Proof of 'deception' is not necessary
Although this offence replaces the offence of obtaining a service by deception under S 1 of the Theft Act 1978, it contains no element of 'deception'. For example, secretly gaining entrance to a football ground to watch a match without paying, although there is no deception, will amount to an offence, since a service has been provided which should have been paid for.

Retaining a Wrongful Credit

S 24A THEFT ACT 1968

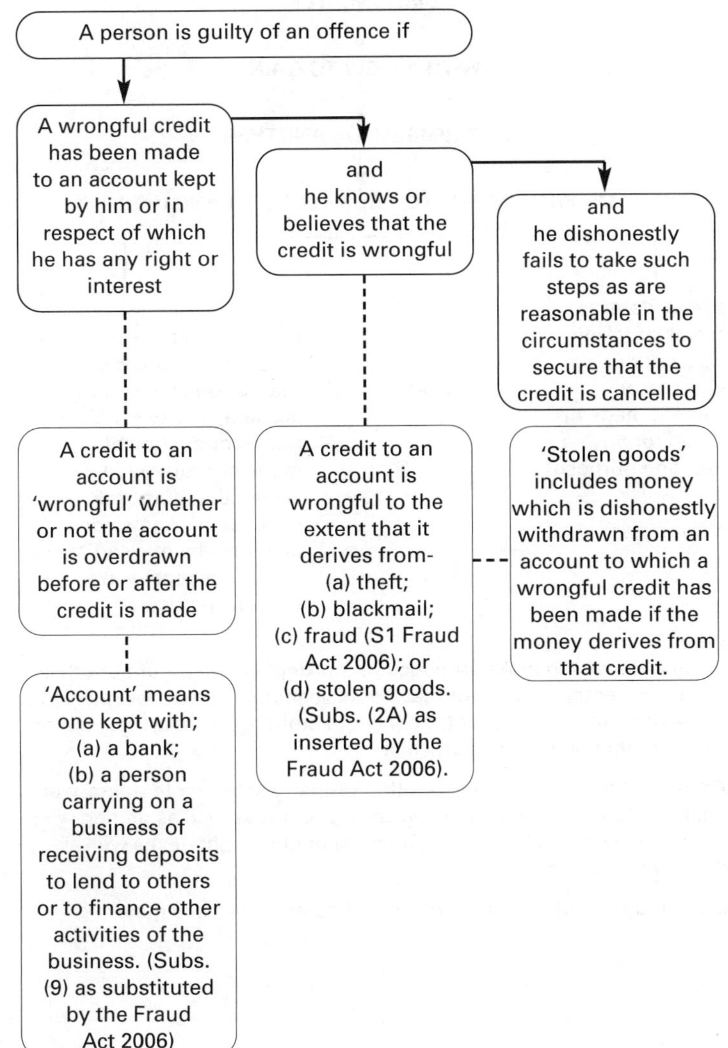

False Accounting

S 17 THEFT ACT 1968

An offence is committed if a person:

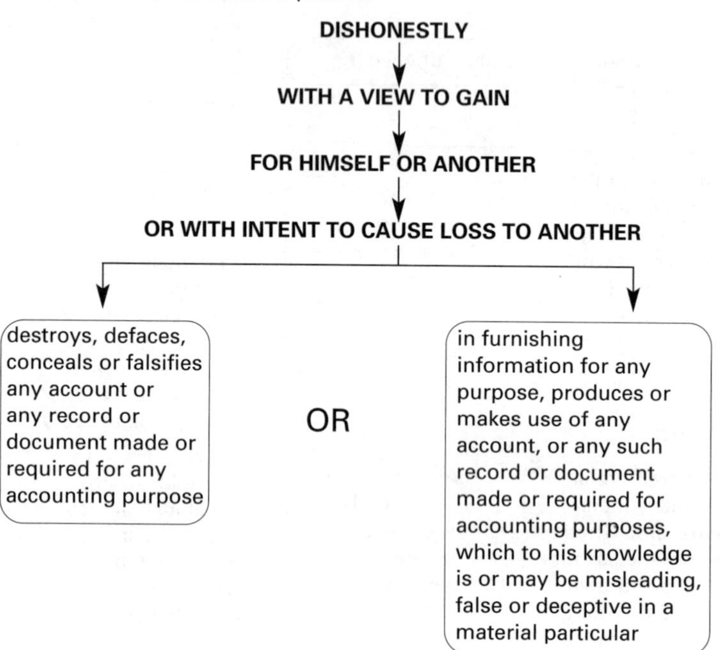

Notes

'Falsifying' means to make (or concur in making) in an account or other document an entry which is or may be misleading, false or deceptive in a material particular, or to omit (or concur in omitting) from an account or other document, a material particular.

'Gain or loss' means in money or other property, whether temporary or permanent. **'Gain'** includes keeping what one has as well as getting what one has not. **'Loss'** includes not getting what one might get as well as parting with what one has.

'Record' may include, for example, a taximeter or turnstile meter.

Liability of Company Officers

S 18 THEFT ACT 1968

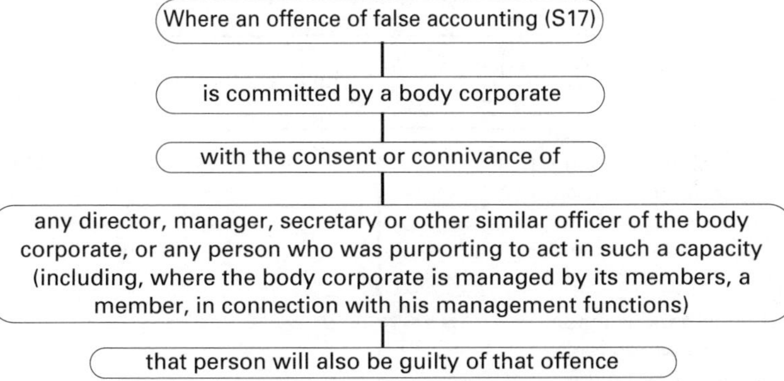

False Statements by Company Directors

S 19 THEFT ACT 1968

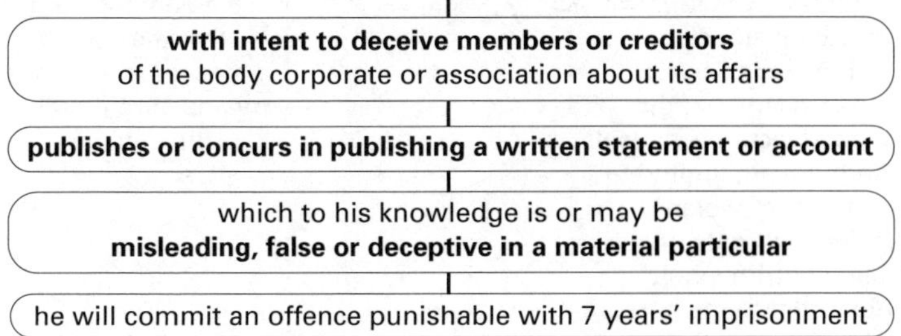

Blackmail

S 21 THEFT ACT 1968

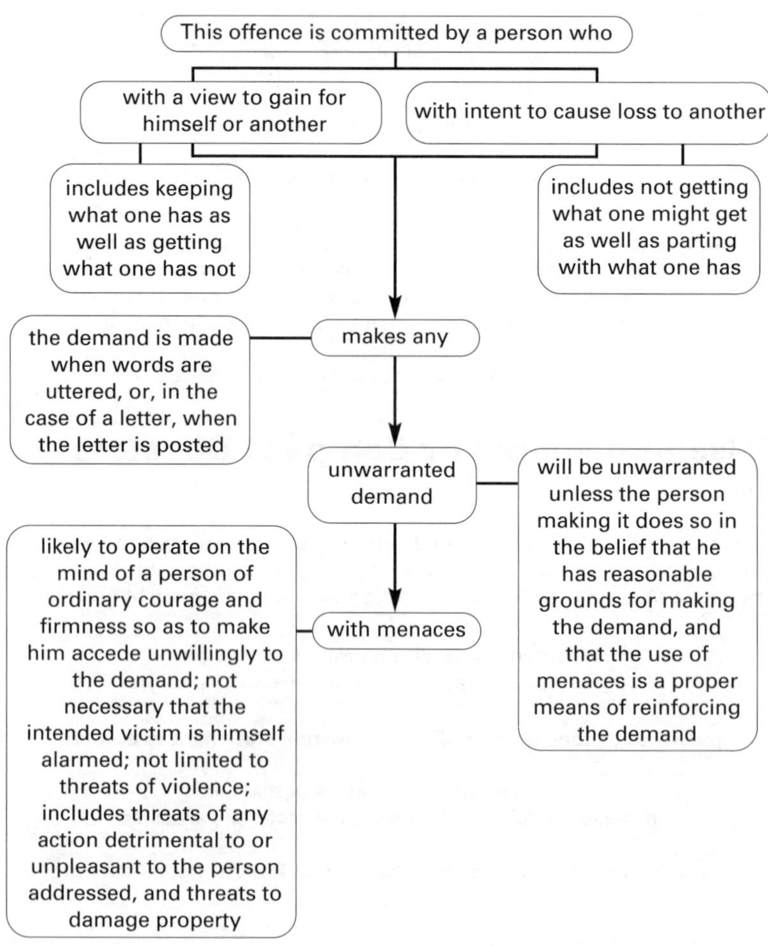

Suppression etc of Documents

S 20 THEFT ACT 1968

DESTRUCTION, CONCEALMENT, ETC

A person who, dishonestly, with a view to gain for himself or another or with intent to cause loss to another

- destroys
- defaces, or
- conceals

any

- valuable security
- will or other testamentary document, or
- original document of or belonging to, or filed or deposited in any court of justice or any government department

shall be guilty of an offence punishable with 7 years' imprisonment.

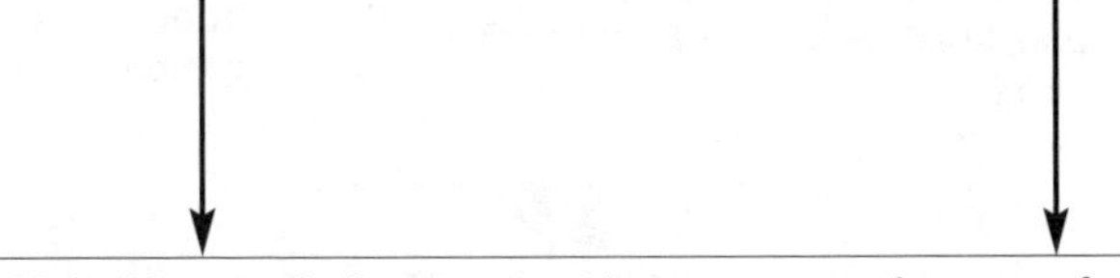

'**Valuable security**' means any document creating, transferring, surrendering or releasing

- any right to, in or over property, or
- authorising the payment of money or delivery of any property, or evidence of the creation, transfer, surrender or release of any such right, or
- the payment of money or delivery of any property, or
- the satisfaction of any obligation.

'**Gain or loss**' has the same meaning as in S17 (see earlier).

Making Off Without Paying

S 3 THEFT ACT 1978

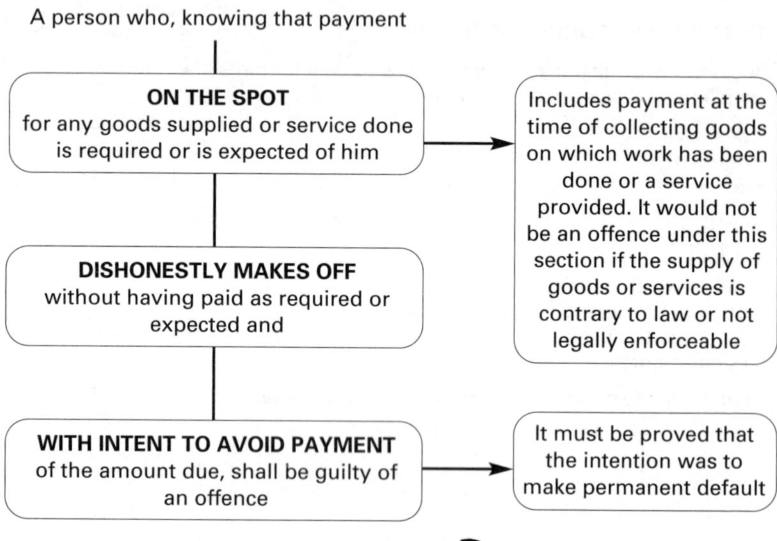

Handling Stolen Goods

S 22 THEFT ACT 1968

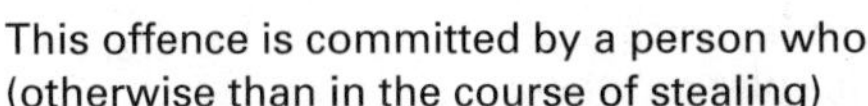

This offence is committed by a person who (otherwise than in the course of stealing)

KNOWING OR **BELIEVING** →

Mere suspicion that they were stolen is not sufficient. There must be either 'knowledge' or 'belief'. **Knowledge** may be implied when he was told that the goods were stolen by someone with first hand knowledge (e.g. the thief or burglar). **Belief** is where he does not know for certain, but there can be no other reasonable conclusion in the light of all the circumstances.

THEM TO BE

STOLEN →

- By theft, blackmail or by way of fraud within the meaning of the Fraud Act 2006 (or a like offence committed outside England and Wales)
- The thief must be guilty
- Goods cease to be stolen after they have been restored to lawful possession or custody, or any rights to restitution have ceased

GOODS →

Money and all other property except land (unless severed from the land), including any proceeds from the original stolen goods, S 34(2)

DISHONESTLY →

- Was he aware of the theft?
- Did he believe the goods to be stolen?
- Did he suspect them to be stolen and deliberately shut his eyes to the obvious?

A) **Receives** the goods (guilty knowledge must exist at the time of receiving, not formed afterwards)

B) **Undertakes** the retention, removal, disposal or realisation of the goods by or for the benefit of another person

C) **Assists** in the retention, removal, disposal or realisation of the goods by or for the benefit of another person, or

D) **Arranges** to do A to C above

Going Equipped

S 25 THEFT ACT 1968

Assault

In the case of *Fagan v Metropolitan Police Commissioner*, 1968, 'assault' was defined as:

> **'Any act which intentionally or recklessly causes another person to apprehend immediate and unlawful personal violence.'**

A person is responsible for injuries which result from inducing into another's mind an immediate sense of danger which causes that person to injure himself in trying to escape.

There are varying degrees of assault which are governed by the seriousness of the injury, the harm done and the attendant circumstances.

Specific offences are discussed on the following pages and reflect the charging standards in assault cases issued by the Crown Prosecution Service in August 1994.

Common Assault

S 39 CRIMINAL JUSTICE ACT 1988

An incident is referred to as being a common assault where the injury is either non-existent or of a negligible nature, e.g. grazes, minor bruising, black eye, etc. The police do not normally institute proceedings for this type of occurrence, thus affording the aggrieved person the choice of taking proceedings either criminally or by civil action to obtain damages. Common assault and battery are two separate summary offences. Both require a mental element of an intention, or recklessness, causing another person to apprehend immediate and unlawful violence.

Actual Bodily Harm

S 47 OFFENCES AGAINST THE PERSON ACT 1861

This includes any hurt or injury calculated to interfere with the health or comfort of the victim. It need not be a permanent injury but must be more than something which is only momentary and trifling, e.g. lost teeth, minor fractures, loss of consciousness. It may include shock which causes injury to the victim's state of mind. 'Harm' also includes psychological harm but does not include mere emotions such as fear, distress or panic. The making of a telephone call could amount to this offence if the victim was apprehensive and was caused psychological damage. No foresight or foreseeability of the consequences is required.

Defences to Assault

Consent

But only a defence if:

a) An illegal purpose is not involved, e.g. a duel or injecting illegal drugs

b) Violence or injury is not excessive

c) Consent is not obtained by fear, fraud or ignorance or the facts

Lawfully justified

For example:

Defence of oneself, a close relative or one's property. But only sufficient force may be used to repel the attack

Legal right

For example:

In the course of a lawful arrest, prevention of a breach of the peace, or serious crime.

But only such force as is necessary to achieve the result may be used.

Wounding or Inflicting Grievous Bodily Harm

S 20 OFFENCES AGAINST THE PERSON ACT 1861

IT IS AN OFFENCE TO
UNLAWFULLY AND MALICIOUSLY

WOUND OR INFLICT ANY GRIEVOUS BODILY HARM

WITH OR WITHOUT ANY
WEAPON OR INSTRUMENT

These charges should be used for injuries involving permanent disability, serious permanent disfigurement, loss of sensory function, broken bones, substantial loss of blood or lengthy treatment, including psychiatric injury.

The defendant must have foreseen that his act would cause harm, even if not of the seriousness which actually resulted.

Wounding or Causing Grievous Bodily Harm With Intent

S 18 OFFENCES AGAINST THE PERSON ACT 1861

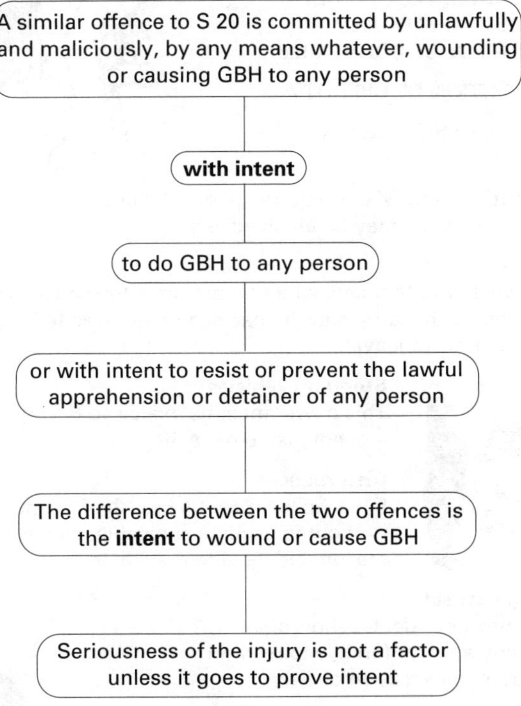

Assault on the Police

S 89 POLICE ACT 1996

IT IS AN OFFENCE TO ASSAULT
OR TO RESIST OR WILFULLY
OBSTRUCT A POLICE CONSTABLE

IN THE EXECUTION OF HIS DUTY

OR A PERSON ASSISTING HIM

'In the execution of duty' covers a range of activities in which the constable may be involved, e.g.

On premises
Unless specifically authorised, when on premises the constable is not acting in the execution of his duty once he has been requested to leave (but he must be given time to leave).

Stopping vehicles
This power must be exercised lawfully e.g. not just to get a lift.

Disturbances
If it is believed that a breach of the peace is about to occur, a constable may use reasonable force to prevent it.

Questioning suspects
There is no power to detain short of an arrest, and any attempt forcibly to restrain cannot amount to execution of duty.

It is also an offence to assault ANY PERSON with intent to resist or prevent the lawful apprehension or detainer of himself or another for any offence (S 38 Offences Against the Person Act 1861).

Female Genital Mutilation

FEMALE GENITAL MUTILATION ACT 2003

A person is guilty of an offence if he:

(a) excises, infibulates or otherwise mutilates the whole or any part of a girl's labia majora, labia minora or clitoris (S 1(1));

(b) aids, abets, counsels or procures a girl to excise, infibulate or otherwise mutilate the whole or any part of her own labia majora, labia minora or clitoris (S 2);

(c) aids, abets, counsels or procures a person who is not a United Kingdom national or permanent United Kingdom resident to do an act of female genital mutilation outside the U.K. which would, if done in the U.K., amount to an offence under S 1. (S 3)

Acts done outside the United Kingdom

Sections 1 to 3 above extend to any act done outside the United Kingdom by a United Kingdom national or permanent United Kingdom resident. In such cases, proceedings may be taken, and the offence may be treated as having been committed, in any place in England and Wales or Northern Ireland. (S 4)

Exemptions

1. No offence is committed by:

(a) a registered medical practitioner who performs a surgical operation which is necessary for the girl's physical or mental health (S 1(2)(a)), (it is immaterial whether she or any other person believes the operation is required as a matter of custom or ritual) (S 1(5));

(b) a registered medical practitioner, a registered midwife or a person undergoing training to become such a practitioner or midwife, who performs a surgical operation on a girl in any stage of labour or birth, for purposes connected with the labour or birth (S 1(2)(b)); or

(c) a person who performs a surgical operation as in (a) or (b) above outside the United Kingdom and who exercises functions corresponding to those of such an approved person (S 1(4)).

Homicide

As far as the criminal law is concerned, there are four types of unlawful killing.

MURDER COMMON LAW

This is committed when a sane person over 10 years of age, through some deliberate act or omission causes the death of a human being, either intending to kill that person or some other person, or to cause grievous bodily harm, or to expose someone to a known serious risk of death or grievous bodily harm resulting from acts committed deliberately and without lawful excuse. It does not matter whether those consequences were intended or not.

Threats

It is also an offence to threaten to kill some person, intending that the person to whom the threat is made will fear that the threat will be carried out.

MANSLAUGHTER S 5 OFFENCES AGAINST THE PERSON ACT 1861, COMMON LAW

This is the unlawful killing of another without the intention to kill or cause grievous bodily harm. Manslaughter is usually described as being voluntary or involuntary:

Voluntary

Where death follows an intended injury (but if the injury is serious, then this may be murder). It normally occurs as a result of a sudden 'fraying of temper' or following some degree of provocation.

Involuntary

Where injury is not intended, but is nevertheless caused through gross negligence or an unlawful act.

INFANTICIDE S 1 INFANTICIDE ACT 1938

Committed by a mother who, by any wilful act or omission, causes the death of her child (under 12 months old) whilst being mentally unbalanced through childbirth or milk fever.

CHILD DESTRUCTION S 1 INFANT LIFE (PRESERVATION) ACT 1929

Committed by any person who, by any wilful act, intentionally causes the death of a child capable of being born alive (this is presumed after 28 weeks pregnancy) before it has had a life independent of its mother.

CONCEALING THE BIRTH OF A CHILD S 60 OFFENCES AGAINST THE PERSON ACT 1861

Although not one of the above offences of unlawful killing, this offence is akin and worth a mention. It is committed by any person who endeavours to conceal the birth of a child by any secret disposition of the dead body of the child, whether it died before, at, or after its birth. The concealment must be with the intention to keep the world at large ignorant of the birth and not just to escape individual anger.

Causing Death of Child or Vulnerable Adult

S 5 DOMESTIC VIOLENCE, CRIME AND VICTIMS ACT 2004

A person (D) is guilty of an offence if:

a) a **child or vulnerable adult** (V) dies as a result of the **unlawful act** of a person who:
   i) was a **member of the same household** as V, and
   ii) had frequent contact with him,
b) D was such a person at the time of that act,
c) at that time there was a significant risk of **serious physical harm** being caused to V by the unlawful act of such a person, and
d) either D was the person whose act caused V's death, or
   i) D was, or ought to have been, aware of the risk mentioned in paragraph (c),
   ii) D failed to take such steps as he could reasonably have been expected to take to protect V from the risk, and
   iii) the act occurred in circumstances of the kind that D foresaw or ought to have foreseen.

The prosecution does not have to prove whether it is the first alternative in paragraph (d), or the second in sub-paragraphs (i) – (iii) that applies.

If D was not the mother or father of V:

a) D may not be charged with this offence if he was under the age of 16 at the time of the act which caused the death; and
b) for the purposes of sub-paragraph (d)(ii) above, D could not have been expected to take any such step as is referred to there before attaining that age.

Member of the same household includes a person who does not live in that household if he visits it so often and for such periods of time that it is reasonable to regard him as a member of it. Where V lived in different households at different times, 'the same household' means that in which V was living at the time of the act which caused his death.

Unlawful act means one which (a) constitutes an offence, or (b) (except for an act of D), would constitute an offence but for being the act of a person under the age of 10, or a person entitled to rely on a defence of insanity.

Act includes a course of conduct as well as an omission.

Child means a person under the age of 16.

Serious harm means harm amounting to grievous bodily harm for the purposes of the Offences against the Person Act 1861.

Vulnerable adult means a person aged 16 or over whose ability to protect himself from violence, abuse or neglect is significantly impaired through physical or mental disability or illness, through old age or otherwise.

Damage

S 1(1) CRIMINAL DAMAGE ACT 1971

DAMAGE
IS THE OFFENCE
COMMITTED BY ANY
PERSON WHO WITHOUT

LAWFUL EXCUSE ➤

He will be treated as having a lawful excuse if he believed he had consent of a person entitled to consent, or he would have consented had he known of the circumstances; or if he caused, or threatened to cause damage in protection of his own or another's property

DESTROYS ➤

If a building: to pull down or demolish

If growing things: to lay waste

If machinery: to break up

If animals: to kill

OR

DAMAGES ➤

Nothing need be actually broken or deformed, eg uncoupling the brake pipe on a car; tampering with machinery so that it will not work; watering milk

PROPERTY ➤

Whether real or personal. Including wild animals which have been tamed or are ordinarily kept in captivity but does not include mushrooms growing wild on any land or flowers, fruit or foliage from wild plants

BELONGING TO ANOTHER ➤

Property belongs to any person having custody or control of it, having a right or interest in it, or having a charge on it

INTENDING ➤

If he intends or foresees damage to property, he may be liable where he in fact causes damage to other property which he had not intended or foreseen

TO DESTROY OR DAMAGE ANY SUCH PROPERTY OR BEING RECKLESS AS TO WHETHER ANY SUCH PROPERTY WOULD BE DESTROYED OR DAMAGED. IF THIS OFFENCE IS COMMITTED BY FIRE, IT WILL BE ARSON.

Damage With Intent to Endanger Life

S 1(2) CRIMINAL DAMAGE ACT 1971

This offence is committed by a person who:

without lawful excuse destroys or damages any property, whether belonging to himself or another

↓

intending to destroy or damage any property or being reckless as to whether any property would be destroyed or damaged

↓

intending by the destruction or damage to endanger the life of another or being reckless as to whether the life of another would be thereby endangered

Arson

S 1(3) CRIMINAL DAMAGE ACT 1971

An offence of damage or endangering life by damage, **by destroying or damaging property by fire** shall be charged as 'arson'.

Threats to Damage

S 2 CRIMINAL DAMAGE ACT 1971

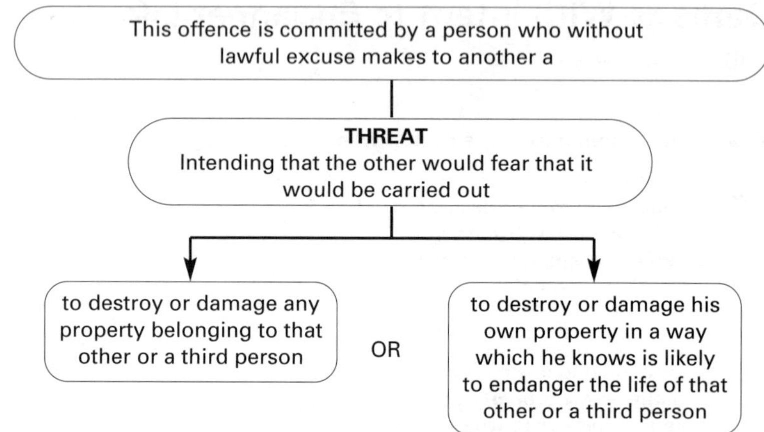

Possession With Intent to Damage

S 3 CRIMINAL DAMAGE ACT 1971

This offence is committed by a person who has
ANYTHING
in his custody or control intending
WITHOUT LAWFUL EXCUSE
to use or cause or permit another to use it

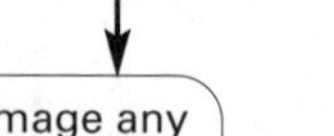

to destroy or damage any property belonging to some other person

OR

to destroy or damage his own or the user's property in a way which he knows is likely to endanger the life of some other person

Sale of Paint Aerosols to Children

S 54 ANTI-SOCIAL BEHAVIOUR ACT 2003

A person commits an offence if he sells an aerosol paint container to a person under 16.

Drugs

The Misuse of Drugs Act 1971 creates a number of offences relating to

Controlled drugs

This means any substance or product listed in one of the three classes (A, B or C) in Sched 2 to the Act. The main significance in classifying drugs as 'A', 'B' or 'C' lies in the punishment to which the offender is liable.

Whilst drugs are listed in their basic form it is clear that other forms of the drug and esters or salts are also included. Both the natural substances and any substance resulting from chemical transformation are controlled drugs.

S 28 of the Act contains a general defence which applies to the following sections referred to later: S 4 (production and supply), S 5 (possession), S 6 (cultivation of cannabis), and S 9 (opium). It will be a defence for the defendant to prove that he neither knew of, nor suspected, nor had reason to suspect, the existence of some fact which the prosecution must prove.

Powers to arrest are contained in the Police and Criminal Evidence Act 1984. It also provides wide powers of search, and contains specific defences.

A variety of aspects are listed below and dealt with in more detail in the following pages:

Import and export	**49**
Production	**49**
Supply	**50-51**
Possession	**52-53**
Cannabis	**53**
Use of premises	**54**
Opium	**55**
Search and arrest	**56**
Closure of premises used for drugs	**57**

Import & Export

S 3 MISUSE OF DRUGS ACT 1971

The import or export of controlled drugs is prohibited unless authorised under the regulations.

Sched 5 of the Misuse of Drugs Regulations 2001 lists certain substances and preparations to which this section does not apply.

Being concerned with the improper import or export, and the fraudulent evasion of prohibition or restriction are all offences under S50 the Customs and Excise Management Act 1979.

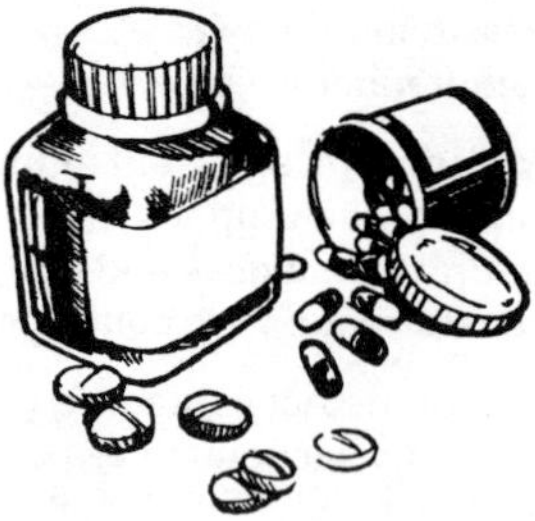

Production

S 4(2) MISUSE OF Drugs Act 1971

IT IS AN OFFENCE TO

UNLAWFULLY

(to be lawful it must be authorised by regulations, eg manufacturers)

PRODUCE

by manufacture, cultivation or any other method, e.g. cultivating or growing

BE CONCERNED IN THE PRODUCTION BY ANOTHER OF

(actual participation is not necessary. All that needs to be proved is an interest, e.g. hiring premises)

A CONTROLLED DRUG

Supply of Articles

S 9A MISUSE OF DRUGS ACT 1971

It is an offence for a person to supply or offer to supply any article which may be used or adapted to be used in the administration of a controlled drug to himself or another, believing that the article is to be so used in circumstances where the administration is unlawful.

The above does not apply to a hypodermic syringe or part of one.

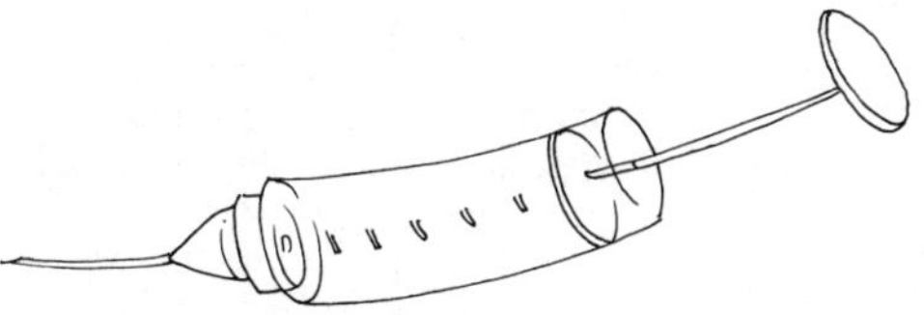

An offence is also committed if the article supplied or offered may be used to prepare a controlled drug for administration.

Any administration of a controlled drug is unlawful except:
- where the production or supply of the drug is not unlawful under S 4(1); or
- possession of the drug is not unlawful under S 5(1).

Supplying Drugs

S 4(3) MISUSE OF DRUGS ACT 1971, S 1 DRUGS ACT 2005

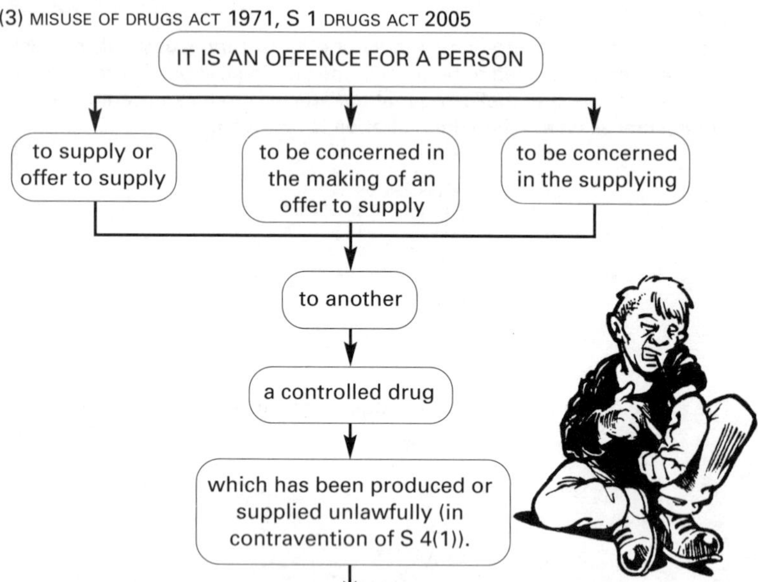

Notes

Lawful supply: The Misuse of Drugs Regulations 2001 contains a list of persons who may lawfully supply, etc, controlled drugs, e.g. pharmacists, vets and masters of ships who do not carry a doctor. It also lists the drugs which they may possess and the circumstances in which they may possess them. **'Supplying'** includes distributing. **'Offer to supply'** includes where the substance in possession is not a controlled drug. It also includes where an offer is made regardless of whether he intends to actually supply the drug. **'Concerned in'** is designed to include the "trafficker" and persons who connive in the supply, as well as persons who may be some distance from the actual making of the offer. **Exemption:** This offence does not include the supply of poppy-straw.

Aggravation of the offence (S 4A)

The court will treat the offence as being more serious if the offender is 18 or over, and (a) the offence is committed in the vicinity of a school at any time when persons under 18 are using the school, and one hour before the start and one hour after the end of such time, or (b) the offender used a courier who was under 18.

Possession

S 5(2) MISUSE OF DRUGS ACT 1971

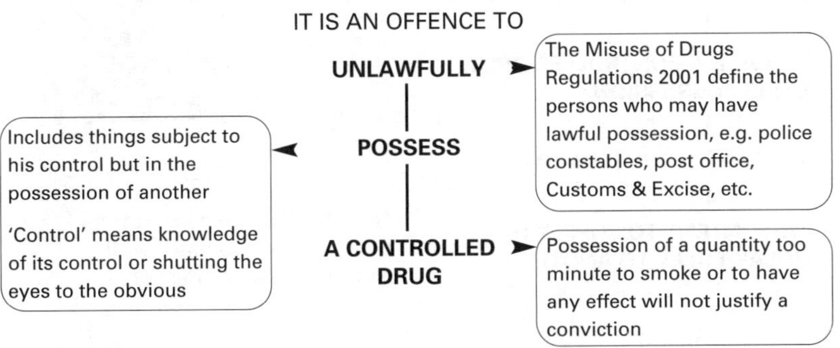

Defence

S 5(4) MISUSE OF DRUGS ACT 1971

It is a defence to a charge of possession to prove that, knowing or suspecting it to be a controlled drug, he took possession of it for the purpose of:

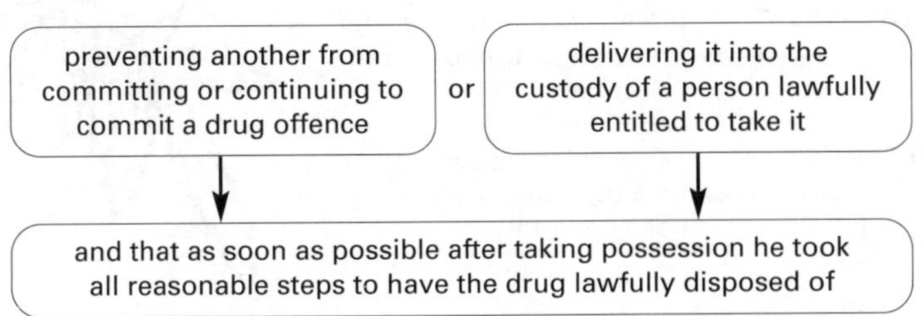

Possession With Intent to Supply

S 5(3) MISUSE OF DRUGS ACT 1971

IT IS AN OFFENCE FOR A PERSON

TO HAVE A CONTROLLED DRUG IN HIS POSSESSION

WHETHER LAWFULLY OR NOT

WITH INTENT TO SUPPLY IT UNLAWFULLY TO ANOTHER → The offence may be committed by a person who has lawful possession, eg a chemist

Cannabis – Cultivating

S 6(2) MISUSE OF DRUGS ACT 1971

IT IS AN OFFENCE TO

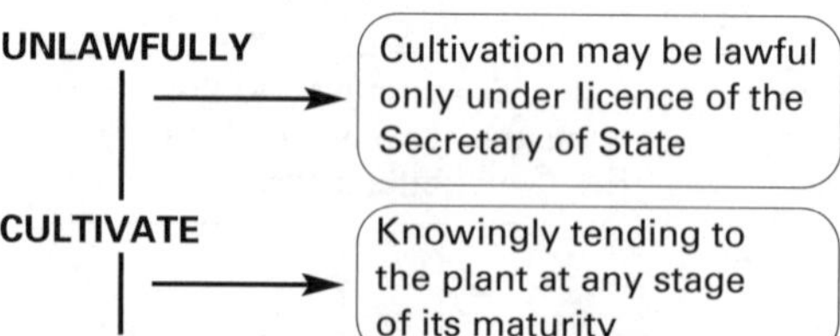

ANY PLANT OF THE GENUS 'CANNABIS'

by whatever name, e.g. hashish, gunjah, bhang, marijuana. It also includes any part of the plant after it has been separated from the rest of the plant except mature stalk, mature stalk fibre or seed.

Use of Premises

S 8 MISUSE OF DRUGS ACT 1971

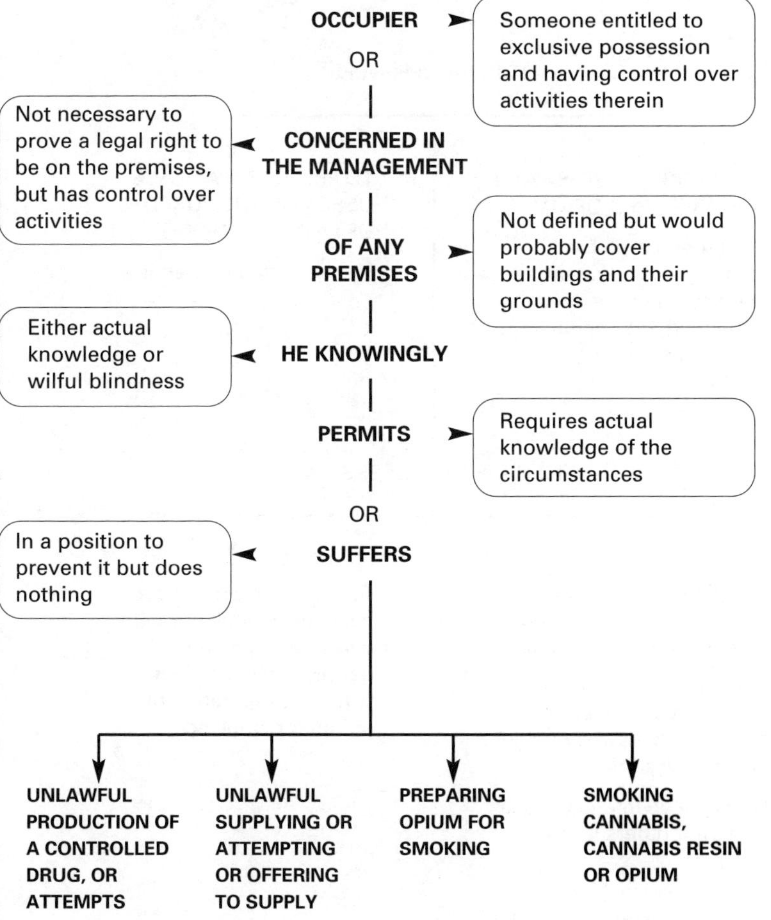

Opium

S 9 MISUSE OF DRUGS ACT 1971

IT IS AN OFFENCE

TO SMOKE OR OTHERWISE USE PREPARED OPIUM

Opium prepared for smoking, including dross and any other residues remaining after opium has been smoked

TO FREQUENT A PLACE USED FOR THE PURPOSE OF OPIUM SMOKING

Not restricted to premises

TO HAVE IN POSSESSION

any pipes or other utensils made for use in connection with the smoking of opium

Being pipes or utensils which have been used by him or with his knowledge and permission

Or which he intends to use or permit others to use

Any utensils which have been used by him or with his knowledge and permission in connection with the preparation of opium for smoking

Police Powers

SEARCH

S 23(2) MISUSE OF DRUGS ACT 1971

If a constable has reasonable grounds to suspect that any person is unlawfully in possession of a controlled drug, he may:

Search that person
and detain him for the purpose of searching him

Search any vehicle or vessel in which the constable suspects that the drug may be found
and require the vehicle to be stopped for that purpose
and seize and detain anything found in the course of the search which appears to the constable to be evidence of an offence under this Act

It is an offence to intentionally obstruct a person exercising these powers

The following provisions of the Police and Criminal Evidence Act 1984 should be noted.

Where the power is exercised to search a person or vehicle without making an arrest, then **before** the search is commenced:

THE FOLLOWING INFORMATION SHOULD BE BROUGHT TO THE ATTENTION OF THE APPROPRIATE PERSON

- Constable's name and his police station. If not in uniform, documentary evidence of being a constable
- Object and grounds of proposed search
- Where a record of the search is made, his entitlement to a copy within 12 months if he asks for it

Where an unattended vehicle is searched, a notice should be left stating that it has been searched and giving the officer's name and station, the right to apply for compensation for any damage caused and his right to a copy of the search record. The notice is to be left inside the vehicle unless not practicable.

For power to test a detained person for drugs see under 'Testing for Drugs' later.

Closure of Premises used for Drugs

Ss 1 – 11 ANTI-SOCIAL BEHAVIOUR ACT 2003

A Closure Notice may be issued by a superintendent or above in relation to premises (including land and outbuildings) if he has reasonable grounds for believing:

(a) that at any time during the preceding 3 months the premises have been used in connection with the **unlawful use, production or supply of a Class A drug**; and
(b) the use of the premises is associated with **disorder or serious nuisance** to members of the public.

The local authority must be consulted and reasonable steps must be taken to attempt to identify the person who lives on or has control of the premises.

The notice is served by affixing it to the premises and serving it on the person having control over the building or living there.

Within 48 hours of serving the notice, an application must be made to a magistrates' court for the issue of a **Closure Order**.

A Closure Order prohibits the entry of all persons to the premises for a maximum period of 3 months (extendable to not more than 6 months). The order is subject to such provisions relating to access and parts of the building as the court thinks fit. It authorises constables to enter the premises by force if necessary.

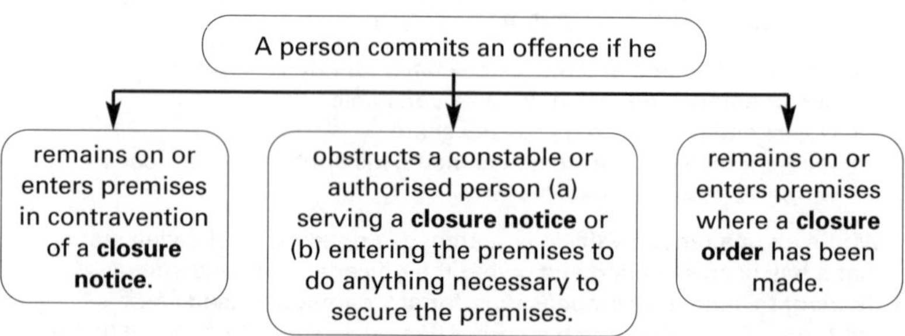

For the purpose of serving a closure notice by affixing it to the premises, a constable may enter any premises using reasonable force if necessary. (SCHED. 1 DRUGS ACT 2005).

Chapter 2

Sexual Offences

Rape

S 1 SEXUAL OFFENCES ACT 2003

A person (A) commits an offence if

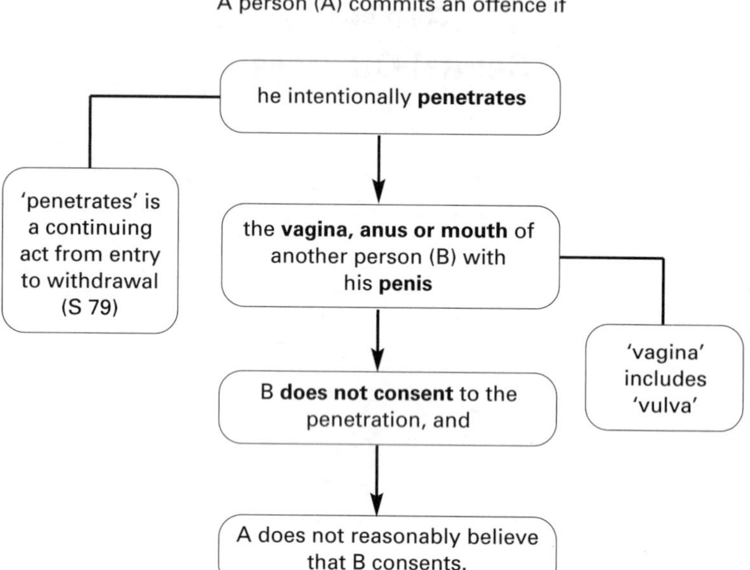

Reasonable belief
Whether a belief is reasonable is to be determined having regard to all the circumstances, including any steps A has taken to ascertain whether B consents.

Consent
A person consents if he agrees by choice, and has the freedom and capacity to make that choice. (S 74)

Presumptions about consent
The absence of the complainant's consent and/or the absence of the defendant's reasonable belief that the complainant consented may be presumed, depending on the circumstances (Ss 75 & 76). See later under 'Presumptions about Consent'.

THIS IS AN ARRESTABLE OFFENCE – LIFE

Assault by Penetration

S 2 SEXUAL OFFENCES ACT 2003

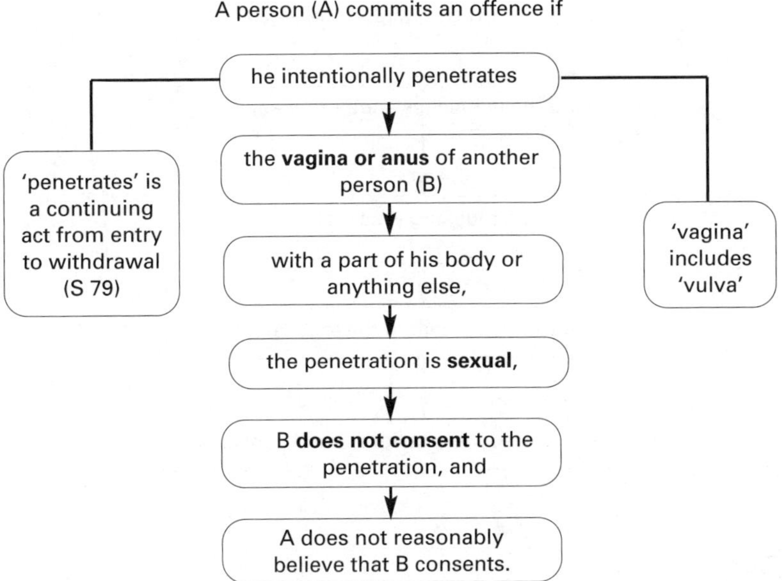

Reasonable belief
Whether a belief is reasonable is to be determined having regard to all the circumstances, including any steps A has taken to ascertain whether B consents.

Consent
A person consents if he agrees by choice, and has the freedom and capacity to make that choice. (S 74)

Presumptions about consent
The absence of the complainant's consent and/or the absence of the defendant's reasonable belief that the complainant consented may be presumed, depending on the circumstances (Ss 75 & 76). See later under 'Presumptions about Consent'.

Sexual
See later under 'Sexual Offences – Interpretation'

Sexual Assault

S 3 SEXUAL OFFENCES ACT 2003

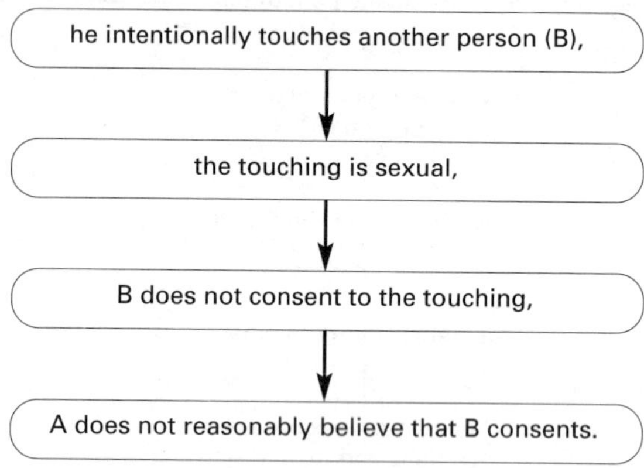

Touches
Includes touching with any part of the body, with anything else, and through anything. In particular it includes touching amounting to penetration. (S 79)

Reasonable belief
Whether a belief is reasonable is to be determined having regard to all the circumstances, including any steps A has taken to ascertain whether B consents.

Presumptions about consent
The absence of the complainant's consent and/or the absence of the defendant's reasonable belief that the complainant consented may be presumed, depending on the circumstances (Ss 75 & 76). See later under 'Presumptions about Consent'.

Sexual
See later under 'Sexual Offences – Interpretation'

Engaging in Sexual Activity Without Consent

S 4 SEXUAL OFFENCES ACT 2003

A person (A) commits an offence if

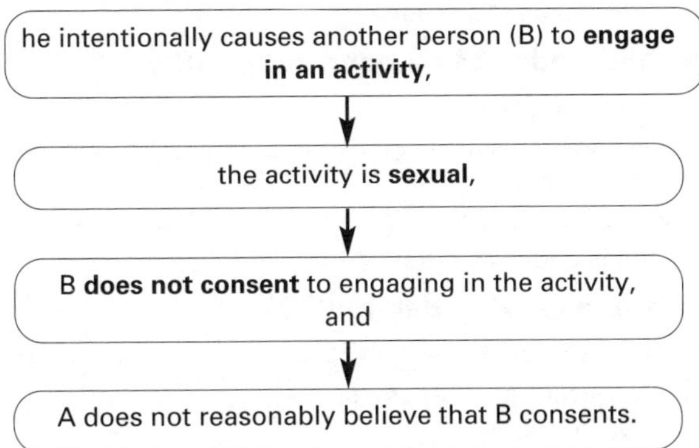

Reasonable belief
Whether a belief is reasonable is to be determined having regard to all the circumstances, including any steps A has taken to ascertain whether B consents.

Presumptions about consent
The absence of the complainant's consent and/or the absence of the defendant's reasonable belief that the complainant consented may be presumed, depending on the circumstances (Ss 75 & 76). See later under 'Presumptions about Consent'.

Sexual
See later under 'Sexual Offences – Interpretation'

Exposure

S 66 SEXUAL OFFENCES ACT 2003

A person commits an offence if:

a) he intentionally exposes his genitals, and
b) he intends that someone will see them and be caused alarm or distress.

Offences Against Children Under 13

Ss 5 – 8 SEXUAL OFFENCES ACT 2003

Rape (S 5)

A person commits an offence if:

(a) he intentionally penetrates the vagina, anus or mouth of another person with his penis, and

(b) the other person is under 13. (Life)

Assault of a child under 13 by penetration (S 6)

A person commits an offence if:

(a) he intentionally penetrates the vagina or anus of another person with a part of his body or anything else,

(b) the penetration is sexual, and

(c) the other person is under 13. (Life)

Sexual assault of a child under 13 (S 7)

A person commits an offence if:

(a) he intentionally touches another person,

(b) the touching is sexual, and

(c) the other person is under 13. (14 years)

Causing or inciting a child under 13 to engage in sexual activity (S 8)

A person commits an offence if:

(a) he intentionally causes or incites another person (B) to engage in an activity,

(b) the activity is sexual, and

(c) B is under 13. (14 years, unless the offence involves penetration, in which case, life)

Note

It will be noted that the main difference between these offences and those against sections 1 to 4 is that consent is irrelevant.

Touches
Includes touching with any part of the body, with anything else, and through anything. In particular it includes touching amounting to penetration. (S 79)

Penetration
See under Ss 1-4.

Sexual
See later under 'Sexual Offences – Interpretation'

Child Sex Offences

Ss 9 – 12 SEXUAL OFFENCES ACT 2003

The following offences are committed by a person aged 18 or over (A):

Sexual Activity with a child (S 9)

(a) if he intentionally touches another person (B),

(b) the touching is sexual, and

(c) either
 (i) B is under 16 and A does not reasonably believe that B is 16 or over, or
 (ii) B is under 13.

(14 years)

Causing or inciting a child to engage in sexual activity (S10)

(a) if he intentionally causes or incites another person (B) to engage in an activity,

(b) the activity is sexual, and

(c) either
 (i) B is under 16 and A does not reasonably believe that B is 16 or over, or
 (ii) B is under 13.

(14 years)

Engaging in sexual activity in the presence of a child (S 11)

(a) if he intentionally engages in an activity,

(b) the activity is sexual,

(c) for the purpose of obtaining sexual gratification, he engages in it
 (i) when another person (B) is present or is in a place from which A can be observed, and
 (ii) knowing or believing that B is aware, or intending that B should be aware, that he is engaging in it, and

(d) either
 (i) B is under 16 and A does not reasonably believe that B is 16 or over, or
 (ii) B is under 13.

(10 years)

Causing a child to watch a sexual act (S12)

(a) if for the purpose of obtaining sexual gratification, he intentionally causes another person (B) to watch a third person engaging in an activity, or to look at an image of any person engaging in an activity,

(b) the activity is sexual, and

(c) either
 (i) B is under 16 and A does not reasonably believe that B is 16 or over, or
 (ii) B is under 13.

(10 years)

Child Sex Offences

Ss 14 – 15 SEXUAL OFFENCES ACT 2003

Arranging or facilitating commission of a child sex offence (S 14)

A person commits an offence if:

(a) he intentionally arranges or facilitates something that he intends to do, intends another person to do, or believes that another person will do, in any part of the world, and

(b) doing it will involve the commission of an offence under any of sections 9 to 13 of this Act.

Defence – he arranged or facilitated the act without intending it to be carried out, and he was acting for the protection of a child.

Protection of a child – means one of the following acts:

(a) protecting the child from sexually transmitted infection,

(b) protecting the physical safety of the child,

(c) preventing the child from becoming pregnant, or

(d) promoting the child's emotional well-being by the giving of advice, and not for the purpose of obtaining sexual gratification or for the purpose of causing or encouraging the activity constituting the offence under sections 9 to 13.

(14 years)

Meeting a child following sexual grooming etc. (S 15)

A person aged 18 or over (A) commits an offence if:

(a) having met or communicated with another person (B) on at least 2 earlier occasions, he:
   (i) intentionally meets (B), or
   (ii) travels with the intention of meeting B in any part of the world,

(b) at the time, he intends to do anything to or in respect of B, during or after the meeting and in any part of the world, which if done will involve the commission by A of a relevant offence,

(c) B is under 16, and

(d) A does not reasonably believe that B is 16 or over.

(10 years)

Met means in any part of the world.

Communicated means from, to or in any part of the world by any means.

Relevant offence means:

(a) an offence under this part of the Act (Sections 1 – 79)

(b) an offence under paragraphs 61 – 92 of Sched. 3 (mainly sexual offences in Northern Ireland), or

(c) anything done outside England and Wales and Northern Ireland which is not an offence in (a) or (b) but would be an offence under (a) if done in England and Wales.

Abuse of Position of Trust

Ss 16 – 19 SEXUAL OFFENCES ACT 2003

The following offences are very similar in nature to Ss 9 – 12 committed by persons aged 18 or over (see earlier). The main difference is that they are **committed by a person who is in a position of trust** (described on the following page). The effect in each case is to reduce the maximum penalty to 5 years.

Sexual activity with a child (S 16)

Committed where a person in a position of trust (A) intentionally touches another person (B) and the touching is sexual. Unlike the related offence (S 9), this offence requires that either:

a) B is under 18 and A does not reasonably believe that B is 18 or over, or
b) B is under 13.

There is a presumption that A did not reasonably believe that B was 18 or over unless sufficient evidence to the contrary is adduced.

Causing or inciting a child to engage in sexual activity (S 17)

Committed where a person in a position of trust (A) intentionally causes or incites another person (B) to engage in sexual activity. As with S 16, unlike the corresponding offence (S 10) this offence requires that either:

a) B is under 18 and A does not reasonably believe that B is 18 or over, or
b) B is under 13.

There is a similar presumption that A did not reasonably believe that B was 18 or over unless sufficient evidence to the contrary is adduced.

Sexual activity in the presence of a child (S 18)

Committed where a person in a position of trust (A) intentionally, and for the purpose of obtaining sexual gratification, engages in a sexual activity when another person (B) is present or is in a position to see. Again, unlike the similar offence (S 11), either:

a) B is under 18 and A does not reasonably believe that B is 18 or over, or
b) B is under 13.

Similarly, there is a presumption that A did not reasonably believe that B was 18 or over unless sufficient evidence to the contrary is adduced.

Causing a child to watch a sexual act (S 19)

Committed where a person in a position of trust (A) intentionally, and for the purpose of obtaining sexual gratification, causes another person (B) to watch a third person engaging in a sexual activity, or to look at an image of a person so engaging. In line with the above offences, this offence differs from the comparable offence (S 12) in that either:

a) B is under 18 and A does not reasonably believe that B is 18 or over, or
b) B is under 13.

A like presumption exists that A did not reasonably believe that B was 18 or over unless sufficient evidence to the contrary is adduced.

Defences

No activity will constitute an offence contrary to sections 16 – 19 above where:

a) B is 16 or over and A and B are **lawfully married**, or
b) immediately before a position of trust arose **a sexual relationship existed** between A and B (provided it was lawful).

Position of Trust – Meaning

S 21 SEXUAL OFFENCES ACT 2003

For the purposes of sections 16 – 19 a person (A) is in a position of trust in relation to another person (B) if any of the following apply:

B's situation	A's activity	Location
Detained by a court order or enactment	Looks after persons under 18 so detained	Institution
Resident in a home etc.	Looks after persons under 18 who are resident	Accommodation and maintenance provided by a local authority or voluntary organisation
Accommodated and cared for	Looks after persons under 18 accommodated and cared for	Hospital, independent clinic, care home etc., community home etc, children's home, or residential family centre
Receiving education	Looks after persons receiving education	Educational institution
Under guardianship	Guardian	Northern Ireland
Training for employment	Looks after B on an individual basis in the provision of services	–
Accommodated by local authority	Has regular unsupervised contact with B	Local authority accommodation
Subject to a court welfare report	Reporting on B and has regular unsupervised contact	–
Subject to local authority assessment	Appointed as personal adviser to B on an individual basis	–
Subject of care order, supervision order or education supervision order	Exercising the functions of the order and looks after B on an individual basis	–
Interests being safeguarded by the court or an enactment	Appointed to safeguard B's interests and has regular unsupervised contact with him	–
Subject to requirements on release from detention for a criminal offence, or a court order made in criminal proceedings	Looks after B on an individual basis in pursuance of the requirements	–

Familial Child Sex Offences

Ss 25 & 26 SEXUAL OFFENCES ACT 2003

Sexual Activity with Child Family Member (S 25)

A person commits an offence if:

(a) he intentionally touches another person (B),
(b) the touching is sexual,
(c) the relation of A to B is within S 27 (see following page),
(d) A knows or could reasonably be expected to know that his relation to B is of such a description, and
(e) either –
  (i) B is under 18 and A does not reasonably believe that B is 18 or over, or
  (ii) B is under 13.

Inciting a Child Family Member to Engage in Sexual Activity (S 26)

A person (A) commits an offence if:

(a) he intentionally incites another person (B) to touch, or allow himself to be touched by A,
(b) the touching is sexual,
(c) the relation of A to B is within S 27 (see following page),
(d) A knows or could reasonably be expected to know that his relation to B is of such a description, and
(e) either –
  (i) B is under 18 and A does not reasonably believe that B is 18 or over, or
  (ii) B is under 13.

Touches
Includes touching with any part of the body, with anything else, and through anything. In particular it includes touching amounting to penetration. (S 79)

Sexual
See later under 'Sexual Offences – Interpretation'

Defences
No activity will constitute an offence contrary to sections 25 or 26 above where:

(a) B is 16 or over and A and B are lawfully married, or
(b) the relationship between A and B is not one of parent, grandparent, brother, sister, half-brother, half-sister, aunt, uncle or foster parent, and immediately before the relation between them fell within S 27, a sexual relationship existed between A and B (provided it was lawful). (Ss 28 & 29)

Presumptions
The defendant is to be taken not to have reasonably believed the other was 18 or over, and to have reasonably believed that his relation to B was within S 27 (see following page), unless, in either case, evidence is adduced to the contrary.

Family Relationships – Meaning

S 27 SEXUAL OFFENCES ACT 2003

The relation of one person (A) to another (B) is within this section if:
(a) it is within one of the subsections below, or
(b) it would be within one of those subsections but for S 67 of the Adoption and Children Act 2002 (which states that the adopted person is treated in law as if born as the child of the adopter(s)).

(a) The relation of A to B is within this subsection if:
- (i) one of them is the other's parent, grandparent, brother, sister, half-brother, half-sister, aunt or uncle, or
- (ii) A is or has been B's foster parent.

(b) The relation of A to B is within this subsection if A and B live or have lived in the same household, or A is or has been regularly involved in caring for, training, supervising or being in sole charge of B, and:
- (i) one of them is or has been the other's step-parent,
- (ii) A and B are cousins,
- (iii) one of them is or has been the other's stepbrother or stepsister, or
- (iv) the parent or present or former foster parent of one of them is or has been the other's foster parent.

(c) The relation of A to B is within this subsection if:
- (i) A and B live in the same household, and
- (ii) A is regularly involved in caring for, training, supervising or being solely in charge of B.

Aunt
Means the sister or half-sister of a person's parent.

Uncle
Has a corresponding meaning to 'aunt'.

Cousin
Means the child of an aunt or uncle.

Foster parent
Means the person with whom the child has been placed by a local authority or voluntary organisation; or the person who fosters the child privately.

Step-parent
Includes a parent's partner.

Step-brother and step-sister
Includes the child of a parent's partner.

Partner
Persons (whether of the same sex or different sexes) who live together as partners in an enduring family relationship.

Offences Against Persons with a Mental Disorder Impeding Choice

Ss 30–33 SEXUAL OFFENCES ACT 2003

A person (A) commits an offence if:

Sexual activity with mentally disordered person (S 30).
he intentionally touches another person (B) and the touching is sexual,

OR

Causing a person with mental disorder to engage in sexual activity (S 32).
he intentionally causes or incites another person (B) to engage in an activity and the activity is sexual,

OR

Engaging in sexual activity in presence of mentally disordered person (S 32).

(a) he intentionally engages in an activity and the activity is sexual,
(b) for the purpose of obtaining sexual gratification, he engages in it-
- (i) when another person (B) is present or is in a place from which A can be observed, and
- (ii) knowing or believing that B is aware, or intending that B should be aware, that he is engaging in it,

OR

Causing a person with mental disorder to watch a sexual act (S 33).

(a) for the purpose of obtaining sexual gratification, he intentionally causes another person (B) to watch a third person engaging in an activity, or to look at an image of any person engaging in an activity,
(b) the activity is sexual

AND

(a) B is unable to refuse because of or for a reason related to a mental disorder, and
(b) A knows or could reasonably be expected to know that B has a mental disorder and that because of it or for a reason related to it B is likely to be unable to refuse.

B is unable to refuse if:

(a) he lacks the capacity to choose whether to agree to the touching (whether he lacks sufficient understanding of the nature or reasonably foreseeable consequences of what is being done, or for any other reason), or
(b) he is unable to communicate such a choice to A.

Inducements etc to Persons with a Mental Disorder

Ss 34–37 SEXUAL OFFENCES ACT 2003

A person (A) commits an offence if:

by means of an **inducement** offered or given, a **threat** made or a **deception** practiced by A for the purpose, he-

Sexual activity with person with mental disorder (S 34).

with the agreement of another person (B), intentionally sexually touches that person

OR

Causing person with mental disorder to engage in sexual activity (S 35).

intentionally causes another person (B) to engage in, or to agree to engage in, a sexual activity

Engaging in sexual activity in the presence of a person with a mental disorder (S 36).

procures another person (B) to be in a place and then intentionally engages in a sexual activity and for the purpose of sexual gratification he engages in it:
(a) when B is present or is in a place from which A can be observed, and
(b) knowing or believing that B is aware, or intending that B should be aware, that he is engaging in it

OR

Causing a person with a mental disorder to watch a sexual act (S 37).

for the purpose of sexual gratification, intentionally causes another person (B) to watch a third person engaging in a sexual activity, or to look at an image of any person engaging in a sexual activity

AND

B has a mental disorder, and A knows or could reasonably be expected to know that B has a mental disorder.

Care Workers for Persons with a Mental Disorder

Ss 38–44 SEXUAL OFFENCES ACT 2003

The following offences are very similar to Ss 30 – 33 (see earlier). The main differences are that they are **committed by care workers** (described below) and there is no need to prove that the mental disorder impeded choice.

Each of the offences are committed where a person (A) is involved in another person's care (B), B has a mental disorder, and A knew, or could reasonably be expected to know, that B had a mental disorder. Unlike the related offences, these offences presume that A knew or could reasonably have been expected to know that A had a mental disorder unless contrary evidence is adduced.

Care workers: sexual activity with a person with a mental disorder (S 38)

Committed when A intentionally touches B and the touching is sexual.

Care workers: causing or inciting sexual activity (S 39)

Committed where A intentionally causes or incites B to engage in sexual activity.

Care workers: sexual activity in the presence of a person with a mental disorder (S 40)

Committed where A intentionally, and for the purpose of obtaining sexual gratification, **engages in a sexual activity when B is present** or is in a position from which A can be observed, knowing or believing that B is aware, or intending that B should be aware, that he is engaging in it.

Care workers: causing a person with a mental disorder to watch a sexual act (S 41)

Committed where A intentionally, and for the purpose of obtaining sexual gratification, causes B to watch a third person engaging in a sexual activity, or to look at an image of a person so engaging.

Defences (Ss 43 & 44)

No activity will constitute an offence contrary to sections 38 – 41 above where:

(a) B is 16 or over and A and B are **lawfully married**, or

(b) immediately before the position of care arose, **a sexual relationship existed** between A and B (provided it was lawful).

Care workers – meaning (S42)

A person (A) is involved in the care of another person (B) if:

(a) B is accommodated and cared for in a care home, community home, voluntary home or children's home, and A regularly has face to face contact with B in the home in the course of A's employment, or

(b) B is a patient for whom services are provided by a National Health Service body, an independent medical agency, or in an independent clinic or independent hospital, and A regularly has face to face contact with B in the course of A's employment, or

(c) whether or not in the course of employment, A provides care, assistance or services to B in connection with his mental disorder and has regular face to face contact with him.

Abuse of Children through Prostitution or Pornography

Ss 47–51 SEXUAL OFFENCES ACT 2003

A person (A) commits an offence in any of the circumstances listed below if either:

(a) the other person (B) is under 18 and B does not reasonably believe that A is 18 or over, or

(b) B is under 13.

Paying for sexual services of a child (S 47)
If he intentionally obtains for himself the sexual services of another person, and before obtaining those services he has made or promised payment for those services to B or a third person, or knows that another person has made or promised such payment.

Causing or inciting child prostitution or pornography (S 48)
If he intentionally causes or incites another person (B) to become a prostitute, or to be involved in pornography, in any part of the world.

Controlling a child prostitute or a child involved in pornography (S 49)
If he intentionally controls any of the activities of another person (B) relating to B's prostitution or involvement in pornography in any part of the world.

Arranging or facilitating child prostitution or pornography (S 50)
If he intentionally arranges or facilitates the prostitution or involvement in pornography in any part of the world of another person (B).

Involvement in photography means the recording of an indecent image of that person. (S 51)

Prostitute means a person (A) who on at least one occasion, and whether or not compelled to do so, offers or provides sexual services to another person in return for payment or a promise of payment to A or a third person. (S 51)

Payment means any financial advantage, including the discharge of an obligation to pay, or the provision of goods or services (including sexual services) gratuitously or at a discount. (S 51)

Indecent Photographs

S 1 PROTECTION OF CHILDREN ACT 1978 AS AMENDED BY S 84 CRIMINAL JUSTICE AND PUBLIC ORDER ACT 1994 AND S 45 SEXUAL OFFENCES ACT 2003

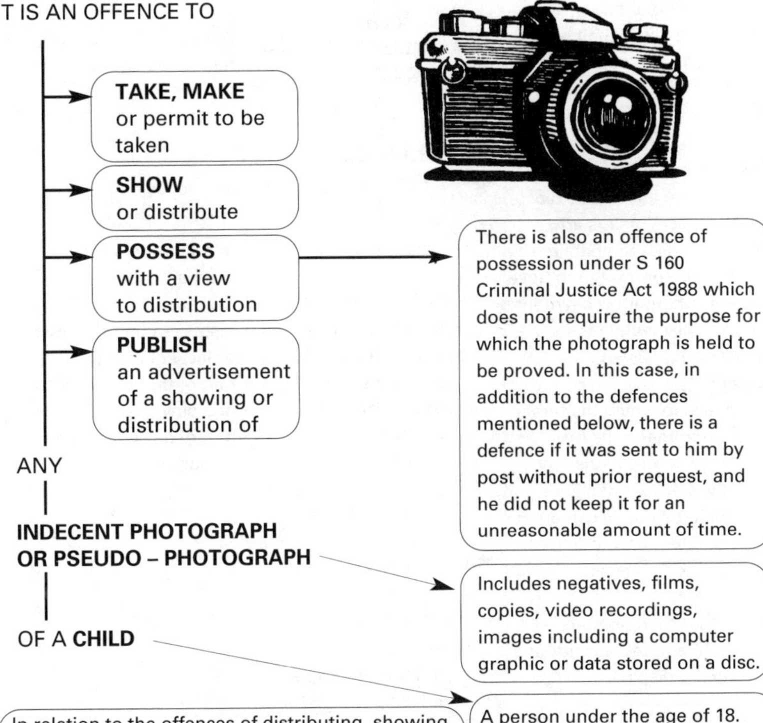

A person under the age of 18. But, irrespective of the actual age, if the impression conveyed by a pseudo-photograph is that of a child, it will be treated as showing a child, even if some of the characteristics shown are those of an adult.

In relation to the offences of distributing, showing, or possessing with a view to doing so, it shall be a **defence** if the accused proves that:

- there is a legitimate reason for distribution or possession
- he had not seen the photographs and neither knew nor suspected they were indecent
- at the time of the offence the child was 16 or over and they were married or living together as partners in an enduring family relationship, or
- it was for the purposes of crime prevention, detection or investigation

'Distribution' means parting with possession of it to, or exposes or offers it for acquisition by, another person.

Indecent Displays

S 1 INDECENT DISPLAYS (CONTROL) ACT 1981

If any INDECENT MATTER is PUBLICLY displayed the person making the display and any person causing or permitting the display to be made shall be guilty of an offence

Indecent matter: Any part of the matter not exposed to view shall be disregarded. Account may be taken of juxtaposing one thing with another.

Indecent matter: Does not include the human body or any part thereof

Publicly displayed: Displayed in or so as to be visible from any public place. **'Public place'** means any place to which the public have or are permitted to have access (whether on payment or otherwise) while the matter is displayed.

Except

a) a place to which the public are admitted only on payment for the display,

b) a shop or part of a shop which the public can enter only after passing a warning **notice** as indicated

if in either case persons under 18 are not permitted during the display.

WARNING
Persons passing beyond this notice will find material on display which they may consider indecent. No admittance to persons under 18 years of age.

The offence does not apply to matter:

- in a TV broadcast
- in an art gallery or museum
- displayed by the Crown or local authority
- part of the performance of a play
- part of a licensed cinema exhibition

Police Powers

A constable may seize any article which he has reasonable grounds for believing to be indecent matter used in the commission of an offence.

Obscene Publications

OBSCENE PUBLICATIONS ACTS 1959 & 1964

IT IS AN OFFENCE TO

PUBLISH
(to distribute, circulate, sell, let on hire, give, lend; show, play or project matter to be looked at or a record; or transmit electronically stored data)

WHETHER OR NOT FOR GAIN

or

HAVE
(ownership, possession or control)

FOR PUBLICATION FOR GAIN
(to the offender or any other person accruing benefit either directly or indirectly)

ANY

OBSCENE → A tendency to deprave or corrupt those who are likely to read, see or hear the matter contained in it.

ARTICLE → Anything containing matter to be read or looked at; any sound, record, film, or other record of a picture or pictures, whether intended to be used alone or as one of a set, or for the reproduction or manufacture of such articles, e.g. negatives, printing blocks, etc.

DEFENCES

The offender had not examined the article and had no reasonable cause to suspect that his having it was an offence, or its publication was justifiable as being for the public good in the interests of science, literature, art or learning, or of other objects of public concern. In the case of a moving picture film or soundtrack, its publication was justified as being for the public good in the interests of drama, opera, ballet or any other art, or of literature or learning.

Harmful Publications

CHILDREN AND YOUNG PERSONS (HARMFUL PUBLICATIONS) ACT 1955

It is an offence to

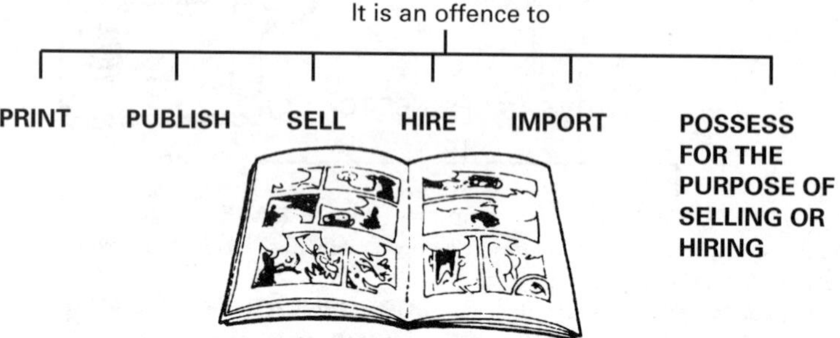

any book, magazine or other like work which is likely to fall into the hands of a child (under 14 years) or young person (under 18 years) and which consists wholly or mainly of stories told in pictures (with or without written material)

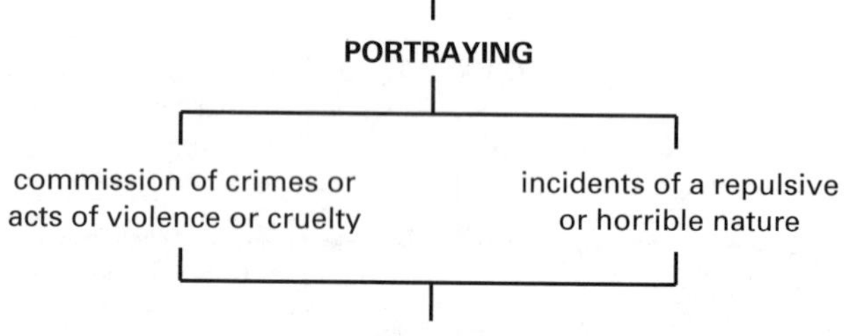

such that the whole work would tend to

CORRUPT

A CHILD OR YOUNG PERSON

into whose hands it might fall

DEFENCE (applies only to selling or hiring or having in possession for that purpose.) That the accused had not examined the work and had no reasonable cause to suspect that it constituted an offence.

Prostitution

S 1 STREET OFFENCES ACT 1959 AS AMENDED BY THE SEXUAL OFFENCES ACT 2003

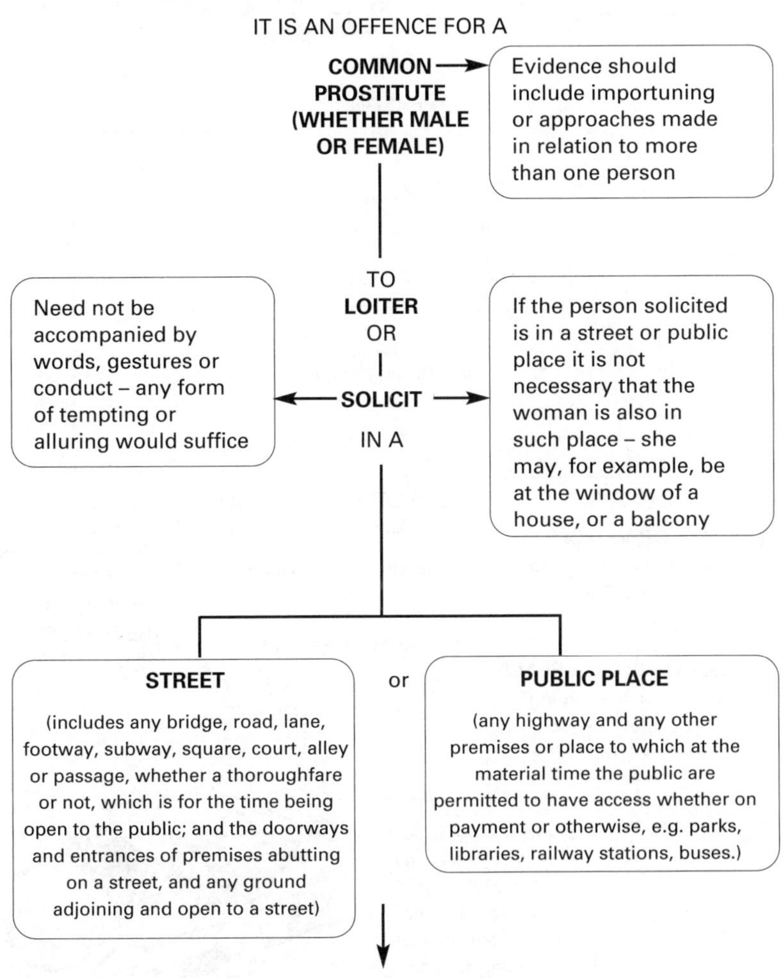

Kerb-Crawling

S 1 SEXUAL OFFENCES ACT 1985 AS AMENDED BY THE SEXUAL OFFENCES ACT 2003

An offence is committed by a

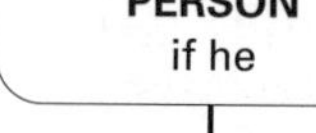

PERSON
if he

SOLICITS

ANOTHER PERSON
for the purpose of

PROSTITUTION

FROM A
MOTOR VEHICLE
(has the same meaning as in the Road Traffic Act)
WHILE IT IS IN A
STREET OR PUBLIC PLACE
(has the same meaning as in the Street Offences Act (see previous page))

IN A STREET OR PUBLIC PLACE WHILE IN THE
IMMEDIATE VICINITY
OF A
MOTOR VEHICLE
WHICH HE HAS JUST GOT OUT OF OR OFF

persistently or in such circumstances as to be likely to cause annoyance to the person solicited, or nuisance to other persons in the neighbourhood

PERSISTENTLY SOLICITS ANOTHER PERSON IN A STREET OR PUBLIC PLACE FOR THE PURPOSE OF PROSTITUTION
(S 2)

Advertising Prostitution

S 46 CRIMINAL JUSTICE AND POLICE ACT 2001

A person commits an offence if he places on, or in the immediate vicinity of,

a public telephone

an advertisement relating to prostitution

and he does so with the intention that the advertisement should come to the attention of any other person or persons

It will relate to prostitution if it:

(a) is for the services of a prostitute, whether male or female; or
(b) indicates that premises are premises at which such services are offered.

Any advertisement which a reasonable person would consider to be an advertisement relating to prostitution shall be presumed to be such an advertisement unless it is shown not to be.

Means:

(a) any telephone which is located in a public place and made available for use by the public, or a section of the public, and
(b) where such a telephone is located in or on, or attached to, a kiosk, booth, acoustic hood, shelter or other structure, that structure.

'Public place' means any place to which the public have or are permitted to have access, whether on payment or otherwise, other than:

(a) any place to which children under the age of 16 years are not permitted to have access, whether by law or otherwise, and
(b) any premises which are wholly or mainly used for residential purposes.

Brothels

S 33 SEXUAL OFFENCES ACT 1956

IT IS AN OFFENCE FOR A PERSON TO KEEP A

A brothel is a place where people of opposite sexes are allowed to resort for illicit sexual intercourse. The women need not necessarily be prostitutes. However, S 6 of the Sexual Offences Act 1967 extended this to include premises to which people resort for lewd homosexual practices.

Evidence of sexual intercourse is not necessary to prove 'assisting in the management'. It is sufficient to prove that more than one woman offered herself for physical acts of indecency or sexual gratification.

or to manage, or act or assist in the management of, a brothel.

To be 'assisting in the management' it is not necessary to show that some sort of control was exercised over the management, nor that there was a specific act of management.

A new offence was inserted by S 55 Sexual Offences Act 2003 of managing etc. a brothel used for practices of prostitution, whether or not also used for other practices (S 33A).

Circumstances where premises WILL NOT be a brothel

A house occupied by a woman and used by her for her own prostitution, but not used by other women, is not a brothel.

Two flats in one building separately let to two prostitutes will not be a brothel.

Circumstances where premises WILL be a brothel

Two women, one being the occupier, both used the premises.

A block of flats inhabited by different women for prostitution.

Three rooms in close proximity separately let to prostitutes.

Premises used by a team of prostitutes but not more than one per day used them.

Premises Used for the Purposes of Sex

SEXUAL OFFENCES ACT 1956 AS AMENDED BY THE SEXUAL OFFENCES ACT 2003

Landlord Letting Premises for Use as Brothel (S 34)
It is an offence for the lessor or landlord of any premises or his agent to let the whole or part of the premises with the knowledge that it is to be used as a brothel, or, where it is being so used, to be a wilful party to that use continuing.

The premises must be used by more than one prostitute.

Tenant Permitting Premises to Be Used as a Brothel (S 35)
It is an offence for the tenant or occupier, or person in charge, of any premises knowingly to permit the whole or part of the premises to be used as a brothel.

Tenant Permitting Premises to Be Used for Prostitution (S 36)
It is an offence for the tenant or occupier of any premises knowingly to permit the whole or part of the premises to be used for the purposes of habitual prostitution (whether any prostitute involved is male or female).

A woman who is the sole occupier cannot be convicted of this offence if she uses the premises for her own habitual prostitution.

Exploitation of Prostitution

Ss 52–54 SEXUAL OFFENCES ACT 2003

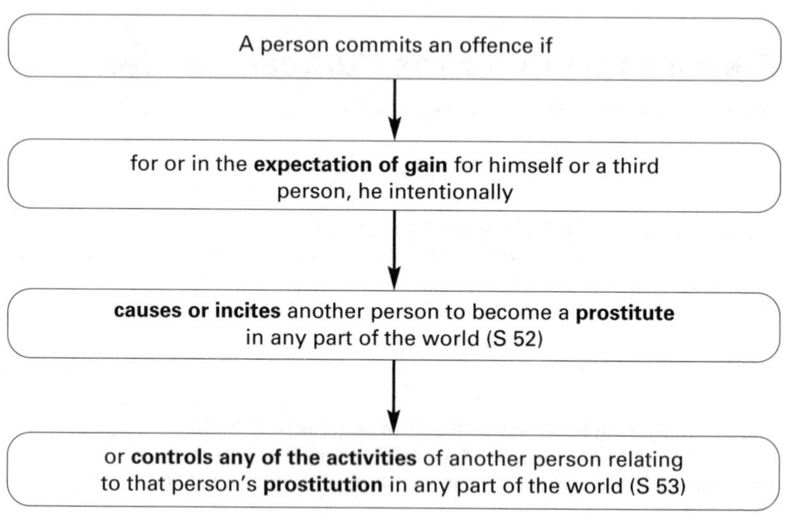

Gain means

(a) any financial advantage, including the discharge of an obligation to pay or the provision of goods or services (including sexual services) gratuitously or at a discount, or

(b) the goodwill of any person which is or appears likely in time, to bring financial advantage. (S 54)

Prostitute means a person (A) who on at least one occasion, and whether or not compelled to do so, offers or provides sexual services to another person in return for payment or a promise of payment to A or a third person. (S 51)

Payment means any financial advantage, including the discharge of an obligation to pay, or the provision of goods or services (including sexual services) gratuitously or at a discount. (S 51)

Trafficking for Sexual Exploitation

Ss 57–59 SEXUAL OFFENCES ACT 2003

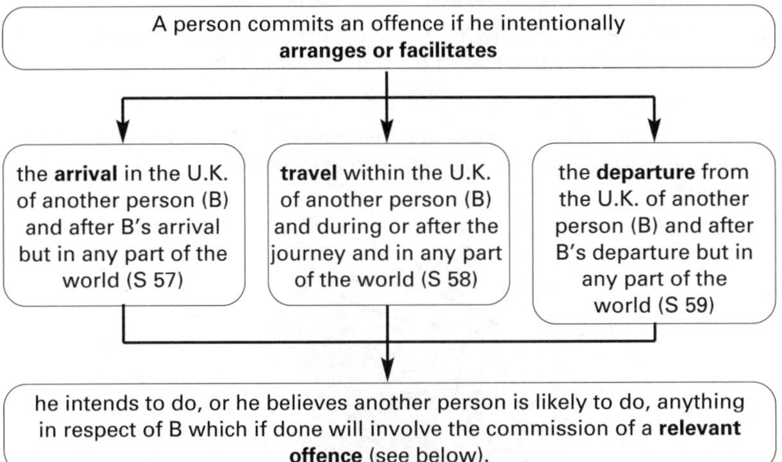

These offences apply to anything done

(a) in the U.K., or

(b) outside the U.K., by a body incorporated under the law of a part of the U.K. or by an individual who is a British citizen, a British overseas territories citizen, a British National (Overseas), a British Overseas citizen, a person who is a British subject under the British Nationality Act 1981, or a British protected person within the meaning of S 50(1) of that Act.

Relevant offence means

(a) any offence under Ss 1–72 of the Sexual Offences Act 2003,

(b) indecent photographs of children (S1(1) Protection of Children Act 1978),

(c) offences listed in Sched. 1 to the Criminal Justice (Children) (Northern Ireland) Order 1978,

(d) an offence under Art. 3(1)(a) of the Protection of Children (Northern Ireland) Order 1978, or

(e) anything done outside England and Wales and Northern Ireland which is not an offence in paragraphs (a) to (d) above but would be if done in England and Wales and Northern Ireland.

Preparatory Offences

Ss 61–63 SEXUAL OFFENCES ACT 2003

Administering a substance with intent (S 61)

A person commits an offence if he intentionally administers a substance to, or causes a substance to be taken by, another person (B)

(a) knowing that B does not consent and,

(b) with the intention of stupefying or overpowering B, so as to enable any person to engage in a sexual activity that involves B.

(10 years)

Committing an offence with intent to commit a sexual offence (S 62)

A person commits an offence under this section if he commits any offence with the intention of committing any offence under Ss 1–72 of this Act (including aiding, abetting, counselling or procuring such an offence).

Life (if the offence involves kidnapping or false imprisonment) or 10 years.

Trespass with intent to commit a sexual offence (S 63)

A person commits an offence if

(a) he is a trespasser on any premises,

(b) he intends to commit any offence under Ss 1–72 of this Act on the premises, and

(c) he knows that, or is reckless as to whether, he is a trespasser.

Premises includes a structure or part of a structure.

Structure includes a tent, vehicle or vessel or other temporary or moveable structure.

(10 years)

Sex with an Adult Relative

Ss 64 & 65 SEXUAL OFFENCES ACT 2003

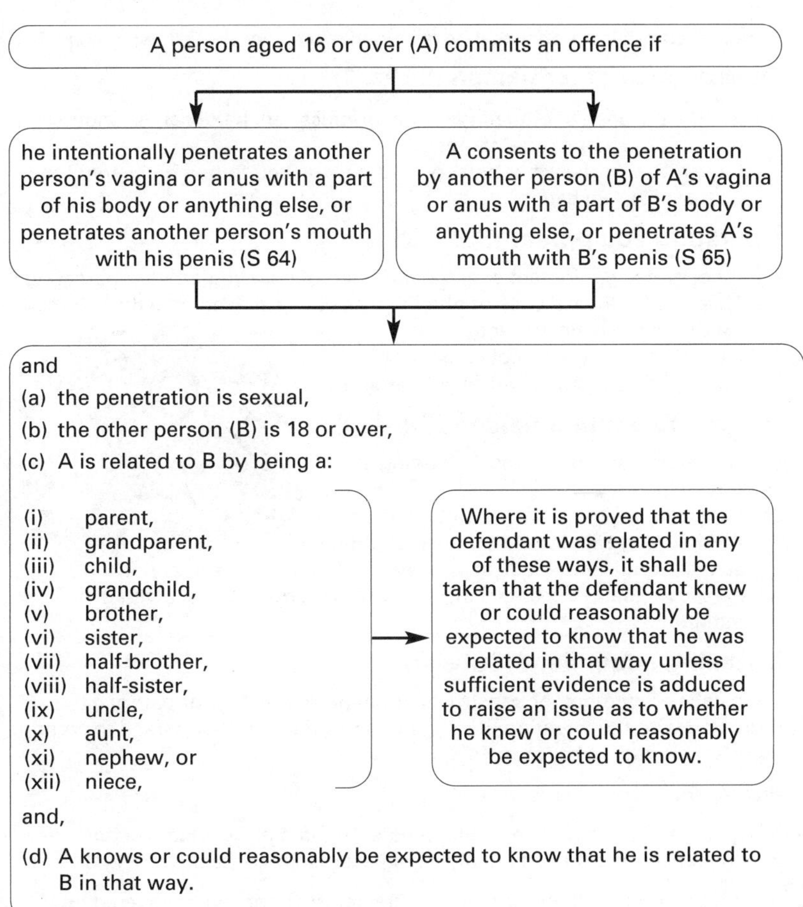

Uncle means the brother of the person's parent, and **aunt** has a corresponding meaning.

Nephew means the child of a person's brother or sister, and **niece** has a corresponding meaning.

Voyeurism

S 67 SEXUAL OFFENCES ACT 2003

A person commits an offence if he is involved in any of the following activities

Observing another person (Subs. 1)

(a) For the purpose of obtaining sexual gratification, he observes another person doing a private act, and
(b) he knows that the other person does not consent to being observed for his sexual gratification.

Operating equipment (Subs. 2)

(a) He operates equipment with the intention of enabling another person to observe, for the purpose of obtaining sexual gratification, a third person (B) doing a private act, and
(b) he knows that B does not consent to his operating equipment with that intention.

Recording another person (Subs. 3)

(a) He records another person (B) doing a private act,
(b) he does so with the intention that he or a third person will, for the purpose of obtaining sexual gratification, look at an image of B doing the act, and
(c) he knows that B does not consent to his recording the act with that intention.

Installing equipment (Subs. 4)

He installs equipment, or constructs or adapts a structure or part of a structure, with the intention of enabling himself or another person to commit an offence under subs. 1 above

Private act

A person is doing a private act if the person is in a place which, in the circumstances, would reasonably be expected to provide privacy, and

(a) the person's genitals, buttocks or breasts are exposed or covered only with underwear,
(b) the person is using a lavatory, or
(c) the person is doing a sexual act that is not of a kind ordinarily done in public.

Structure includes a tent vehicle or vessel or other temporary or moveable structure.

Intercourse with an Animal

S 69 SEXUAL OFFENCES ACT 2003

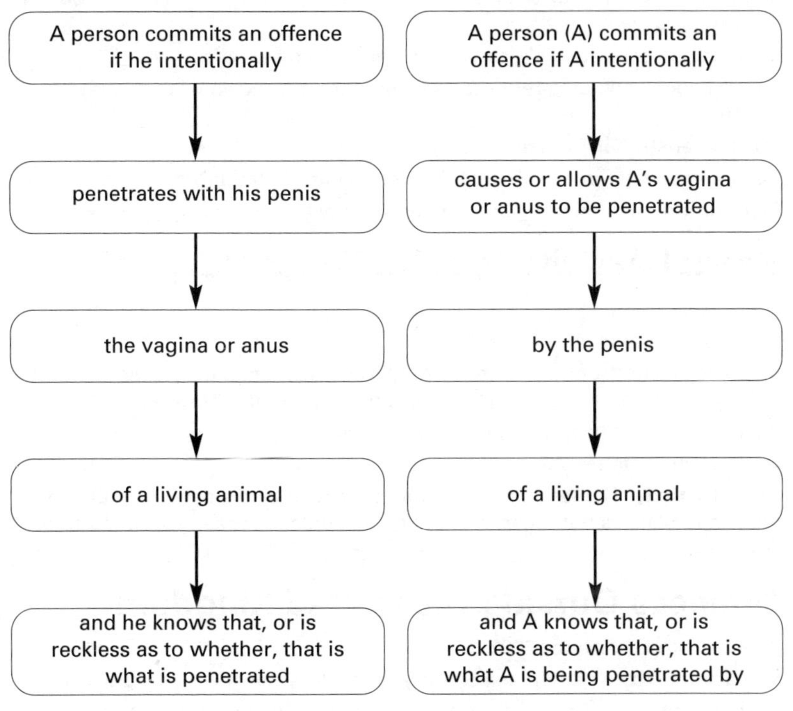

references to the vagina or anus include references to a similar part

Sexual Penetration of a Corpse

S 70 SEXUAL OFFENCES ACT 2003

A person commits an offence if:

(a) he intentionally performs an act of penetration with a part of his body or anything else,

(b) what is penetrated is a part of the body of a dead person,

(c) he knows that, or is reckless as to whether, that is what is penetrated, and

(d) the penetration is sexual.

Sexual – see later under 'Sexual Offences – Interpretation'

Penetration – a continuing act from entry to withdrawal.

Sexual Activity in a Public Lavatory

S 71 SEXUAL OFFENCES ACT 2003

A person commits an offence if:

(a) he is in a lavatory to which the public or a section of the public has or is permitted to have access, whether on payment or otherwise,

(b) he intentionally engages in an activity, and,

(c) the activity is sexual.

Sexual activity. The test for this is whether a reasonable person would, in all the circumstances but regardless of any person's purpose, consider it to be sexual.

Offences Outside the United Kingdom

S 72 SEXUAL OFFENCES ACT 2003

Any act done by a person in a country or territory outside the U.K. which:

(a) constituted an offence under the law in force in that country or territory, and

(b) would constitute an offence to which this section applies if it had been done in England and Wales or in Northern Ireland,

constitutes that sexual offence under the law of that part of the U.K.

The sexual offences to which this section applies in England and Wales are:

(a) Ss 5–15 of this Act (offences against children under 13 or under 16),

(b) Ss 1–4, 16–41, 47–50, and 61 of this Act, where the victim was under 16, Ss 62 or 63 of this Act where the intended victim was under 16, or

(c) S 1 Protection of Children Act 1978, or S 160 Criminal Justice Act 1988 (indecent photographs of children under 16).

Incitement to Commit Sexual Offences Outside the UK

SEXUAL OFFENCES (CONSPIRACY AND INCITEMENT) ACT 1996

A person will be guilty of incitement triable in England and Wales if each of the following conditions is satisfied:

(a) The course of action involves:
 (i) an act which would have been a listed sexual offence (see below) if committed in England or Wales,
 (ii) the whole or part of what he had in view was intended to take place outside the U.K.

(b) What he had in view is an offence in that other country or territory.

Any act of incitement by means of a message (however communicated) is to be treated as done in England and Wales if the message is sent or received in England or Wales.

Listed Sexual Offences

Indecency with Children Act 1960:
 S 1 indecent conduct towards a young child

Presumptions about Consent

Ss 75 & 76 SEXUAL OFFENCES ACT 2003

In proceedings for an offence to which this section applies (see below), **the complainant is to be taken not to have consented and the defendant is to be taken not to have reasonably believed that the complainant consented** (unless, in either case, sufficient contrary evidence is adduced to raise an issue), if:

(a) the defendant did the relevant act (see below), and

(b) any of the below circumstances existed, and the defendant knew they existed.

Offence	Relevant Act (in each case intentionally)
S 1 (Rape)	Penetrating, with his penis, the vagina, anus or mouth of another person
S 2 (Assault by penetration)	Sexually penetrating with part of his body or anything else the vagina or anus of another person
S 3 (Sexual assault)	Sexually touching another person
S 4 (Sexual activity without consent)	Causing another person to engage in a sexual activity

Circumstances

Violence
Any person was, at the time of the relevant act, or immediately before it began, using violence against the complainant or causing him to fear that immediate violence would be used against him.

Fear of violence against another person
Any person was, at the time of the relevant act or immediately before it began, causing the complainant to fear that violence was being used, or that immediate violence would be used, against another person.

Unlawfully detained
The complainant was, and the defendant was not, unlawfully detained at the time of the relevant act.

Unconscious
The complainant was asleep or unconscious at the time of the relevant act.

Unable to consent through physical disability
Because of the complainant's physical disability, he would not have been able at the time of the relevant act to communicate to the defendant whether he consented.

Administering a stupefying or overpowering substance
Any person had administered to or caused to be taken by the complainant, without the complainant's consent, a substance which, having regard to when it was administered or taken, was capable of causing or enabling the complainant to be stupefied or overpowered at the time of the relevant act.

Conclusive presumptions about consent S 76
It is to be conclusively presumed that the complainant did not consent to the relevant act (as above) and that the defendant did not believe that the complainant consented if

(a) the defendant intentionally deceived the complainant as to the nature or purpose of the relevant act, or

(b) the defendant intentionally induced the complainant to consent to the relevant act by impersonating a person known personally to the complainant.

Sexual Offences – Interpretation

Consent
A person consents if he agrees by choice, and has the freedom and capacity to make that choice (S 74).

Sexual
Penetration, touching or any other activity is sexual if a reasonable person would consider that:

(a) whatever its circumstances or any person's purpose in relation to it, it is because of its nature sexual, or

(b) because of its nature it may be sexual and because of its circumstances or the purpose of any person in relation to it (or both) it is sexual. (S 78)

This definition does not apply to S 71 (sexual activity in a public lavatory).

Penetration
This is a continuing act from entry to withdrawal. (S 79)

Part of the body
Includes a part surgically constructed (in particular through gender reassignment surgery). (S 79)

Image
A moving or still image and includes an image produced by any means and, where the context permits, a three dimensional image. (S 79)

Image of a person
Includes an image of an imaginary person. (S 79)

Mental disorder
Means the same as in S 1 Mental Health Act 1983 – "mental illness, arrested or incomplete development of mind, psychopathic disorder and any other disorder or disability of mind". (S 79)

Observation
However expressed, means either direct or by looking at an image. (S 79)

Touching
Includes touching with any part of the body, with anything else, or through anything, and in particular includes touching amounting to penetration. (S 79)

Vagina
Includes vulva. In relation to an animal, references to a vagina or anus includes reference to any similar parts. (S 79)

Notification Requirements

Ss 80–91 SEXUAL OFFENCES ACT 2003

Persons subject to notification requirements (S 80)
A person is subject to notification requirements if:
(a) convicted of a Sched. 3 offence (see later),
(b) found not guilty of such an offence by reason of insanity,
(c) found to be under a disability and to have done the act charged against him in respect of such an offence, or
(d) cautioned for such an offence.

Notification requirements: initial notification (S 83)
The offender must, within 3 days of the relevant date (see below), notify to the police:
(a) date of birth,
(b) national insurance number,
(c) name and any other names used on the relevant date,
(d) home address on the relevant date,
(e) name and any other names used on the date of notification,
(f) home address on the date of notification,
(g) address of any other premises in the U.K. where he regularly resides or stays

The period of 3 days will not include time in court custody; imprisonment or service detention; detained in hospital; or outside the U.K.

Any changes to the above must be notified to the police within 3 days. (S 84)

Method of notification (S 87)
Notification is given by:
(a) attending a local police station prescribed by the Secretary of State, and
(b) giving oral notification to any police officer or other authorised person.

For the purpose of verifying the identity of the offender a photograph may be taken of any part of him and his fingerprints taken.

Young offenders; parental directions (S 89)
Where the offender is under 18, the court may direct that obligation for notification may be placed on the parent responsible for him and the offender must attend the police station with the parent.

Offences relating to notification (S 91)
A person commits an offence if he fails to comply with the above requirements or gives false information.

Persons formerly subject to the Sex Offenders Act 1997 (S 81)
A person will still be subject to notification requirements if he was subject to the old law in respect of a Sched. 3 offence if the conviction, caution, etc. occurred before 1.9.97.

Relevant date (S 82)
This means:
(a) the date of **conviction** (for person convicted of Sched. 3 offence),
(b) the date of the **finding** (for a person found not guilty by reason of insanity, or for a person suffering from a disability but to have done the act),
(c) the date of the **caution** for a person who has been cautioned for the offence, or
(d) the **corresponding relevant date** for a person subject to an order under the Sex Offenders Act 1997.

Notification Requirements – Schedule 3 Offences

Schedule 3 of the SEXUAL OFFENCES ACT 2003 (Amendment of Schedules 3 and 5) Order 2007

Listed below are the offences under the Sexual Offences Act 2003 for the purposes of notification of details to the police

Section(s)	Circumstances of offence
1 or 2	Rape or assault by penetration
3	Sexual assault (and condition (a) below)
4 to 6	Causing sexual activity without consent, rape of under 13 or assault by penetration of under 13
7	Sexual assault child under 13– offender over 18 or sentenced to 12 months
8 to 12	Sexual activity with child under 13 or child sex offences by adults
13	Child sex offences by child or young person & sentenced to 12 months
14	Arranging child sex– offender 18 or over, or sentenced to 12 months
15	Meeting child following grooming
16 to 19	Abuse of position of trust & imprisoned, detained in hospital, or community sentence for 12 months or more
25 or 26	Familial child sex, offender over 18 or sentenced to 12 months or more
30 to 37	Offences against persons with mental disorder
38 to 41	Care workers for persons with mental disorder (and condition (a) below)
47	Paying for sex with child (victim under 16 and offender either 18 or over, or sentenced to 12 months or more)
48	Causing or inciting child prostitution or pornography (and condition (d) below)
49	Controlling a child prostitute or a child involved in pornography (and condition (d) below)
50	Arranging or facilitating child prostitution or pornography (and condition (d) below)
61	Administering substance with intent
62 or 63	Trespassing with intent to commit sexual offence (and condition (a) below)
64 or 65	Sex with adult relative (and condition (b) below)
66	Exposure (and condition (a) below)
67	Voyeurism (and condition (a) below)
69 or 70	Intercourse with animal or penetration of a corpse (and condition (b) below)

In addition, the following offences which were included in the (now revoked) Sex Offenders Act 1997 are also included in the Sched. 3 offences

S 1 Protection of Children Act 1978 or S 160 of the Criminal Justice Act 1988	Indecent photographs of child under 16 (and condition (c) below)
S170 Customs and Excise Management Act 1979	Importation of indecent photographs of child under 16 (and condition (c) below)

Conditions

(a) Either (i) offender under 18 and sentenced to at least 12 months imprisonment, or (ii) in any other case, either the victim under 18, or the offender sentenced to imprisonment, detained in hospital, or subject of a community sentence of at least 12 months.

(b) Either (i) offender under 18 and sentenced to at least 12 months imprisonment, or (ii) in any other case offender sentenced to imprisonment or detained in a hospital.

(c) Either (i) the conviction, finding or caution was before the commencement of this Act in 1979, or (ii) the offender was over 18 or sentenced to imprisonment for at least 12 months.

(d) Either the offender was (i) 18 or over, or (ii) is or has been sentenced in respect of the offence to imprisonment for a term of at least 12 months.

Chapter 3

Firearms and Explosives

Firearms – Definitions

S 57 FIREARMS ACT 1968

The term 'firearm' includes any:

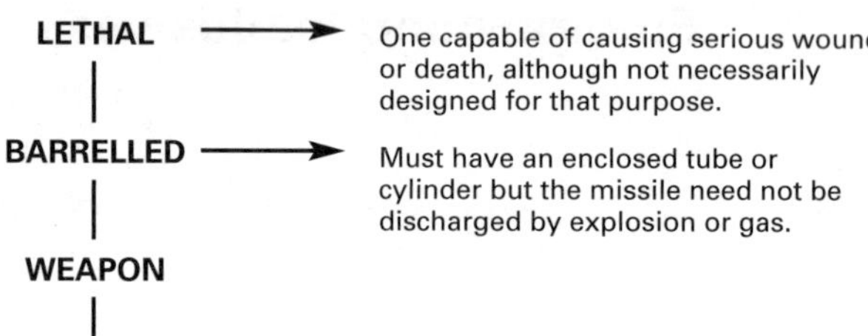

of any description from which any shot, bullet or other missile can be discharged and including any:

- **Prohibited weapon** whether it is lethal or not.
- **Component part** of such lethal or prohibited weapon.
- **Accessory** to such weapons designed or adapted to diminish the noise or flash caused by firing the weapon.

'Ammunition' means ammunition for any firearm and includes grenades, bombs and other like missiles, whether capable of use with a firearm or not, and also includes prohibited ammunition.

The term **'imitation firearm'** means anything which has the appearance of being a firearm (other than a weapon designed or adapted for the discharge of any noxious liquid, gas or other thing) whether or not it is capable of discharging any shot, bullet or other missile.

Prohibited Weapons

S 5(1) FIREARMS ACT 1968

A person commits an offence if, without the authority of the Secretary of State, he has in his possession, or purchases or acquires, or manufactures, sells or transfers:

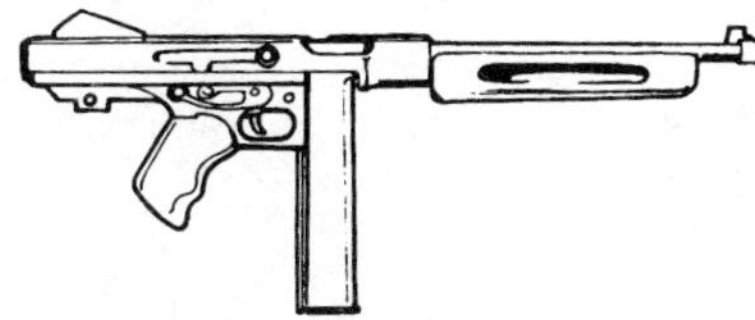

- any firearm which is so designed or adapted that two or more missiles can be successively discharged without repeated pressure on the trigger
- any self-loading or pump-action rifled gun other than one which is chambered for .22 rim-fire cartridges
- any firearm which either has a barrel less than 30 cm or less than 60 cm overall (disregarding any detachable, folding, retractable or other moveable butt-stock) other than an air weapon, a muzzle-loading gun or a firearm designed as signalling apparatus
- any self-loading or pump action smooth-bore gun which is not an air weapon or chambered for .22 rim-fire cartridges and either:
  a) has a barrel less than 24″ in length, or an air weapon, or
  b) is less than 40″ in overall length
- any smooth-bore revolver gun other than one which is chambered for 9 mm rim-fire cartridges or a muzzle loading gun
- any rocket-launcher, or any mortar, for projecting a stabilised missile, other than a launcher or mortar designed for line-throwing or pyrotechnic purposes or as signalling apparatus
- any air rifle, air gun or air pistol which uses, or is designed or adapted for use with, a self-contained gas cartridge system
- any weapon of whatever description designed or adapted for the discharge of any noxious liquid, gas or other thing

(CONTINUED ON NEXT PAGE)

Prohibited Weapons – Cont.

- any cartridge with a bullet designed to explode on or immediately before impact, any ammunition containing or designed or adapted to contain any such noxious thing mentioned above and, if capable of being used with a firearm of any description, any grenade, bomb (or other like missile), or rocket or shell designed to explode on or immediately before impact

Prohibited Weapons Subject to Exemptions (S 5A)

Exemptions exist (but a Firearm Certificate is still required) in relation to slaughtering instruments, humane killing of animals, starting pistols, trophies of war acquired before 1.1.46, part of a collection and manufactured before 1.1.19, firearms of rare or historic importance or firearms for shooting vermin or treating animals.

Exemptions also exist in relation to holders of certificates or authority, firearms collectors, bodies concerned in cultural or historical aspects of firearms, slaughtering instruments, and registered firearms dealers.

Other Prohibitions (S 5(1A))

Subject to S 5A above, a person commits an offence if, without the authority of the Secretary of State he has in his possession, or purchases or acquires, or sells or transfers:

- Any firearm which is disguised as another object
- Any rocket or ammunition which consists in or incorporates a missile designed to explode on or immediately before impact and is for military use
- Any launcher or other projecting apparatus designed to be used with any rocket or ammunition for the discharge of any noxious gas, liquid or other thing
- Any ammunition for military use which consists of or incorporates a missile designed so that a substance contained in the missile will ignite on or immediately before impact, or which is designed, on account of its having a jacket or hardcore, to penetrate armour plating, armour screening or body armour
- Any ammunition which incorporates a missile designed or adapted to expand on impact
- Anything which is designed to be projected as a missile from any weapon and is designed to be, or had been, incorporated in any ammunition as mentioned above

The expressions **'prohibited weapons'** and **'prohibited ammunition'** mean weapons and ammunition specified in this page and the preceding page, including anything designed to be projected as a missile from any weapon and designed to be, or has been, incorporated in any ammunition.

Prohibited Weapons and Ammunition – Exemptions

S 5A FIREARMS ACT 1968

The following exemptions apply only to those weapons listed under 'Prohibited Weapons Subject to Exemptions' (see facing page).

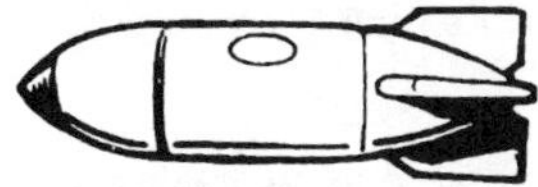

The authority of the Secretary of State is not required for:

a) possession, purchase or acquisition for activities recognised by another member state as a collector of firearms, or a body concerned in the cultural or historical aspects of weapons;

b) possession, purchase, acquisition, sale or transfer of any expanding ammunition or the missile for such ammunition if he is authorised by a firearm certificate or visitor's firearm permit for it, but restricted to the following uses:

- lawful shooting of deer;
- shooting of vermin;
- shooting other wildlife in the course of managing an estate;
- humane killing of animals; or
- shooting animals for the protection of other animals or humans;

c) possession of any expanding ammunition or missile for such ammunition designed to be used with a slaughtering instrument, if he is entitled under S 10 of this Act to possess a slaughtering instrument and ammunition;

d) sale or transfer of expanding ammunition or the missile for such ammunition to any person authorised to purchase or acquire it; or

e) a firearms dealer or his servant to possess, purchase, acquire, sell or transfer, any expanding ammunition or the missile for such ammunition.

'Expanding ammunition' means any ammunition which incorporates a missile designed to expand on impact.

Firearms Certificates

S 1(1) FIREARMS ACT 1968 AS AMENDED BY THE FIREARMS (AMENDMENT) ACT 1988

Subject to any exemption under the act, it is an offence for a person to **purchase**, or **acquire** (to hire, accept as a gift or borrow), or **possess** (to have ultimate control over it, and not necessarily in physical possession):

(a) any AMMUNITION except:

- **cartridges** containing 5 or more shot, none of which exceeds .36" diameter
- ammunition for an **air weapon**
- **blank cartridges** not more than 1" diameter

(b) a FIREARM except:

- a **shotgun** (not being an air gun) which is a smooth-bore gun:
  - having a barrel not less than 24" in length nor more than 2" in diameter;
  - having either no magazine or a non-detachable magazine incapable of holding more than 2 cartridges (if adapted to have such a magazine, it must bear an approval mark); and
  - not being a revolver gun
- an **air weapon** (air rifle, air gun, air pistol not being a prohibited weapon and not declared by the Secretary of State to be specially dangerous). It will be specially dangerous if it:
  - is capable of discharging a missile so that it has, on being discharged from the muzzle, kinetic energy in excess, in the case of an air pistol, of 6ft lb or, in the case of an air weapon other than an air pistol, of 12ft lb, or
  - which is disguised as another object

without holding an in-force firearm certificate, or otherwise than as authorised by such a certificate. It is an offence to fail to comply with a condition subject to which the certificate is held.

Imitation firearms

FIREARMS ACT 1982

S 1 of the 1968 Act will apply to an imitation firearm if it has the appearance of a S 1 firearm and it is constructed or adapted as to be readily convertible into such a firearm.

Exemptions

In addition to registered firearms dealers, operators of miniature rifle ranges, and persons in the service of the Crown, who may be authorised to possess, purchase and acquire firearms, shotguns and ammunition, provision is made for the following exemptions:

- **Police permit:** The holder of a **police permit** may possess a firearm and ammunition in accordance with the terms of his permit (S 7(1))
- **Firearms dealers:** If registered, the dealer and his servant may possess, purchase or acquire firearms and ammunition in the course of the business. (Not restricted to the place of business)
- **Auctioneer:** An **auctioneer, carrier** or **warehouseman**, or servant of such may possess or deliver a firearm and ammunition in the course of his business (S 9(1)). The auctioneer may also **sell** if he holds a police permit (S 9(2))
- **Slaughterman:** A **licensed slaughterman** may possess a slaughtering instrument and ammunition in a slaughterhouse or knacker's yard where he is employed. (Also applies to the **proprietor**). (S 10(1) & (2))
- **Sport:** A person may **carry for another** a firearm or ammunition, under instruction from, and for the use of, that other person for sporting purposes only (S 11(1))
- **Starter: A starter at an athletic** meeting may possess a firearm for starting races (S 11(2))
- **Persons temporarily in GB:** for not more than 30 days in the preceeding 12 months may possess, purchase or acquire a shotgun certificate (S 14)
- **Ranges:** User of air rifles and miniature rifles at a **miniature rifle range** or shooting gallery may possess such weapons (S 11(4))
- **Clubs:** A **member of a rifle club** or miniature rifle club approved by the Secretary of State (certain types of weapons may be specified in the approval) (S 15 1988 Act)

(CONTINUED ON NEXT PAGE)

Exemptions – Cont.

- **Private premises:** A person may borrow a **shotgun** from the occupier of **private premises** and use it on those premises in the occupier's presence (S 11(5)). A person over 17 years of age may borrow a **rifle** from the occupier of **private premises** if the occupier holds a certificate and he or his servant is present (S 16 1988 Act)
- **Approved:** A person may use a shotgun at police-approved meetings for **shooting at artificial targets** (S 11(6))
- **Theatres:** Persons taking part in **theatrical performances** or rehearsals, or production of films, may possess firearms and, if approved by the Secretary of State, prohibited weapons (S 12(1) & (2))
- **Signalling equipment: Signalling apparatus** on an aircraft or at an aerodrome, or firearms or ammunition on board a ship, as equipment of such (S 13(1))
- **Northern Ireland:** The holder of a **Northern Ireland firearm certificate** (S 15)
- **Crown service:** Persons in the **service of the Crown** (includes police officers in their capacity as such) (S 54)
- **Proof houses:** Possession of a firearm going to, at, or coming from a specified **proof house** where they are tested (S 58).
- **Visitor's permit:** The holder of a **visitor's firearms or shotgun permit** (S 17 1988 Act)
- **Antique firearms:** See page 105

Shotguns

S 2(1) FIREARMS ACT 1968

IT IS AN OFFENCE FOR A PERSON TO

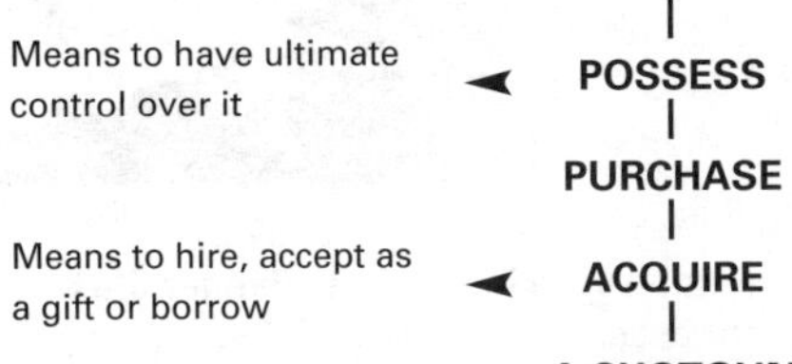

Means to have ultimate control over it ← **POSSESS**

PURCHASE

Means to hire, accept as a gift or borrow ← **ACQUIRE**

A SHOTGUN

(A smooth-bore gun with a barrel not less than 24" in length, not being an air gun. But component parts and sound moderators are not included. It must be a complete shotgun. A certificate would not be required for a part, e.g. a barrel)

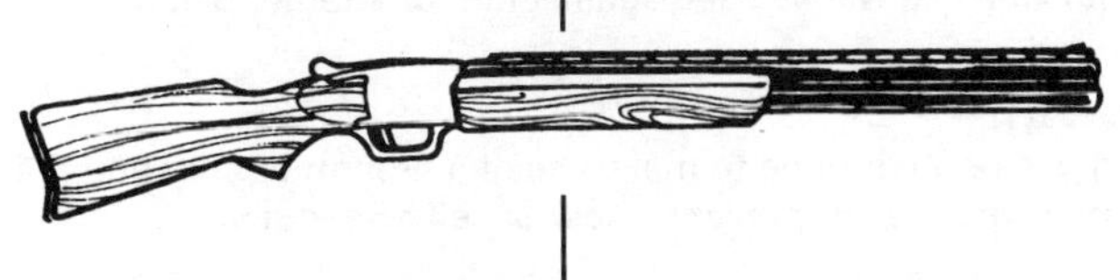

WITHOUT HOLDING A CERTIFICATE AUTHORISING HIM TO POSSESS SHOTGUNS

IT IS AN OFFENCE TO FAIL TO COMPLY WITH A CONDITION SUBJECT TO WHICH A SHOT GUN CERTIFICATE IS HELD

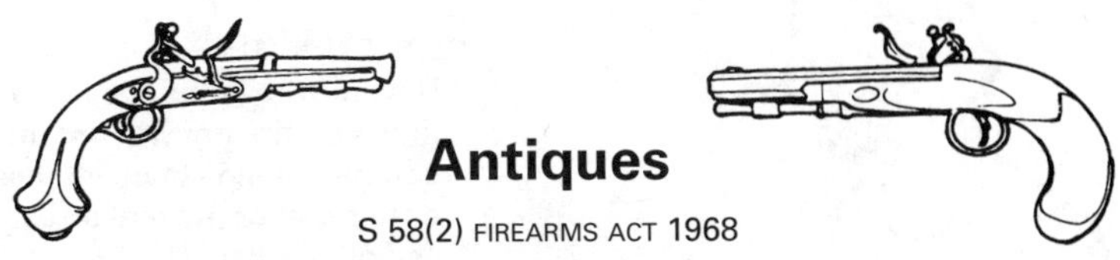

Antiques

S 58(2) FIREARMS ACT 1968

Nothing in the Act relating to firearms shall apply to an antique rifle or shotgun which is sold, transferred, purchased, acquired or possessed **as a curiosity or ornament.**

The term 'antique' is not defined. But for practical purposes, a breach-loading weapon capable of firing a metallic cartridge would probably not be an antique.

A genuine antique used for target practice would not be possessed as a curio and, therefore, would require a certificate.

Criminal Use of Firearms

FIREARMS ACT, 1968

The law attempts to prevent the criminal use and possession of firearms and imitation firearms in the following provisions:

SECTION 16

Possession of a firearm or ammunition with **intent to endanger life** or enable another to do so (injury not essential)

SECTION 16A

Possession of a firearm or imitation firearm with intent by means thereof, or to enable another by means thereof, to cause any person to believe that **unlawful violence** will be used against him or another person.

SECTION 17(1)

Making use or attempting to make use of a firearm or imitation firearm with **intent to resist or prevent arrest** of self or another

SECTION 17(2)

Possession of a firearm or imitation firearm **at time of committing or of arrest for Schedule 1 offence** (see following page)

SECTION 18(1)

Having with him a firearm or imitation firearm with **intent to commit an indictable offence** or to resist or prevent arrest of self or another

Schedule 1 to the Firearms Act 1968

The offences listed below are those referred to in section 17(2) of the Firearms Act 1968

1 Offences under S 1 of the Criminal Damage Act 1971

2 Offences under any of the following provisions of the Offences Against the Person Act 1861:
- Ss 20-22 (Inflicting bodily injury; garroting; criminal use of stupefying drugs)
- S 30 (Laying explosive to building, etc.)
- S 32 (Endangering railway passengers by tampering with track)
- S 38 (Assault with intent to commit felony or resist arrest)
- S 47 (Criminal assaults)

3 Offences under the Child Abduction Act 1984, Pt 1

4 Theft, robbery, burglary, blackmail and any offence under S 12(1) (taking of motor vehicle or other conveyance without the owner's consent) of the Theft Act 1968

5 Offences under S 89(1) of the Police Act 1996 or S 41 Police (Scotland) Act 1967 (assaulting a constable in the execution of his duty)

6 An offence under S 90(1) of the Criminal Justice Act 1991 (assaulting a prisoner custody officer)

7 An offence under S 13(1) of the Criminal Justice and Public Order Act 1994 (assaulting a secure training centre custody officer)

8 Offences under any of the following provisions of the Sexual Offences Act 2003:
- S 1 (rape)
- S 2 (assault by penetration)
- S 4 (sexual activity without consent, involving penetration)
- S 5 (rape of child under 13)
- S 6 (assault of child under 13 by penetration)
- S 8 (causing or inciting child under 13 to engage in sexual activity involving penetration), and
- S 30 & S 31 (sexual activity with a person with a mental disorder impeding choice, involving penetration)

9 Aiding and abetting the commission of any offence specified in the foregoing sections, and attempts to commit them

Firearms Dealers

S 3(1) FIREARMS ACT 1968

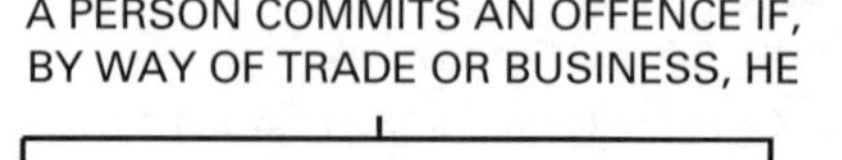

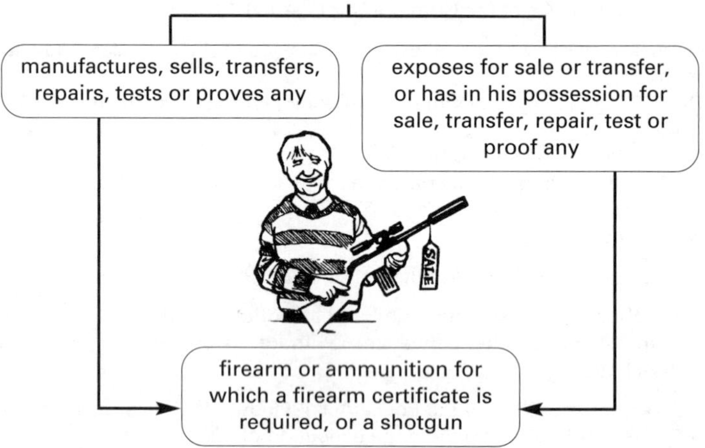

Does not include air weapons, cartridges containing 5 or more shots, none of which exceeds .36" dia. But does include ammunition capable of being fired from a shotgun or smooth-bore gun for which a firearms certificate is required (S 5 FIREARMS (AMENDMENT) ACT 1988)

unless he is registered as a firearms dealer

He must keep a register in which the prescribed particulars are recorded within 24 hours of the transaction. Inspection of the register must be allowed by a police officer authorised in writing by the chief constable

The main **exemptions** cover auctioneers, miniature rifle ranges and proof houses.

It is an **offence** for a person to sell or transfer to another person in the UK, or to repair, test or prove a firearm or ammunition to which S 1 applies unless that other person holds a certificate authorising his possession, or is exempt.

It is an **offence** for a pawnbroker to accept a S 1 firearm or ammunition, or a shotgun, as pawn.

Possession of Firearms

FIREARMS ACT 1968

A person commits an offence if, without lawful authority or reasonable excuse (the proof whereof lies on him), he has with him in a **public place:**

- a loaded shotgun
- an air weapon, whether loaded or not
- any other firearm, whether loaded or not, together with ammunition suitable for use in that firearm; or
- an imitation firearm (S 19)

'Public place' includes any highway and any other premises or place to which at the material time the public have, or are permitted to have, access, whether on payment or otherwise.

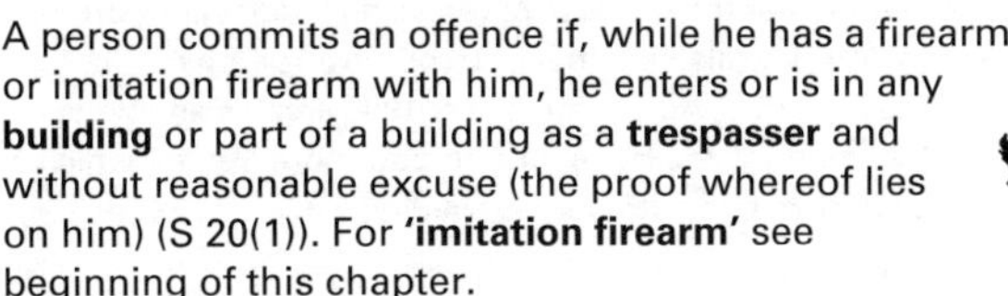

A person commits an offence if, while he has a firearm or imitation firearm with him, he enters or is in any **building** or part of a building as a **trespasser** and without reasonable excuse (the proof whereof lies on him) (S 20(1)). For **'imitation firearm'** see beginning of this chapter.

Trespassing
A person commits an offence if, while he has a firearm or imitation firearm with him, he enters or is on any **land** as a **trespasser** and without reasonable excuse (the proof whereof lies on him) (S 20(2)). **'Land'** includes land covered with water.

A person who has been sentenced to serve 3 years or more **imprisonment** or detention, shall not have a firearm or ammunition in his possession **at any time.** A person who has been sentenced to borstal training, to corrective training, or to imprisonment for 3 months or more but less than 3 years, shall not have a firearm or ammunition in his possession for **5 years** from the date of his release. A child or young person convicted of a serious crime and who has been released on licence; or a person who is bound over to keep the peace or be of good behaviour, or is subject to a probation order, a condition of which in any of those cases prohibits him from possessing a firearm, shall not possess a firearm for the duration of the licence or is so subject (S 21).

Miscellaneous Offences

DRUNKENNESS

S 12 LICENSING ACT 1872

It is an offence to be drunk when in possession of any **loaded** firearm, and such a person may be apprehended. Includes air guns. **Note:** there is no mention of public place, highway, etc.

HIGHWAYS

S 161(2) HIGHWAYS ACT 1980

S 28 TOWN POLICE CLAUSES ACT 1847 (if adopted in that locality)

It is an offence, without lawful authority or excuse, to discharge any firearm within 50 feet of the centre of a highway if a user of the highway is injured, interrupted or endangered.

SHORTENING BARRELS, ETC

S 4(1) FIREARMS ACT 1968

It is an offence to shorten the barrel of a shotgun to a length less than 24" (except registered dealers, who may shorten it for the purpose of replacing a defective part, to produce a barrel of not less than 24"). It is also an offence to possess, purchase or acquire such a weapon. S 6 of the Firearms (Amendment) Act 1988 creates an offence (unless a dealer) to shorten to less than 24" the barrel of a smooth-bore gun for which a firearm certificate is required (other than one with bore exceeding 2").

CONVERTING

S 4(3) FIREARMS ACT 1968

It is an offence (other than as a registered dealer) to convert into a firearm anything which, though having the appearance of being a firearm, is so constructed as to be incapable of discharging any missile through its barrel, S 4(3). It is also an offence to possess, purchase or acquire such a weapon, S 4(4).

SUPPLYING TO DRUNK OR UNSOUND PERSON

S 25 FIREARMS ACT 1968

It is an offence to sell or transfer any firearm or ammunition to, or repair, prove or test any firearm or ammunition for another person whom he knows or has reasonable cause for believing to be drunk or of unsound mind.

RESTRICTION ON SALE AND PURCHASE OF PRIMERS

S 35 VIOLENT CRIME REDUCTION ACT 2006

It is an offence to purchase or sell a cap-type primer designed for use in metallic ammunition for a firearm; or an empty cartridge case incorporating such a primer unless he: is a registered firearms dealer, sells such primers by way of trade or business, has a certificate authorising possession by himself or another, is a person in the service of Her Majesty and is authorised to have possession, or is otherwise authorised under regulations.

Firearms – Ages

FIREARMS ACT 1968

	Under 17 but over 14	Under 15	Under 14
Firearms and ammunition	• May not purchase or hire • Offence to sell or let on hire to, S 22(1), S 24(1) • May accept as a gift or loan if both parties have firearms certificates		• May not possess except as gun bearer, member of rifle club or miniature rifle range or shooting gallery, S 22(2) • Offence to make a gift to, lend to, or part with possession to, S 24(4)
Shotguns	• May not purchase or hire • Offence to sell or let on hire to, S 22(1)	• May not have with him an assembled shotgun except: i) under supervision of a person over 21, or ii) when so covered with a securely fastened gun cover that it cannot be fired, S 22(3) • offence to make a gift to, S 24(3)	
Air weapons	• May not have with him an air weapon or ammunition unless under the supervision of a person over 21; but if on premises may not fire any missile beyond the premises • If over 14 may have with him on private premises with the consent of the occupier but may not fire any missiles beyond the premises • May have with him as a member of an approved rifle club • May use at a shooting gallery if an air rifle or miniature rifle not over .23″ calibre • It is an offence to make a gift of an air weapon or ammunition to a person under 17 • It is an offence, except as mentioned above, to part with possession of an air weapon or ammunition to a person under 17		May not have with him an air weapon or ammunition unless under the supervision of a person over 21; but if on premises may not fire any missile beyond the premises

IT IS AN OFFENCE TO SELL OR LET ON HIRE ANY FIREARM OR AMMUNITION TO A PERSON UNDER THE AGE OF 17

Police Powers

FIREARMS ACT 1968

Stop and Search S 47

Where a constable has reasonable cause to suspect a person:

a) of having a firearm, with or without ammunition, with him in a public place or
b) to be committing or about to commit, elsewhere than in a public place, an offence of carrying firearms with criminal intent (S 18(1)) or trespassing with a firearm (S 20)

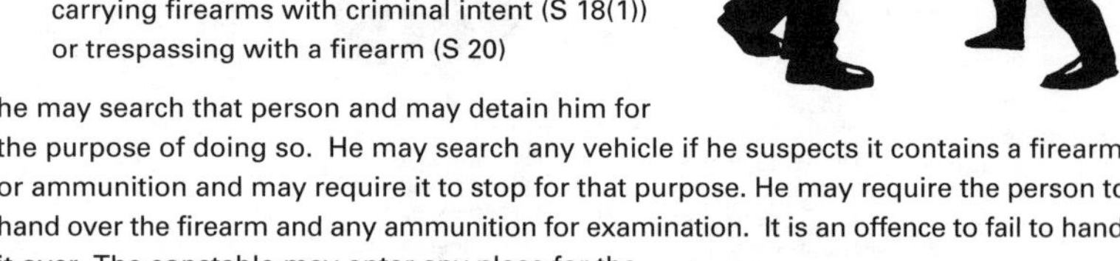

he may search that person and may detain him for the purpose of doing so. He may search any vehicle if he suspects it contains a firearm or ammunition and may require it to stop for that purpose. He may require the person to hand over the firearm and any ammunition for examination. It is an offence to fail to hand it over. The constable may enter any place for the purpose of exercising these powers.

Production of Certificate S 48(1)

A constable may demand from any person whom he believes to be in possession of a firearm or ammunition for which a certificate is required, or of a shotgun, the production of his firearm certificate or, as the case may be, his shotgun certificate.

Where appropriate the constable may demand the corresponding document issued by another European state (S 48(1A)).

If he fails to produce the certificate or to permit the constable to read it, or to show that he is exempt from the requirement to hold one, the constable may seize and detain the firearm, ammunition or shotgun, and demand the person to declare to him immediately his name and address.

It is an offence for a person to fail to produce a certificate; or refuse to declare, or to fail to give his true name and address.

Chapter 4
Licensing

Gambling – the Principles

GAMBLING ACT 2005

The **objectives** of the Act are to-

(a) prevent gambling from being a source of, or being associated with, crime or disorder, or being used to support crime,

(b) ensure gambling is conducted in a fair and open way, and

(c) protect children and other vulnerable persons from being harmed or exploited by gambling.

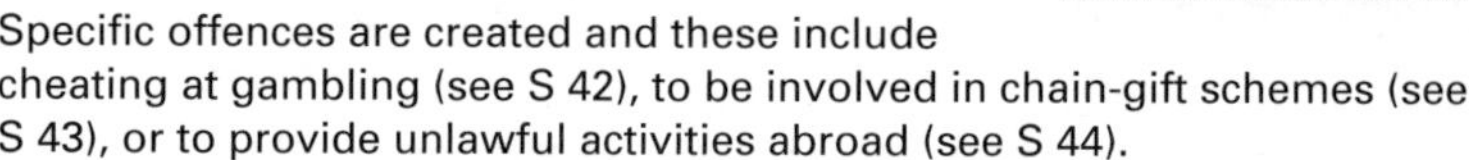

Specific offences are created and these include cheating at gambling (see S 42), to be involved in chain-gift schemes (see S 43), or to provide unlawful activities abroad (see S 44).

In relation to children and young persons, it is an offence–

(a) to invite a child or young person to gamble (see S 46),

(b) to invite a child or young person to enter premises (see S 47),

(c) for a young person to gamble (see S 48),

(d) for a young person to enter premises (see S 49),

(e) for a young person to provide facilities for gambling (see S 50),

(f) to employ a child or young person in gambling, lottery, football pools, bingo, gaming machines, or casino facilities (see Ss.51–57).

Gambling activities are **licensed** by licensing authorities and it is unlawful to provide facilities or use premises without the appropriate licence or to act in contravention of any conditions attached.

'Gambling' (S 3) is defined as–

(a) gaming (see S 6),

(b) betting (see S 9), and

(c) participating in a lottery (see S 14).

'Remote gambling' (S.4) means gambling by means of–

(a) the internet,

(b) telephone,

(c) television,

(d) radio, or

(e) any other kind of electronic or other technology for facilitating communication.

Gambling Licences

GAMBLING ACT 2005

Need for a licence
A person commits an offence if he-

(a) provides facilities for gambling unless he holds an **operating licence** (see S 33),

(b) uses premises to operate a casino, play bingo, provide gaming machines, provide other facilities for gaming, or provide facilities for betting, unless he holds a **premises licence** (see S 37), or

(c) manufactures, supplies installs or adapts gambling software unless he holds an **operating licence** (see S.41),

(d) performs the functions of a specified management office or specified operational function connected with the provision of facilities for gambling unless he holds a **personal licence** (see Ss 80 & 127).

'Facilities for gambling' (S 5)
A person provides facilities if he-

(a) invites others to gamble in accordance with arrangements made by him,

(b) provides, operates or administers arrangements for gambling by others, or

(c) participates in the operation or administration of gambling by others.

But he will not provide facilities by virtue only of-

(a) providing an article other than a gaming machine in the course of any of the activities in (a), (b) or (c) above,

(b) providing, otherwise than in the course of (b) or (c) above, an article for gambling, or

(c) making facilities for remote communication by persons carrying on any of those activities, or by persons gambling in response to any of those activities.

But the exception provided by (c) above will not apply if-

(a) remote communication facilities are available,

(b) they are adapted or presented in such a way as to facilitate or draw attention to the possibility of their use for gambling, and

(c) they cannot reasonably be expected to be used for any other purpose and they are intended to be used wholly or mainly for gambling.

Operating licence (S 65)

N.B. The issue of an operating licence does not affect the possibility that a premises licence may be required.
An operating licence states that it authorises the licensee

(a) to operate a casino a **'casino operating licence'**, (including the betting on the outcome of a virtual game, race, competition or other event or process, and any game of chance other than bingo (a **'combined licence'** (S 68)),

(b) to provide facilities for playing bingo, a **'bingo operating licence'**,

(c) to provide facilities for betting other than pool betting a **'general betting operating licence'** (including betting on the outcome of a virtual race, competition or other event or process other than a game of chance (a **'combined licence'** (S 68)),

(d) to provide facilities for pool betting, a **'pool betting operating licence',**

(e) to act as a betting intermediary, a **'betting intermediary operating licence',**

(f) to make gaming machines available for use in an adult gaming centre, a **'gaming machine general operating licence' for an adult gaming centre,**

(g) to make gaming machines available for use in a family entertainment centre, a **'gaming machine general operating licence' for a family entertainment centre,**

(h) to manufacture, supply, install, adapt, maintain or repair a gaming machine, or part of a gaming machine, **'gaming machine technical operating licence',**

(i) to manufacture, supply, install or adapt gambling software, a **'gambling software operating licence',** or

(j) to promote a lottery a **'lottery operating licence'**.

The inclusion of gaming machines (S 68)
The following types of licence, in addition to the authorised activities, allow the use of one or more gaming machines within categories A to D (see later)-

(a) a non-remote casino operating licence,

(b) a non-remote bingo operating licence,

(c) a non-remote general betting operating licence, and

(d) a non- remote pool betting operating licence.

Operating Licence – Cont.

GAMBLING ACT 2005

No other kind of operating licence (other than a gaming machine general operating licence) may authorise the use of gaming machines.

An operating licence specifies the person to whom it is issued, the period of validity, and any conditions attached to it (S 66). It may also be of a type which authorises more than one of the above activities (a combined licence) (S 68). It must also state whether it is a 'remote operating licence' or not. (S 67).

A **'remote operating licence'** authorises remote gambling activities, or activities by means of remote communication (see S 5 above). A remote operating licence may not also authorise activity which is neither in respect of remote gambling nor carried on by means of remote communication (S 67).

Production of operating licence (S 108).
A constable or enforcement officer may require the holder of an operating licence to produce it within a specified period. A licensee commits an offence if he fails, without reasonable excuse to comply with such a requirement (S 108).

Premises licence (Ss 37 & 150)

A person commits an offence if, when not authorised by a premises licence, he uses premises, or causes or permits premises to be used to-

(a) operate a casino (needs **a casino premises licence,** which may relate to 'regional', 'large' or 'small' casinos),

(b) provide facilities for the playing of bingo (needs **a bingo premises licence**),

(c) make a Category B gaming machine available for use (needs **an adult gaming centre premises licence**),

(d) make a Category C gaming machine available for use (needs **a family entertainment centre premises licence**),

(e) provide facilities for betting (whether by making or accepting bets, by acting as a betting intermediary or by providing other facilities for the making or accepting of bets) (needs **a betting premises licence**), or

(f) provide other facilities for gaming.

Exceptions
The offence will not be committed in relation to-

(a) accepting bets on a track where the use is authorised by a premises licence,

(b) a casino being used for bingo or betting authorised under S 174(3) (a casino premises licence),

(c) the use of premises to provide facilities to be used only by persons who are either acting in the course of a business, or are not on the premises,

(d) an 'occasional use notice' for track betting (S 39),

(e) football pools authorised under S 93(3) (S 40),

(f) a temporary use notice under S 214,

(g) gaming machines authorised under S 247 (a category D machine used at a family entertainment centre), S 248 (a gaming machine where there is no prize), and S 249 (a gaming machine where the prize is limited to nothing in excess of what is paid to use the machine),

(h) clubs and miners' welfare institutes authorised under Ss 269, 271 and 273,

(i) premises with an alcohol licence authorised under Ss 279, 282 and 283,

(j) travelling fairs using category D machines as an ancillary amusement (S 287),

Premises Licence – Cont.

GAMBLING ACT 2005

(k) prize gaming authorised under Ss 289 to 292,

(l) private gaming and betting authorised under S 296, and

(m) non-commercial gaming authorised under S 298.

Gambling software (S 41)
A person commits an offence if in the course of a business he manufactures, supplies, installs or adapts gambling software except as authorised by an operating licence. But the offence is not committed if facilities for remote communication or non-remote communication are made available to another, and they are used by the other person to supply or install gambling software.

Gambling software means computer software for use in connection with remote gambling, but does not include anything used solely in connection with a gaming machine.

Personal licence

A 'personal licence' is defined by S 127 as a licence which authorises an individual to perform the functions of a specified management office or a specified operational function in connection with gambling. It may be a 'remote licence'.

Under Ss 75 and 77 the Commission may specify conditions to be attached to operating licences unless it applies to a 'small scale operator' (where there are no more than three qualifying positions, each held by a qualified person (SI 3266/2006)). S 80 requires the Commission to ensure that in respect of each operating licence at least one person-

(a) occupies a specified management office, and

(b) holds a **personal licence** authorising the functions of the office.

The holder of such a licence must act in accordance with any conditions attached to the operating licence. The requirement for a personal licence does not apply in relation to a bingo operating licence issued to a members' club or a miners' welfare institute.

Production of personal licence (S 134)
A constable or enforcement officer may require a person who holds a personal licence (including a small scale operator) to produce the licence either within a specified period, or immediately where a licensed activity is being carried on.

Gaming

GAMBLING ACT 2005

Gaming (S 6) means playing a game of chance for a prize.

Game of chance

(a) includes (i) a game that involves both an element of chance and an element of skill, (ii) a game that involves an element of chance that can be eliminated by superlative skill, and (iii) a game that is presented as involving an element of chance, but

(b) does not include a sport.

Playing a game of chance means participating in a game of chance-

(a) whether or not there are other participants in the game, and

(b) whether or not a computer generates images or data taken to represent the actions of other participants in the game.

Playing a game of chance for a prize means-

(a) playing a game of chance and thereby acquiring a chance of winning a prize, and

(b) whether or not he risks losing anything at the game.

Prize (except in the context of a gaming machine)-

(a) means money or money's worth, and

(b) includes both a prize provided by a person organising gaming and winnings of money staked.

Casino (S 7) means an arrangement whereby people are given an opportunity to participate in one or more casino games.

Casino game means a game of chance which is not "equal chance gaming" (see below).

It is immaterial-

(a) whether an arrangement is provided on one set of premises or more than one;

(b) whether an arrangement is provided wholly or partly by means of remote communication.

Equal chance gaming (S 8) means-

(a) it does not involve playing or staking against a bank, and

(b) the chances are equally favourable to all participants.

Gaming – Cont.

GAMBLING ACT 2005

It is immaterial how the bank is described and whether or not a bank is controlled or administered by a player.

Exempt gaming (S 269)
Sections 33 (illegal provision of facilities for gambling) and 37 (illegal use of premises) do not apply to the provision of equal chance gaming which satisfies the below conditions by a members' club, a commercial club or a miners' welfare institute. The conditions are-

(a) the prescribed amounts for stakes and prizes must be satisfied,

(b) no amount may be deducted or levied from sums staked or won,

(c) the prescribed fee for participation is not exceeded,

(d) a game played on one set of premises may not be linked with one played on another set of premises, and

(e) persons participating must (i) have applied for membership, have been nominated for membership, or have become a member at least 48 hours beforehand, or (ii) be a guest of such a member (but under S 272 a person may not be a guest of a member if they have not previously been acquainted and it is done only to enable the person to take advantage of gaming).

The disapplication of S 33 by this section does not apply to 'high turnover bingo' (aggregate stakes and aggregate prizes exceed GBP2,000 in any period of 7 days) (S 275).

Club gaming permit (S 271)
Sections 33 (illegal provision of facilities for gambling), 37 (illegal use of premises) and 242 (illegal use of gaming machines), do not apply to the provision of facilities for gambling in accordance with a club gaming permit. This is issued by the licensing authorities and authorises the provision of facilities for gaming (a) on a members' club or on a miners' welfare club premises, and (b) in the course of their activities. It contains conditions that restrict participation to members and guests, and excludes children and young persons from using Category B or C gaming machines.

In particular the permit authorises-

(a) up to three gaming machines of Category B, C or D,

(b) facilities for gaming which satisfies the conditions listed in S 269 (see above) except for the first one, and

Gaming – Cont.

GAMBLING ACT 2005

(c) facilities for prescribed games of chance in accordance with the following conditions (i) no participation fee may be charged except as provided by regulations, (ii) no amount is deducted or levied from stakes or winnings except as provided by regulations, (iii) the public is excluded from any area of the premises where gaming is taking place, and (iv) children and young persons are excluded from any area of the premises where gaming is taking place.

The disapplication of S 33 by this section does not apply to 'high turnover bingo' (aggregate stakes and aggregate prizes exceed GBP2,000 in any period of 7 days) (S 275).

The occupier of the premises commits an offence if he fails without reasonable excuse to produce the permit on request to a constable or enforcement officer (Sched. 12).

Club machine permit (S 273)
Sections 37 (illegal use of premises) and 242 (illegal use of gaming machines), do not apply to the provision of gaming machines in accordance with a club machine permit. The permit is issued by the licensing authority and authorises up to three gaming machines of Categories B, C or D on premises which are a members' club, a commercial club or a miners' welfare club, in the course of their activities. Like the club gaming permit it contains conditions which restrict participation to members and guests, and restrict children and young persons to Category B and C machines.

The occupier of the premises commits an offence if he fails without reasonable excuse to produce the permit on request to a constable or enforcement officer (Sched. 12).

Gaming – Cont.

GAMBLING ACT 2005

Exempt gaming where an alcohol licence has effect (S 279)
Sections 33 (illegal provision of facilities for gambling) and 37 (illegal use of premises) do not apply to the provision of equal chance gaming which takes place on premises in respect of which an on-premises alcohol licence or relevant Scottish licence has effect, which contains a bar for the consumption of alcohol, at a time when alcohol may be supplied. Certain conditions must be complied with. These are

(a) the prescribed amounts for stakes and prizes must be satisfied,

(b) no amount may be deducted or levied from sums staked or won,

(c) no participation fee may be charged,

(d) a game played on one set of premises may not be linked with one played on another set of premises, and

(e) children and young persons are excluded from participation.

The disapplication of S 33 by this section does not apply to 'high turnover bingo' (aggregate stakes and aggregate prizes exceed GBP2,000 in any period of 7 days) (S 275).

Gaming machines: automatic entitlement where an alcohol licence has effect (S 282)
Sections 37 (illegal use of premises) and 242 (illegal use of gaming machines) do not apply to the provision of one or two gaming machines of Category C or D on premises mentioned above in S 279 provided-

(a) the licensee sends the licensing authority a written notice of his intention to make the machines available, together with the prescribed fee, and

(b) any relevant code of practice about the location and operation of machines is complied with.

The exemption from sections 37 and 242 do not apply in relation to premises when gaming machines are made available in reliance on a club gaming or machine permit.

Gaming – Cont.

GAMBLING ACT 2005

Licensed premises gaming machine permits (S 283)
Sections 37 (illegal use of premises) and 242 (illegal use of gaming machines) do not apply to the provision of a gaming machine of Category C or D on premises mentioned above in S 279 if it is made available in accordance with a licensed premises gaming machine permit. This is issued by the licensing authority and is subject to the condition that the holder complies with any relevant code of practice about its location and operation.

The exemption from Sections 37 and 242 do not apply in relation to premises when gaming machines are made available in reliance on a club gaming or machine permit.

The occupier of the premises commits an offence if he fails without reasonable excuse to produce the permit on request to a constable, enforcement officer or authorised local authority officer (Sched. 13).

Travelling fairs: gaming machines (S 287)
Sections 37 (illegal use of premises) and 242 (illegal use of gaming machines) do not apply to the provision of one or more gaming machines of Category D for use at a travelling fair if the machine(s) and facilities for gambling (whether by gaming machine or otherwise) together amount to no more than an ancillary amusement at the fair.

Prize gaming (S 288)
Gaming is prize gaming if neither the nature nor the size of a prize played for is determined by (a) the number of persons playing, or (b) the amount paid for or raised by the gaming.

Prize gaming permits (S 289)
Sections 33 (illegal provision of facilities for gambling) and 37 (illegal use of premises) do not apply to the provision of facilities for prize gaming if they are provided in accordance with a prize gaming permit issued by a licensing authority, and the following conditions are satisfied-

(a) the prescribed limits of participation fees must be complied with,

(b) (i) the chances to participate must be acquired or allocated on one day and in the place where it is played, (ii) the game must be played entirely on that day, and (iii) the result must be made public in the place where the game is played and as soon as reasonably practicable after the game ends, and in any event on that day,

Gaming – Cont.

GAMBLING ACT 2005

(c) a prize or the aggregate of prizes must not exceed the prescribed amount or value, and

(d) participation in a game does not entitle the participant or another to participate in any other gambling (whether or not he or the other person would have to pay to participate in the other gambling).

The occupier of the premises commits an offence if he fails without reasonable excuse to produce the permit on request to a constable, enforcement officer or authorised local authority officer (Sched. 14).

Gaming and entertainment centres (S 290)
Sections 33 (illegal provision of facilities for gambling) and 37 (illegal use of premises) do not apply to the provision of facilities for prize gaming if the gaming satisfies the conditions applicable to S 289 (see above) and the facilities are provided in an adult gaming centre or a licensed family entertainment centre. Neither would Ss 33 and 37 be contravened by providing facilities for equal chance prize gaming if the said conditions are satisfied and the facilities are provided on premises where a family entertainment centre gaming machine permit has effect.

Gaming and bingo halls (S 291)
Sections 33 (illegal provision of facilities for gambling) and 37 (illegal use of premises) do not apply to the provision of facilities for prize gaming in premises where a bingo premises licence has effect. Conditions relating to the nature and circumstances of the game may be attached.

Gaming and travelling fairs (S 292)
Sections 33 (illegal provision of facilities for gambling) and 37 (illegal use of premises) do not apply to the provision of facilities for equal chance prize gaming if the facilities are provided at a travelling fair and the facilities for gambling (in whatever form) amount together to no more than an ancillary amusement at the fair. The conditions applicable to prize gaming permits under S 289 (see above) also apply to this section.

Private gaming and betting: definition (Sched. 15)
Gaming is private if it is in a private dwelling on a domestic occasion and-

(a) no charge is made for participation and (i) it is immaterial how a charge is described, (ii) it is immaterial whether the charge is money or money's worth, (iii) an amount deducted or levied from sums staked or won is a charge, (iv) a charge for admission to premises shall be a charge, and (v) a stake is not a charge,

Gaming – Cont.

GAMBLING ACT 2005

(b) it must be equal chance gaming, and

(c) it must not occur in a place to which the public have access (whether or not on payment).

Betting is private if it is domestic betting or workers' betting.
Domestic betting is betting made on premises in which each party to the transaction lives. This means the person habitually resides in any part of the premises (whether or not there are other premises in which he also habitually resides). **Workers' betting** is betting made between persons each of whom is employed under a contract of employment with the same employer.

Private gaming and betting exemption (S 296)
Section 33 (illegal provision of facilities for gambling) does not apply to the provision of facilities for private gaming or private betting.

Section 37 (illegal use of premises) does not apply to the use of premises to carry on private gaming or private betting.

Neither section 33 nor section 37 applies to the making or accepting a bet, or by offering to make or accept a bet, if he acts otherwise than in the course of a business.

Non-commercial gaming: definition (S 297)
Gaming is non-commercial if it takes place at a non-commercial event (whether as an incidental activity or as the principal or only activity).
An **event** is non-commercial if the arrangements are such that no part of the proceeds is to be appropriated for the purpose of private gain. The **proceeds** of an event are (i) the sums raised (whether by way of fees for entrance or for participation, by way of sponsorship, by way of commission from traders or otherwise), minus (ii) amounts deducted in respect of costs reasonably incurred in organising the event.

Non-commercial betting: definition (S 302)
A betting transaction is non-commercial betting if no party to the transaction-

(a) enters it in the course of a business, or

(b) holds himself out as being in business in relation to the acceptance of bets.

Gaming – Cont.

GAMBLING ACT 2005

Non-commercial gaming and betting: exception (S 298)
Sections 33 (illegal provision of facilities for gambling) and 37 (illegal use of premises) do not apply to the provision of facilities or the use of premises for non-commercial prize gaming, or non-commercial equal chance gaming. In each case, certain conditions must be complied with as follows-

Non-commercial prize gaming (S 299)

(a) players must be informed that the purpose of the gaming is to raise money for a specified purpose other than that of private gain,

(b) profits must be applied for a purpose other than that of private gain,

(c) the non-commercial event does not take place (i) on premises, other than a track, in respect of which a premises licence has effect, (ii) on a track at a time when activities are carried on in reliance on a premises licence, or (iii) on premises at a time when activities are being carried on in reliance on a temporary use notice, and

(d) gaming is not remote.

'Profits' means (i) the aggregate of amounts paid by way of stakes or otherwise accruing to the organiser, minus (ii) amounts deducted for the provision of prizes or other reasonably incurred organising costs.

Non-commercial equal chance gaming (S 300)
The conditions are the same as for S 299 (see above) plus-

(e) regulations governing (i) limiting the amounts staked, (ii) limiting participation fees, (iii) limiting other amounts paid in connection with the gaming, (iv) limiting a combination of any of the aforementioned matters in (i) to (iii), (v) limiting the amount or value of a prize, and (vi) limiting the aggregate amount or value of prizes, must be complied with.

Misusing profits of non-commercial prize gaming (S 301)
A person commits an offence if he uses, or permits to be used, any part of the profits of non-commercial prize gaming or non-commercial equal-chance gaming, for a purpose other than that specified.

Betting

GAMBLING ACT 2005

Betting (S 9) means making or accepting a bet on-

(a) the outcome of a race, competition or other event or process,

(b) the likelihood of anything occurring or not occurring, or

(c) whether anything is or is not true.

A transaction that relates to the outcome of a race, competition or other event or process may be a 'bet' despite the facts that-

(a) race, competition, event or process has already occurred or been completed, and

(b) one party to the transaction knows the outcome.

A transaction that relates to the likelihood of anything occurring or not occurring may be a 'bet' despite the facts that-

(a) the thing has already occurred or failed to occur, and

(b) one party to the transaction knows that it has already occurred or failed to occur.

Spread bets, etc (S 10): A 'bet' for the purposes of S 9 does not include a bet which is a regulated activity within S 22 of the Financial Services and Markets Act 2000 (investments or property activities made by way of business).

Prize competitions (S 11): For the purposes of S 9 a person makes a 'bet' (despite the fact that he does not deposit a stake in the normal way of betting) if-

(a) he participates in an arrangement where the participants are required to guess (including using skill or judgement) any of the matters referred to in S 9 (a), (b) or (c) above,

(b) he is required to pay to participate, and

Betting – Cont.

GAMBLING ACT 2005

(c) if his guess is accurate, or more accurate than other guesses, he (i) wins a prize, or (ii) enters a class among whom one or more prizes are to be allocated (whether or not wholly by chance). 'Prize' includes any money, articles or services, (a) whether or not described as a prize, and (b) whether or not consisting wholly or partly of money paid, or articles or services provided, by the members of the class among whom the prizes are allocated.

Pool betting (S 12) means betting made on terms that all or part of winnings-

(a) shall be determined by reference to the aggregate of stakes paid or agreed to be paid by the persons betting,

(b) shall be divided among the winners, or

(c) shall or may be something other than money.

'Pool betting' is 'horse-race pool betting' if it relates to horse-racing in Great Britain.

Betting intermediary (S 13) means a person who provides a service designed to facilitate the making or accepting of bets between others. Such activities constitute 'providing facilities for betting'.

Lotteries

GAMBLING ACT 2005

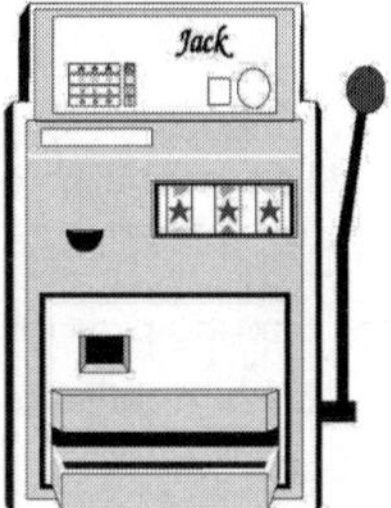

Lottery (S 14) means an arrangement, irrespective of how it is described, if it is a 'simple' or a 'complex' lottery as described below.

A simple lottery is where-
(a) persons are required to pay in order to participate in the arrangement,
(b) in the course of the arrangement one or more prizes are allocated to one or more members of a class, and
(c) the prizes are allocated by a process which relies wholly on chance.

A complex lottery is where-
(a) persons are required to pay in order to participate in the arrangement,
(b) in the course of the arrangement one or more prizes are allocated to one or more members of a class,
(c) the prizes are allocated by a series of processes, and
(d) the first of those processes relies wholly on chance.

Prize in relation to lotteries includes any money, articles or services-
(a) whether or not described as a prize, and
(b) whether or not consisting wholly or partly of money paid, or articles or services provided, by the members of the class among whom the prize is allocated.

Wholly on chance will include a process which requires a person to exercise skill or judgement or to display knowledge, if the requirement cannot reasonably be expected to prevent a significant proportion of participants, or persons wishing to participate, from receiving a prize, and

National Lottery (S 15) will not be regarded as gambling for the purposes of this Act except in relation to S 42 (the offence of cheating) and S 335 (enforceability of gambling contracts).

Lotteries – Cont.

GAMBLING ACT 2005

Promoting a lottery (S 252)
A person promotes a lottery if he makes or participates in making the arrangements for a lottery. In particular he promotes a lottery if he-

(a) makes arrangements for printing tickets,

(b) makes arrangements for printing promotional material,

(c) arranges for the distribution or publication of promotion material,

(d) possesses promotional material,

(e) makes other arrangements to advertise a lottery,

(f) invites a person to participate in a lottery,

(g) sells or supplies a lottery ticket,

(h) offers to sell or supply a lottery ticket,

(i) possesses a lottery ticket with a view to its sale or supply,

(j) does or offers to do anything whereby a person becomes a member of a class among whom prizes are to be allocated, or

(k) uses premises for the purpose of allocating prizes or for any other purpose connected with the administration of a lottery.

Offence of promoting a lottery (S 258)
A person commits an offence if he promotes a lottery unless he holds (or acts on behalf of a person who holds) an operating licence authorising the activity and he acts in accordance with its terms and conditions.

A lottery is exempt (Sched. 11) if it is an **incidental non-commercial lottery** (where no sum is appropriated for private gain) and the following conditions are satisfied-

(a) not more than the prescribed sum may be deducted from the proceeds for the cost of the prizes or for organising the lottery,

(b) it must be wholly for a purpose other than private gain,

(c) it must not include a rollover,

(d) the tickets must be sold on the premises on which the event takes place and while it is taking place, and

(e) the results must be made public while the event is taking place,

Lotteries – Cont.

GAMBLING ACT 2005

Facilitating a lottery (S 259)
A person commits an offence if he facilitates a lottery (by printing tickets, printing promotional material, or advertising) unless he acts in accordance with the terms and conditions of an operating licence. But no offence is committed if it is exempt under Sched. 11 (see above).

Misusing profits of a lottery (S 260)
A person commits an offence if he uses, or permits the use of, any part of the profits for a purpose other than that which the promoter has stated.

Misusing profits of an exempt lottery (S 261)
A person commits an offence if he uses, or permits the use of, any part of the profits of-

(a) an incidental non-commercial lottery,

(b) a private society lottery, or

(c) a small society lottery

for a purpose other than one for which the lottery is permitted to be promoted in accordance with Sched. 11.

Small society lottery: breach of condition (S 262)
A non-commercial society commits an offence if (a) a lottery is promoted when the society is not registered with the local authority, (b) the society fails to comply with para. 39 of Sched. 11 by not supplying full details of the lottery, or (c) the society provides false or misleading information required under para. 39.

Cross-category activities

GAMBLING ACT 2005

Sometimes an activity may satisfy more than one definition. Sections 16 to 18 stipulate how they shall be treated and these are contained in the following table-

Section	Activity	To be treated as-
16	Betting (S 9) and Gaming (S 6)	If it is pool betting within the meaning of section 12 it shall be **Betting,** not **Gaming.** Any other transaction shall be **Gaming** and not **Betting**.
17	Game of chance (S 6) and Lottery (S 14)	If the person who pays in order to join the class amongst whose members prizes are allocated, is required to participate in, or be successful in, more than three processes before becoming entitled to a prize, the arrangement will be treated as a **Game of Chance** and not as a **Lottery**. But, subject to the above, it will be regarded as a **Lottery** and not a **Game of Chance** if it falls within any of the following provisions of Sched. 11- (a) an exempt lottery incidental to a non-commercial event (para.1), (b) a private society lottery (para. 10), (c) a work lottery (para. 11), (d) a residents' lottery (para. 12), (e) a customer lottery (para. 20), (f) a small society lottery (para. 30), or (g) it is promoted in reliance on a lottery operating licence. Any other arrangement shall be treated as a **Game of Chance** and not as a **Lottery**.
18	Lottery (S 14) and (a) Pool Betting (S 12), or (b) Betting (S 9) by virtue of it being a Prize Competition (S 11).	Shall be treated as a **Lottery** and not **Betting** if it satisfies any of the items (a) to (g) relating to a Game of Chance and a Lottery above. Any other transaction shall be regarded as **Betting** and not a **Lottery**.

Gaming Machines

GAMBLING ACT 2005

Definition (S235)
'Gaming machine' means a machine which is designed or adapted for use by individuals to gamble (whether or not it can also be used for other purposes). But it will not be a gaming machine if it is-

(a) a domestic or dual-use computer which can be used to participate in remote gambling,

(b) a telephone or other machine for communicating which can be used to participate in remote gambling,

(c) a machine designed or adapted for use to bet on future events,

(d) a machine which dispenses lottery tickets or otherwise enables a person to enter a lottery provided that the results of the lottery are not determined by the machine and are not announced by the machine without a prescribed interval,

(e) a machine designed or adapted for playing bingo by way of prize gaming and used in accordance with conditions attached to a bingo operating licence,

(f) a machine designed or adapted for playing bingo by way of prize gaming and used in accordance with conditions attached to a gaming machine general operating licence,

(g) a machine designed or adapted for playing bingo by way of prize gaming, made available under a family entertainment centre gaming machine permit or a prize gaming permit, and any requirements prescribed by a code of practice are complied with,

(h) a machine designed or adapted to be controlled or operated by an employee arranging for others to play a real game of chance, or used in connection with a real game of chance controlled or operated by an individual, or

(i) a machine designed or adapted to enable individuals to play a real game of chance if it is not required to be controlled or operated by an employee or an individual and used in accordance with a condition attached to a casino operating licence.

Gaming Machines – Cont.

GAMBLING ACT 2005

Maximum number of machines (S 172)
Under S 172, the relevant licence holder may make the following number of gaming machines available for use on the premises-

adult gaming centre premises licence:
(a) up to four Category B,

(b) any number of Category C,

(c) any number of Category D,

family entertainment centre premises licence:
(a) any number of Category C,

(b) any number of Category D,

casino premises licence for a regional casino using at least 40 gaming tables: not more than 25 times the number of gaming tables used in the casino, and in any case not more than 1250, of Category A, B, C or D,

casino premises licence for a large casino using at least one gambling table, or a regional casino with fewer than 40 gambling tables: not more than five times the number of gaming tables used in the casino, and in any case not more than 150, of Category B, C or D,

casino premises licence for a small casino using at least one gambling table: not more than twice the number of gaming tables used in the casino, and in any case not more than 80, of Category B, C or D,

bingo premises licence:
(a) up to four Category B,

(b) any number of Category C,

(c) any number of Category D,

betting premises licence: up to four of Category B, C or D (but this applies to a betting premises licence in respect of a track only if the holder also holds a **pool betting operating licence**).

Gaming Machines – Cont.

GAMBLING ACT 2005

Offences

Making machine available for use (S 242)
A person commits an offence if he makes a gaming machine available for use by another unless it is in accordance with an operating licence. Exceptions are contained in

(a) S 247 (Category D machine under a family entertainment centre gaming machine permit),

(b) S 248 (a no prize gaming machine where the player does not acquire an opportunity to win a prize),

(c) S 249 (a limited prize gaming machine where the player can not win a prize in excess of the amount he paid to use the machine),

(d) S 271 (a club gaming permit for a members' club or miners' welfare institute),

(e) S 273 (a club machine permit which authorises up to three gaming machines of Category B, C or D in a members' club, a commercial club or a miners' welfare institute, for use by members and their guests),

(f) S 282 (an on-premises alcohol licence which automatically entitles the use of one or two gaming machines of Category C or D),

(g) S 283 (a licensed premises gaming machine licence which authorises the use of Category C or D machines), and

(h) S 287 (a travelling fair where one or more Category D machines is used as an ancillary amusement).

An offence is also committed if a machine is made available for use in contravention of S 240 (regulations controlling use).

Manufacture, supply etc (S 243).
A person commits an offence if he manufactures, supplies, installs, adapts, maintains or repairs a gaming machine or part of a gaming machine unless he has an operating licence or is exempt under S 248 (a no prize gaming machine) or S 250 (a single machine supply and maintenance permit).

He also commits an offence if he fails to comply with regulations under S 241 (controlling such activities).

Offences under S 243 do not apply to scrap machines or machines which are incidental to the sale, etc of property.

Gaming Machines – Cont.

GAMBLING ACT 2005

Virtual gaming (S 173)

The holder of a **casino premises licence** or a **betting premises licence** may make facilities available for betting on the outcome of a virtual game, race, competition or other event or process.

Casino premises licence (S 174)
A casino premises licence may only be issued for-

(a) a regional casino,

(b) a large casino, or

(c) a small casino,

and authorises the holder to make available

(a) any number of games of chance other than casino games, and

(b) provision of facilities for (i) bingo, (ii) betting, or (iii) both (except in the case of a small casino which is restricted to betting).

Temporary use of Premises

GAMBLING ACT 2005

Where the holder of an operating licence wishes to use premises to carry on an activity which is authorised under his licence, he may give notice (a 'temporary use notice') of his intention to do so to the licensing authority for the area in which the premises are situated (S 214). An endorsed copy of the notice is returned to the licensee either in its original form or with amendments (S 227). A copy of the notice must be displayed on the premises to which it relates when an activity is being carried on. The notice must be produced on request to a constable, customs and excise officer, enforcement officer or authorised local authority officer. Failure to do so is an offence (S 229).

General Offences

GAMBLING ACT 2005

Cheating (S 42)
A person commits an offence if he cheats at gambling or does anything to enable or assist another to cheat at gambling. It is immaterial whether a person who cheats (a) improves his chance of winning, or (b) wins anything. Cheating at gambling may, in particular, consist of actual or attempted deception or interference in connection with

(a) the process by which gambling is conducted, or (b) a real or virtual game, race or other event or process to which gambling relates.

Chain-gift schemes (S 43)
A person commits an offence if he-

(a) invites another to join a chain-gift scheme, or

(b) knowingly participates in the promotion, administration or management of a chain-gift scheme.

Chain-gift means an arrangement where-

(a) in order to participate a person must make a payment to one or more other participants (a 'joining fee'), and

(b) each person who participates (i) is required or invited to invite others to participate, and (ii) is encouraged to believe that he will receive the joining fees, or part of the joining fees, of other participants, to an amount in excess of the joining fee paid by him.

Payment means money or money's worth but does not include the provision of goods and services. It is immaterial whether a payment is made directly or through a person responsible for managing or administering the scheme.

Provision of unlawful facilities abroad (S 44)
A person commits an offence if he does anything in GB, or uses remote gambling equipment situated in GB, to invite or enable a person in a prohibited territory to participate in gambling.

Prohibited territory means a country or place designated by the Secretary of State.

Protection of Children and Young Persons

GAMBLING ACT 2005

Child means an individual who is less than 16 years old.

Young person means an individual who is not a child but who is less than 18 years old.

Invitation to gamble (S 46)
A person commits an offence if he invites, causes or permits a child or young person to gamble.

But the offence does not apply to-

(a) private or non-commercial entertainment,

(b) private or non-commercial betting,

(c) lottery,

(d) football pools,

(e) category D gaming machines,

(f) equal chance gaming under a prize gaming permit,

(g) equal chance gaming at a licensed family entertainment centre,

(h) prize gaming at a non-licensed family entertainment centre, or

(i) prize gaming at a travelling fair under S 292.

Inviting includes intentionally-

(a) sending to a child or young person any document which advertises gambling, or

(b) bringing to the attention of a child or young person information about gambling with a view to encouraging him to gamble.

The offence is committed by the person whose name or contact details for payment or information is given in the document or information.

Invitation to enter premises (S 47)
A person commits an offence if he invites or permits a child or young person to enter any of the following.

(a) Premises where a **casino** premises licence is in force and the premises are being used as such at that time. But the offence does not apply where he is permitted to enter a part of premises which are being used for a regional casino, and that part is not being used for gambling at that time.

Protection of Children and Young Persons – Cont.

GAMBLING ACT 2005

(b) Premises other than a track if a **betting** premises licence is in force and the premises are being used as such at that time.

(c) Premises if an **adult gaming centre** premises licence is in force and the premises are being used as such at that time.

(d) An area from which they are required to be excluded under S 182 **(betting or gaming machine areas on a track)**.

(e) Part of licensed **family entertainment centre** premises where there is access to a category C gaming machine which is in use or is available for use.

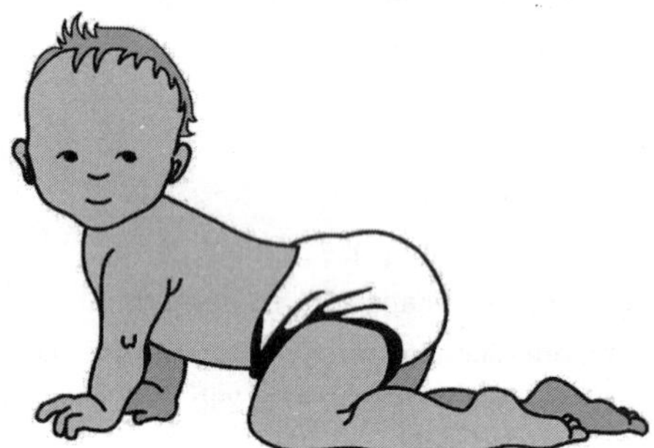

A young person commits an offence if he **enters premises** under the above circumstances (S 49).

Gambling (S 48)
A young person commits an offence if he gambles. There are exceptions to the offence and these are the same as for 'Invitation to gamble' under S 46 above.

Provision of facilities for gambling (S 50).
A young person commits an offence if he provides facilities for gambling, except-

(a) private or non-commercial gambling,

(b) private or non-commercial betting,

(c) lottery,

(d) football pools, or

(e) prize gaming at a travelling fair under S 292

Employment offences

A person commits an offence if he employs a person in the following circumstances-

Section	Employed	Activity	Exceptions
51	Child or young person	Provide facilities for gambling.	Private or non-commercial gaming. Private or non-commercial betting. Lottery. Football pools. Prize gaming at travelling fair (S 292)
52	Child	Provide facilities for gambling in connection with a lottery, or football pools.	National Lottery.
53	Child	Perform any function on premises where, and at a time when, facilities are provided for bingo, or club gaming permit or club machine permit.	
54	Child or young person	On premises where a category A, B, C or D gaming machine is situated, perform any function in connection with the gaming machine. An employed young person also commits the offence.	
55	Child or young person	Perform any function on premises where there is a casino premises licence, a betting premises licence, or an adult gaming centre premises licence in effect. An employed young person also commits the offence.	(a) Employment when no activity under the premises licence is being carried out. (b) Employment on a part of premises being used for a regional casino when that part is not being used for gambling facilities.

Invitation to participate in lottery (S 56)
A person commits an offence if he invites, causes or permits a child to participate in a lottery other than-

(a) an incidental non-commercial lottery exempt by S 258 & Sched.11,

(b) a private lottery (whether private society, work, or residents' lottery) exempt by S 258 & Sched.11, or

(c) the National Lottery.

Invitation to participate in football pools (S 57)
A person commits an offence if he invites, causes or permits a child to participate in football pools.

Enforcement

GAMBLING ACT 2005

Production of copy of authorisation (S 316)
A constable or enforcement officer may require the holder of an operating licence or a casino premises licence to produce within a specified period a copy of any authorisation given by the holder of the licence to his agent. Similarly, the agent may be required to produce a copy of the authorisation, within a specified time or immediately. Failure to do so without reasonable excuse is an offence.

Assessing compliance (S 305)
A constable, enforcement officer or authorised person may undertake activities to assess compliance with provisions of the Act and whether an offence is being committed.

Entry to premises (S 306)
A constable or enforcement officer may enter premises if he reasonably suspects that an offence under this Act may be-

(a) being committed on the premises, or

(b) about to be committed on the premises.

Where there are reasonable grounds to suspect that-

(a) an offence under the Act has been committed on the premises,

(b) evidence of the commission of the offence may be found on the premises, and

(c) at least one of the following conditions is satisfied-

- (i) admission to the premises has been refused,
- (ii) admission to the premises is likely to be refused unless a warrant is produced,
- (iii) the purpose of entry may be frustrated or seriously prejudiced unless immediate entry can be secured,
- (iv) there is likely to be nobody at the premises capable of granting admission,

a justice of the peace may on the application of a constable of enforcement officer issue a warrant authorising entry to the premises.

Enforcement – Cont.

Other powers of entry

There are other specific powers of entry as depicted in the table below.

Section	Premises	Purpose
307	Where it is suspected facilities are, are about to be, or have been provided.	To discover whether facilities for gambling other than private and non-commercial or betting may be being provided, may be about to be provided or have been provided.
308	Reasonably believed to be used by the licensee wholly or partly connected with the licensed activities.	To determine whether the licensed activities are being carried on in accordance with the terms and conditions of the operating licence.
309(1)	Where an application has been made for a family entertainment centre gaming machine permit.	For a purpose connected with the application.
309(2)	Where a family entertainment centre gaming machine permit has effect.	To determine whether the gaming machines used on the premises comply with requirements.
310(1)	Where an application has been made for an alcohol licensed premises gaming machine permit.	For a purpose connected with the application.
310(2)	Where an alcohol licensed premises gaming machine permit has effect.	To determine whether gaming carried on satisfies the conditions.
311(1)	Where an application has been made for a prize gaming permit.	For a purpose connected with the application.
311(2)	Where a prize gaming permit has effect.	To determine whether gaming carried on satisfies the conditions.

Enforcement – Cont.

312(1)	Reasonably believed to be used by a members' club, a commercial club or a miners' welfare club.	To determine whether gaming is taking place, or is about to take place.
313(1)	Where an application for a premises licence has been made.	To assess the likely effects of activity carried on in reliance on the premises licence.
313(2)	Where a premises licence has effect.	For a purpose connected with a review.
315(1)	Where a temporary use notice has been given.	To assess the likely effects of activities carried on in reliance on the temporary use notice.
315(2)	Where a temporary use notice has effect.	To determine whether an activity is being carried on in accordance with the temporary use notice.

Entry to premises (S 317)
A constable, enforcement officer or authorised person exercising a power to enter premises relating to inspection (Part 5 of the Act) may-

(a) inspect any part of the premises and any machine or other thing on the premises;

(b) question any person on the premises;

(c) require access to any written or electronic record kept on the premises;

(d) require to be supplied with a copy, in such form as he directs, of an entry in a written or electronic record which is kept on the premises;

Enforcement – Cont.

(e) remove and retain anything if he reasonably believes that it constitutes or contains evidence of (i) the commission of an offence under this Act, or (ii) the breach of a term or condition of a licence issued under this Act; and

(f) remove and retain anything if he reasonably believes that it is being used or has been used in the commission of an offence under this Act.

Dwellings (S 318)
A power to enter premises without warrant does not apply in relation to a dwelling.

Use of force (S 323)
A constable may use reasonable force for the purpose of entering premises in pursuance of a power under this part of the Act (Part 5 which deals with inspections). An enforcement officer may use force in relation to Ss 306 or 307. An authorised officer may use force in relation to S 307. Where force is used, on leaving the premises they must be as secure as when they were entered.

Obstruction (S 326)
A person commits an offence if without reasonable excuse he obstructs, or fails to cooperate with, a constable, enforcement officer or authorised person exercising a power under this part of the Act (inspections).

Enforcement – Cont.

Provision of information (Gambling Act 2005 (Inspection) (Provision of Information) Regs. 2007).

Persons who exercise their powers of entry and inspection must

(a) ensure that anyone accompanying them produces evidence of identity (Reg. 3),

(b) inform the person of their right to a written record of the visit (Reg. 4),

(c) inform the person of the inspector's right to question persons on the premises, and of the offence of obstruction if the person refuses to answer questions (Reg. 5), and

(d) provide a written record of the inspection on request (Reg. 6).

Gambling – Mandatory Premises Conditions

GAMBLING ACT 2005 (MANDATORY AND DEFAULT CONDITIONS) (ENGLAND AND WALES) REGULATIONS 2007.

These Regulations attach conditions to premises licensed under the Act as contained in the following table-

Type of premises	Conditions
All premises (Reg. 3)	Summary of licence to be displayed. No sale of private or customer lottery tickets. No gambling between 6 am and noon (but this may be excluded by the licensing authority (Reg. 9)).
All casino premises (Reg. 4)	Principal entrance from a street and not from premises used by children or young persons. Gap of at least 2 m between ordinary gambling table (not automated) and any other equipment, etc. used for gambling. No more than 40 separate player positions for automated gaming tables at any one time. Rules for each type of game to be displayed. Any cash machine must be placed so a customer must stop gambling in order to use it.
Regional casino premises (Reg. 5)	Notice stating no under 18s permitted to enter. Gambling area not to be seen by children or young persons. Table gaming floor area not to be less than 1,000 m^2 and must be non-gambling floor area of not less than 1,500 m^2. Where payment is made for a card game, notice to be displayed setting out terms. Where betting is provided there must be a notice setting out terms of betting. No more than 40 betting positions may be available.
Large casino premises (Reg. 6)	Notice stating no under 18s permitted to enter. Table gaming floor area not less than 1,000 m^2 and only table gaming allowed. Must have a non-gambling floor area not less than 500 m^2. Where betting is provided must be a notice setting out terms of betting. No more than 40 betting positions may be available.
Small casino premises (Reg. 7)	Notice stating no under 18s permitted to enter. Table gaming floor area not less than 500 m^2 and only table gaming allowed. Must have a non-gambling floor area not less than 250 m^2. Where betting is provided there must be a notice setting out terms of betting. No more than 40 betting positions may be available.
Converted casino premises (Reg. 8)	Notice stating no under 18s permitted to enter. Table gambling floor area not less than 200 m^2 and non-gambling floor area of not less than 10 % of that.

Bingo premises (Reg. 10)	Notice stating no under 18s permitted to play bingo. No direct entry from a casino, adult gaming centre or betting premises. Where children and young persons are permitted entry and Category B or C gaming machines are available, that area must be separated from the rest of the premises; supervised to ensure those persons do not enter; and a notice displayed stating under 18s not permitted. Notice of admission charges to be displayed. Rules for each type of game to be available to customers. Any cash machine must be placed so a customer must cease gambling in order to use it. No gambling (except gaming machines) between midnight and 9 am (but this may be excluded by the licensing authority (Reg. 11)).
Adult gaming centre (Reg. 12)	Notice stating no under 18s permitted to enter. No access from any other premises licensed under the Act. Any cash machine must be placed so a customer must cease gambling in order to use it. No alcohol to be consumed whilst gambling facilities are provided and a notice to that effect displayed.
Family entertainment centre (Reg. 13)	No direct access from a casino, adult gaming centre or betting premises. Any cash machine must be placed so a customer must cease gambling in order to use it. Where Category C gaming machines are available, that area must be separated from the rest of the premises; supervised to ensure those persons do not enter; and a displayed stating under 18s are not permitted. No alcohol to be consumed whilst gambling facilities are provided and a notice to that effect displayed.
Betting premises (other than track betting) (Reg. 14)	Notice stating no under 18s permitted to enter. Access to be from a street or other betting premises. Not to be used for any purposes other than those permitted by the Act. Any cash machine must be placed so a customer must cease using a gaming or betting machine in order to use it. No apparatus (either by sound or visual) used for making information available except information about (a) betting on a sporting event, or any information incidental to such an event; or (b) betting events which are effected on the premises. No publications, except racing or betting, to be sold on the premises. No music, dancing or other entertainment, except relating to betting, provided. No alcohol consumed whilst gambling facilities are provided and such a notice effect displayed. Notice stating terms of betting to be displayed. No gambling between 10 pm and 7 am (but this may be excluded by the licensing authority (Reg. 15)).

All track premises (Reg. 16)	No access from casino or adult gaming centre. Notice stating no under 18s permitted to bet. Notice stating terms of betting displayed. Betting operators to have an operating licence. Persons accepting unauthorised bets to be removed from the premises. Any cash machine must be placed so a customer must cease gambling in order to use it. No gambling between 10 pm and 7 am, except when a sporting event is taking place on the premises when transactions can take place at any time that day (but this may be excluded by the licensing authority (Reg. 17)).

Licensable Activities

S 1 & 2 LICENSING ACT 2003

The following are licensable activities requiring a premises licence, a temporary event notice, or a club premises certificate:

(a) the sale by retail of alcohol;
(b) the supply of alcohol by or on behalf of a club to a member of the club (including the sale to a guest of a member for consumption on the premises, and the provision of regulated entertainment for members and guests);
(c) the provision of regulated entertainment; and
(d) the provision of late night refreshment.

But the following are exempt activities:

(a) at certain locations (aboard an aircraft, hovercraft or railway vehicle, a vessel on an international journey, approved wharf at a port, an examination station at an airport, a royal palace, armed forces premises, or certificated premises exempt for national security (S 173 & 174);
(b) a lottery where prizes (none of which are money prizes) consist of alcohol (in a sealed container) and promoted as an incident of an exempt entertainment not run for private gain, the result being announced during the entertainment and the lottery not being the only inducement to attend. (S 175)

'Provision of regulated entertainment' (Sched. 1) means the provision of:

(a) entertainment consisting of a play, film, indoor sporting event, boxing or wrestling, live or recorded music, dancing, or similar entertainment; or
(b) entertainment facilities for making music, dancing, or similar entertainment

where, in either case, it is provided for members of the public, members of a club, or for profit. But the following activities are exempt:

(a) film exhibitions for advertisement, information, education, etc.;
(b) film exhibitions for the purposes of a museum or art gallery;
(c) music incidental to certain other activities;
(d) television or radio broadcasts;
(e) religious services;
(f) garden fetes, etc. for other than private gain;
(g) morris dancing or similar; or
(h) entertainment on a vehicle in motion.

Licensable Activities – Cont.

S 1 & 2 LICENSING ACT 2003

'Provision of late night refreshment' (Sched. 2) means at any time between 11 pm and 5 am, the supply of hot food or hot drink to members of the public on or from any premises for consumption on or off the premises. But the following activities are exempt:

(a) supplying to a member of a recognised club, to a person staying at a hotel or similar premises for the night, to an employee, to a person engaged in a particular trade, profession or vocation, or to a guest of any of the aforementioned;
(b) the premises are used for a licensed public exhibition in London, or which may be near beer premises in London by virtue of a licence; or
(c) hot drink containing alcohol, or from a vending machine, or hot food or drink supplied free (unless a charge is made to enter the premises or for some other item), or from a registered charity, or from a vehicle in motion.

The Premises Licence

S 11, 12, 14, 15, 17 – 19, 24, 26, 33 & 57 LICENSING ACT 2003

The licence
A 'premises licence' authorises the premises to be used for one or more licensable activities (S 11). It is granted by the licensing authority in whose area the premises are situated. (S 12)

The application
An application for a licence includes an operating schedule which describes the licensable activities; the times during which the activities are to take place and any other times when the premises will be open to the public; and, where the activities involve the supply of alcohol, details of the premises supervisor, and whether the supplies are for consumption on or off the premises, or both. (S 17)

Contents of the licence
The licensing authority grants the licence subject to such conditions as are consistent with the operating schedule (which includes opening times) (S 18). The licence includes a plan of the premises and specifies:

(a) the name of the holder;
(b) any limited period of effect;
(c) the licensable activities for which the premises may be used;
(d) the name and address of the premises supervisor; and
(e) the conditions subject to which the licence has effect. (S 24)

Conditions attached
Where the licence authorises the supply of alcohol it must contain a condition that:

(a) alcohol may not be supplied when there is no designated premises supervisor, or when the designated premises supervisor does not hold a personal licence; and
(b) the supply must be made or authorised by a person who holds a personal licence. (S 19)

Validity
A licence is valid until it is revoked, until any limited period of effect has expired, or until it is suspended. (S 26)

The premises licence holder must notify any change in his name or address or the name or address of the premises supervisor (unless the latter does it himself). Failure to comply is an offence. (S 33)

The Premises Licence – Cont.

S 11, 12, 14, 15, 17 – 19, 24, 26, 33 & 57 LICENSING ACT 2003

Display and production
Whenever premises are being used for licensable activities authorised by the licence the holder, they must ensure that the licence or a certified copy of it is kept at the premises, and that the summary of the licence or a certified copy of that summary are prominently displayed at the premises. Failure to do so is an offence. A constable may require production of the licence (or the certified copy) for examination. Failure to produce it is an offence. (S 57)

'Supply of alcohol' means the sale by retail of alcohol or the supply of alcohol to a member of a club. (S 14)

'Designated premises supervisor' means the individual specified in the licence as the premises supervisor. This may be the premises licence holder. (S 15)

The Club Premises Certificate

S 60, 94 & 97 LICENSING ACT 2003

The certificate

This is granted in respect of premises occupied by, and habitually used for the purposes of, a club. It certifies that the premises may be used for one or more specified qualifying club activities and that the club is a qualifying club in relation to each activity (S 60). The application for the certificate is very similar to an application for a licence. The contents of the certificate differ from the licence in that there is no 'designated premises supervisor' and any conditions attached will not include those mandatory conditions applicable to a licence.

Display and production

Very similar provisions exist in relation to the display and production of the certificate as apply to a licence. The secretary of the club commits an offence if he fails to comply. (S 94)

Powers of entry and search

A constable may enter and search premises being used under a club premises certificate if he has reasonable cause to believe:

(a) that an offence under S 4(3)(a), (b) or (c) of the Misuse of Drugs Act 1971 (supplying etc. controlled drugs) has been, is being, or is about to be, committed there, or
(b) that there is likely to be a breach of the peace there. (S 97)

'Qualifying club' in relation to the **provision of regulated entertainment** means one which satisfies the following conditions:

(a) under the rules of the club persons may not be admitted to membership, or be admitted, as candidates for membership, to any of the privileges of membership, without an interval of at least two days between nomination or application and admission;
(b) under the rules of the club persons becoming members without prior nomination or application may not be admitted to the privileges of membership without an interval of at least two days between nomination or application and admission;
(c) the club is established and conducted in good faith as a club;
(d) the club has at least 25 members; and
(e) alcohol is not supplied to members otherwise than by or on behalf of the club. (Ss 61 & 62)

The Club Premises Certificate – Cont.

S 60, 94 & 97 LICENSING ACT 2003

'Qualifying club' in relation to the supply of alcohol to members or guests means one which satisfies conditions (a) to (e) above and in addition, the following:

(a) the purchase of alcohol for the club, and the supply of alcohol by the club, are managed by a committee consisting of members of the club, are over 18 years of age, and are elected by members of the club;
(b) no person is to receive at the expense of the club any commission, percentage or similar payment on purchases of alcohol by the club;
(c) no person is to directly or indirectly derive any pecuniary benefit from the supply of alcohol apart from any benefit accruing to the club as a whole, or any benefit derived indirectly by the supply giving rise to a general gain from the carrying on of the club. (Ss 61 & 64)

Permitted Temporary Activities

S 98, 100, 101, 104, 107-109 LICENSING ACT 2003

Conditions

A licensable activity is a permitted temporary activity if it is carried out in accordance with a notice given to the licensing authority and the police (who may object) no later than 10 working days before the event begins (S 100 & 104) and the following conditions are satisfied:

1. receipt of the notice has been acknowledged by the licensing authority and the police have been notified;
2. the notice has not been withdrawn; and
3. no counter notice has been given by the licensing authority following a police objection or where limits on the number of events are exceeded. (S 98)

Temporary event notice

Where it is proposed to use premises for a licensable activity during a period not exceeding 96 hours, an individual may give the licensing authority notice of the proposal. The notice must give the maximum number of persons (being less than 500) who will be allowed on the premises at the same time. If the activity involves the supply of alcohol, it must state whether it is for consumption on or off the premises, or both, and include a condition that it is all supplied by or under the authority of the premises user (the person who gave the notice). There must be a minimum of 24 hours between any two events (each requiring a separate notice) (S 101). There are limits on the number of event notices which may be granted in a given period. (S 107)

Police powers of entry

A constable may, at any reasonable time, enter the premises to which a temporary event notice relates to assess the likely effect of the notice on the promotion of crime prevention. (S 108)

Permitted Temporary Activities – Cont.

S 98, 100, 101, 104, 107-109 LICENSING ACT 2003

Production of notice

The premises user must prominently display a copy of the notice at the premises, or ensure that it is kept in his custody (or that of another nominated person who is present and working at the premises, in which case a notice to that effect must be displayed). It is an offence to fail to comply. Where a notice is not displayed, a constable may require the premises user (or the other person nominated) to produce the notice for examination. Failure to do so is an offence. (S 109)

Personal Licences

S 111, 115, 120, 125, 127-129, 132, & 135 LICENSING ACT 2003

A personal licence is granted by a licensing authority to an individual authorising that person to supply alcohol, or authorise the supply of alcohol, in accordance with a premises licence. 'Supplying alcohol' means selling alcohol by retail, or supplying it by or on behalf of a club to a member of the club. (S 111)

Period of validity
A licence has effect for an initial period of 10 years and is renewable for periods of 10 years at a time. (S 115)

Grant of licence
The authority must grant the licence if the person is aged 18 or over, possesses a licensing qualification (or is a person of a prescribed description), has not forfeited a licence in the previous five years, and has not been convicted of a relevant offence or foreign offence. (S 120)

Licensing qualification
This means a qualification accredited at that time by the Secretary of State, awarded by an accredited body. It also includes a qualification previously awarded which the Secretary of State certifies is to be treated as a licensing qualification, and an equivalent qualification obtained in Scotland, Northern Ireland or an EEA State. (S 120)

Form of licence
The licence specifies the holder's name and address and identifies the granting authority. It also contains a record of conviction for each relevant offence and foreign offence and the sentence imposed (S 125). Any change of name or address must be notified and failure to do so is an offence. (S 127)

Production of licence to a court
Where the person is charged with a relevant offence he must produce his licence to the court. Failure to comply is an offence (S 128). Where the holder is convicted of a relevant offence the court may either order the forfeiture of the licence, or order its suspension (S 129). Upon conviction, the holder must notify the licensing authority. Failure to do so is an offence (S 132). A list of relevant offences is contained in Sched. 4 and includes a wide range of licensing offences and crimes.

Personal Licences – Cont.

S 111, 115, 120, 125, 127-129, 132, & 135 LICENSING ACT 2003

Production of licence to the police

Where the holder of a licence is on premises to make or authorise the supply of alcohol and such supply is authorised by a premises licence or a temporary event notice, a constable may require the holder to produce the licence for examination. Failure to comply is an offence. (S 135)

Unauthorised Licensable Activities

S 136-139 LICENSING ACT 2003

A person commits an offence if:

(a) he carries on or attempts to carry on a licensable activity on or from any premises otherwise than under and in accordance with an authorisation (meaning a premises licence, a club premises certificate, or a temporary event notice); or

(b) he knowingly allows a licensable activity to be so carried on.

Exemption

Where the activity is regulated entertainment, a person does not commit an offence if his only involvement is that he:

(a) performs in a play;
(b) is a sportsman in an indoor sporting event;
(c) boxes or wrestles in boxing or wrestling entertainment;
(d) performs live music;
(e) plays recorded music;
(f) performs dance; or
(g) does something similar to music, dance, etc.

Exposing alcohol for unauthorised sale

A person commits an offence if, on any premises, he exposes for sale by retail any alcohol in circumstances where such sale would be an unauthorised licensable activity. (S 137)

Keeping alcohol on premises for unauthorised sale

A person commits an offence if he has in his possession or under his control alcohol which he intends to sell by retail or supply in circumstances where that activity would be an unauthorised licensable activity. (S 138)

Defence of due diligence

In any of the above offences except S 136(b) it is a defence that:

(a) the act was due to a mistake, or to reliance on information given to him, or to an act or omission by another person, or to some other cause beyond his control; and

(b) he took all reasonable precautions and exercised all due diligence to avoid committing the offence. (S 139)

Drunkenness and Disorderly Conduct

S 140-144 & 159 LICENSING ACT 2003

Allowing disorderly conduct
A person commits an offence if he knowingly allows disorderly conduct on relevant premises.This offence applies to the persons listed below. (S 140)

Sale of alcohol to person who is drunk
A person commits an offence if, on relevant premises, he knowingly:

(a) sells or attempts to sell alcohol to a person who is drunk; or
(b) allows alcohol to be sold to such a person.

This offence applies to the persons listed below. (S 141)

Failure to leave licensed premises, etc
A person who is drunk or disorderly commits an offence if, without reasonable excuse:

(a) he fails to leave the premises when requested to do so by a constable or by a person listed below; or
(b) enters or attempts to enter premises after a constable or person listed below has requested him not to enter.

On being requested to do so by a person listed below a constable must:

(a) help to expel from the premises any person who is drunk or disorderly; and
(b) help to prevent such person from entering the premises. (S 143)

Keeping smuggled goods

A person commits an offence if he knowingly keeps or allows to be kept, on any relevant premises, any goods which have been imported without payment of duty or which have otherwise been unlawfully imported. (S 144)

The above offences/authorisations apply to:

(a) any person who works at the premises (paid or unpaid) in a capacity which authorises him to prevent the conduct/sell the alcohol concerned/make such a request/keep the goods, as the case may be,
(b) in the case of licensed premises, (i) the holder of a premises licence, and (ii) the designated premises supervisor,

(CONTINUED ON NEXT PAGE)

Drunkenness and Disorderly Conduct – Cont.

S 140-144 & 159 LICENSING ACT 2003

(c) in the case of a club premises certificate, any member or officer of the club who is present on the premises in a capacity which enables him to prevent it/ prevent the sale or supply/make such a request, as the case may be; and
(d) in the case of a temporary event notice, the premises user.

Obtaining alcohol for person who is drunk
A person commits an offence if, on relevant premises, he knowingly obtains or attempts to obtain alcohol for consumption on those premises by a person who is drunk. (S 142)

'Relevant premises' means:
(a) licensed premises; or
(b) premises in respect of which there is in force a club premises certificate; or
(c) premises which may be used for a permitted temporary activity. (S 159)

Children and Alcohol

S 145 LICENSING ACT 2003

Prohibition of unaccompanied children

A person commits an offence if:

(a) knowing that they are 'relevant premises' (see below) he allows an unaccompanied child to be on the premises when they are open for the supply of alcohol for consumption there; or
(b) he allows an unaccompanied child to be on relevant premises between midnight and 5 am when they are open for the supply of alcohol for consumption there.

This offence applies to:

(a) any person who works at the premises (paid or unpaid) in a capacity which authorises him to request the unaccompanied child to leave the premises;
(b) in the case of licensed premises, (i) the holder of a premises licence, and (ii) the designated premises supervisor;
(c) in the case of a club premises certificate, any member or officer of the club who is present on the premises in a capacity which enables him to make such a request; and
(d) in the case of a temporary event notice, the premises user.

Exemption

No offence is committed if the child is on the premises solely for the purpose of passing to or from some place to or from which there is no other convenient means of access or egress.

Defence

That the person (a) believed that the child was over 16 or that the individual accompanying him was over 18, and (b) either (i) he had taken all reasonable steps (i.e. by asking for evidence of his age, and the evidence would have convinced a reasonable person) to establish the individual's age, or (ii) nobody could reasonably have suspected from the individual's appearance that he was under 16 or, as the case may be, 18.

Definitions

'Child' means aged under 16.

'Unaccompanied' means not in the company of an individual aged 18 or over.

Children and Alcohol – Cont.

S 145–148 LICENSING ACT 2003

'Relevant premises' in this section means:

(a) they are exclusively or primarily used for the supply of alcohol for consumption on the premises; or
(b) they are open for the purpose of being used for the supply of alcohol for consumption on the premises under the authority of a temporary event notice, and exclusively or primarily used for such supplies.

'Relevant premises' – for general meaning see earlier.

Sale of alcohol to children

A person commits an offence if he sells alcohol to an individual aged under 18.

A club (and the person supplying) commits an offence if alcohol is supplied by or on its behalf:

(a) to, or to the order of, a member of the club who is aged under 18; or
(b) to the order of a member of the club, to an individual who is aged under 18.

Defence

That the person (a) believed that the individual was aged 18 or over, and either (i) he had taken all reasonable steps (i.e. by asking for evidence of his age, and the evidence would have convinced a reasonable person) to establish the individual's age, or (ii) nobody could reasonably have suspected from the individual's appearance that he was under 18. (S 146)

Allowing the sale of alcohol to children

A person who works on the premises (paid or unpaid) in a capacity which authorises him to prevent the sale commits an offence if he knowingly allows the sale of alcohol on relevant premises to an individual aged under 18.

A person commits an offence if he knowingly allows alcohol to be supplied on relevant premises by or on behalf of a club:

(a) to, or to the order of, a member of the club who is aged under 18, or
(b) to the order of a member of the club, to an individual who is aged under 18.

(CONTINUED ON NEXT PAGE)

Children and Alcohol – Cont.

S 147–149 LICENSING ACT 2003

This offence is committed by:

(a) a person who works on the premises (paid or unpaid) in a capacity which authorises him to prevent the supply; and
(b) any member or officer of the club who is present on the premises in a capacity which enables him to prevent it. (S 147)

Sale of liqueur confectionary to children under 16
Similar offences to the above are committed if liqueur confectionary is sold or supplied to children under 16. Similar defences also exist.(S 148)

Purchase of alcohol by children
An individual aged under 18 commits an offence if:

(a) he buys or attempts to buy alcohol; or
(b) where he is a member of a club, alcohol is supplied to him by some act or default of his, or he attempts to have alcohol supplied to him.

But this offence is not committed where the individual buys or attempts to buy the alcohol at the request of a constable or a weights and measures inspector acting in the course of their duty.

Purchase on behalf of children
A person commits an offence if:

(a) he buys or attempts to buy alcohol on behalf of an individual aged under 18; or
(b) where he is a member of a club, on behalf of an individual aged under 18 he makes arrangements whereby alcohol is supplied to him, or he attempts to make such arrangements.

It is a defence that he had no reason to suspect that the individual was aged under 18.

Purchase on behalf of children for consumption on premises
A person commits an offence if:

(a) he buys or attempts to buy alcohol for consumption on relevant premises by an individual aged under 18; or
(b) where he is a member of a club, by some act or default of his, alcohol is supplied to him for consumption on relevant premises by an individual aged under 18, or he attempts to have alcohol so supplied for such consumption.

Children and Alcohol – Cont.

S 149, 150 & 159 LICENSING ACT 2003

It is a defence that he had no reason to suspect that the individual was aged under 18.

But this offence is not committed where:

(a) the person making, or attempting to make the purchase or supply is 18 or over;
(b) the individual is aged 16 or 17;
(c) the alcohol is beer, wine or cider;
(d) its purchase or supply is for consumption at a table meal on relevant premises; and
(e) the individual is accompanied at the meal by an individual aged 18 or over.

'Table meal' – means a meal eaten by a person seated at a table, or at a counter or other structure which serves the purpose of a table and is not used for the service of refreshments for consumption by persons not seated at a table or structure serving the purpose of a table. (S 159)

Consumption of alcohol by children
An individual aged under 18 commits an offence if he knowingly consumes alcohol on relevant premises.

Allowing consumption of alcohol by children
A person commits an offence if he knowingly allows the consumption of alcohol on relevant premises by an individual aged under 18.

This offence applies:

(a) to a person who works at the premises in a capacity, whether paid or unpaid, which authorises him to prevent the consumption, and
(b) where the alcohol was supplied by a club to a member of the club, to any member or officer of the club who is present at the premises in a capacity which enables him to prevent it.

But this offence is not committed where:

(a) the individual is aged 16 or 17;
(b) the alcohol is beer, wine or cider;

(CONTINUED ON NEXT PAGE)

Children and Alcohol – Cont.

S 150 & 151 LICENSING ACT 2003

(c) its consumption is at a table meal on relevant premises; and
(d) the individual is accompanied at the meal by an individual aged 18 or over. (S 150)

Delivering alcohol to children
A person who works on relevant premises in any capacity, whether paid or unpaid, commits an offence if he knowingly delivers to an individual aged under 18:

(a) alcohol sold on the premises; or
(b) alcohol supplied on the premises by or on behalf of a club to a member of the club. (S 151)

Allowing another to deliver alcohol to children
A person commits an offence if he knowingly allows anybody else to deliver to an individual aged under 18 alcohol sold on relevant premises.

This offence applies to a person who works on the premises in a capacity, whether paid or unpaid, which authorises him to prevent the delivery of the alcohol. A similar offence is committed where the alcohol is supplied by a club, and the liability extends to any member or officer of the club who is present in a capacity which enables him to prevent the supply. (S 151)

Exemption
Offences under S 151 do not apply where:

(a) the alcohol is delivered at a place where the buyer (or the person supplied) lives or works; or
(b) the individual aged under 18 works; on the relevant premises in a capacity, whether paid or unpaid, which involves the delivery of alcohol; or
(c) the alcohol is sold or supplied for consumption on the relevant premises.

'Table meal' – see previous page.

(CONTINUED ON NEXT PAGE)

Children and Alcohol – Cont.

S 152 & 153 LICENSING ACT 2003

Sending a child to obtain alcohol
A person commits an offence if he knowingly sends an individual aged under 18 to obtain:

(a) alcohol sold or to be sold on relevant premises for consumption off the premises; or
(b) alcohol supplied or to be supplied by or on behalf of a club to a member of the club for such consumption.

But no offence will be committed if the individual aged under 18 works on the relevant premises in a capacity, whether paid or unpaid, which involves the delivery of alcohol. Neither is an offence committed where the individual aged under 18 is sent by a constable or a weights and measures inspector acting in the course of their duty. (S 152)

Prohibition of unsupervised sales by children
A responsible person commits an offence if on any relevant premises he knowingly allows an individual aged under 18 to make on the premises:

(a) any sale of alcohol; or
(b) any supply of alcohol by or on behalf of a club to a member of the club

unless the sale or supply has been specifically approved by that or another responsible person.

(CONTINUED ON NEXT PAGE)

Children and Alcohol – Cont.

S 152 & 153 LICENSING ACT 2003

But no offence will be committed where:

(a) the alcohol is sold or supplied for consumption with a table meal;
(b) it is sold or supplied in premises which are being used for the service of table meals (or a part of the premises so used); and
(c) the premises are not used for the sale or supply of alcohol otherwise than to persons having table meals there and for consumption by such a person as an ancillary to his meal.

'Responsible person' means:

(a) in relation to licensed premises, the holder of the premises licence, the designated premises supervisor, or any individual aged 18 or over who is authorised by the holder or supervisor;
(b) in relation to premises where there is a club premises certificate, any member or officer of the club present on the premises in a capacity which enables him to prevent the supply in question; and
(c) in relation to premises where a temporary activity is permitted, the premises user, or any individual aged 18 or over who is authorised by the premises user. (S 153)

'Relevant premises' – for meaning see earlier.

Closure notices for persistently selling alcohol to children

S 169A LICENSING ACT 2003 (INSERTED BY S 24 VIOLENT CRIME REDUCTION ACT 2006)

A relevant officer (which includes a police officer of at least superintendent rank) may give a closure notice relating to premises where the 'responsible person' has committed an offence under S 147A of unlawfully setting alcohol to under 18s on those premises on 3 or more different occasions within a period of 3 consecutive months. (S 147A was inserted by S 23 of the 2006 Act). Such a closure notice proposes a prohibition for a period not exceeding 48 hours on sales of alcohol on the premises; and offers the opportunity to discharge all criminal liability in respect of the offence.

Closure Orders

S 161 & 162 LICENSING ACT 2003

Power to make a closure order
A senior police officer (inspector or above) may make a closure order in relation to any relevant premises if he reasonably believes that:

(a) there is, or is likely imminently to be, disorder on, or in the vicinity of and related to, the premises and their closure is necessary in the interests of public safety; or
(b) a public nuisance is being caused by noise coming from the premises and the closure of the premises is necessary to prevent that nuisance.

The closure order may require the relevant premises to be closed for a period not exceeding 24 hours. It comes into force at a time when a constable gives notice of it to an appropriate person (holder of the premises licence, designated premises supervisor, or premises user in the case of a temporary event notice) who is connected with any of the activities to which the disorder or nuisance relates. The closure order must specify the premises, the period for which it must remain closed, the grounds on which it is made, and state the effect of possible extensions, cancellations, extensions by a magistrates' court, and review of the premises licence.

A person commits an offence if, without reasonable excuse, he permits relevant premises to be open in contravention of a closure order or extension of it.

In determining whether to make a closure order the police officer must have regard, in particular, to the conduct of each appropriate person in relation to the disorder or nuisance.

'Relevant premises' in this section means premises in respect of which there is in effect a premises licence or a temporary event notice. (S 161)

(CONTINUED ON NEXT PAGE)

Closure Orders – Cont.

S 162, 163, 169 & 170 LICENSING ACT 2003

Extension of closure order
Where, before the end of the closure period or an extension of it, the responsible senior police officer reasonably believes that:

(a) a relevant magistrates' court will not have determined whether to exercise its powers relating to a closure order by the end of the closure period; and
(b) closure is necessary in the interests of public safety or prevention of public nuisance (as the case may be)

he may extend the closure period for a further 24 hours beginning with the end of the previous closure period.

The extension comes into force when a constable gives notice of it to an appropriate person, but it must be served before the end of the previous closure period. (S 162)

Cancellation of a closure order
It may be cancelled by the responsible senior police officer at any time after making the order but before a magistrates' court has made a determination relating to a closure. The closure order must be cancelled if the need for it ceases. (S 163)

Enforcement
A constable may use such force as may be necessary for the purpose of closing premises in compliance with a closure order (S 169). A constable is not liable for any damage caused in such enforcement. (S 170)

Exemptions

S 172-175 LICENSING ACT 2003

Relaxation of opening hours – special occasions
The Secretary of State may make a licensing hours order on an occasion of exceptional international, national or local significance. Such an order provides that during the specified relaxation period, premises licences and club premises certificates have effect as if the specified times were included in the opening hours. The order may apply generally or in relation to premises in specified areas. (S 172)

Activities in certain locations

An activity is not a licensable activity if it is carried on:

(a) aboard an aircraft, hovercraft or railway vehicle engaged on a journey;
(b) aboard a vessel engaged on an international journey;
(c) at an approved wharf at a designated port or hoverport;
(d) at an examination station at a designated airport,
(e) at a royal palace;
(f) at premises which are permanently or temporarily occupied by the armed forces of the Crown;
(g) at premises in respect of which a certificate of exemption for national security has been issued under S 174; or
(h) at such other place as may be prescribed. (S 173)

Raffle, tombola, etc.
A lottery which would otherwise be a licensable activity by reason of one or more prizes consisting of alcohol, will not constitute a licensable activity if:

(a) it is promoted as an incident of an exempt entertainment;
(b) the whole proceeds, less expenses, of the entertainment (including those of the lottery) are applied for purposes other than private gain;
(c) it does not include alcohol not in a sealed container;
(d) no prize in the lottery is a money prize;
(e) the ticket or chance in the lottery is sold or issued, and the result of the lottery is declared, at the premises where the entertainment takes place, and during the entertainment; and
(f) the opportunity to participate in a lottery or gaming is not the only or main inducement to attend. (S 175)

Police Powers and Definitions

S 97, 179, 180 & 191 LICENSING ACT 2003

Rights of Entry to Investigate Licensable Activities
Where a constable has reason to believe that any premises are being, or are about to be, used for a licensable activity, he may enter the premises with a view to seeing whether the activity is being, or is to be, carried on under and in accordance with an authorisation (a premises licence, a club premises certificate (but see the proviso below), or a temporary event notice).

A constable exercising this power may, if necessary, use reasonable force.

This section does not apply to premises in respect of which there is a club premises certificate but no other authorisation. (S 179)

Right of entry to investigate offences
A constable may enter and search any premises in respect of which he has reason to believe that an offence under this Act has been, or is about to be committed. He may, if necessary, use reasonable force in exercising this power. (S 180)

A constable may enter and search premises being used under a **club premises certificate** if he has reasonable cause to believe:

(a) that an offence under S 4(3)(a), (b) or (c) of the Misuse of Drugs Act 1971 (supplying etc. controlled drugs) has been, is being, or is about to be, committed there, or
(b) that there is likely to be a breach of the peace there. (S 97)

Meaning of alcohol
"Alcohol" means spirits, wine, beer, cider or any other fermented, distilled or spirituous liquor, but does not include:

(a) alcohol with a strength not exceeding 0.5% at the time of sale or supply;
(b) perfume;
(c) flavouring essences not intended for consumption as or with dutiable alcoholic liquor;
(d) Angostura bitters aromatic flavouring essence;
(e) alcohol which is, or is included in, a medicinal product;
(f) denatured alcohol;
(g) methyl alcohol;
(h) naphtha; or
(i) alcohol contained in liqueur confectionary having not more than 0.2 l of alcohol (strength not over 57 %) per kg of confectionary, and which consists of separate pieces weighing not more than 42 g or is designed to be broken down into such pieces for the purpose of consumption. (S 191)

Drunks in Public Places

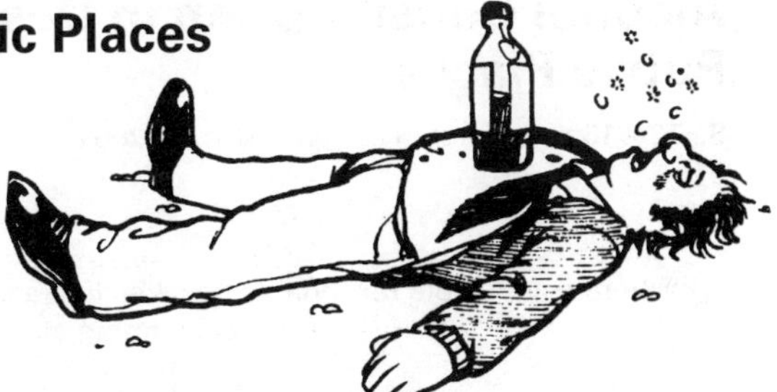

Drunkenness

S 12 LICENSING ACT 1872

It is an offence to be found drunk in any highway or other public place whether a building or not, or any licensed premises. (Public place includes all places where the public have access whether on payment or otherwise.)

Carriage, etc.

S 12 LICENSING ACT 1872

It is an offence to be drunk whilst in charge on any highway or other public place of any horse, cattle, pig, sheep, carriage, motor vehicle, trailer, bicycle or steam engine.

Firearms

S 12 LICENSING ACT 1872

It is an offence, whilst drunk, to be in possession of any loaded firearm (including an airgun).

Children

S 2 LICENSING ACT 1902

It is an offence to be drunk in a highway or other public place, whether a building or not, or any licensed premises, while having the charge of a child apparently under the age of 7 years.

Disorderly

S 91(1) CRIMINAL JUSTICE ACT 1967

It is an offence in a public place to be guilty, whilst drunk, of disorderly behaviour. (Public place includes any highway and any other premises or place to which at the material time the public have, or are permitted to have, access whether on payment or otherwise.)

Alcohol Consumption in Designated Public Places

Ss 12 – 15 CRIMINAL JUSTICE AND POLICE ACT 2001

Where a constable reasonably believes that a person is, or has been, or intends, consuming alcohol

in a designated public place

the constable may require the person:

(a) not to consume in that place anything which the constable believes to be alcohol;

(b) to surrender anything in his possession which he believes to be alcohol, or a container for such liquor.

and may dispose of anything surrendered to him in such manner as he considers appropriate.

It is an offence to fail without reasonable excuse to comply with such a requirement.

The constable must inform the person concerned that failure to comply without reasonable excuse is an offence.

A *'designated public place'* is a public place which is identified in an order made by a local authority.

Public Charitable Collections

S 66 CHARITIES ACT 1992

At the time of going to press, this section was not in force. See following page for current provisions.

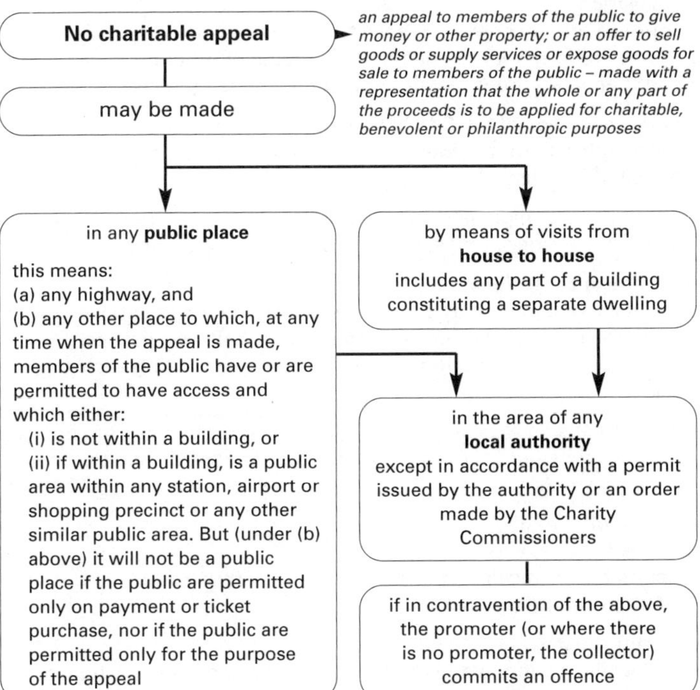

Exceptions

Does not apply to a charitable appeal which:
(a) is made in the course of a public meeting; or
(b) is made:
   (i) on land within a churchyard or burial ground contiguous or adjacent to a place or public worship, or
   (ii) on other land occupied for the purposes of a place of public worship and contiguous or adjacent to it, being in each case land which is enclosed, or substantially enclosed; or
(c) is an appeal to the public to give money or other property by placing it in a receptacle

Street and house to house Collections

POLICE, FACTORIES ETC (MISCELLANEOUS PROVISIONS) ACT 1916; HOUSE TO HOUSE COLLECTIONS ACT 1939; AND HOUSE TO HOUSE COLLECTIONS REGULATIONS 1947

Street collections
It is an offence for any person, in any street or public place, to collect money or sell articles for the benefit of charitable or other purposes otherwise than in accordance with regulations made by:

- the common council of the City of London;
- the police authority for the Metropolitan Police District; or
- the council of that district.

'Street' includes any highway and any public bridge, road, lane, footway, square, court, alley, or passage, whether a thoroughfare or not.

House-to-house collections
It is an offence for a person to promote a collection for a charitable purpose, or to act as a collector for such purpose, unless a licence, certificate or order of exemption has been issued authorising such activities.

'Collection' means an appeal to the public by means of visits from house to house, to give, whether for consideration of not, money or other property.

The promoter must issue to each collector:
- a certificate of authority;
- a prescribed badge; and
- a collecting box or receipt book indicating the purpose of the collection and a distinguishing number.

The collector must:
- sign the certificate and badge and return them when the collection is completed;
- not be under the age of 16;
- not importune or annoy people; and
- only collect money which is placed in the collecting box, or issue a receipt for it.

A collection may be made by envelope if authorised by the Secretary of State.

Police powers
A constable may require a person whom he believes is acting as a collector to declare his name and address and to sign his name. Failure to do so is an offence.

Chapter 5
Animals

Welfare of Animals

ANIMAL WELFARE ACT 2006

Introduction

The act makes provision for the promotion of the welfare of vertebrate animals, other than those in the wild. Care should be taken to ensure that the scope of the offence covers the animal in question. For example cruelty and fighting offences extend to 'protected animals' whereas the welfare offence applies to animals for which the person is 'responsible'. The Act contains offences of causing unnecessary suffering, mutilation, docking of dogs' tails, administration of poisons, and animal fighting. It also creates offences of not ensuring an animal's needs are met, and selling animals to persons under 16. In addition it gives powers to inspectors and the police to take steps to alleviate suffering and to stop and search vehicles.

These provisions are discussed in more depth in the following pages.

The main provisions of the Act do not apply to Scotland.

Meaning of 'animal' (S 1)
'Animal' means a vertebrate other than man. But nothing in the Act applies to an animal while it is in its foetal or embryonic form. 'Vertebrate' means any animal of the Subphylum Vertebrata of the Phylum Chordata. 'Invertebrate' means any animal not of that Subphylum.

Meaning of 'protected animal' (S 2)
An animal is a 'protected animal' if it is-

(a) of a kind which is commonly domesticated in the British Islands,
(b) under the control of man whether on a permanent or temporary basis, or
(c) not living in a wild state.

Responsibility for animals (S 3)
This means a person responsible for an animal whether on a permanent or temporary basis. It includes being in charge of it. A person who owns an animal shall always be regarded as being a person responsible for it. Where a person has actual care and control of a person under 16 years, he will be responsible for any animal for which the under-16 is responsible.

Welfare of Animals – Unnecessary Suffering

S 4 ANIMAL WELFARE ACT 2006

Unnecessary suffering of protected animal

A person commits an offence if-

(a) an act of his, or a failure of his to act, causes an animal (for meaning see previous page) to suffer,

(b) he knew, or ought reasonably to have known, that the act, or failure to act, would have that effect or be likely to do so,

(c) the animal is a protected animal (for meaning see previous page), and

(d) the suffering is unnecessary.

Unnecessary suffering caused by responsible person

A person commits an offence if-

(a) he is responsible (for meaning see previous page) for an animal,

(b) an act, or failure to act, of another person causes the animal to suffer,

(c) he permitted that to happen or failed to take such steps (whether by way of supervising the other person or otherwise) as were reasonable in all the circumstances to prevent that happening, and

(d) the suffering is unnecessary.

Unnecessary suffering

Considerations to determine whether suffering is unnecessary-

(a) whether the suffering could reasonably have been avoided or reduced;

(b) whether the conduct which caused the suffering was in compliance with any relevant enactment or any relevant provisions of a licence or code of practice;

(c) whether the conduct which caused the suffering was for a legitimate purpose, such as (i) benefiting the animal, or (ii) protecting a person, property or another animal;

(d) whether the suffering was proportionate to the purpose of the conduct concerned;

(e) whether the conduct concerned was in all the circumstances that of a reasonably competent and humane person.

Suffering means physical or mental suffering. (S 62).

Welfare of Animals – Mutilation

S 5 ANIMAL WELFARE ACT 2006

Carrying out a prohibited procedure

A person commits an offence if-

(a) he carries out a prohibited procedure on a protected animal (for meaning see earlier);

(b) he causes such a procedure to be carried out on such an animal.

Responsible person permitting a prohibited procedure

A person commits an offence if-

(a) he is responsible for an animal (for meaning see earlier),
(b) another person carries out a prohibited procedure on the animal, and
(c) he permitted that to happen or failed to take such steps (whether by way of supervising the other person or otherwise) as were reasonable in all the circumstances to prevent that happening.

Neither of the above offences apply in such circumstances as the appropriate national authority specify in regulations.

Nor do they apply to the removal of the whole or any part of a dog's tail (but see following page).

Prohibited procedure means the carrying out of a procedure which involves interference with the sensitive tissues or bone structure of the animal, otherwise than for the purpose of its medical treatment.

Welfare of Animals – Docking of Dogs' Tails

S 6 ANIMAL WELFARE ACT 2006
DOCKING OF WORKING DOGS' TAILS REGS. 2007

Removal of dog's tail
A person commits an offence if-
(a) he removes the whole or any part of a dog's tail, otherwise than for the purpose of its medical treatment;
(b) he causes the whole or any part of a dog's tail to be removed by another person, otherwise than for the purpose of its medical treatment.

Responsible person permitting the removal of a dog's tail
A person commits an offence if-
(a) he is responsible (for meaning see earlier) for a dog,
(b) another person removes the whole or any part of the dog's tail, otherwise than for the purpose of its medical treatment, and
(c) he permitted that to happen or failed to take such steps (whether by way of supervising the other person or otherwise) as were reasonable in all the circumstances to prevent that happening.

Neither of these offences apply if the dog is a certified working dog that is not more than five days old.

'Certified' means a veterinary surgeon has certified in accordance with regulations that the dog is of a type specified by regulations (see below), and that he has been produced evidence (it is an offence to produce false evidence) that the dog is likely to be used for work in connection with-

(a) law enforcement,
(b) activities of HM armed forces,
(c) emergency rescue,
(d) lawful pest control, or
(e) the lawful shooting of animals.

Under the **Docking of Working Dogs' Tails (England) Regs. 2007**, such dogs must be microchipped for identification purposes. These regulations also specify the breeds to which the Act applies as being any type or combination of types of hunt point retrievers, spaniels, and terriers

Failure to have dog certified
A person commits an offence if he owns such a dog and fails to take reasonable steps to secure that, before the dog is three months old, it is identified as such in accordance with regulations.

Showing a dog
A person commits an offence if (a) he shows a dog at an event to which members of the public are admitted on payment of a fee, (b) the dog's tail has been wholly or partly removed (in England or Wales or elsewhere), and (c) removal took place on or after the commencement day of this section (6th April 2007).
But this offence will not apply if it is a certified dog shown only to demonstrate its working ability.

Welfare of Animals – Administration of Poisons

S 7 ANIMAL WELFARE ACT 2006

Administering poisons etc

A person commits an offence if, without lawful authority or reasonable excuse, he

(a) administers any poisonous or injurious drug or substance to a protected animal (for meaning see earlier), knowing it to be poisonous or injurious, or

(b) causes any poisonous or injurious drug or substance to be taken by a protected animal, knowing it to be poisonous or injurious.

Responsible person causing or permitting the administering of poisons etc.

A person commits an offence if, being responsible for an animal-

(a) without lawful authority or reasonable excuse, another person administers a poisonous or injurious drug or substance to the animal or causes the animal to take such a drug or substance, and

(b) he permitted that to happen or, knowing the drug or substance to be poisonous or injurious, he failed to take such steps (whether by way of supervising the other person or otherwise) as were reasonable in all the circumstances to prevent that happening.

A poisonous or injurious drug or substance includes a drug or substance which, by virtue of the quantity or manner in which it is administered or taken, has the effect of a poisonous or injurious drug or substance.

It is not necessary to show that the animal did in fact suffer as a result of the action.

Welfare of Animals – Animal Fights

S 8 ANIMAL WELFARE ACT 2006

Being involved with an animal fight
A person commits an offence if he-

(a) causes an animal fight to take place, or attempts to do so;

(b) knowingly receives money for admission to an animal fight;

(c) knowingly publicises a proposed animal fight;

(d) provides information about an animal fight to another with the intention of enabling or encouraging attendance at the fight;

(e) makes or accepts a bet on the outcome of an animal fight or on the likelihood of anything occurring or not occurring in the course of the animal fight;

(f) takes part in an animal fight;

(g) has in his possession anything designed or adapted for use in connection with an animal fight with the intention of its being so used;

(h) keeps or trains an animal for use for or in connection with an animal fight;

(i) keeps any premises for use for an animal fight.

Being present at an animal fight
A person commits an offence if, without lawful authority or reasonable excuse, he is present at an animal fight.

Video recordings of animal fights (Please note that at the time of going to press this provision had not been brought into force)

A person commits an offence if, without lawful authority or reasonable excuse, he

(a) knowingly supplies a video recording of an animal fight (except for inclusion in a programme service),

(b) knowingly publishes a video recording of an animal fight (except by including it in a programme service),

Welfare of Animals – Animal Fights – Cont.

S 8 ANIMAL WELFARE ACT 2006

(c) knowingly shows a video recording of an animal fight to another (except by including it in a programme service), or

(d) possesses a video recording of an animal fight, knowing it to be such a recording, with the intention of supplying it (except for inclusion in a programme service).

The offence does not apply if the video recording is of an animal fight that took place-

(a) outside Great Britain, or

(b) before the commencement date (not yet in force).

Animal fight means an occasion on which a protected animal is placed with an animal, or with a human, for the purpose of fighting, wrestling or baiting. **Programme service** means (a) a television programme service, (b) public teletext, (c) an additional television service, (d) a digital additional television service, (e) a radio programme service, and (f) a sound service provided by the BBC (Communications Act 2003).

Welfare of Animals – Animal Needs

S 9 ANIMAL WELFARE ACT 2006

Ensuring animals' needs are met
A person commits an offence if he does not take such steps as are reasonable in all the circumstances to ensure that the needs of an animal for which he is responsible are met to the extent required by good practice.

An *animal's needs* include-
(a) its need for a suitable environment,
(b) its need for a suitable diet,
(c) its need to be able to exhibit normal behaviour patterns,
(d) any need it has to be housed with, or apart from, other animals, and
(e) its need to be protected from pain, suffering, injury and disease.

The **circumstances** mentioned above include, in particular-
(a) any lawful purpose for which the animal is kept, and
(b) any lawful activity undertaken in relation to the animal.

Welfare of Animals – Sale, etc. to Children

S 11 ANIMAL WELFARE ACT 2006

Sale to child under 16 years
A person commits an offence if he sells an animal to a person whom he has reasonable cause to believe to be under the age of 16 years.

Selling includes transferring, or agreeing to transfer, ownership of the animal in consideration of entry by the transferee into another transaction.

Animals as prizes
A person commits an offence if-
(a) he enters into an arrangement with a person whom he has reasonable cause to believe to be under the age of 16 years, and
(b) the arrangement is one under which that person has a chance to win an animal as a prize.

But this offence will not apply if-
(a) the arrangement is made in the presence of the child and the child is accompanied by a person who is not under 16 years of age,
(b) the arrangement is made not in the presence of the child, but there is a belief that a person who has actual care and control of the child has consented to the arrangement, or
(c) the arrangement is entered into in a family context.

Welfare of Animals – Animals in Distress

S 18 ANIMAL WELFARE ACT 2006

Action to alleviate suffering
If an inspector or constable reasonably believes that a protected animal is suffering he may take, or arrange for the taking of, such steps as appear to him to be immediately necessary to alleviate the animal's suffering. This does not authorise the destruction of an animal. See earlier for definition of 'protected animal'.

Destruction of an animal
If a veterinary surgeon certifies that the condition of a protected animal is such that it should in its own interests be destroyed, an inspector or constable may-

(a) destroy the animal where it is or take it to another place and destroy it there, or

(b) arrange for this to be done.

Destruction in urgent cases
An inspector or constable may destroy or arrange destruction of an animal as above without the certificate of a veterinary surgeon if it appears to him-

(a) that the condition of the animal is such that there is no reasonable alternative to destroying it, and

(b) that the need for action is such that it is not reasonably practicable to wait for a veterinary surgeon.

Welfare of Animals – Animals in Distress – Cont.

S 18 ANIMAL WELFARE ACT 2006

Taking an animal into possession
An inspector or constable may take a protected animal (including any dependent offspring of the animal) into possession if a veterinary surgeon certifies-

(a) that it is suffering, or

(b) that it is likely to suffer if its circumstances do not change.

Taking an animal into possession in urgent cases
An inspector or constable may take possession in the above circumstances without the certificate of a veterinary surgeon if the need for action is such that it is not reasonably practicable to wait for a veterinary surgeon.

Obstructing the exercise of powers
A person commits an offence if he intentionally obstructs a person in the exercise of any of the above powers.

Welfare of Animals – Police Powers

ANIMAL WELFARE ACT 2006

Powers of entry to premises (S 19)
An inspector or constable may enter premises (except premises used as a private dwelling – warrant needed) for the purpose of searching for a protected animal and of exercising any of the above powers if he reasonably believes that there is a protected animal on the premises, and that the animal is suffering or, if the circumstances of the animal do not change, it is likely to suffer. Reasonable force may be used in exercising the power of entry but only if it appears to him that entry is required before a warrant can be obtained and executed.

Seizure of animals involved in fighting offences (S 22)
A constable may seize an animal if it appears to him that it is one in relation to which an offence under S 8(1) or (2) has been committed (taking part in or being present at an animal fight). (See earlier).

Entry and search of premises (S 22)
A constable may enter and search premises (except premises used as a private dwelling - warrant needed) for the purpose of exercising power to seize such an animal if he reasonably believes-

(a) that there is an animal on the premises, and

(b) that the animal is one in relation to which the above power to seize animals is exercisable.

Entry for purposes of arrest (S 24)
S 17(1)(c) of the Police and Criminal Evidence Act 1984 gives constables a power to enter and search premises for the purpose of arresting a person for specified offences. The following offences under the Animal Welfare Act 2006 have been added to that list of offences-

(a) S 4 (unnecessary suffering),

(b) S 5 (mutilation),

(c) S 6(1) & (2) (docking of dog's tails),

(d) S 7 (administering poisons etc.), and

(e) S 8(1) & (2), (taking part in or being present at an animal fight).

Welfare of Animals – Police Powers – Cont.

ANIMAL WELFARE ACT 2006

Power to stop and detain vehicles (S 54)
A constable in uniform may stop and detain a vehicle for the purpose of entering and searching it in the exercise of a power under S 19(1) (entry and search in the case of an animal which is, or is likely to be, suffering) (see above) and S 22(2) (entry and search in the case of an animal subject of an offence by a person of taking part in, or being present at, an animal fight) (see above). This power also includes action taken where a warrant has been issued in the above circumstances.

Cruelty To Wild mammals

WILD MAMMALS (PROTECTION) ACT 1996

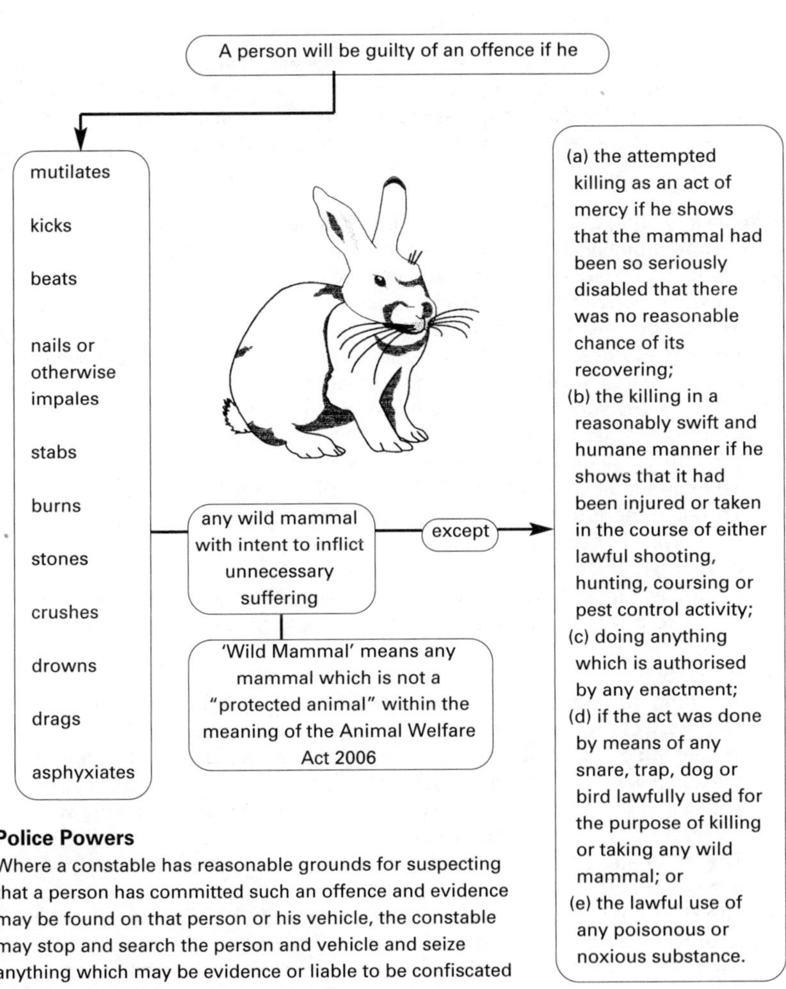

Police Powers

Where a constable has reasonable grounds for suspecting that a person has committed such an offence and evidence may be found on that person or his vehicle, the constable may stop and search the person and vehicle and seize anything which may be evidence or liable to be confiscated by the court (vehicles, equipment, etc.)

Protection of Wild Animals

WILDLIFE AND COUNTRYSIDE ACT 1981

Schedule 5 to this Act lists certain wild animals which are protected. The list is too long to be reproduced here, but includes – adder, bat, beetle, butterfly, wildcat, cricket, dolphin, frog, grasshopper, moth, mussel, newt, otter, porpoise, red squirrel, toad, water vole, walrus and whale.

Offences relating to animals contained in Schedule 5:

1. To intentionally kill, injure or take any wild animal;
2. To have in possession or control any live or dead wild animals or anything derived from such an animal;
3. To intentionally or recklessly-
   - damage or destroy, or obstruct access to, any structure or place which a wild animal uses for shelter or protection, or
   - disturb any such animal while it is occupying a structure or place which it uses for that purpose,

but the above will not be an offence if it takes place in a dwelling house;

4. To intentionally or recklessly disturb a dolphin, whale or basking shark;
5. To sell, offer or expose for sale, or have in possession or transport for the purpose of sale, a live or dead wild animal, or any part of, or anything derived from, such an animal;
6. To publish or cause to be published any advertisement to buy or sell, or intend to buy or sell any such thing as is mentioned in '5' above.

Defences (S 10)

(a) Anything done as a requirement of the Minister of Agriculture, the Secretary of State or an order under the Animal Health Act 1981.

(b) The taking of a disabled animal solely for the purpose of tending it and releasing it when no longer disabled.

(c) The killing of an animal which was so seriously disabled that there was no reasonable chance of it recovering.

(d) The incidental result of a lawful operation and could not reasonably have been avoided.

(e) The killing or injuring of a wild animal by an authorised person, if done to prevent serious damage to livestock, foodstuffs for livestock, crops, vegetables, fruit, growing timber or any other form of property or to fisheries. This defence could only be relied upon if the events were not anticipated – otherwise a licence would be needed.

(CONTINUED ON NEXT PAGE)

Protection of Wild Animals – continued

Prohibited methods of taking and killing any wild animals (S 11(1))

(a) Setting self-locking snares calculated to cause injury to wild animals;
(b) Using self-locking snares (whether or not so calculated), or a bow, crossbow, or explosive;
(c) Using as a decoy any live mammal or bird;
(d) Knowingly causing or permitting any of the above.

Prohibited methods of taking and killing Schedule 6 wild animals (S 11(2)):
Schedule 6 lists certain animals which may not be killed or taken by certain methods. They are: badger, horseshoe bat, typical bat, wildcat, bottle-nosed dolphin, common dolphin, dormouse, hedgehog, pine martin, common otter, polecat, common porpoise, shrew and red squirrel.
The prohibited methods are:

(a) Setting any of the following articles calculated to cause injury: trap, snare, electrical device for killing or stunning or any poisonous, poisoned or stupefying substance;
(b) Using an automatic or semi-automatic weapon, target illuminating device or night sight, artificial light, mirror or dazzling device, or gas or smoke;
(c) Using a mechanically propelled vehicle in pursuit; or
(d) Using for the purpose of killing or taking a wild animal, any of the following articles whether or not calculated to cause injury: trap, snare, electrical device for killing or stunning or any poisonous, poisoned or stupefying substance; or net;
(e) Using as a decoy any sound recording; or
(f) Knowingly causing or permitting any of the above.

Snares (S 11(3))
It is an offence to fail to inspect at least once a day, any snare which has been set in position and which is of such a nature and is so placed as to be calculated to cause bodily injury to any wild animal.

Protection of Plants

S 13 WILDLIFE AND COUNTRYSIDE ACT 1981

Schedule 8 of the Act lists a variety of wild plants which are afforded protection. They are too numerous to list here, but include the following: blackwort, purple colt's foot, wild cotoneaster, numerous forms of gentian, numerous forms of lichen and moss, numerous forms of orchid, fen ragwort and fen violet.

Offences

1. Intentionally picking, uprooting or destroying any wild plant included in the Schedule;
2. not being an authorised person, intentionally uprooting any wild plant not included in the Schedule;
3. selling, offering or exposing for sale, or having in possession or transporting for the purpose of sale any live or dead wild plant included in the Schedule; and
4. publishing or causing to be published an advertisement to buy or sell any of those things.

In relation to offences 1 and 2 above, it is a defence to show that the act was an incidental result of a lawful operation and could not reasonable have been avoided.

Police Powers

S 19 WILDLIFE AND COUNTRYSIDE ACT 1981

If a constable suspects with reasonable cause that any person is committing or has committed an offence under Sections 1, 5, 6, 7 or 8 (protection of wild birds); sections 9 or 11 (protection of wild animals); or Section 13 (protection of wild plants); he may, without warrant:

(a) stop and search that person if the constable suspects with reasonable cause that evidence of the commission of the offence is to be found on him;
(b) search or examine any thing which is in that person's possession if the constable suspects with reasonable cause that evidence of the commission of the offence is to be found on that thing;
(c) seize and detain any thing which may be evidence of the commission of the offence or may be liable to be forfeited (includes vehicles, animals, weapons, etc.).

Sale of Dogs

BREEDING AND SALE OF DOGS (WELFARE) ACT 1999

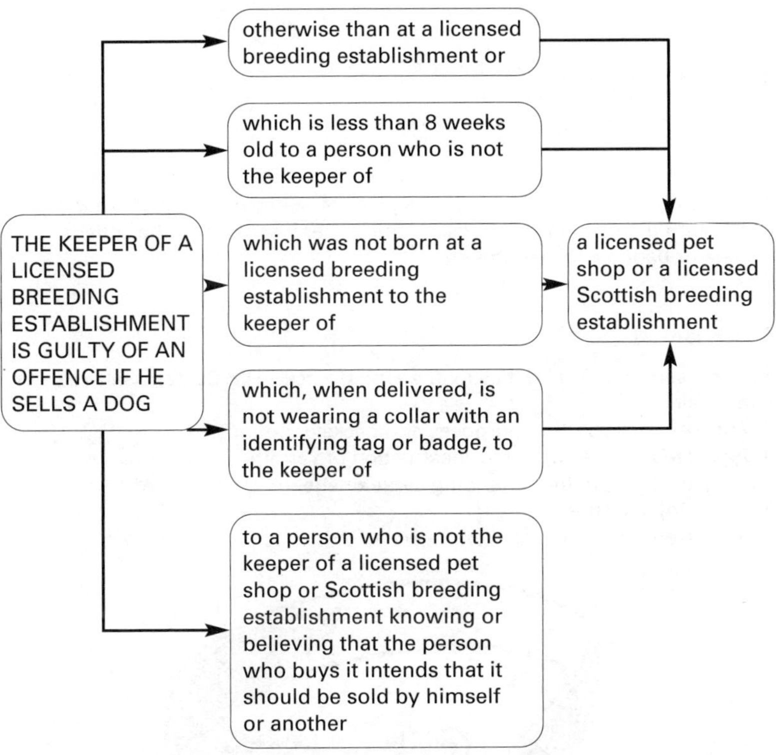

The keeper of a licensed pet shop is guilty of an offence if he sells a dog which, when delivered to him, was wearing a collar with an identifying tag or badge, but is not wearing such a collar when delivered to the person to whom he sells it.

The identifying tag or badge must clearly display the following information:

(a) the date of birth of the dog;
(b) an identifying number, if any, allocated to the dog by the licensed breeding establishment at which it was born; and
(c) the breeding establishment at which it was born.

Dogs

Dog Collars

ARTICLE 1 CONTROL OF DOGS ORDER 1992

Every dog while in a highway or in a place of public resort, shall wear a collar with the name and address of the owner inscribed on the collar or on a plate or badge attached thereto.

Exceptions

- Dogs used on official duties by the armed forces, HM Customs & Excise or the police.
- Dogs used for sporting purposes and packs of hounds
- Dogs used for the capture or destruction of vermin
- Dogs used for driving or tending cattle or sheep
- Guide dogs for the blind
- Dogs used for emergency rescue work

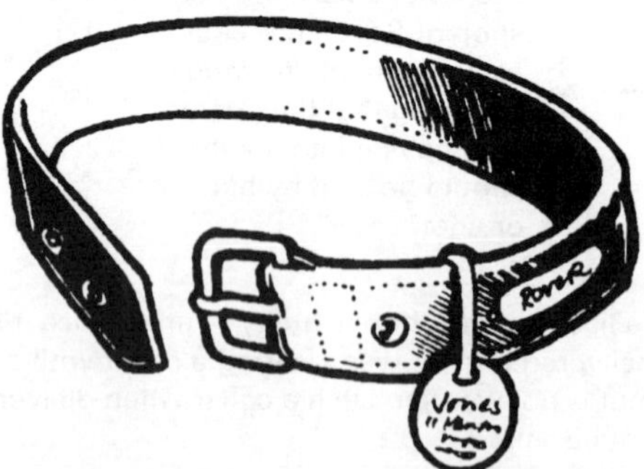

The owner of the dog and any person in charge of it, who, without lawful authority or excuse causes or permits the dog to be on the highway or place of public resort shall each be guilty of an offence. Dogs not wearing a collar may be seized as a stray dog. This order will be executed and enforced by officers of a local authority and not by the police.

Dogs Worrying Livestock

S 1 DOGS (PROTECTION OF LIVESTOCK) ACT 1953 AS AMENDED

If a dog	
worries	Attacking livestock, chasing livestock in such a way as may reasonably be expected to cause injury or suffering, or abortion or loss or diminution of their produce. It is sufficient to prove that the dog ran among the livestock and alarmed them, provided the result is achieved. Also, being at large (not on a lead or under close control) in a field or enclosure where there are sheep
livestock	Means cattle, sheep, goats, swine, horses, fowl, turkeys, geese and ducks
on any agricultural land	Means land used as arable meadow or grazing land, poultry land, pig land, market gardens, allotments, nursery grounds or orchards. It will not be an offence if the livestock are 'trespassing' and the dog belongs to, is in charge of, the owner/occupier of the land, unless he causes it to attack the livestock
the owner of the dog and any other person in charge of it	The owner shall not be convicted if he proves that at the material time the dog was in the charge of some other person whom he reasonably believed to be a fit and proper person
shall be guilty of an offence	A constable who believes that a dog has been worrying livestock as above may seize the dog if no person admits to being the owner or person in charge of it

It is a defence to a charge of killing or injuring a dog to prove that it was done to protect the livestock and the police were informed with 48 hours.

Orders for Controlling Dangerous Dogs

S 2 DOGS ACT 1871

Where a dog is regarded as being dangerous, either because it has attacked someone, or because it has worried livestock and is not kept under proper control, application may be made to the court for an order to be made for the dog to kept by the owner under proper control or destroyed. It is an offence to fail to comply with such an order.

S 28 TOWN POLICE CLAUSES ACT 1847

Where the Town Police Clauses Act 1847 applies, an offence is committed by any person who in any street, to the obstruction, annoyance or danger of residents or passengers, suffers to be at large any unmuzzled ferocious dog, or sets on or urges any dog or other animal to attack, worry or put in fear any person or animal.

Dangerous Dogs

S 1 DANGEROUS DOGS ACT 1991

This section applies to:

- PIT BULL TERRIERS
- JAPANESE TOSAS
- DOGS DESIGNATED BY THE SECRETARY OF STATE
  At the time of going to press, this includes the Dogo Argentina and the Fila Braziliero
  Dangerous Dogs (Designated Types) Order 1991

A person commits an offence if he:
has such a dog in his **POSSESSION** or **CUSTODY** except under a power of seizure or in accordance with an order for its destruction;

BREEDS
or breeds from, any of the above;

SELLS
or exchanges such a dog or offers, advertises or exposes such a dog for sale or exchange;

MAKES A GIFT
(or offers to do so) of such a dog or advertises or exposes such a dog as a gift;

ALLOWS
such a dog of which he is the owner or of which he is for the time being in charge to be in a **PUBLIC PLACE** without being **MUZZLED** and **KEPT ON A LEAD**;
(**'Muzzled'** means sufficient to prevent it biting someone, and **'kept on a lead'** means securely held by a person not less than 16 years. S 7)

ABANDONS
such a dog of which he is the owner;

Allows such a dog to **STRAY**, being the owner or for the time being in charge.

Control of Dogs

S 3 DANGEROUS DOGS ACT 1991

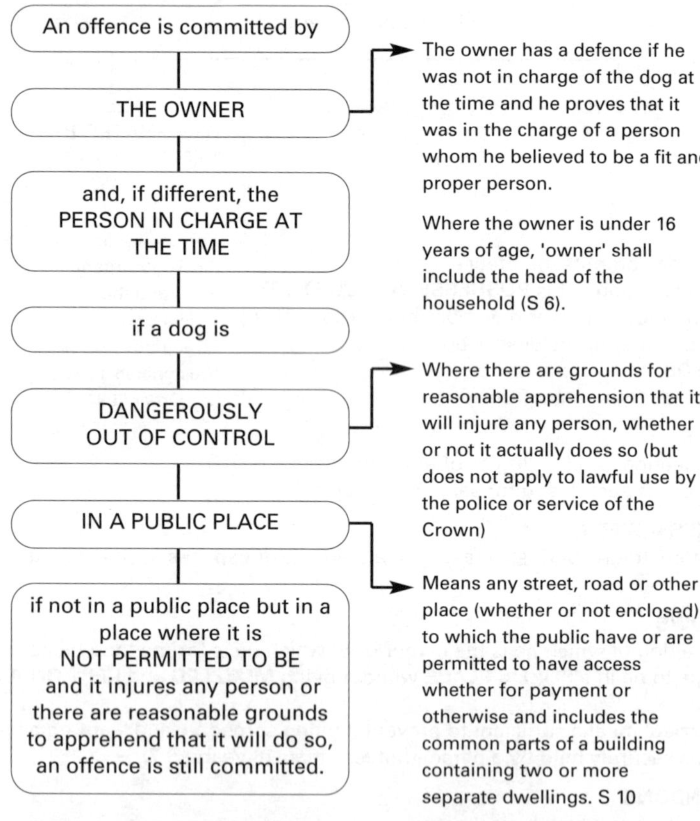

If the dog **injures someone** whilst out of control an aggravated offence is committed for which heavier penalties are liable

POLICE POWERS

S 5 DANGEROUS DOGS ACT 1991

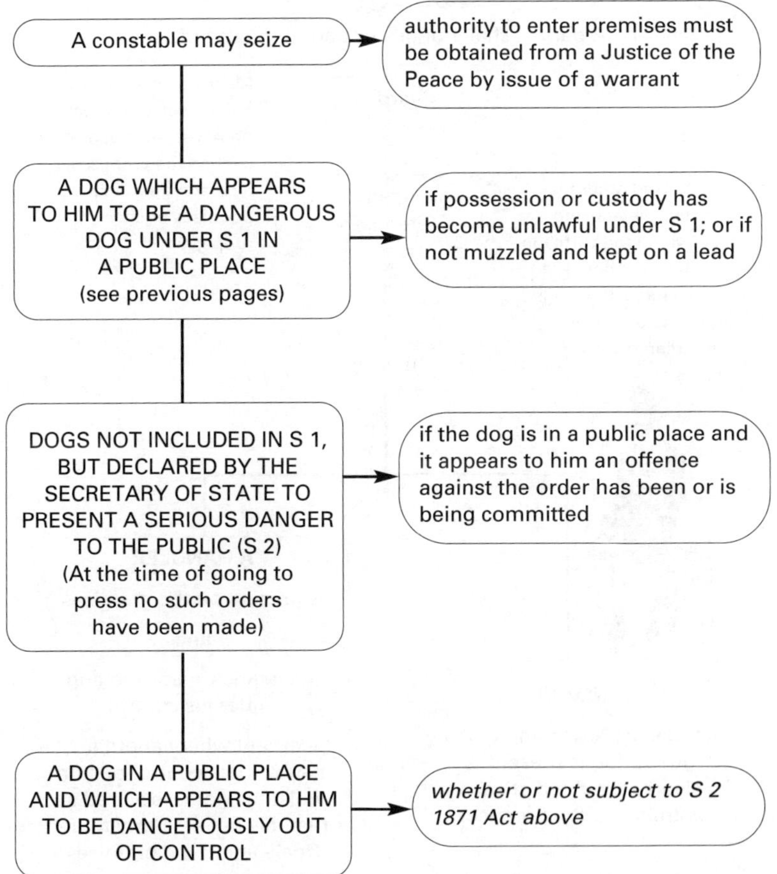

Guard Dogs

S 1 GUARD DOGS ACT 1975

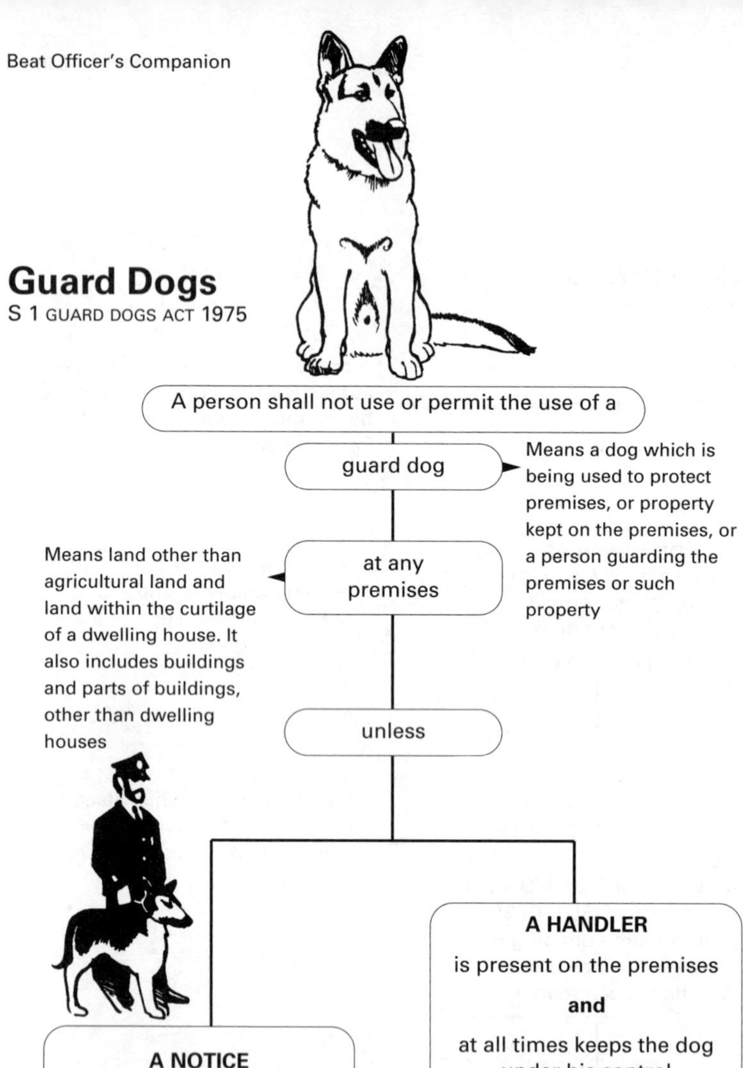

Dangerous Wild Animals

S 1 DANGEROUS WILD ANIMALS ACT 1976

No person is allowed to keep a dangerous wild animal unless he has been granted a licence to do so by the local authority (S 1).

A 'dangerous wild animal' is one which is specifically mentioned in the Act. Many animals are mentioned but the following list gives a guide to the type of animal referred to:

Alligators, crocodiles, ostriches, apes, poisonous snakes, lions, tigers, leopards, bears, wild dogs and wolves.

The provisions of this Act do not apply to:

- Zoos
- Circuses
- Licensed pet shops
- Premises authorised to be used for experiments (S 5)

Animals on Highways

S 155 HIGHWAYS ACT 1980

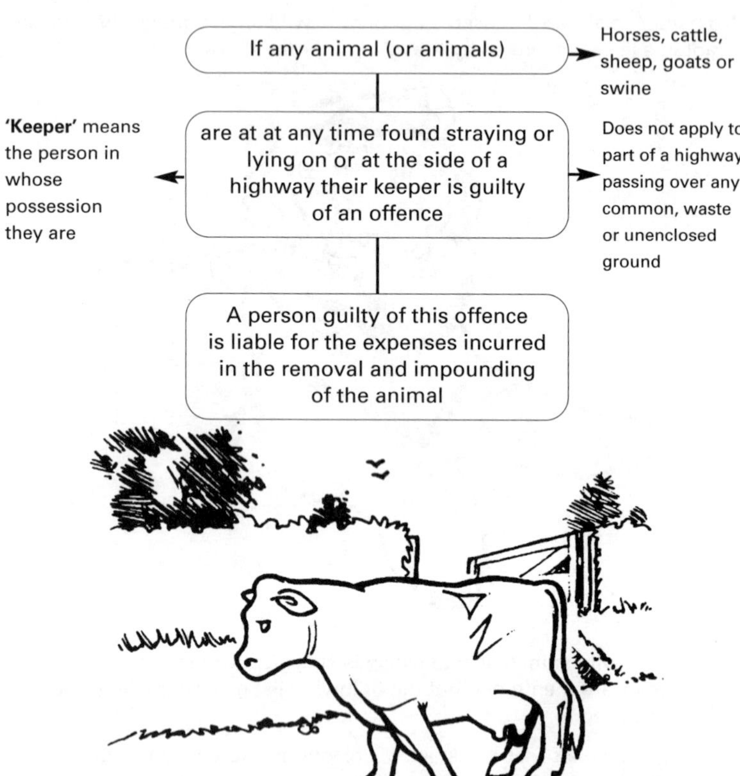

Dogs to be kept on lead
Where a local authority has designated a road upon which dogs must be kept on a lead, a person who causes or permits a dog to be on the road in contravention of the order shall be guilty of an offence

Dogs fouling land
Where a local authority has designated land in that area, it is an offence for a person in charge of a dog to fail to remove faeces deposited by the dog forthwith.

Diseases of Animals

ANIMAL HEALTH ACT 1981

NOTIFICATION S 15(1)
Any person having possession or charge of a diseased animal shall keep it separate from unaffected animals and notify the police with all practicable speed.

'INFECTED AREAS'
If necessary, the veterinary inspector who is called to visit the infected place declares the premises and the area surrounding the premises to be an infected area.

MOVEMENT
Movement of animals from and to infected areas is then restricted to those authorised by licence. Various powers are then given to the minister and the local authority to make orders and regulations to control the situation.

POWER OF ARREST S 60
If a person is seen or found committing, or is reasonably suspected of being engaged in committing, an act which has been declared to be an offence against the Act or an order of the minister or a regulation of the local authority, a constable may stop and detain him and if his name and address are not given to the satisfaction of the constable, he **may be apprehended in accordance with** the provisions of the Police and Criminal Evidence Act 1984.

ANIMALS AND PROPERTY
Irrespective of the stopping or apprehension of the person the constable may stop, detain and examine any animal, vehicle, boat or thing to which the offence relates, and require the same to be returned to any place from which it was unlawfully removed, and he may execute and enforce that requisition.

OBSTRUCTION S 60
A person who obstructs or impedes or assists to obstruct or impede a constable or other officer in the execution of this Act or of orders or regulations made in consequence of it, may be arrested by the constable or officer.

POWERS OF ENTRY
In areas where constables are appointed as local authority inspectors, they also have power to enter land and buildings where they suspect that diseased animals are or have been kept or where provisions of the Act are not being complied with.

Diseases of Animals – continued

ANIMAL HEALTH ACT 1981

Meaning of 'Animals'

Animal means:

- cattle, sheep and goats,
- all other ruminating animals and swine,
- any mammals except whales, dolphins, porpoises, seals, dugongs, and manatees, and
- poultry (domestic fowls, turkeys, geese, ducks, guinea-fowls, pigeons, pheasants and partridges and all other birds).

'Cattle' means bulls, cows, steers, heifers and calves.

Meaning of 'Disease'

Disease means:

- african swine fever,
- anthrax,
- aujeszky's disease,
- bovine leukosis,
- brucellosis,
- brucellosis suis,
- cattle plague,
- equine viral arteritis,
- foot and mouth disease,
- infectious diseases of horses,
- pleuro-pneumonia,
- rabies,
- sheep pox,
- sheep scab,
- swine fever,
- swine vesicular disease,
- tuberculosis,
- tularaemia, and
- warble fly

and in relation to poultry means:

- fowl cholera,
- fowl paralysis,
- fowl pest,
- fowl plague,
- fowl pox,
- fowl typhoid,
- infectious bronchitis,
- infectious laryngotracheitis,
- Newcastle disease,
- paramyxovirus 1 in pigeons, and
- pullorum disease

Rabies

Ss 15, 61 & 62 ANIMAL HEALTH ACT 1981, S17 POLICE AND CRIMINAL EVIDENCE ACT 1984

The powers conferred by these sections are without prejudice to the diseases of animals powers given on the previous pages.

Offences specific to this disease involve landing or attempting to land or importing, or attempted importation through the channel tunnel, animals in contravention of the order introduced to prevent the introduction of rabies into GB; the failure by the person having charge or control of any vessel or boat to discharge any obligation imposed on him by such an order; and the unlawful movement of any animal into, within or out of an infected area or place.

Any person who knows or suspects that an animal is affected with rabies shall give notice of that fact to a constable (S 15).

POLICE POWERS

For the purpose of arresting a person a constable may enter (if need be by force) and search any vessel, boat, hovercraft, aircraft or vehicle of any other description in which that person is or where the constable reasonably suspects him to be.

The above power of entry also applies in exercising the power to seize any animal.

Under S 17 of PACE, a constable may enter and search premises for the purposes of arresting a person for any of the above offences.

Importation of Animals

ARTs. 4 & 4A RABIES (IMPORTATION OF DOGS, CATS AND OTHER MAMMALS) ORDER 1974

This order applies to a wide variety of mammals which can be found in Sched. 1 to the Order. It includes dogs, cats, lions, tigers, hedgehogs, shrews, moles, rabbits, kangaroos, monkeys, baboons, apes, rats and mice.

The landing in GB of an animal brought from a place outside GB is prohibited except:

1. An animal brought to GB from Northern Ireland, Republic of Ireland, Channel Islands or Isle of Man, provided that, if the animal was taken to one of those places from another country (other than GB), the prohibition **will** apply unless:
   - it was imported from another member state or Norway in accordance with Council Directive 92/65/EEC; or
   - in any other case it has been detained and quarantined for at least 6 months before coming to GB.
2. An animal brought to GB from Northern Ireland, Republic of Ireland, Channel Islands or Isle of Man, provided:
   - if it was admitted there under Regulation EC 998 2003; and
   - in the case of a dog, cat or ferret, it has been treated against Echinococcus Multilocularis and ticks between 24 and 48 hours before embarkation to that place.
3. An animal landing under the authority of a licence granted by the Minister.

Specified Ports listed below must be used for landing animals except:

- specifically authorised in the licence mentioned in para. 3 above;
- an animal to which para. 1 above applies;
- landing at Cheriton through the Channel Tunnel; or
- the vessel/aircraft has been diverted to another port/airport by an inspector in the interests of safety or other exceptional circumstances.

The ports are: Dover Eastern Docks; Harwich and Parkeston Quay; Hull; Portsmouth; and Southampton.

The airports are: Birmingham; Edinburgh; Gatwick; Glasgow; Heathrow; Leeds; Manchester; and Prestwick.

Animals taken from GB, Northern Ireland, Republic of Ireland, Channel Islands or Isle of Man, to a place outside those countries (whether or not landed at that place, or coming into contact with another animal), shall be deemed to be an animal brought from a place outside GB and therefore subject to the above rules.

Animals imported from a member State other than the Republic of Ireland are not subject to the prohibition on landing, nor the use of specified ports as above if imported in accordance with Council Directive 92/65/EEC or the Animal and Animal Products (Import and Export) Regulations 2004 (concerning the import, export or transport for intra community trade of certain animals and animal products).

Animals imported under the Non-Commercial Movement of Pet Animals Regulations 2004 or Regulation (EC) 998/2003 (which also deals with animal health requirements for the non-commercial movement of pet animals) are not subject to the provisions of this order. For provisions of the 2004 Regulations, see the following page.

Pet Travel Scheme

NON COMMERCIAL MOVEMENT OF PET ANIMALS (ENGLAND) REGULATIONS 2004

A pet animal may be brought into England without complying with the Rabies (Importation of Dogs, Cats and other Mammals) Order 1974 (quarantine, etc.) provided the Community Regulation (998/2003) and these Regulations are complied with. The regulations do not apply to Wales or Scotland, but where an animal has been brought into England in accordance with the regulations, it can then be taken to Wales or Scotland. (Reg. 4).

2004 Regulations

1. Pet dogs, cats and ferrets must be **identifiable by microchip**. (Reg. 6).
2. A blood test must be carried out at least 6 months before arrival in England. (Reg.7).
3. Pet dogs, cats and ferrets must be brought into England by an **authorised carrier**. (Reg. 8).
4. Between 24 and 48 hours before embarkation to England, dogs, cats and ferrets must have been **treated by a vet** against Echinococcus Multilocularis and ticks. This is in addition to the Community Regulation requirement to be vaccinated against rabies, and lasts until 2009. (Reg. 9).
5. In addition to the **certification** required by the Community Regulation, the passport or health certificate shall also specify the manufacturer, product and date of administration of the treatment. (Reg. 9).

Exclusion. The above exemption from quarantine, etc. does not apply to the movement to England of:

1. more than 5 pet animals if they are travelling together and they come from a country other than Andorra, Iceland, Liechtenstein, Monaco, Norway, San Marino, Switzerland or The Vatican;
2. prairie dogs originating in or travelling from the US;
3. cats travelling from Australia accompanied by an Australian Government Veterinary Certificate (but a cat in transit through Australia by air shall not be treated as travelling from Australia if it does not leave the airport). (Reg. 5).

Community Regulation 998/2003

Applies to the non commercial movement of pet animals which are dogs, cats, ferrets, invertebrates (except bees and crustaceans), ornamental tropical fish, amphibia, reptiles, birds (all species except poultry covered by other Council Directives), and mammals (rodents and domestic rabbits), between member states or from 3rd countries (Art. 2).

"**Pet Animals**" means those listed above which are accompanying their owners or other responsible person on their behalf and not intended to be sold or transferred to another person. (Art. 3).

Pet animals which are **dogs, cats or ferrets** being coming into the U.K. must be microchipped and have a passport issued by a vet. certifying valid antirabies vaccination (Art 5), and certifying a satisfactory blood test (Art. 6).

"**Passport**" means any document enabling it to be clearly identified and enabling the points relating to its status to be checked. (Art. 3).

Other pet animals which are: invertebrates (except bees and crustaceans), ornamental tropical fish, amphibia, reptiles, birds (all species except poultry covered by other Council Directives), and mammals (rodents and domestic rabbits) coming to the U.K. from a member state or from Andorra, Iceland, Liechtenstein, Monaco, Norway, San Marino, Switzerland or The Vatican, of shall not be subject to any requirements with regard to rabies. However, they may need a certificate and have their numbers limited. (Art. 7).

Game Licences

S 1 HARES ACT 1848, S 4 GAME LICENCES ACT 1860, S 4 GROUND GAME ACT 1880

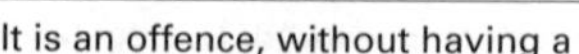

It is an offence, without having a **GAME LICENCE** 1860 ACT

to take, kill or pursue by any means whatever, or to use any dog, gun, net or other engine for the purpose of taking, killing or pursuing any

hare, pheasant, partridge, grouse, heath or moor game, black game, woodcock, snipe, rabbit or deer

Except

A game licence is not required for any of the following purposes:

- taking woodcock or snipe with nets or snares
- taking or destroying rabbits by the proprietor of a warren or grounds, or the tenant of land, or by his permission
- pursuing hares by coursing with greyhounds, or killing hares by hunting with beagles or other hounds
- taking, killing or destroying hares on enclosed land by the owner, occupier and person authorised by them in writing
- pursuing and killing of deer by hunting with hounds
- taking and killing of deer in enclosed lands by the owner or occupier of lands or by his permission

The following persons are exempt from the requirement to hold a licence:

- the royal family
- any person appointed as gamekeeper on behalf of Her Majesty
- a person aiding or assisting the holder of a licence
- a person authorised to kill hares under the Hares Act 1848
- the occupier of the land upon which the game is taken or killed, and persons authorised by him.

A police officer may demand production of the licence and, if not produced, require the person's name and address. Failure to produce the licence or, in default, to give the correct name and address, is an offence. S 31A

Game – Out of Season

S3 GAME ACT 1831

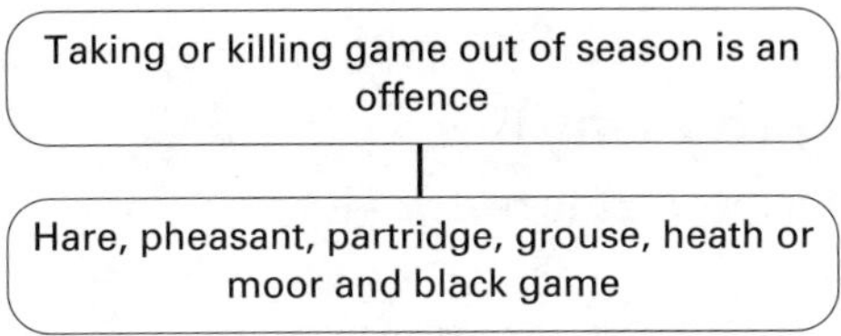

Close Season

Sundays

Christmas Day

Partridge	1 February	to	1 September
Pheasant	1 February	to	1 October
Black Game*	10 December	to	20 August
Grouse	10 December	to	12 August
Bustard	1 March	to	1 September

**(except in Somerset, Devon or the New Forest of Hampshire, where the close season is between 10 December and 1 September)*

Eggs

S 24 GAME ACT 1831

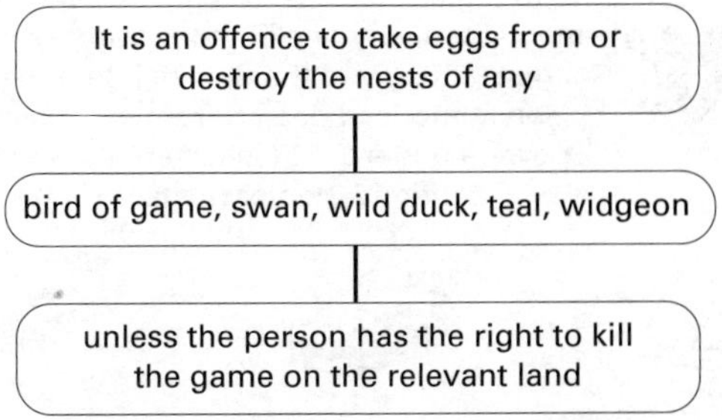

Havings such eggs in one's possession or control is also an offence (see further restrictions under 'birds')

Poaching

Poaching (by Day)

Ss 30, 31, 32 & 35 GAME ACT 1831

It is an offence by day

'Day' begins 1 hour before sunrise until 1 hour after sunset

to trespass on any land in search or pursuit of

hares, pheasants, partridges, grouse, heath and moor game, black game, woodcocks, snipe or rabbits

An additional penalty is payable if 5 or more persons together are found on any land for the purpose of poaching

A further offence is committed if 5 or more together trespass to search for the above mentioned, any one of them being armed with a gun, and any of them, with intent to prevent an authorised person from exercising his powers under S 31 (see later), uses violence, intimidation or menace (S 32)

Poaching (by Night)

S 1 NIGHT POACHING ACT 1828 AS AMENDED

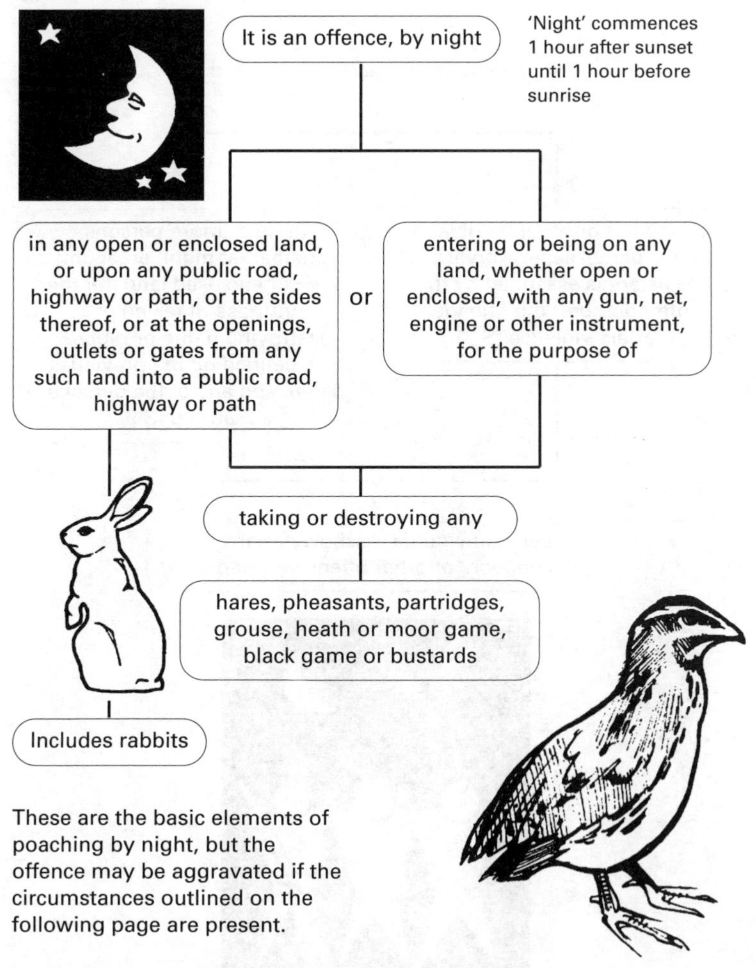

These are the basic elements of poaching by night, but the offence may be aggravated if the circumstances outlined on the following page are present.

Poaching (by Night) – continued

Ss 2 & 9 NIGHT POACHING ACT 1828

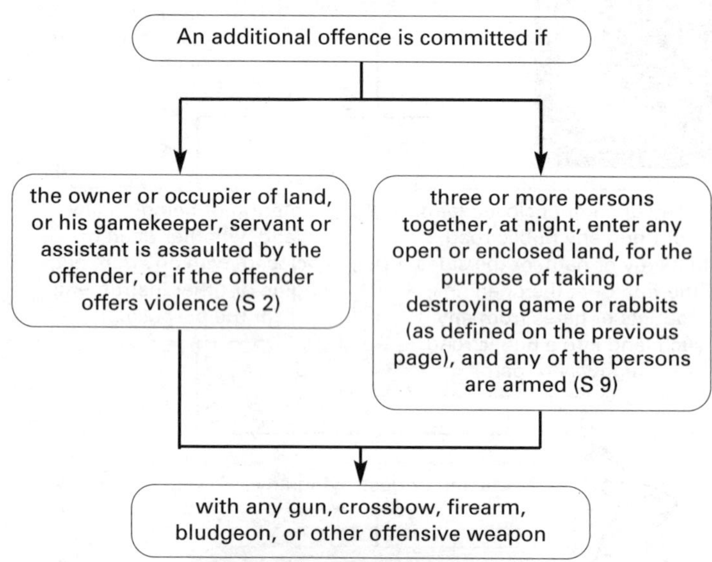

Police Powers

On Land S 2 GAME LAWS (AMENDMENT) ACT 1960

A constable may enter land if he has reasonable grounds for suspecting that a person is trespassing on the land, by day or night, for the purpose of taking or destroying game or rabbits.

Night S 2 GAME LAWS (AMENDMENT) ACT 1960

Where a constable has reasonable grounds for suspecting that a person is committing an offence on any land under Ss 1 or 9 of the Night Poaching Act 1828, he may enter the land for the purpose of requiring him to quit and to give his name and address.

Daytime Ss 31 & 31A GAME ACT 1831

A constable may require any person he finds on any land in search or pursuit of game, woodcocks, snipe or rabbits, to quit the land and give his name and address. Any subsequent arrest must be in accordance with the Police and Criminal Evidence Act 1984. There is also power to enter the land for the above purpose under S 2 Game Laws (Amendment) Act, 1960. S 31 also applies to anyone having the right to kill game on the land, occupiers, persons authorised by the aforementioned, gamekeepers or servants, and wardens, rangers and others employed in a similar capacity in royal forests and parks, etc.

Street or Public Place S 2 POACHING PREVENTION ACT 1862

A constable may, in any public place, **search** any person whom he has good cause to **suspect** of coming from any land where he has been unlawfully in pursuit of game, and having in his possession any game, gun, ammunition, nets, snares, traps or other device for killing or taking game, and also to **stop** and **search** any cart or other conveyance which the constable has good cause to suspect is carrying any game or article mentioned above, and the constable may **seize** and detain any game or article found on the person or in the conveyance. Proceedings are then taken by **summons**. There is no power of arrest.

A similar power to search and seize property and game is provided under S 4, Game Laws (Amendment) Act 1960, where the constable is arresting an offender under S 24, Police and Criminal Evidence Act 1984.

Deer

DEER ACT 1991

Poaching of Deer

S 1

It is an offence

without the consent of the

OWNER
or
OCCUPIER
or
OTHER LAWFUL AUTHORITY

to ENTER any land in search or pursuit of any deer with the intention of TAKING, KILLING OR INJURING IT

it shall be a defence if the person believed that

- he would have the consent of the owner or occupier of the land if they knew of it, or
- he has other lawful authority to do it

- to intentionally take, kill or injure, or attempt to take, kill or injure any deer
- to search for or pursue any deer with the intention of taking, killing or injuring any deer, or
- to remove the carcass of any deer

WHILST ON ANY LAND

Land includes buildings and other structures, land covered with water, and any interest, etc. over the land

If an offence is suspected by the owner or occupier or any person authorised by him or having the right to kill deer on the land, he may require the offender to give his name and address and to quit the land forthwith. Failure to comply is an offence.

Close Season

S 2 AND SCHED 1 DEER ACT 1991

It is an offence to intentionally take or kill, or attempt to take or kill, any deer in the close season:

RED DEER (*Cervus elaphus*)

Stags	1 May to 31 July inclusive
Hinds	1 March to 31 October inclusive

FALLOW DEER (*Dama dama*)

Buck	1 May to 31 July inclusive
Doe	1 March to 31 October inclusive

ROE DEER (*Capreolus capreolus*)

Buck	1 November to 31 March inclusive
Doe	1 March to 31 October inclusive

SIKA DEER (*Cervus nippon*)

Stags	1 May to 31 July inclusive
Hinds	1 March to 31 October inclusive

There is an exemption for businessmen keeping marked deer on enclosed land for meat, other foodstuffs, skin or other by-products, or breeding stock.

Night

It is an offence to take or intentionally kill any deer between the expiry of the first hour after sunset and the beginning of the last hour before sunrise (S 3).

Possession of prohibited weapons and articles

It is an offence to have in possession for the purpose of committing the above: any trap, snare, poisoned or stupefying bait; net, arrow, spear or similar missile; or any missile whether discharged from a firearm or otherwise carrying or containing any poison, stupefying drug or muscle relaxing agent; or any firearm or ammunition (S 5).

Use of Weapons etc S 4

It is an offence:

- To set any **traps, snare, or poisoned or stupefying bait** calculated to **cause bodily injury** to any deer.
- To use any **trap, snare, or poisoned or stupefying bait, or any net** for the purpose of **taking or killing** any deer.
- To use, for the purpose of **taking, killing or injuring** any deer:
  1. Any smooth-bore gun.
  2. Any rifle having a calibre of less than .240 inches or a muzzle energy of less than 2,305 joules (1,700 ft/lbs).
  3. Any air gun, air rifle or air pistol.
  4. Any cartridge for use in a smooth-bore gun.
  5. Any bullet for use in a rifle other than a soft-nosed or hollow-nosed bullet.
  6. Any arrow, spear or similar missile.
  7. Any missile, whether discharged from a firearm or otherwise, carrying or containing any poison, stupefying drug or muscle-relaxing agent.
- To **discharge any firearm**, or project any missile, from any **mechanically propelled vehicle** at any deer.
- To use any **mechanically propelled vehicle** for the purpose of **driving deer**.
- To attempt to commit any of the above offences (S 5).

It shall be a defence to either of the last two offences if the act is done with the written authority of the occupier of any enclosed land in relation to deer usually kept on that land.

Other miscellaneous defences to this and previous sections are contained in Ss 6, 7 and 8 (e.g. to prevent suffering, causing damage to crops, and for nature conservancy).

Sale of Venison s 10

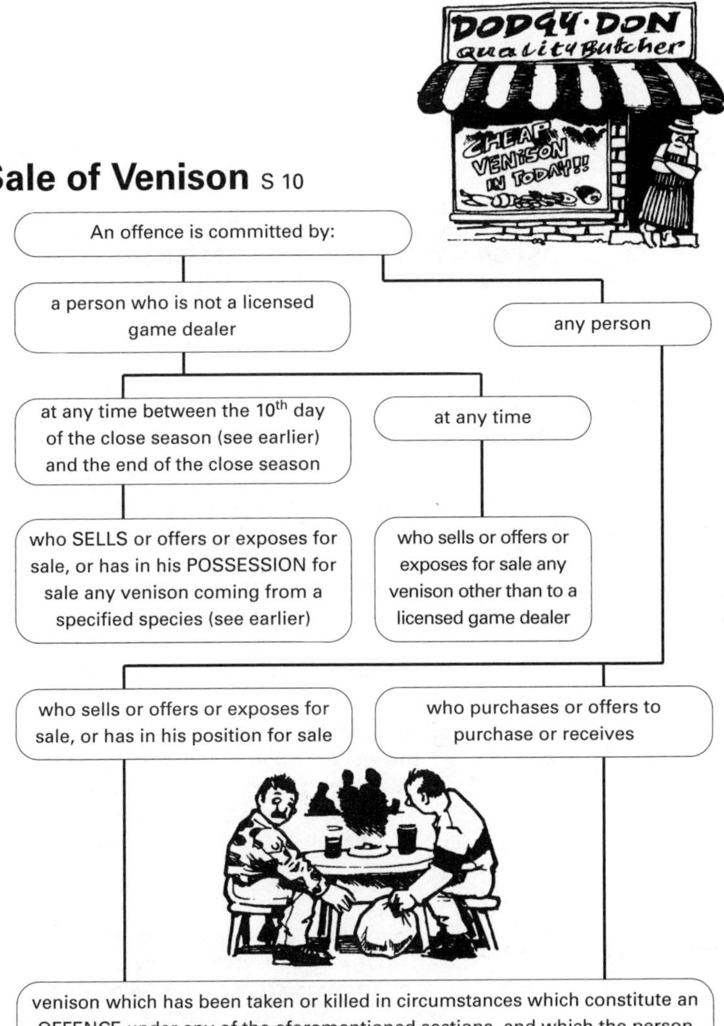

Sale includes barter and exchange

Police Powers S 12

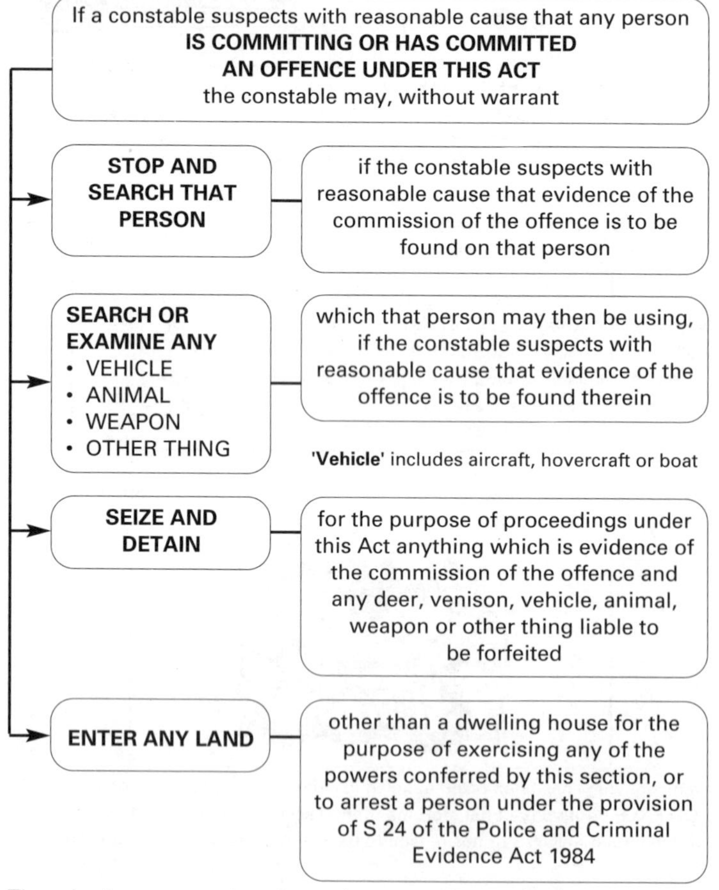

There is also a power to sell any deer or venison seized.

Badgers

PROTECTION OF BADGERS ACT 1992

Killing etc S 1(1)
It is an offence to wilfully kill, injure, take or attempt to kill, injure or take a badger.
(See next page for exceptions)

Firearms S 2
It is an offence to use for killing a badger any firearm except: a smooth bore weapon of not less than 20 bore, or a rifle using ammunition of muzzle energy not less than 160ft/lbs and bullet weighing not less than 38 grains.
See next page for exceptions

Sale, possession, etc S 4
It is an offence to sell, offer for sale, or have in possession or under control, any live badger.
See next page for exceptions

Possession, etc S 1(3)
It is an offence to have in possession or under control any dead badger or any part of, or anything derived from a dead badger unless it was not killed in contravention of this Act.
See next page for exceptions

Cruelty, etc
It is an offence to:
- Cruelly ill-treat a badger S 2
- Use any badger tongs in the course of taking or killing a badger S 2
- Dig for a badger S 2
- Mark or ring a badger, unless authorised by a licence S 5
- Interfere with a badger sett by:
  a) damaging a sett or part of it;
  b) destroying a sett;
  c) obstructing access to any entrance of a sett;
  d) causing a dog to enter a badger sett; or
  e) disturbing a badger when it is occupying a sett.
  Except: if necessary to prevent serious damage to crops, land or poultry (but licence must have been applied for); obstructing for fox hunting purposes (but only if done by hand); or incidental and unavoidable result of a lawful operation.

Exceptions

A person will not be guilty of the offences of killing, etc if:

- He is a 'licensed person' S 10, or
- A badger is found disabled and it is taken for the purpose of tending it S 6, or
- A badger is so seriously injured or in such a condition that to kill it would be an act of mercy S 6, or
- Where the killing or injuring was an unavoidable result of a lawful action S 6
- Authorised under the Animals (Scientific Procedures) Act 1986 (S 6)
- The act was necessary to prevent serious damage to land, crops or poultry (but if such damage foreseeable then a licence must have been applied for).

A person shall not be guilty of having a live badger in his possession under S 4 if:

- He has possession of it in the course of his business as a carrier
- He is a licensed person, or
- It is necessary to keep it in possession for the purpose of tending to its disability.

Police powers

Where a police constable has reasonable cause to suspect that an offence against the Act has been or is being committed he may:

- stop and search that person and search any vehicle or article he may have with him. Order the person to quit the land and to give his name and address. Failure to do so is an offence.
- seize and detain anything which may be evidence, any badger, whether dead or alive, and any weapon or article in that person's possession.

Birds

WILDLIFE AND COUNTRYSIDE ACT 1981

The law relating to birds broadly covers restrictions on killing and taking wild birds; the prohibition of certain methods of killing or taking them; restrictions on the sale of birds and their eggs; and the prevention of disturbance to nesting birds. The various aspects are discussed in the following pages but for ease of reference the four categories into which birds are placed may be exemplified at this point.

Schedule 1
These are birds which are protected by special penalties
Part 1 At all times – e.g. barn owl, eagle, purple heron, osprey, stone curlew
Part 2 During the close season – e.g. goldeneye, greylag goose, pintail goose

Schedule 2
These are birds which may be taken or killed outside the close season – e.g. coot, mallard, woodcock.

Schedule 3
These are birds which may be sold
Part 1 Alive at all times if ringed and bred in captivity – e.g. blackbird, chaffinch, magpie, barn owl, starling
Part 2 Dead at all times – e.g. wood pigeon
Part 3 Dead from 1 Sept to 28 Feb – e.g. tufted duck, mallard, snipe, woodcock

Schedule 4
These are birds which must be registered and ringed if kept in captivity – e.g. falcon, hawks, osprey, crested tit, kestrel, woodlark.

Birds

WILDLIFE AND COUNTRYSIDE ACT 1981

'Wild bird' means of a species which is ordinarily resident in or is a visitor to the European territory of any member state in a wild state but does not include poultry or game bird, nor does it include any bird which has been bred in captivity.

'Poultry' means domestic fowl, geese, ducks, guinea fowl, pigeons, quails and turkeys.

'Game bird' means pheasant, partridge, grouse (or moor) game, black (or heath) game or ptarmigan.

S 1
It is an offence for any person intentionally to

- kill, injure or take any wild bird
- have in possession or control any live or dead wild bird or part of one
- take or destroy an egg of a wild bird or have in his possession or control an egg or part of one
- take, damage or destroy the nest of a wild bird whilst in use or being built

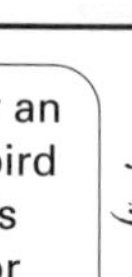

- disturb any wild bird listed in Sched 1 while it is building a nest or is in, on or near a nest containing eggs or young; or disturb dependent young of such a bird (but if the bird is included in Part 2 of the Sched, the offence is only committed during the close season)

But see following page for exceptions.

Exceptions S 2

KILLING, etc.

A person shall not be guilty of an offence under S 1 by reason of the killing or taking of a bird included in part 2 of Sched 2 (see earlier) or the taking, damaging or destruction of a nest of such a bird, or the taking or destruction of an egg of such a bird, when done in any case by an authorised person.

A person shall not be guilty of an offence under S 1 by reason of the killing, injuring or taking of a bird included in part 1 of Sched 2 (see earlier) outside the close season for that bird.

CLOSE SEASON

CAPERCAILLIE AND WOODCOCK (except Scotland)
1 February to 30 September

SNIPE 1 February to 11 August

WILD DUCK OR WILD GEESE (in any area below high water mark of ordinary spring tides) 21 February to 31 August

ANY OTHER CASE 1 February to 31 August

AUTHORISED PERSONS

An authorised person will not be guilty of an offence of killing or injuring a wild bird, other than a bird included in Sched 1, if he shows that it was necessary:

- For preserving public health or public or air safety;
- For preventing the spread of disease; or
- For preventing serious damage to livestock, foodstuffs for livestock, crops, vegetables, fruit, growing timber, fisheries or inland waters.

GENERAL

A person shall not be guilty of an offence by reason of:

- Taking a wild bird which has been disabled and which was taken to tend it and release when no longer disabled;
- Killing a wild bird so seriously disabled that it would not recover; or
- Any act which was the incidental result of a lawful operation and could not have been avoided. S 4

Prohibited Methods of Killing etc

S 5 WILDLIFE AND COUNTRYSIDE ACT 1981

Unless authorised by licence, it is an offence for any person to:

Set in position any article to cause bodily injury to any wild bird coming into contact with it, i.e. springe, trap, gin, snare, hook and line, any electrical device for killing, stunning or frightening, or any poisonous, poisoned or stupefying substance.

Use for the purpose of taking or killing any wild bird any article as aforesaid, or any net, baited board, gas, bird-lime or other like substance.

Use as a decoy, for the purpose of killing or taking a wild bird, any sound recording or any live bird or other animal which is tethered or similarly secured, or which is blind, maimed or injured.

Use for the purpose of killing or taking any wild bird

- A bow or crossbow
- Explosive other than ammunition
- An automatic weapon
- Shotgun over 1 ¾" dia. barrel
- An illuminating or night sighting device
- A lighting or dazzling device
- Gas or smoke
- A chemical wetting agent

Use any mechanically propelled vehicle in immediate pursuit of a wild bird for the purpose of killing or taking it.

But it shall not be unlawful: a) for an authorised person to use a cage-trap or net to take a bird included in part 2 of Sched 2; b) to use nets for taking wild duck in a duck decoy which was in use immediately before the passing of the Protection of Birds Act 1954; or c) to use a cage-trap or net for taking any game bird for the purpose of breeding.

But it will not be lawful to use a net for taking birds in flight, or a net projected or propelled other than by hand for taking birds on the ground.

Restrictions on Sale

S 6 WILDLIFE AND COUNTRYSIDE ACT 1981

It is an offence to sell, offer or expose for sale, or have in possession or transport for the purpose of sale, or advertise the buying or selling of

live birds

other than a bird included in part 1 of Sched 3 (see earlier)

dead birds

other than a bird included in part 2 or 3 of Sched 3, or any part of, or anything derived from, such a wild bird

unless he is for the time being registered so to do

eggs

of a wild bird or any part of such an egg

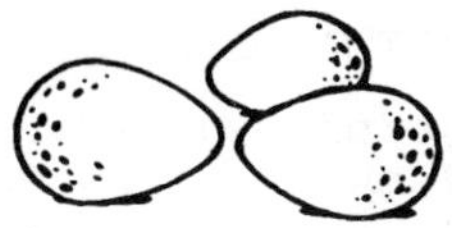

It is an offence to show or cause or permit to be shown in a competition any live bird other than a bird included in part 1 of Sched 3; or a bird one of whose parents was such a wild bird.

Specific Offences

WILDLIFE AND COUNTRYSIDE ACT 1981

REGISTRATION OF CAPTIVE BIRDS (S 7)

It is an offence to keep or have in possession or have under control any bird included in Schedule 4, which has not been registered and ringed or marked in accordance with regulations. It is also an offence to have a Schedule 4 bird within 3 or 5 years (depending on the nature of the offence) of a conviction for certain offences relating to wild birds.

CONFINING (S 8)

It is an offence to keep or confine any bird in any cage or receptacle which does not allow sufficient room for the bird to stretch its wings freely.

But this offence does not apply to:

- Domestic fowl, ducks, geese, guinea fowl, pigeons and turkeys;
- Any bird whilst being conveyed, publicly exhibited (provided the time does not exceed 72 hours), or whilst undergoing veterinary treatment.

SHOOTING EVENTS (S 8)

It is an offence to be in any way involved in any event in which captive birds are liberated for the purpose of being shot immediately after their liberation.

Police Powers

S 19 WILDLIFE AND COUNTRYSIDE ACT 1981

In relation to any offence against the Act (this includes taking or killing birds or eggs; using illegal methods of taking or killing, etc; unlawful selling, etc; confining; and disturbing nesting birds) a constable may without warrant

STOP AND SEARCH

any person if the constable suspects that evidence of the commission of the offence is to be found on that person

and examine anything which that person may then be using or have in his possession if the constable suspects that evidence of the commission of the offence is to be found on that thing. The constable may, for the purpose of exercising these powers or arresting a person under S 24 Police and Criminal Evidence Act 1984, enter any land other than a dwelling house. A warrant to enter and search premises may be granted by a justice of the peace if the offence attracts a special penalty

and may SEIZE AND DETAIN

for the purpose of proceedings, any thing which may be evidence of the commission of the offence or may be liable to be forfeited under this Act

Fish

S 32 AND SCHED 1 THEFT ACT 1968

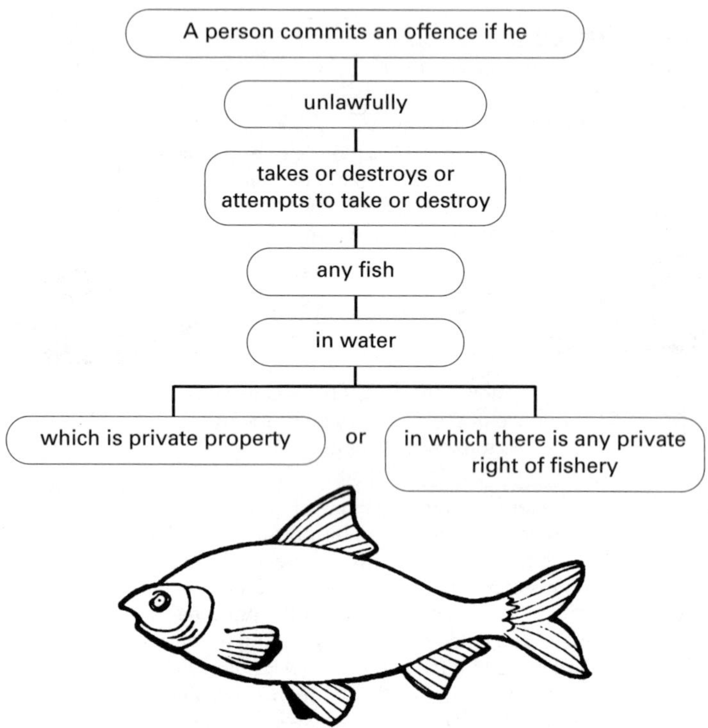

Offences

SALMON AND FRESHWATER FISHERIES ACT 1975

The following are offences connected with salmon, trout or freshwater fish:

Nets

To use nets with meshes smaller than 2" between knots, or to use two nets of requisite mesh close together, or to work a draft net across more than ¾ of the width of any waters for salmon or migatory trout (S 3).

Poison, etc

To cause or knowingly permit any poisonous or injurious substances to flow in, or be put into, any waters containing fish (S 4).

Damage/ Explosives

To use in or near any waters any explosive substance, any poison or other noxious substance, or any electrical device, with intent to take or destroy fish; or without lawful excuse destroy or damage any dam, flood-gate or sluice with intent to take or destroy fish (S 5).

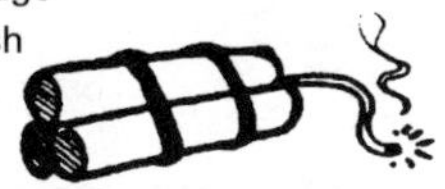

Instruments

Using any firearm; an otter lath or jack, wire or snare; a crossline or setline; a spear, gaff, stroke-haul, snatch or other like instrument; or a light for the purpose of taking or killing salmon, trout or freshwater fish; or to have same in possession with intent to use for taking or killing such fish or to throw or discharge any stone or other missile for the purpose of taking or killing salmon, trout or freshwater fish (S 1).

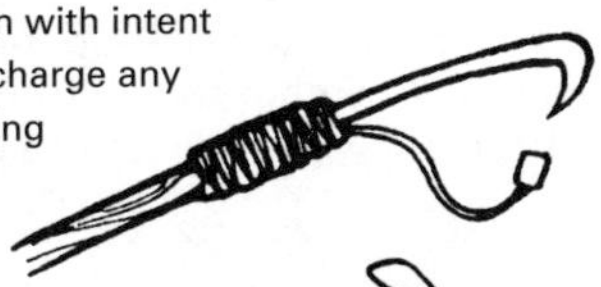

Roe

To use fish roe for fishing, or to buy, sell or have salmon or trout roe for that purpose (S 2).

Young fish

To wilfully disturb any spawn or spawning fish.
To knowingly take, buy, sell or have in possession any unclean or immature fish (S 2).

Weirs

No fishing weir or mill dam may be used, which was not in use on 6.8.1861, for the purpose of taking salmon or migratory trout (S 7).

Fishing Licences

Ss 25, 27 & 35 SALMON AND FRESHWATER FISHERIES ACT 1975

Water authorities are required to control fishing for

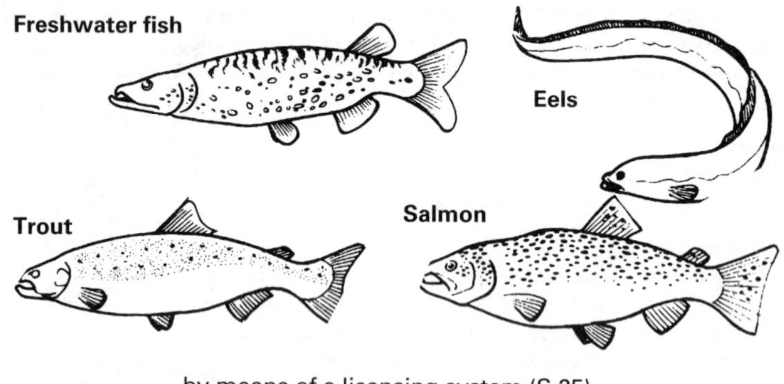

by means of a licensing system (S 25).

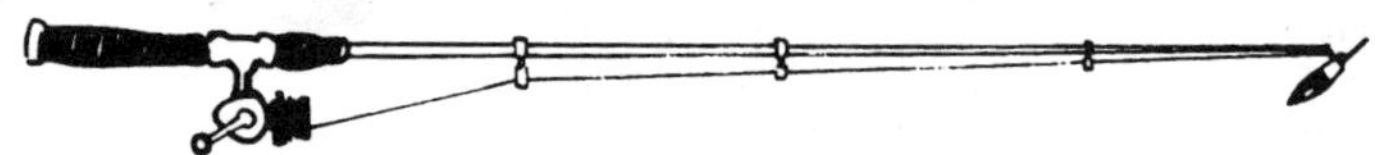

It is an offence to fish for or take fish otherwise than by means of an instrument authorised in the licence, or to have in possession such an instrument with intent to use it (S 27)

Production

A constable, water bailiff, or person producing his authority may require any person found fishing or whom he reasonably suspects to be about to fish, or to have within the preceding half-hour fished, to produce his licence and give his name and address. Failure to comply is an offence but if the person produces his licence within 7 days of the request at the water authority office he will not be convicted of the offence (S 35).

Close Season (Fish)

S 19 & SCHED 1 SALMON AND FRESHWATER FISHERIES ACT 1975

Unless there is a bylaw to the contrary, it is an offence to fish for, take, kill or attempt to take or kill at the following times:

Salmon

By rod and line	31 Oct – 1 Feb
By any other method	31 Aug – 1 Feb

The weekly close time is from 6 am Saturday to 6 am Monday

Trout

By rod and line	30 Sep – 1 March
By any other method	31 Aug – 1 March

The weekly close time is from 6 am Saturday to 6 am Monday

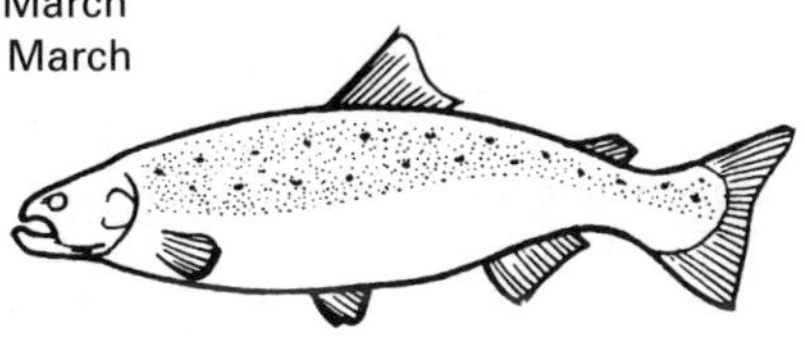

Freshwater fish
(other than salmon, trout, eels and migratory fish)
14 March – 16 June

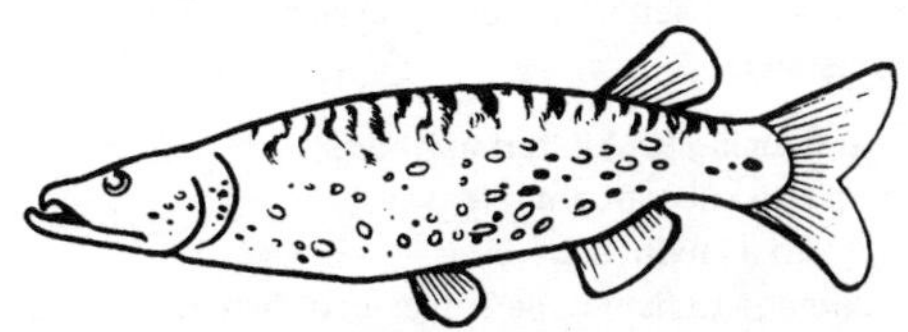

Rainbow trout
The close season is fixed by bylaws.

Seals

CONSERVATION OF SEALS ACT 1970

It is an offence to

use for the purpose of killing or taking any seal, any poisonous substance, or, use for the purpose of killing, injuring or taking any seal, any firearm other than a rifle using ammunition having a muzzle energy of not less than 600 ft/lbs pounds and a bullet not less than 45 grains.

wilfully kill, injure or take a seal during the close season: **Grey Seals** – 1 September to 31 December; **Common Seals** – 1 June to 31 August.

wilfully kill, injure or take a seal in contravention of a prohibition order (for conservation) made by the Secretary of State. (Such an order has been made.)

attempt to commit any of these offences.

Apprehension of Offenders

A constable may stop any person he suspects with reasonable cause of committing the above offence and may search any vehicle or boat which that person may be using at that time, and seize any seal, seal skin, firearm, ammunition or poisonous substance.

Defences (to offences other than using prohibited methods)

Disabled seal taken for tending and subsequent release.
Unavoidable killing resulting from a lawful act.
To prevent the seal causing damage to fishing nets, tackle, or fish in any net, provided the seal was in the vicinity of the net or tackle.

Defence (to all the above offences)

Killing any seal which was so seriously disabled that there was no reasonable chance of its recovering.

Hunting

HUNTING ACT 2004

A person commits an offence if he hunts a wild mammal with a dog unless his hunting is exempt. (S. 1). For the meaning of 'wild mammal' see the end of this section.

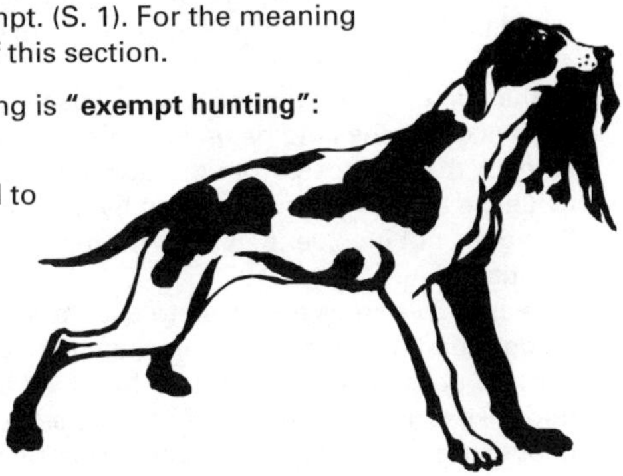

By S 2 and Sched. 1, the following is **"exempt hunting"**:

1. stalking or flushing out;
2. the use of dogs below ground to protect birds for shooting;
3. rats;
4. rabbits;
5. retrieval of hares;
6. falconry;
7. recapture of wild mammal;
8. rescue of wild mammal; and
9. research and observation.

These will now be explained in more depth.

1. Stalking a wild mammal or flushing it out of cover is exempt if the following conditions are met:

1. it is done for the purposes of:
   - (a) preventing or reducing serious damage which the wild mammal would otherwise cause to livestock, game birds, wild birds, food for livestock, crops, growing timber, fisheries, other property, or the biological diversity of an area;
   - (b) obtaining meat for human or animal consumption;
   - (c) participation in a field trial (a competition, other than hare coursing, in which dogs are assessed as to their usefulness in flushing animals out of cover, or in retrieving an animal which has been shot);
2. it takes place on land: (a) which belongs to the person doing the stalking or flushing out, or (b) which he has been given permission to use for the purpose by the occupier or owner;
3. not more than 2 dogs are used;
4. it does not involve the use of a dog below ground otherwise than under the conditions outlined under "use of dogs below ground", in the next section;
5. as soon as possible after being found or flushed out, the wild mammal is shot dead by a competent person, and dogs are kept under sufficient control not to prevent that happening.

(CONTINUED ON NEXT PAGE)

Hunting – continued

HUNTING ACT 2004

2. The use of a dog below ground for stalking or flushing out of cover is exempt if the following conditions are met:

1. it is done for the purpose of reducing or preventing serious damage to game birds or wild birds being kept or preserved for the purpose of being shot;
2. the person doing the stalking or flushing out: (a) has with him written evidence that the land belongs to him, or that he has permission to use the land for that purpose, from the owner or occupier: and (b) he makes that evidence available for inspection by a constable;
3. it does not involve the use of more than one dog below ground at any one time;
4. reasonable steps are taken to ensure that (a) as soon as possible after being found the wild mammal is flushed out from below ground, (b) as soon as possible thereafter it is shot dead by a competent person, (c) the dog is kept under sufficient control so as not to obstruct or prevent that happening, (d) injury is prevented from being caused to the dog, and (e) the manner in which the dog is used complies with any code of practice issued by the Secretary of State.

3. & 4. The hunting of rats or rabbits is exempt if it takes place on land which (a) belongs to the hunter, or (b) which he has been given permission to use for that purpose by the owner or occupier.

5. The hunting of a hare which has been shot is exempt if it takes place on land which (a) belongs to the hunter, or (b) which he has been given permission to use for that purpose by the owner or occupier.

6. Falconry is exempt if it consists of flushing a wild mammal from cover for the purpose of enabling a bird of prey to hunt the wild mammal, and it takes place on land which (a) belongs to the hunter, or (b) which he has been given permission to use for that purpose by the owner or occupier.

7. The hunting of a wild mammal which has escaped or been released from captivity or confinement is exempt if the following conditions are satisfied:

1. the hunting takes place on land which (a) belongs to the hunter, or (b) which he has been given permission to use for that purpose by the owner or occupier or (c) with the authority of a constable;

Hunting – continued

HUNTING ACT 2004

2. reasonable steps are taken to ensure that (a) as soon as possible after being found, it is either recaptured or shot dead by a competent person and (b) each dog used in the hunt is kept under sufficient control so as not to prevent or obstruct that happening;
3. the wild mammal was not released (or permitted to escape) for the purpose of being hunted.

8. The hunting of a wild mammal for the purpose of rescuing it is exempt if the following conditions are satisfied:

1. the hunter reasonably believes that the wild mammal is, or may be, injured;
2. the hunting is for the purpose of relieving the wild mammal's suffering;
3. it does not involve the use of more than 2 dogs;
4. it does not involve the use of a dog below ground;
5. the hunting takes place on land which (a) belongs to the hunter, or (b) which he has been given permission to use for that purpose by the owner or occupier or (c) with the authority of a constable;
6. reasonable steps are taken to ensure that (a) as soon as possible after being found, appropriate action is taken to relieve its suffering and (b) each dog used in the hunt is kept under sufficient control so as not to prevent or obstruct that happening;
7. the wild mammal was not harmed for the purpose of enabling it to be hunted in reliance on this exemption.

9. The hunting of a wild mammal for research and observation is exempt if the following conditions are satisfied:

1. hunting is for the purpose of or in connection with the observation or study of the wild animal;
2. it does not involve the use of more than 2 dogs;
3. it does not involve the use of a dog below ground;
4. the hunting takes place on land which (a) belongs to the hunter, or (b) which he has been given permission to use for that purpose by the owner or occupier;
5. each dog used in the hunt must be kept under sufficiently close control to ensure that it does not injure the wild animal.

Hunting; assistance (S 3)

(a) **Use of land.** A person commits an offence if he knowingly permits land which belongs to him to be entered or used in the course of the commission of an offence under S 1.

(b) **Use of dogs.** A person commits an offence if he knowingly permits a dog which belongs to him to be used in the course of an offence under S 1.

Hunting – continued

HUNTING ACT 2004

Hunting: Defence (S 4)
It is a defence for a person charged with an offence under S 1 in respect of hunting to show that he reasonably believed that the hunting was exempt.

Hare coursing (S 5)
A person commits an offence if he:

(a) participates in a hare coursing event;
(b) attends a hare coursing event;
(c) knowingly facilitates a hare coursing event; or
(d) permits land which belongs to him to be used for the purpose of a hare coursing event.

If a dog participates in a hare coursing event, an offence is committed by any person who:

(a) enters the dog for the event;
(b) permits the dog to be entered; or
(c) controls or handles the dog in the course of or for the purposes of the event.

A hare coursing event is a competition in which dogs are, by the use of live hares, assessed as to skill in hunting hares.

Search and seizure (S 8)
This section applies where a constable reasonably suspects that a person is committing or has committed an offence under S 1 – 5 of this Act.

If the constable believes that evidence of the offence is likely to be found on the suspect, or on or in a vehicle, animal or other thing in his possession or control, the constable may stop and search him, the vehicle, animal or other thing, as the case may be.

A constable may seize and detain a vehicle, animal or other thing if he reasonably believes that it may be used in evidence.

For the purpose of exercising these powers a constable may, without warrant, enter land, premises other than a dwelling, or vehicle.

Wild mammal includes, in particular:
(a) one which has been bred or tamed for any purpose;
(b) one which is in captivity or confinement;
(c) one which has escaped or been released from captivity or confinement; and
(d) one which is living wild. (S 11)

Chapter 6
People

Children and Young Persons

S 107 CHILDREN AND YOUNG PERSONS ACT 1933

TERMS

Child
Under the age of 14 years

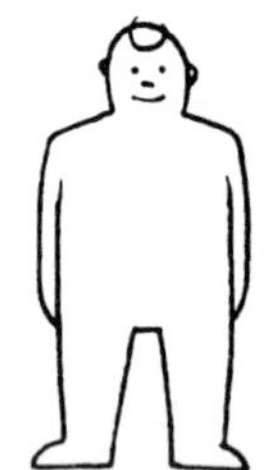

Young person
Attained the age of 14 years but under 17 years (changed to 18 years by the Criminal Justice Act 1991 – when in force)

Guardian
Any person who has, in the opinion of the court, for the time being the care of the child or young person

Street
Any highway and any public bridge, road, lane, footway, square, court, alley, or passage, whether a thoroughfare or not

Public place
Any public park, garden, sea, beach, railway station, and any ground to which the public have or are permitted to have access, whether on payment or otherwise

Cruelty

S 1 CHILDREN AND YOUNG PERSONS ACT 1933, AS AMENDED BY THE CHILDREN ACT 1989

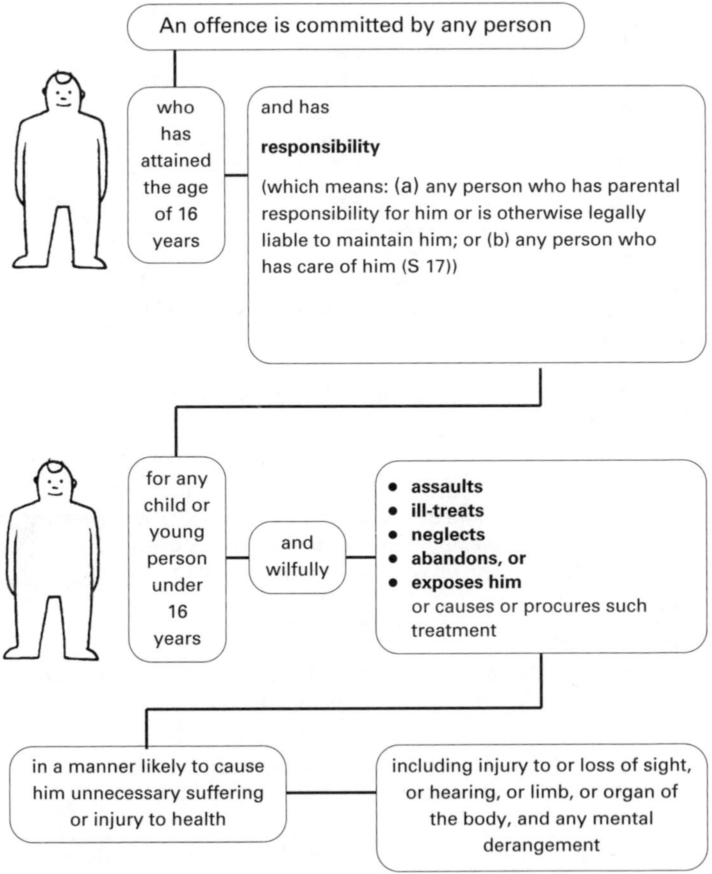

Employment

S 18 CHILDREN AND YOUNG PERSONS ACT 1933 AS AMENDED BY THE C & YP ACT 1963, THE CHILDREN ACT 1972 AND SI 1998/276.

Subject to any byelaws, it is an offence to employ a child of compulsory school age

who is under the age of 14 years; or

to do any work other than light work; or

Light work is work which is not likely to be harmful to the safety, health, development or education of the child.

if it is a day on which he is required to attend school, before the close of school hours or for more than 2 hours; or

for more than 2 hours on any Sunday; or

before 7 am or after 7 pm on any day; or

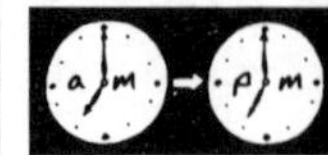

for more than 8 hours or, if he is under 15 years, for more than 5 hours in any day:
(a) on which he is not required to attend school and,
(b) which is not a Sunday, or

for more than 35 hours, or if under 15 years, 25 hours, in any week in which he is not required to attend school, or

for more than 12 hours in any week in which he is required to attend school, or

for more than 4 hours in any one day without a rest break of 1 hour or

at any time in a year unless he has at least 2 weeks without employment during the period when he is not at school

The offence is committed by the employer and any person (other than the person employed) to whose act or default this contravention is attributable

Tattoos

TATTOOING OF MINORS ACT 1969

It is an offence to tattoo a person under the age of 18 years except for medical reasons by a medical practitioner or by a person working under his direction. But it is a defence to show that there was reasonable cause to believe that the person was 18 or over and he did in fact so believe.

Tobacco

S 7 CHILDREN AND YOUNG PERSONS ACT 1933
CHILDREN AND YOUNG PERSONS (SALE OF TOBACCO, ETC.) ORDER 2007 (effective from 1.10.07)

It is an offence for a person to sell to a person under the age of 18 years any tobacco or cigarette papers, whether for his own use or not

It is an offence to sell loose (unpackaged) cigarettes to any person.

It is the duty of a constable in uniform to seize any tobacco or cigarette papers from persons apparently under 18 years found smoking in a street or public place

An order may be made by a court for the removal of any automatic cigarette machine which has been used by any person under 18 years

Alcohol S 5

It is an offence for any person to give or cause to be given to any child under the age of 5 years any alcohol (for meaning see earlier, but excluding items (f) to (i)).

Truancy

S 16 CRIME AND DISORDER ACT 1998

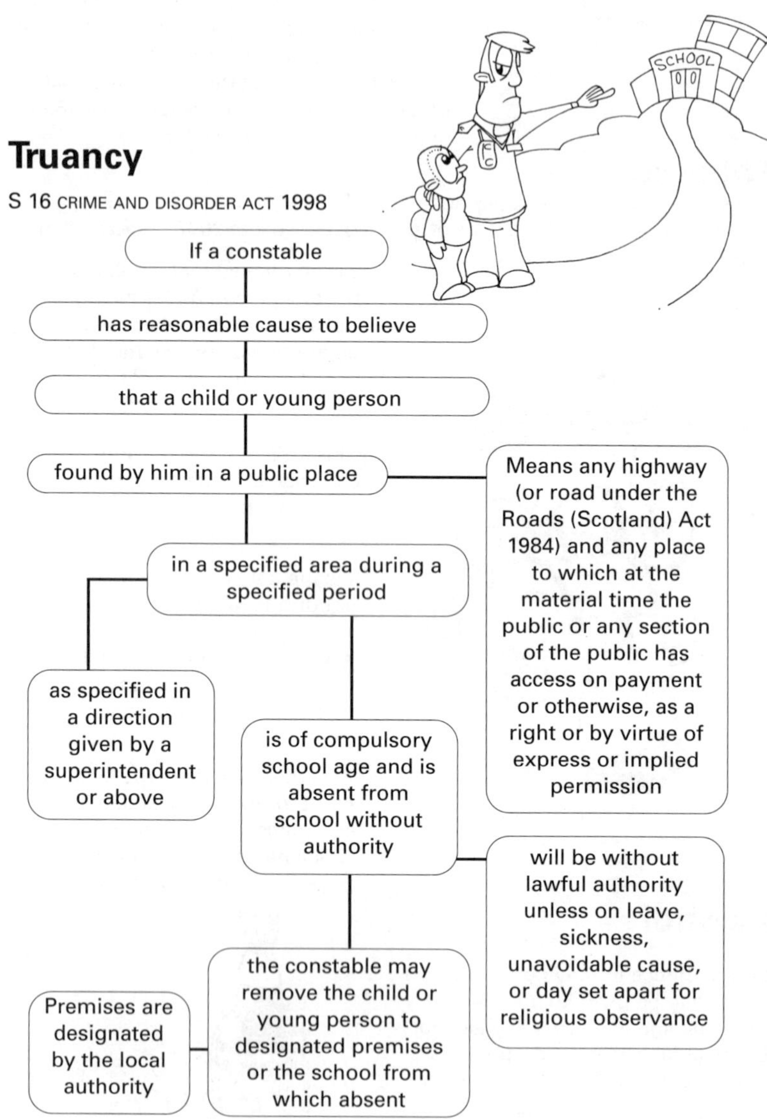

Education

S 7 EDUCATION ACT 1966

The parent of every child of compulsory school age (5-16) shall cause him to receive efficient full-time education suitable to his age, ability, aptitude and subject to any special educational needs.

Begging

S 4 CHILDREN AND YOUNG PERSONS ACT 1933

It is an offence for any person to cause or procure any child or young person under 16 years, or having responsibility for such a child or young person, to allow him to be in any street, premises or place for the purpose of begging or receiving or inducing the giving of alms (whether or not there is any singing etc.)

Burning

S 11 CHILDREN AND YOUNG PERSONS ACT 1933

If a person who has attained the age of 16 years, having responsibility for any child under the age of 12 years

allows the child to be in any room containing an open fire grate or any heating appliance liable to cause injury to any person

not sufficiently protected to guard against the risk of being burnt or scalded, without taking reasonable precautions against the risk

and by reason thereof the child is killed or suffers serious injury

then that person commits an offence

Brothels

S 3 CHILDREN AND YOUNG PERSONS ACT 1933

It is an offence for a person having the responsibility for a person

who has attained the age of 4 years and is under the age of 16 years

to allow that person to reside in or frequent a brothel

Police Protection

S 46 CHILDREN ACT 1989

Where a constable has reasonable cause to believe that a **child** would otherwise be likely to

SUFFER SIGNIFICANT HARM

he may

remove the child to **suitable accommodation** and keep him there	or	take such steps as are reasonable to ensure that the child's removal from any hospital or other place in which he is then being accommodated is prevented

The child is then referred to as having been taken into

POLICE PROTECTION ⟶ No child may be kept in police protection for more than 72 hours

As soon as reasonably practicable thereafter the constable shall:

- inform the local authority of the reasons for the steps taken or to be taken and give details of the place where the child is being accommodated
- inform the child (if he can understand) of the reasons for the steps taken or to be taken
- take steps to discover the wishes and feelings of the child
- secure that the case is enquired into by a designated officer
- where the place to which the child was taken was not provided by a local authority or an official refuge, secure that he is moved to such accommodation
- take such steps as are reasonably practicable to inform:
  - (a) the child's parents;
  - (b) every person who is not a parent of his but who has parental responsibility for him; and
  - (c) any other person with whom the child was living immediately before being taken into police protection.

Armed Forces

Absentees and Deserters

S 186 ARMY ACT 1955; S 186 AIR FORCE ACT 1955; S 105 NAVAL DISCIPLINE ACT 1957

A constable may arrest without warrant any person whom he has reasonable cause to suspect of being a member of the regular forces who has deserted or is absent without leave. This provision also applies to **visiting forces** but only where a request is made by the appropriate authority of the country to which he belongs (S 13 VISITING FORCES ACT 1952).

Uniforms

S 2 & S 3 UNIFORMS ACT 1894

It is an offence for any person not serving in Her Majesty's forces to wear without Her Majesty's permission the uniform of any of those forces, or any dress having the appearance, or bearing any of the regimental or other distinctive marks of any such uniform

but there is an exemption in the case of stage plays in properly authorised places for public performances, music halls, circus performances or any bona fide military representation

It is an offence for a person not serving in Her Majesty's Forces to wear any such uniform, etc. in such a manner and under such circumstances as to bring contempt on that uniform, or to employ anyone so to do.

The unauthorised use of any official uniform to gain admission to a prohibited place is an offence under the Official Secrets Act 1920, S 1.

The impersonation of a constable is an offence under the Police Act 1996, S 90 and the British Transport Commission Act 1962, S 43.

The unauthorised wearing of a merchant navy uniform is an offence under the Merchant Shipping Act 1995, S 57.

Decorations and Badges etc

S 197 ARMY AND AIR FORCE ACTS 1955

An offence is committed by any person who:

Uses or wears any military decoration or badge, wound stripe or emblem supplied or authorised by the defence council; or any decoration, etc. so nearly resembling an official one as to be calculated to deceive; or falsely represents himself to be a person who is or has been entitled to wear any official decoration etc.

but this does not prohibit the use or wearing of ordinary regimental badges or of brooches or ornaments representing them

and

A person shall be guilty of an offence if he

purchases, takes in pawn, solicits or procures any person to sell or pledge,

or

acts for any person in the sale or pledging of

any naval, military or air force decoration awarded to any member of Her Majesty's forces. But it shall be a defence to prove that at the time of the alleged offence the person to whom the decoration was awarded was dead or had ceased to be a member of those forces.

'Decoration' includes medals, medal ribbons, clasps and good conduct badges

Immigration

Ss 1–3 Immigration Act 1971

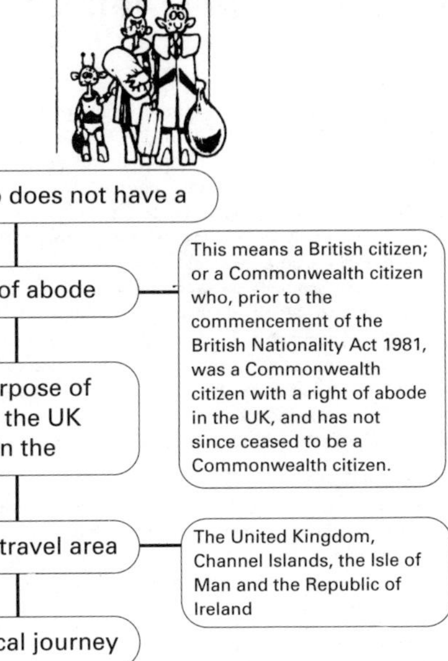

A person who does not have a

right of abode

- This means a British citizen; or a Commonwealth citizen who, prior to the commencement of the British Nationality Act 1981, was a Commonwealth citizen with a right of abode in the UK, and has not since ceased to be a Commonwealth citizen.

who enters the UK for the purpose of living, working or settling in the UK otherwise than from within the

common travel area

- The United Kingdom, Channel Islands, the Isle of Man and the Republic of Ireland

on a local journey

- A journey which begins and ends in the common travel area and does not call in the course of the journey at a place not therein

must obtain leave to enter from an immigration officer

There may be conditions attached regarding:

- Employment
- Police registration
- Accommodation and maintenance of himself and his dependants without recourse to public funds

Leave may be subject to a time limit

Except that persons exercising **European Community** rights and nationals of Member States (currently Austria, Belgium, Czech Republic, Denmark, Estonia, Finland, France, Germany, Greece, Hungary, Iceland, Ireland, Italy, Latvia, Liechtenstein, Lithuania, Luxembourg, Malta, Netherlands, Norway, Poland, Portugal, Republic of Cyprus, Slovakia, Spain, Sweden and the UK) do not require leave to enter or remain.

Immigration Offences

IMMIGRATION ACT 1971

Illegal entry, etc (S 24)

A person who is not a British citizen, or a Commonwealth citizen who has the right of abode in the UK, commits an offence if:

(a) he knowingly enters the UK in breach of a deportation order or without leave;

(b) having only a limited leave to enter the UK, he knowingly either remains beyond the time limit, or fails to observe a condition of the leave;

(c) having lawfully entered the UK as a member of the crew of a ship or aircraft, he fails to leave at the expiry of the time allowed;

(d) without reasonable cause he fails to comply with a requirement to report to a medical officer of health or to submit to a test or examination;

(e) without reasonable excuse he fails to observe any restriction imposed as to residence, employment or occupation, or as to reporting to the police or immigration officer;

(f) he disembarks in the UK from a ship or aircraft after being placed on board with a view to his removal from the UK; or

(g) he embarks in contravention of a restriction not to do so made by an Order in Council.

Deception (S 24A)

A person who is not a British citizen, or a Commonwealth citizen who has the right of abode in the UK, commits an offence if, by means of deception:

(a) he obtains or seeks to obtain leave to enter or remain in the UK; or

(b) he secures or seeks to secure the avoidance, postponement or revocation of enforcement action against him.

'Enforcement action' means:

(a) directions for his removal from the UK under this Act or the Immigration and Asylum Act 1999;

(b) the making of a deportation order under this Act; or

(c) his removal from the UK in consequences of directions or a deportation order.

Assisting illegal entry, and harbouring (S 25)

An offence is committed by any person knowingly concerned in making or carrying out arrangements for securing or facilitating:

(a) entry into the UK of anyone he knows or has reasonable cause for believing to be an illegal entrant (whether the act was done in or outside the UK);

(b) entry into the UK of anyone he knows or has reasonable cause for believing to be an asylum claimant (whether the act was done in or outside the UK); or

(c) the obtaining by anyone of leave to remain in the UK by means which he knows or has reasonable cause for believing to include deception.

Subsection (b) above will not apply to anything done:

(a) to a person who has been detained or granted temporary admission under this Act;

(b) by a person otherwise than for gain; or

(c) by a person in the course of his employment by a bona fide organisation whose purpose is to assist such claimants.

An offence is committed by any person knowingly harbouring anyone whom he knows or has reasonable cause to believe to be an illegal entrant or to have committed an offence under S 24(1)(b) or (c) above.

Refugees

The UN Convention relating to the status of refugees provides that illegal entrants should not be prosecuted for offences, eg forged travel documents, if they are coming directly from a territory where their life or freedom was threatened provided they present themselves without delay and show good cause for their illegal entry or presence. This was followed by the Divisional Court in *R v Uxbridge Magistrates' Court, ex p Adimi.*

Hotels etc

ARTS 3 & 4 IMMIGRATION (HOTEL RECORDS) ORDER 1972

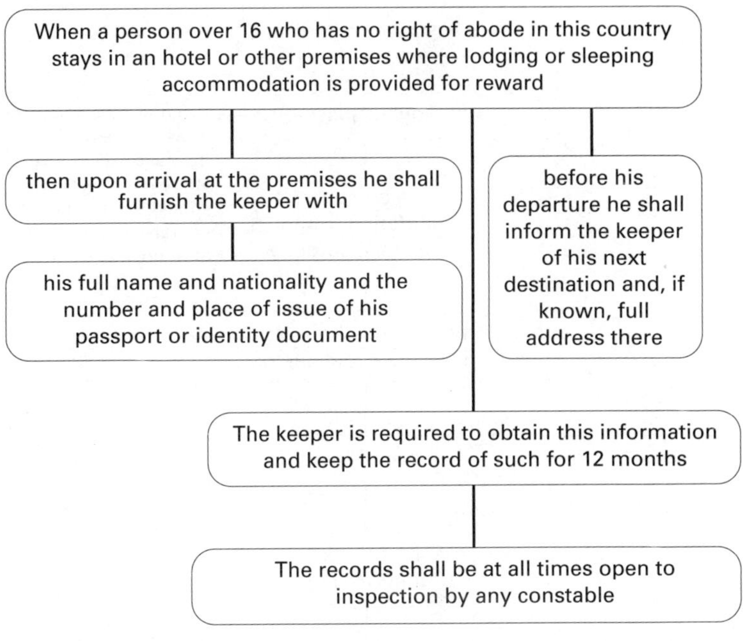

Mental Health

S 136 MENTAL HEALTH ACT 1983

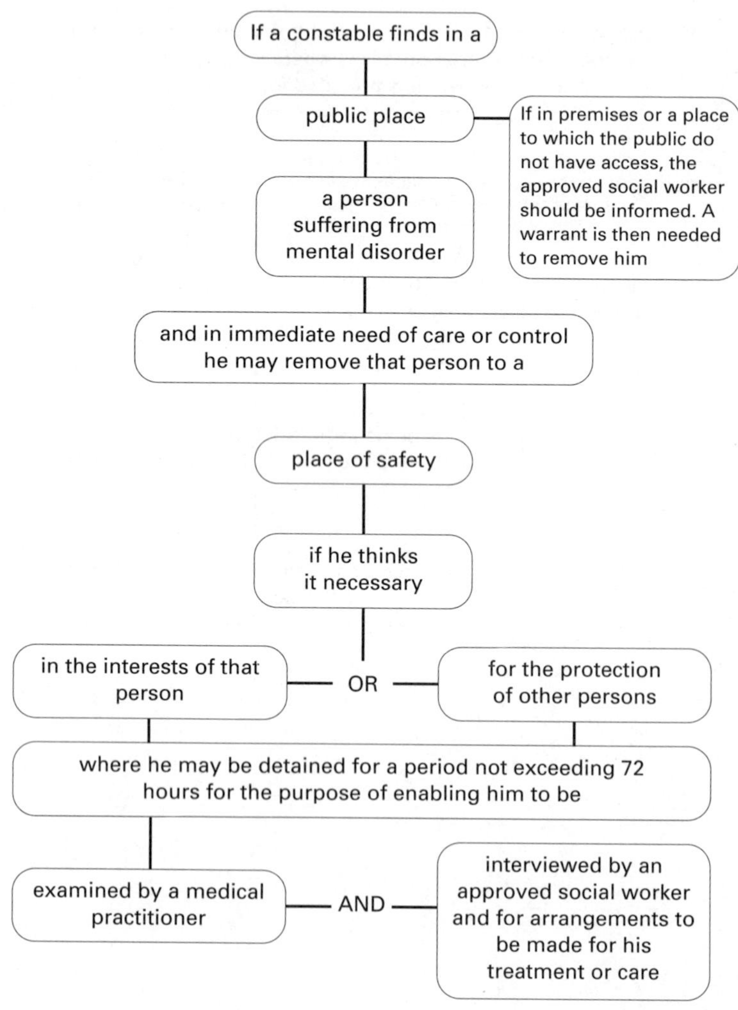

Pedlars

PEDLARS ACT 1871

A 'pedlar' is defined as:
any pedlar, hawker, petty chapman, tinker, caster of metals, mender of chairs, or other person who, without any horse or other beast bearing or drawing burden, **travels and trades on foot** and goes from town to town or to other people's houses, carrying to sell, or exposing for sale any goods, wares or merchandise, or procuring orders for goods immediately to be delivered, or selling or offering for sale his skill in handicrafts (S 3).
The Act does not apply to commercial travellers or other persons selling or seeking orders for goods to or from dealers for resale; or to agents authorised by publishers selling or seeking orders for books; or sellers of vegetables, fish, fruit or victuals; or persons selling at any public market, etc (S 23).

Any person who acts as a pedlar must obtain a certificate. It is an offence to act without one (S 4)

It is an offence to fail to produce the certificate to a justice, police officer, person to whom he offers goods, or a person on whose private grounds or premises he is found (S 17)

It is also an offence to lend, borrow, forge or fail to produce a certificate (S 10)

Scrap Metal Dealers

SCRAP METAL DEALERS ACT 1964

A scrap metal dealer is defined as:

a person who carries on a business of **buying** and **selling** scrap metal, whether the scrap metal is sold in the form in which it is bought or otherwise (S 9)

'Scrap metal' includes any old metal, manufactured articles made wholly or partly from metal and any metallic wastes.

S 2 **At each scrap metal store, the dealer must keep a book in which he must enter particulars of:**

1) All scrap metals received at that place

2) All scrap metal either processed at or despatched from that place

The particulars which must be recorded immediately after the processing or despatch are:

Received

- Description and weight of the scrap metal
- Date and time of receipt
- Full name and address of person from whom received
- The price payable (if known)
- Where price is not known, the value as estimated by the dealer
- The registration mark of any vehicle used to deliver the metal

Processed or Despatched

- Description and weight of the scrap metal
- Date of processing or despatch and, if applicable, the process applied
- The full name and address of the person to whom it was sold or exchanged and the consideration given for it
- If processed or despatched other than on sale or exchange, the value of the scrap metal immediately before despatch, as estimated by the dealer

These particulars may be kept in two separate books if preferred. In any case the books must be kept for 2 years from the date of completion

A constable has a right at all reasonable times to enter a scrap metal dealer's business premises and inspect scrap metal, record books and receipts (S 6)

It is an offence to obstruct the exercise of the powers of entry and inspection conferred by these provisions (S 6)

It is an offence for a person selling scrap metal to a scrap metal dealer to give him a false name and address (S 5)

It is an offence for a scrap metal dealer to acquire scrap metal from a person apparently under the age of 16 years (S 5)

Motor Salvage Operators

VEHICLE (CRIME) ACT 2001

A motor salvage operator is a person who carries on a business which consists:
1. wholly or partly in recovery for re-use or sale of salvageable parts from motor vehicles and the subsequent sale or other disposal for scrap of the remainder of the vehicles;
2. wholly or mainly in the purchase of written-off vehicles and their subsequent repair and resale;
3. wholly or mainly in the sale or purchase of motor vehicles which are to be the subject of any of the above activities;
4. wholly or mainly in activities which fall within 2 or 3 above.

A person who carries out the business of a motor salvage operator must **register** with the local authority. It is an offence to make false statements in an application for registration.

Entry and Inspection of Premises
A constable may at any reasonable time enter and inspect **registered** premises which are occupied by an operator as a motor salvage yard. (Force may not be used in executing any warrant to enter.)

Requirement to Keep Records
Records (electronic or manual) must be kept at the premises of details relating to the vehicle, the supplier or person receiving (including proof of identity), condition of vehicle, date of transaction and date details were entered on the record.

Inspection of Records
A constable may at any reasonable time:
1. require production of, and inspect, any motor vehicles or salvageable parts kept on **registered** premises; and
2. require production of, inspect and take copies of or extracts from any records which the operator is required to keep.

Warrant to Enter Premises
In order to secure compliance with regulations, or to ascertain whether provisions are being complied with, a Justice of the Peace may issue a warrant authorising a constable to enter and inspect specified premises. (Other than as mentioned above, reasonable force may be used to execute a warrant). If required by the owner or occupier of the premises, the constable shall produce evidence of his identity and his authority for entering, before doing so.

Giving False Particulars
A person who sells a motor vehicle to a motor salvage operator commits an offence if he gives him a false name or address.

Vagrancy

The following are offences under the VAGRANCY ACT 1824, AMENDED BY THE VAGRANCY ACT 1935

LODGING IN OUTHOUSES

Every person who wanders abroad and lodges in any barn or otherwise, or in any deserted or unoccupied building or in the open air, or under a tent, or in any cart or wagon, and not giving a good account of himself

AND

- he has been directed to a reasonably accessible place of free shelter and has failed to apply or has refused shelter there; or
- he persistently wanders abroad and there is a reasonably accessible place of free shelter; or
- he has caused damage to property, infection with vermin, or other offensive consequence, or lodges in such circumstances as to appear to be likely to do so (S 4).

Vagrancy – Cont.

VAGRANCY ACT 1824

FOUND ON ENCLOSED PREMISES

Every person being found in or upon any dwelling house, warehouse, stable or outhouse, or in any enclosed yard, garden or area for any unlawful purpose (S 4)

EXPOSING WOUNDS

Every person who wanders abroad and endeavours by **exposing wounds or deformities** to obtain or gather alms (S 4)

POWER TO ARREST ONLY IN ACCORDANCE WITH THE POLICE AND CRIMINAL EVIDENCE ACT 1984

BEGGING

Every person who wanders abroad, or places himself in any public place, street, highway, court or passage, **to beg or gather alms** or causing, procuring or encouraging any child to do so (S 3)

FRAUDULENT COLLECTIONS

Any person who goes about as a gatherer or collector of alms, or endeavours to procure charitable contributions of any nature or kind, under any false or fraudulent pretence (S 4)

Police

S 90 POLICE ACT 1996

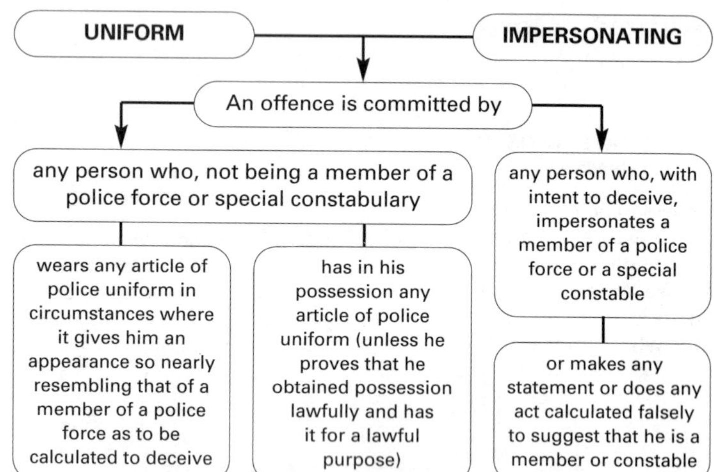

The unauthorised use of any uniform to gain admission to a 'prohibited place' is an offence under S 1 Official Secrets Act 1920

'Article of police uniform' means any article of uniform or any distinctive badge, mark or identification document (or any thing having the appearance of such article, etc)

ASSAULT, etc S 89

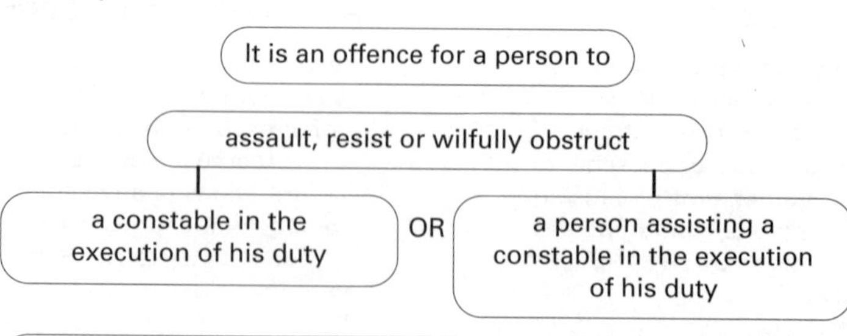

It is a common law offence to refuse to aid and assist a constable in the execution of his duty when called upon to do so, if the person is physically capable of helping and has no lawful excuse for refusing

Chapter 7
Public Order

Litter

S 5 LITTER ACT 1983,
S 87 ENVIRONMENTAL PROTECTION ACT 1990

It is an offence to — wilfully remove or otherwise interfere with any **LITTER BIN** or notice board provided or erected under S 5 of the Litter Act 1983 or S 185 of the Highways Act 1980

THROW DOWN — includes to drop or otherwise deposit

in, into or from

ANY PUBLIC OPEN PLACE OR ANY PLACE

which is:
a highway or road repairable at public expense; land in the open air which is open to the public and owned or controlled by the Crown, a designated undertaker, an education authority, a principal litter authority or within the litter control area of a local authority

a 'public open place' is a place in the open air to which the public have access without payment; and any covered place open to the air on at least one side and available for public use.

AND LEAVE

anything whatsoever in such circumstances as to cause, contribute to, or tend to lead to

DEFACEMENT BY LITTER — unless authorised by law or consent is obtained from the owner, occupier or person having control of that place

Abandoning Vehicles etc.

S 2 REFUSE DISPOSAL (AMENITY) ACT 1978

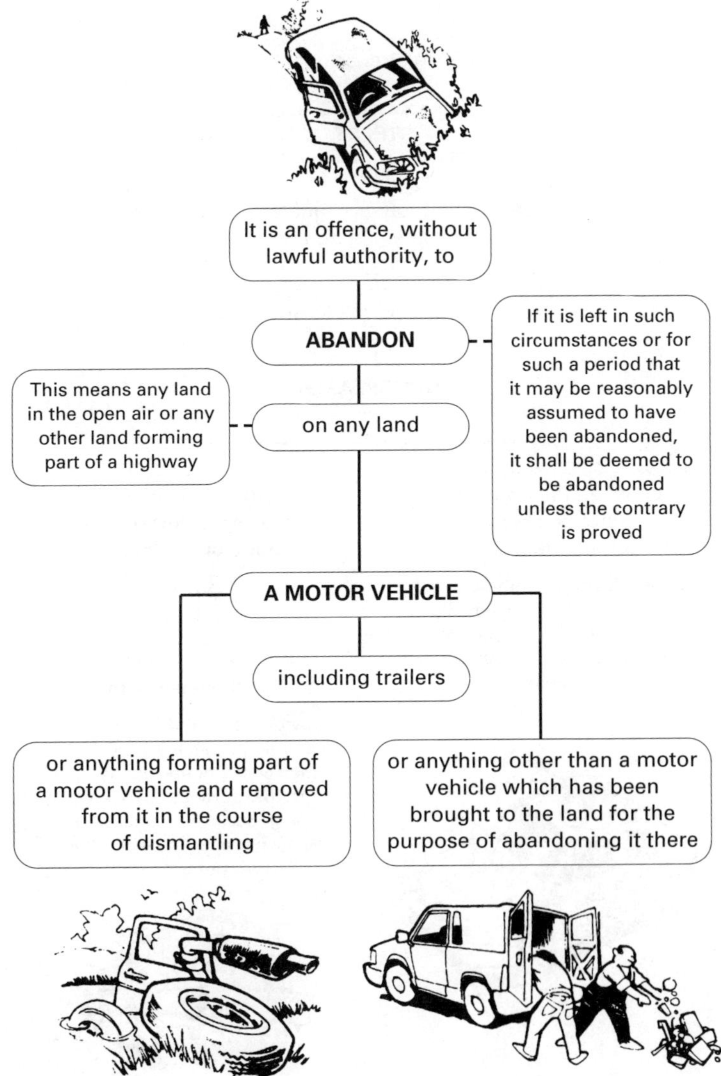

Noise

S 62 CONTROL OF POLLUTION ACT 1974

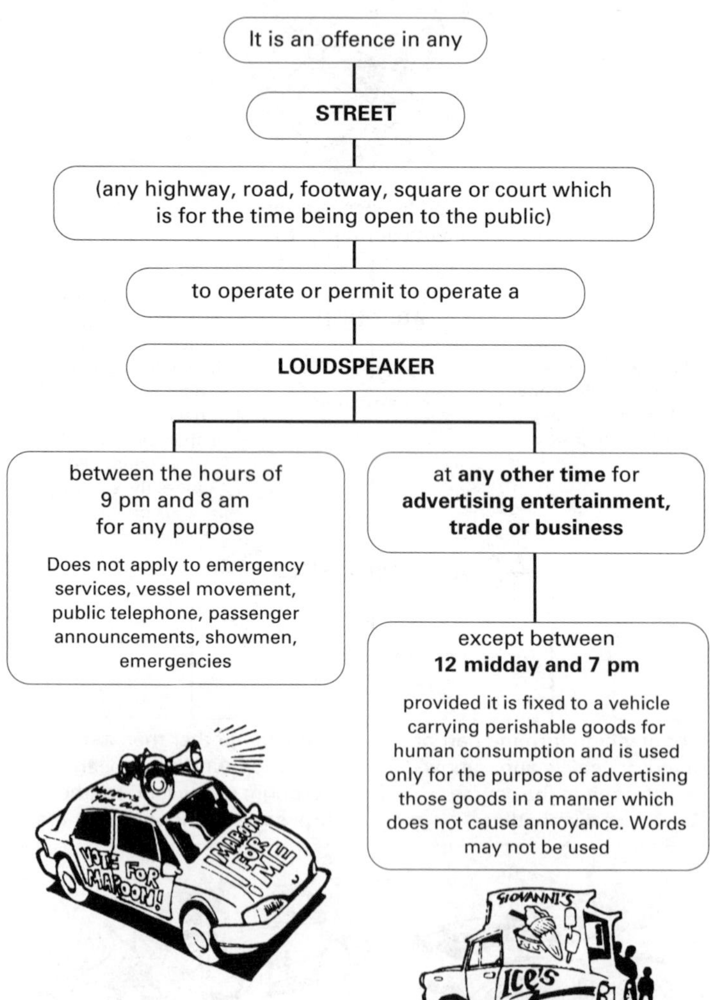

Trade Disputes

S 241 TRADE UNION AND LABOUR RELATIONS (CONSOLIDATION) ACT 1992

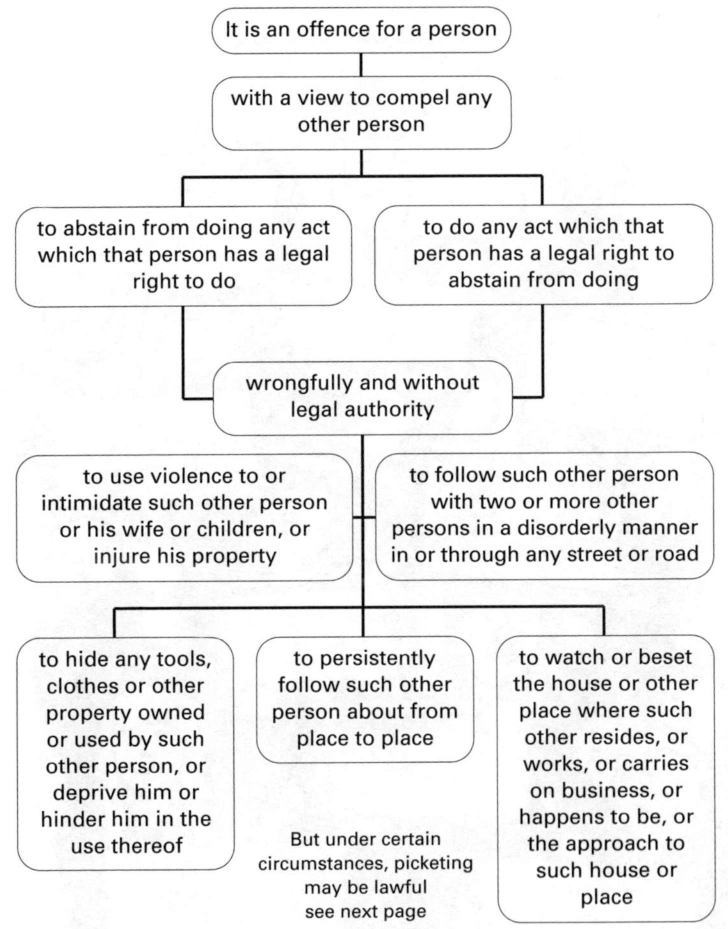

Peaceful Picketing

S 220 TRADE UNION AND LABOUR RELATIONS (CONSOLIDATION) ACT 1992

Fear or Provocation of Violence

S 4 PUBLIC ORDER ACT 1986

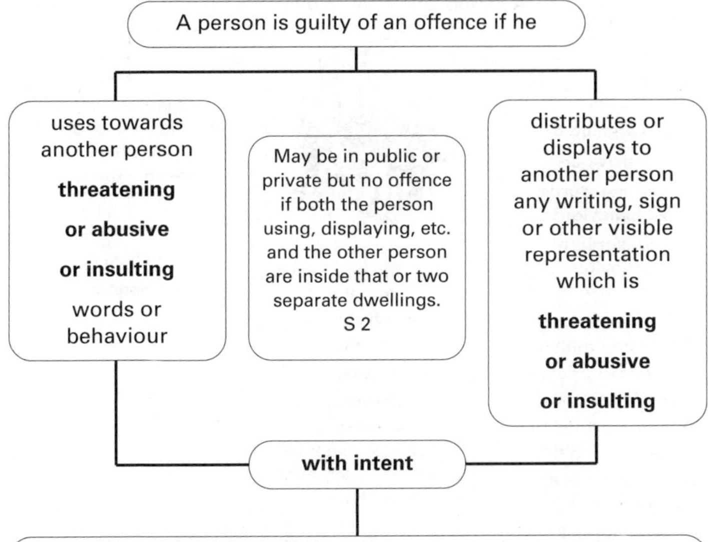

- to cause that person to believe that immediate unlawful violence will be used against him or another by any person, or
- to provoke the immediate use of unlawful violence by that person or another, or
- whereby that person is likely to believe that such violence will be used or it is likely that such violence will be provoked

Violence includes conduct towards property. Need not cause, or be intended to cause, injury or damage (S 8)

Harassment, Alarm or Distress

S 5 PUBLIC ORDER ACT 1986

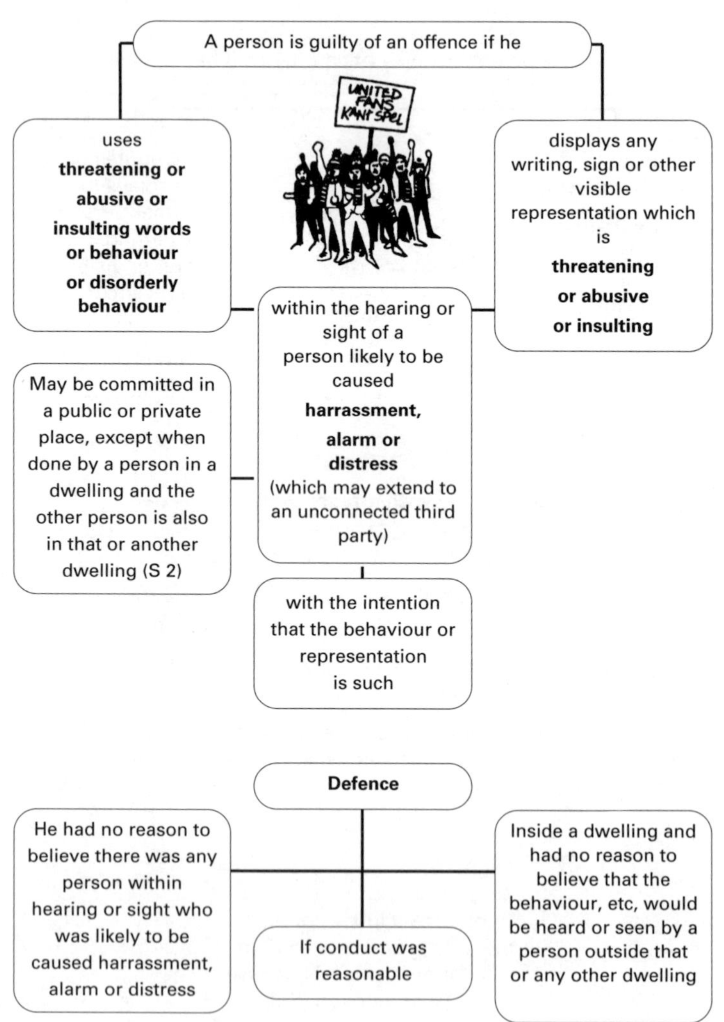

Intentional Harassment, Alarm or Distress

S 4A PUBLIC ORDER ACT 1986 (INSERTED BY S 154 CRIMINAL JUSTICE AND PUBLIC ORDER ACT 1994)

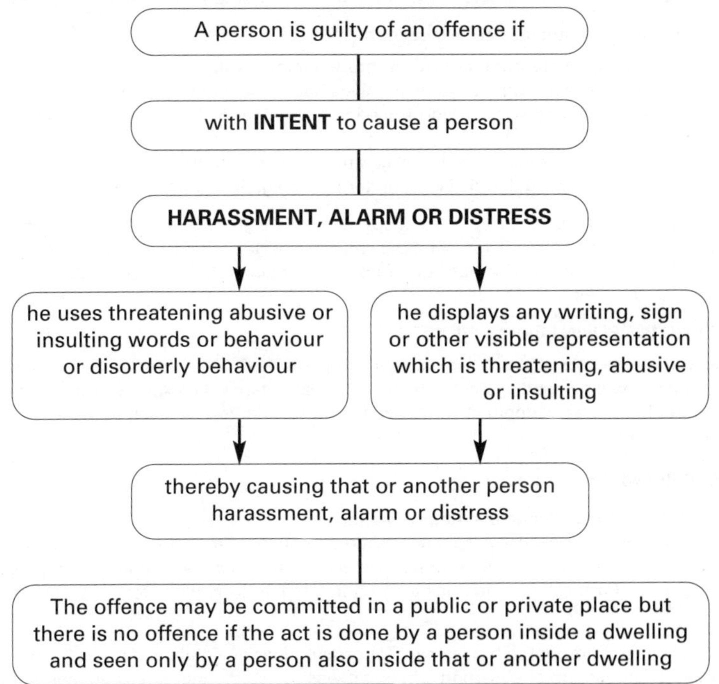

Defences:
(i) he was inside the dwelling and had no reason to believe that the act would be seen or heard by someone outside the dwelling
(ii) the conduct was reasonable.

Harassment Intended to Deter Lawful Activities

PROTECTION FROM HARASSMENT ACT 1997 (AS AMENDED BY THE SERIOUS ORGANISED CRIME AND POLICE ACT 2005)

PROHIBITION OF HARASSMENT

A person must not pursue a course of conduct:

(a) which amounts to harassment of another, and
(b) which he knows or ought to know amounts to harassment. (S 1(1))

A person must not pursue a course of conduct:

(a) which involves harassment of two or more persons, and
(b) which he knows or ought to know involves harassment of those persons, and
(c) by which he intends to persuade any person (whether or not those mentioned above):
    (i) not to do something that he is required or entitled to do, or
    (ii) to do something that he is not under any obligation to do. (S 1(1A))

A person who pursues such a course of conduct will be guilty of an offence. An actual or apprehended breach of S 1 may be the subject of a claim in civil proceedings by the victim. This may result in damages or a restraining injunction, in relation to S 1(1), or a restraining injunction for S 1(1A).

PUTTING PEOPLE IN FEAR OF VIOLENCE

A person whose course of conduct causes another to fear, on at least two occasions, that violence will be used against him is guilty of an offence if he knows or ought to know that his course of conduct will cause the other so to fear on each of those occasions. (S 4).

INTERPRETATION

Presumption of knowledge of course of action

A person ought to know that a course of action amounts to or includes harassment (or, in the case of S 4, causes another to fear violence) if a reasonable person in possession of the same information would think it amounted to harassment (or fear of violence).

Defence

Conduct will not amount to harassment (or causing fear of violence) if it was for the purpose of preventing or detecting crime; if it was pursued under any enactment; or if it was reasonable in the circumstances.

'Harassing' includes alarming or causing distress.

'Course of conduct' must involve:

(a) if relating to a single person, conduct on at least 2 occasions in relation to that person, or
(b) if relating to 2 or more persons, conduct on at least one occasion in relation to each person.

'Conduct' includes speech.

Harassment in the Home – Prevention

S 42 CRIMINAL JUSTICE AND POLICE ACT 2001

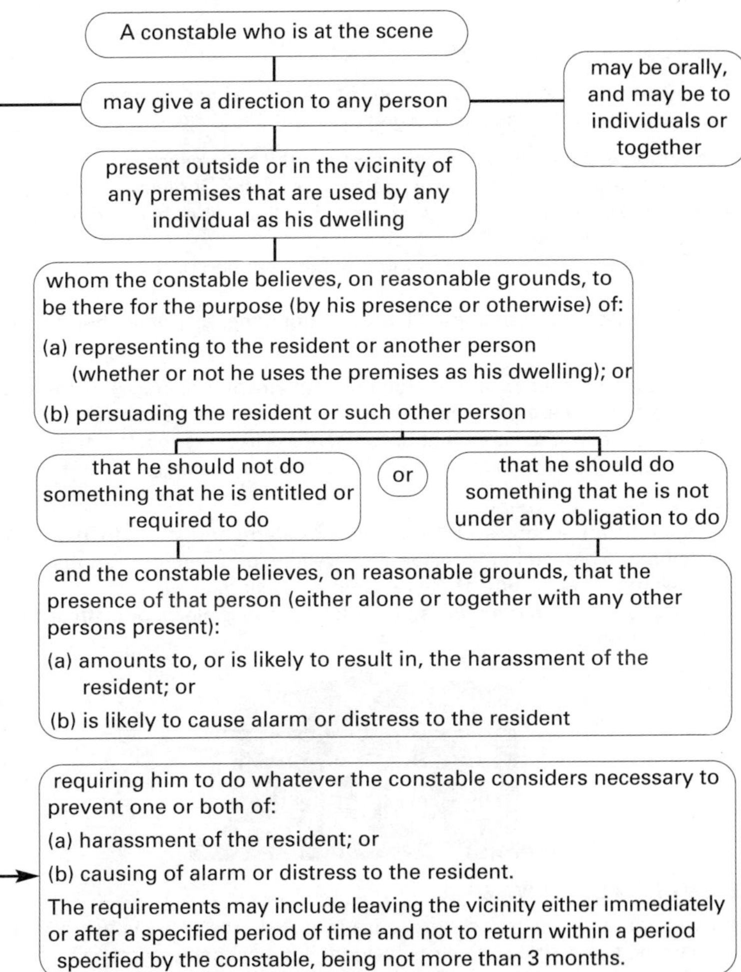

Harassment in the Home – Offence

S 42A CRIMINAL JUSTICE AND POLICE ACT 2001

A person commits an offence if:

(a) that person is present outside or in the vicinity of any premises that are used by an individual as his dwelling;

(b) that person is present there for the purpose (by his presence or otherwise) of representing to the resident or another individual (whether or not one who uses the premises as his dwelling), or of persuading the resident or such another individual:
- (i) that he should not do something that he is entitled or required to do; or
- (ii) that he should do something that he is not under any obligation to do;

(c) that person:
- (i) intends his presence (either alone or with any other person) to amount to the harassment of, or cause alarm or distress to, the resident, or
- (ii) knows or ought to know that his presence is likely to result in the harassment of, or to cause alarm or distress to, the resident, and

(d) the presence of that person:
- (i) amounts to the harassment of, or causes alarm or distress to, the resident, a person in the resident's dwelling, or a person in another dwelling in the vicinity of the resident's dwelling, or
- (ii) is likely to result in the harassment of, or to cause alarm or distress to, any such person.

PRESUMPTION OF KNOWLEDGE

A person ought to know that his presence is likely to result in the harassment of, or to cause alarm or distress to a resident if a reasonable person in possession of the same information would think that his presence would have that effect.

Animal Research Organisations – Protection

S 145 SERIOUS ORGANISED CRIME AND POLICE ACT 2005

A person (A) commits an offence if, with the intention of harming an animal research organisation, he:

(a) does a relevant act, or

(b) threatens that he or someone else will do a relevant act,

in circumstances in which that act or threat is intended or likely to cause a second person (B):

(a) not to perform any contractual obligation owed by B to a third person (C) (whether or not such non-performance amounts to a breach of contract);

(b) to terminate any contract B has with C;

(c) not to enter into a contract with C.

Relevant act means:

(a) an act amounting to a criminal offence, or

(b) a tortuous act causing B to suffer loss or damage of any description (except one which only induces another person to break a contract with B).

Contract includes any other arrangement.

Harm means:

(a) to cause the organisation to suffer loss or damage of any description, or

(b) to prevent or hinder the carrying out by the organisation of any of its activities.

Application. This section does not apply to any act done wholly or mainly in contemplation or furtherance of a trade dispute.

Animal research organisation. See following page.

Animal Research Organisations – Intimidation

S 146 SERIOUS ORGANISED CRIME AND POLICE ACT 2005

A person (A) commits an offence if, with the intention of causing a second person (B) to abstain from doing something which B is entitled to do (or to do something which B is entitled to abstain from doing):
(a) A threatens B that A or somebody else will do a relevant act, and
(b) A does so wholly or mainly because B is a person falling within the table below, **relating to an animal research organisation**:

(a)	an employee or officer
(b)	a student at an educational establishment
(c)	a lessor or licensor of premises
(d)	a person with financial interest in, or provides financial assistance to
(e)	a customer or supplier
(f)	a person contemplating becoming someone in (c), (d) or (e)
(g)	a person who is, or is contemplating becoming a customer or supplier of a person in (c), (d), (e) or (f)
(h)	an employee or officer of someone in (c), (d), (e), (f) or (g)
(i)	a person with financial interest in, or who provides financial assistance to, a person in (c), (d), (e), (f) or (g)
(j)	a spouse, civil partner, friend, or relative of, or a person who is personally known to, a person in (a) to (i)
(k)	a person who is, or is contemplating becoming, a customer or supplier of a person in (a), (b), (h), (i) or (j)
(l)	an employer of someone in (j)

Officer includes, where the organisation or person is:
(a) **a body corporate** – a director, manager or secretary,
(b) **a charity** – a charity trustee,
(c) **a partnership** – a partner.

Relevant act means:
(a) an act amounting to a criminal offence, or
(b) a tortuous act causing B or another person to suffer loss or damage of any description.

Application. This section does not apply to any act done wholly or mainly in contemplation or furtherance of a trade dispute.

Animal research organisation means any person who, or organisation which:
1. is the owner, lessee or licensee of premises constituting or including:
   (a) a place specified in a licence granted under the Animals (Scientific Procedures) Act 1986,
   (b) a scientific procedure establishment designated under S 6 of that Act, or
   (c) a breeding or supplying establishment designated under S 7 of that Act; or
2. employs, or engages under a contract for services, any of the following in his capacity as such:
   (a) the holder of a personal licence granted under S 4 of that Act,
   (b) the holder of a project licence granted under S 5 of that Act,
   (c) a person specified under S 6(5) or 7(5) of that Act.

Dispersal of Groups

S30 ANTI-SOCIAL BEHAVIOUR ACT 2003

AUTHORISATION

Where a superintendent or above has reasonable grounds for believing:

(a) that any members of the public have been intimidated, harassed, alarmed or distressed as a result of the presence or behaviour of groups of 2 or more persons in public places; and

(b) that anti-social behaviour is a significant and persistent problem,

he may give an authorisation to a constable in uniform for a period not exceeding 6 months.

PROCESS

Any authorisation must be in writing, signed by the officer and must specify the relevant locality, the grounds and period the powers are exercisable. Consultation must take place with the relevant local authority and publicity must be given before the powers are exercisable.

CONSTABLE'S DIRECTION

Where an authorisation has been given, if the constable has reasonable grounds for believing that the presence or behaviour of such persons has resulted, or is likely to result in intimidation, harassment, alarm or distress, he may give a direction:

(a) requiring the group to disperse;

(b) requiring any person who does not live within that locality to leave the locality; and/or

(c) prohibiting persons who do not live in the locality from returning for up to 24 hours.

EXCEPTIONS

A direction may not be given to persons engaged in lawful trade union activities or lawful processions.

FAILURE TO COMPLY

Any person who fails to comply with a direction commits an offence.

UNSUPERVISED PERSONS UNDER 16

If a constable in uniform finds a person under 16 in a public place in the relevant locality between 9pm and 6am and not under the effective control of a parent or responsible person over 18, he may remove him to his home unless he believes he would be likely to suffer significant harm by taking him there.

DEFINITIONS

S 30 'Anti-social behaviour' means behaviour by a person which causes or is likely to cause harassment, alarm or distress to one or more other persons not of the same household as that person.

'Public place' means any highway and any place to which at the material time the public or any section of the public has access, on payment or otherwise, as of right or by virtue of express or implied permission.

Seizure of Vehicles Causing Annoyance etc.

S 59 POLICE REFORM ACT 2002

POLICE (RETENTION AND DISPOSAL OF MOTOR VEHICLES) REGULATIONS 2002

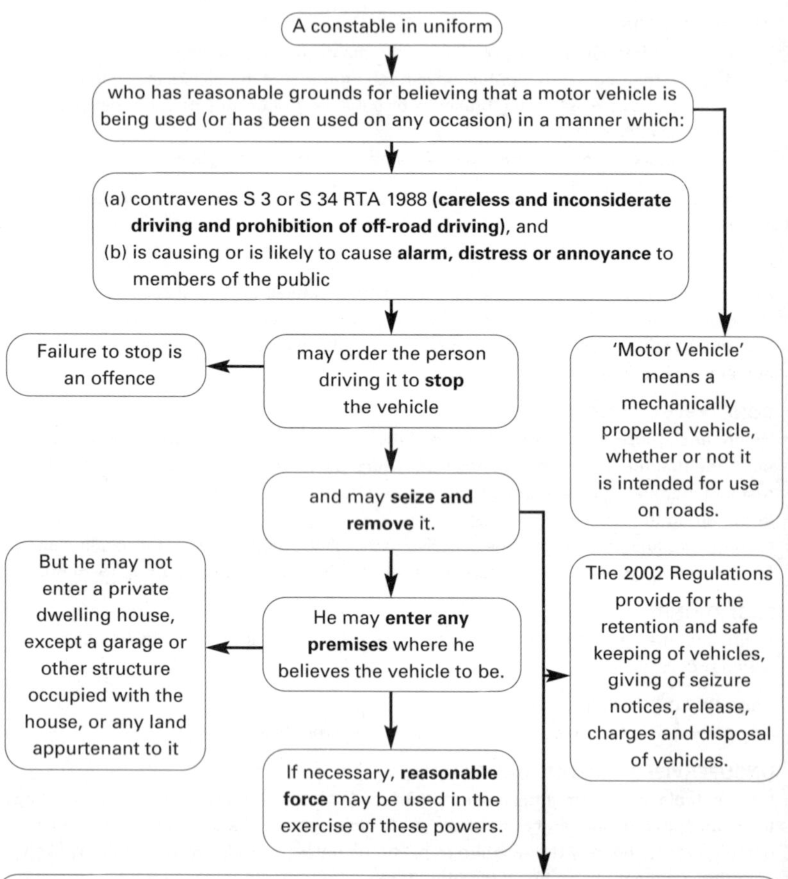

But he must first warn him that he will seize it if such use continues or is repeated; and the use has continued or been repeated after the warning. But a warning need not be given if: (a) it is impracticable for him to give the warning; (b) he has already given a warning on that occasion in respect of the use of that vehicle or another vehicle by that or another person; (c) he believes that such a warning has been given on that occasion by someone else; or (d) the person has already been warned by him or someone else within the previous 12 months whether or not it was in respect of the same vehicle or the same or similar use.

Football Offences

FOOTBALL (OFFENCES) ACT 1991

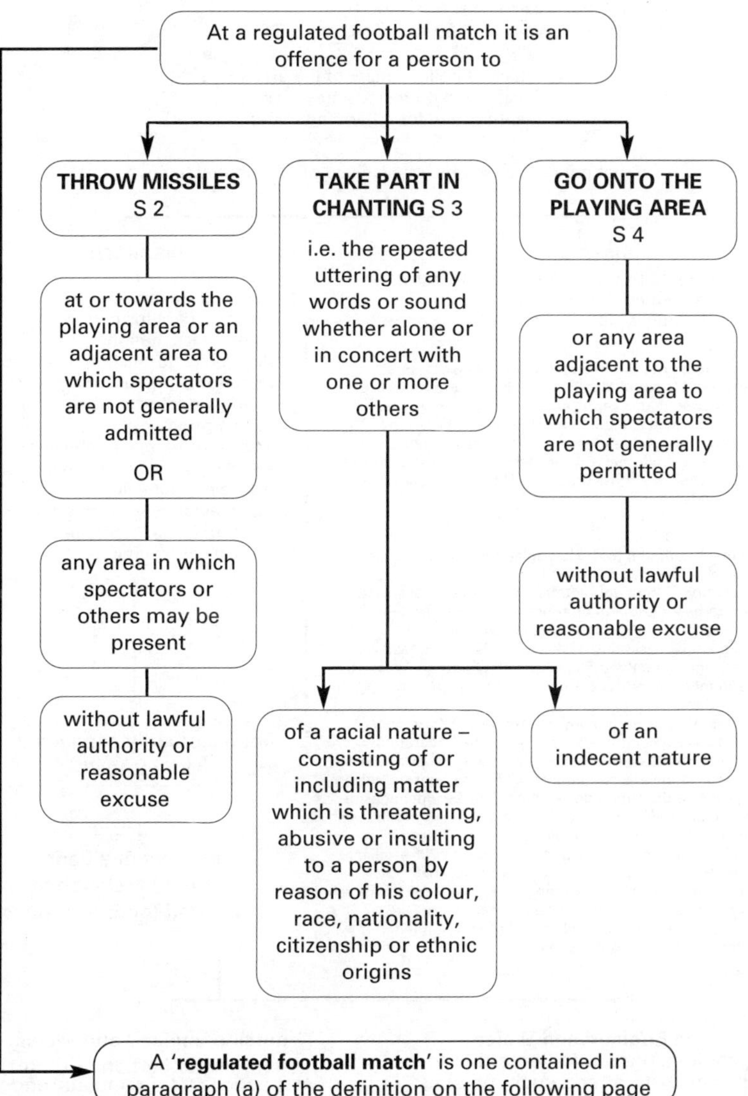

Banning Orders

FOOTBALL SPECTATORS ACT 1989
FOOTBALL (DISORDER) ACT 2000
FOOTBALL SPECTATORS (PRESCRIPTION) ORDER 2004
FOOTBALL SPECTATORS (PRESCRIPTION) (AMENDMENT) ORDER 2006

The chief police officer of the area in which a person resides may make an application for a **Banning Order**

if that person has at any time caused or contributed to any

VIOLENCE
(against persons or property, including threatening violence and doing anything which endangers life)

or

DISORDER
Including:
(a) stirring up hatred against a group of persons defined by colour, race, nationality (including citizenship) or ethnic or national origins, or against an individual as a member of such a group;
(b) using threatening, abusive or insulting words or behaviour or disorderly behaviour;
(c) displaying any writing or other thing which is threatening, abusive or insulting.

not necessarily connected with football

A **regulated match (in England and Wales)** is an association football match in which one or both of the participating teams represents:
(a) a club which is a full or associate member of the Football League, the Football Association Premier League, the Football Conference or the League of Wales;
(b) a club whose home ground is situated outside England and Wales, or
(c) a country or territory.

A **regulated match (outside England and Wales)** is an association football match involving:
(a) a national team appointed by the Football Association to represent England or appointed by the Football Association of Wales to represent Wales;
(b) a team representing a club which is a full or associate member of the Football League, the Football Association Premier League, the Football Conference or the League of Wales;
(c) a team representing any country or territory whose football association is a member of the Federation Internationale de Football Associations (FIFA) where the match is part of a competition or tournament organised by FIFA or the Union des Associations Europeennes de Football (UEFA); and is one in which a team mentioned in (a) above is eligible to participate; or
(d) a team representing a club which is a full or associate member of, or affiliated to, a national football association which is a member of FIFA, where the match is part of a competition or tournament organised by FIFA or UEFA; and is one in which a team mentioned in (b) above is eligible to participate.

The effect of a Banning Order in relation to **regulated football matches**

in England and Wales
prohibits the person entering any premises to attend such matches

outside England and Wales
requires the person to report at a police station and surrender his passport

Sporting Events – Control of Alcohol, etc

SPORTING EVENTS (CONTROL OF ALCOHOL etc.) ACT 1985, THE SPORTS GROUNDS AND SPORTING EVENTS (DESIGNATION) ORDER 2005

COACHES AND TRAINS (S 1)

Where a public service vehicle or railway passenger vehicle is being used to carry passengers for the whole or part of a journey to or from a designated sporting event, an offence is committed by any person who:

(a) is the operator of a public service vehicle (or his servant or agent), or is a person who has hired a vehicle (or his servant or agent) and knowingly causes or permits alcohol to be carried on the vehicle;
(b) has alcohol in his possession while on the vehicle; or
(c) is drunk on the vehicle.

OTHER VEHICLES (S 1A)

Where a vehicle is not a public service vehicle but is adapted to carry more than eight passengers, and is being used to carry two or more passengers for the whole or part of a journey to or from a designated sporting event, an offence is committed by any person who:

(a) is its driver, or is not its driver but is its keeper or a servant or agent of the keeper, or a person by whom it is made available (by hire, loan or otherwise) or his servant or agent and knowingly causes or permits alcohol to be carried on the vehicle;
(b) has alcohol in his possession while on the vehicle; or
(c) is drunk on the vehicle.

SPORTS GROUNDS (S 2)

A person commits an offence if he has in his possession alcohol or (except for holding a medicinal product) a bottle, can or other portable container (including if crushed or broken), which is for holding any drink and which, when empty, is normally discarded, etc.,

(a) during the period of a designated sporting event (see later) when he is in any area of a designated sports ground from which the event may be directly viewed; or
(b) while entering or trying to enter a designated sports ground during the period of a designated sporting event at that ground.

A person also commits an offence if he is drunk:

(a) in a designated sports ground during a designated sporting event; or
(b) while entering or trying to enter such a ground during such time.

Sporting Events – Control of Alcohol, etc. – Cont.

FIREWORKS etc. (S 2A)

A person commits an offence if he has in his possession any article or substance whose main purpose is the emission of a flare for illuminating or signalling, or the emission of smoke or a visible gas, and in particular, distress flares, fog signals, and pellets and capsules used as fumigators or for testing pipes (but does not include matches, cigarette lighters or heaters) or any firework:

(a) during the period of a designated sporting event when he is in any area of a designated sports ground from which the event may be directly viewed; or
(b) while entering or trying to enter a designated sports ground during the period of a designated sporting event at that ground.

POWERS OF ENFORCEMENT (S 7)

A constable may, during a designated sporting event at any designated sports ground, enter any part of the ground for the purpose of enforcing the above provisions. A constable may search a person he has reasonable grounds to suspect is committing or has committed any of these offences. A constable may stop a public service vehicle or a motor vehicle mentioned in S 1A above and may search such a vehicle or railway passenger vehicle if he has reasonable grounds to suspect that an offence under that section is being or has been committed.

Designated sports grounds means any sports ground in England or Wales used wholly or partly for sporting events where accommodation is provided for spectators.

Designated sporting events means:

(a) at any designated sports ground, association football matches in which one or both of the teams represents a club which is a full or associate member of the Football League, the Football Association Premier League, the Football Conference National Division, the Scottish Football League or Welsh Premier League, or represents a country or territory. It also includes association football matches in competition for the Football Association Cup (other than in a preliminary qualifying round); and
(b) association football matches at a sports ground outside England and Wales in which one or both of the teams represents a club which is for the time being a full or associate member of the Football League, the Football Association Premier League, the Football Conference National Division, the Scottish Football League or Welsh Premier League, or represents the Football Association or the Football Association of Wales.

Exemption. The Act does not apply to any sporting event where all competitors take part otherwise than for reward, and all spectators are admitted free of charge.

Football Ticket Touts.

S 166 CRIMINAL JUSTICE AND PUBLIC ORDER ACT 1994 (AS AMENDED BY THE VIOLENT AND SERIOUS CRIME ACT 2006)
TICKET TOUTING (DESIGNATION OF FOOTBALL MATCHES) ORDER 2007

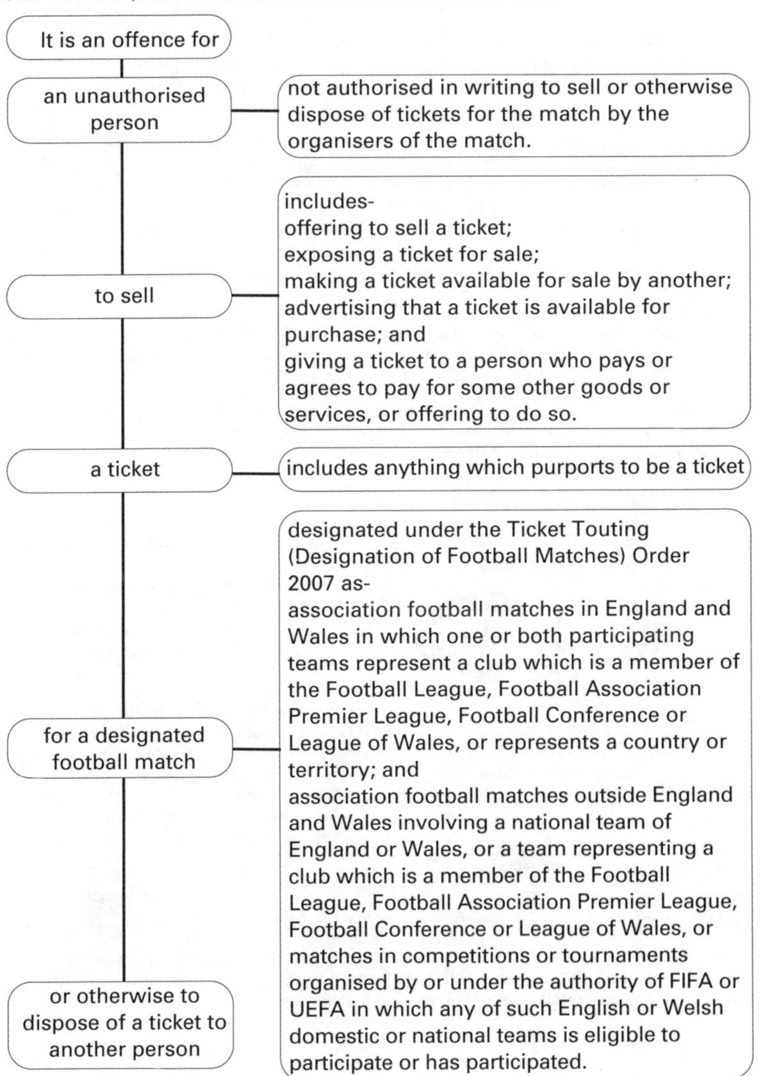

Offensive Weapons

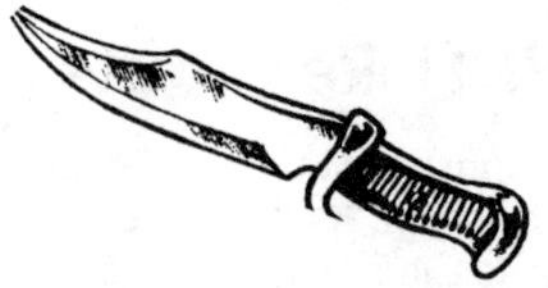

S 139 CRIMINAL JUSTICE ACT 1988

It is an offence to have an article which has a **blade** or which is **sharply pointed**

Folding pocket-knives are exempt provided the cutting edge of the blade is not longer than 3".

In a public place
(i.e. any place to which at the material time the public has or is permitted access, whether on payment or otherwise)

It shall be a **defence** to show that he had good reason or lawful authority for having it, or that he had it with him for use at work, for religious reasons, or as part of a national costume.

School Premises
An additional offence was created by the Offensive Weapons Act 1996 to include possession of the above article (or offensive weapons as described below) whilst on **school premises** (S 139A Criminal Justice Act 1988).

A constable may **enter** (using reasonable force if necessary) and **search** school premises for weapons if he suspects this offence is being, or has been, committed and to **seize** such articles.

S 1 PREVENTION OF CRIME ACT 1953

It is an offence to have an **offensive weapon**

Offensive weapons will normally be one of two types:

- Any article **made or adapted** for causing injury
- Or other articles **intended to be used** for such purposes

whilst in a **public place** without lawful authority or reasonable excuse

Unless acting in the capacity of Crown servant, police, armed services, etc. (Public place means any highway and any other place to which at the material time the public have or are permitted access, whether on payment or otherwise.)

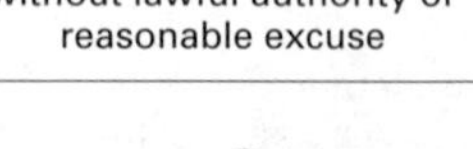

RESTRICTION OF OFFENSIVE WEAPONS ACTS 1959 & 1961

It is an offence for any person to manufacture, import, sell, hire, offer for sale or hire, or expose or have in possession for the purpose of sale or hire, or lend or give to any other person a **flick knife, flick gun or gravity knife**.

Offensive Weapons – Sale or Supply

S 141 CRIMINAL JUSTICE ACT 1988 AND CRIMINAL JUSTICE ACT 1988 (OFFENSIVE WEAPONS) ORDER 1988

It is an offence to
import, manufacture, sell or hire, offer for sale or hire, expose or have in possession for the purpose of sale or hire or lend or give to any other person

ANY OF THE FOLLOWING WEAPONS

not being antiques (manufactured more than 100 years before the date of the offence)

Balisong, or butterfly knife
being a blade enclosed by its handle, which is designed to split down the middle, without the operation of a spring or other mechanical means, to reveal the blade;

Knuckleduster
that is, a band of metal or other hard material worn on one or more fingers, and designed to cause injury, and any weapon incorporating a knuckleduster;

Telescopic truncheon
being a truncheon which extends automatically by hand pressure applied to a button, spring or other device in or attached to its handle;

Push dagger
being a knife the handle of which fits within a clenched fist and the blade of which protrudes from between two fingers;

Shuriken, shaken, or death star
being a hard non-flexible plate having three or more sharp radiating points and designed to be thrown;

Handclaw
being a band of metal or other hard material from which a number of sharp spikes protrude, and worn around the hand;

Footclaw
being a bar of metal or other hard material from which a number of sharp spikes protrude, and worn strapped to the foot;

(CONTINUED ON NEXT PAGE)

Offensive Weapons – Cont.

Manrikigusari, or kusari
being a length of rope, cord, wire or chain fastened at each end to a hard weight or hand grip;

Swordstick
that is, a hollow walking-stick or cane containing a blade which may be used as a sword;

Hollow kubotan
being a cylindrical container containing a number of sharp spikes;

Blowpipe, or blowgun
being a hollow tube out of which hard pellets or darts are shot by the use of breath;

Kusari gama
being a length of rope, cord, wire or chain fastened at one end to a sickle;

Kyoketsu shoge
being a length of rope, cord, wire or chain fastened at one end to a hooked knife;

Belt buckle knife
being a buckle which incorporates or conceals a knife;

Disguised knife
being any knife which has a concealed blade or concealed sharp point and is designed to appear to be an everyday object of a kind commonly carried on the person or in a handbag, briefcase, or other hand luggage (such as a comb, brush, writing instrument, cigarette lighter, key, lipstick or telephone);

Stealth knife
being a knife or spike, which has a blade, or sharp point, made from a material which is not readily detectable by apparatus used for detecting metal and which is not designed for domestic use or for use in the processing, preparation or consumption of food or as a toy;

Truncheon
being a straight, side handled or friction-lock truncheon (sometimes known as a baton).

Sale to Persons Under 16

S 141A CRIMINAL JUSTICE ACT 1988

Any person who sells to a person under the age of **16 years** any knife, knife blade, razor blade, axe, or any other article which has a blade or is sharply pointed, and made or adapted for causing injury to any person shall be guilty of an offence.

Marketing of Knives

KNIVES ACT 1997, S 60 CRIMINAL JUSTICE AND PUBLIC ORDER ACT 1994

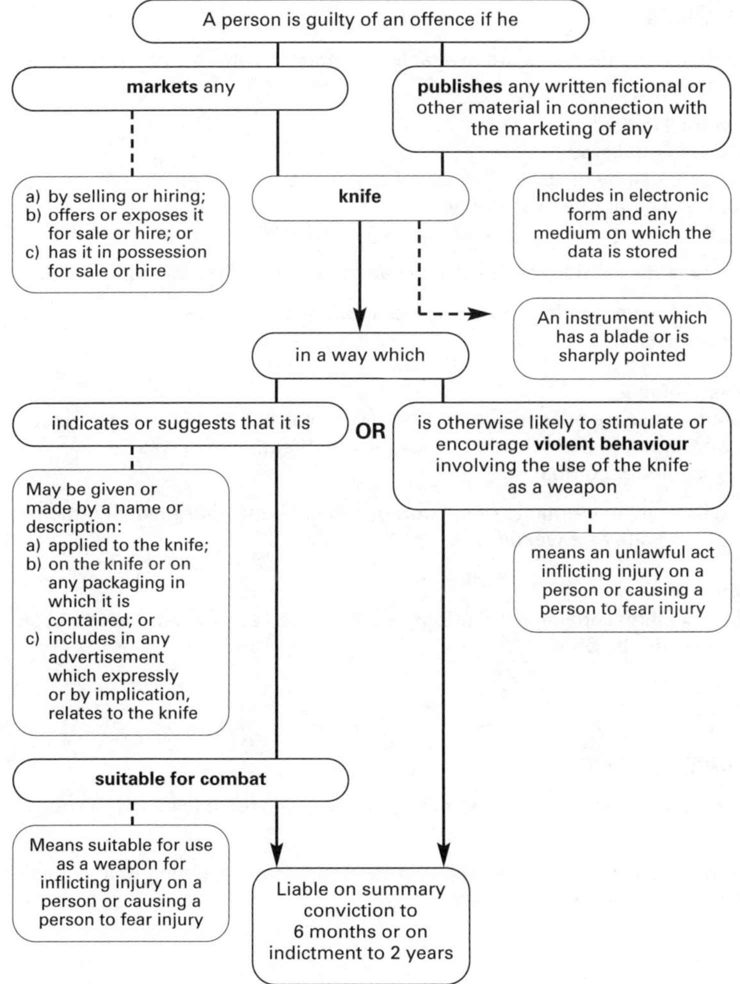

Marketing of Knives – Cont.

DEFENCES

The following defences are available to persons charged with an offence on the preceding page:

Exempt Trades:

a) It was marketed:
   i) for use by the armed forces of any country;
   ii) as an antique or curio; or
   iii) as falling within such other category (if any) as may be prescribed;

b) It was reasonable for the knife to be marketed in that way; and

c) There were no grounds to suspect that it would be used for an unlawful purpose.

Other defences:

He did not know or suspect that the way in which the knife was marketed:

a) amounted to an indication or suggestion that the knife was suitable for combat; or

b) was likely to stimulate or encourage violent behaviour involving the use of the knife as a weapon.

General:

He took all reasonable precautions and exercised all due diligence to avoid committing the offence.

POLICE POWERS

A justices' warrant is required to search premises for knives and to seize them.

An Inspector or above may authorise stopping and searching in anticipation of violence (see following page).

Stop and Search for Knives or Offensive Weapons

S 60 CRIMINAL JUSTICE AND PUBLIC ORDER ACT 1994
AS AMENDED BY S 8 THE KNIVES ACT 1997

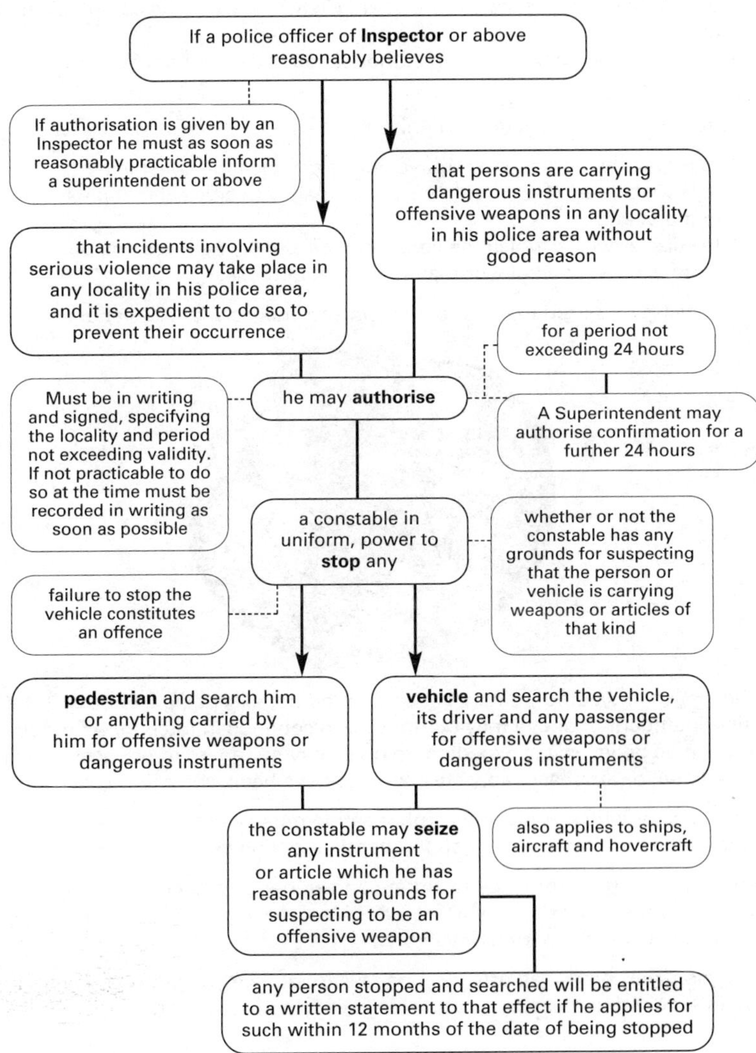

Removal of Disguises

S 60AA CRIMINAL JUSTICE AND PUBLIC ORDER ACT 1994

If a police officer of or above the rank of inspector reasonably believes:

(a) that activities may take place that are likely to involve the commission of offences, and
(b) that it is expedient to give an authorisation to prevent or control those activities,

he may authorise a constable in uniform:

(a) to require any person to remove any item which the constable reasonably believes is worn wholly or mainly to conceal that person's identity; and
(b) to seize any item which the constable reasonably believes any person intends to wear wholly or mainly for that purpose.

Any articles so seized may be retained in accordance with regulations.

The inspector's authority may be for a period not exceeding 24 hours, but a superintendent or above may authorise it to continue in force for a further 24 hours if he believes it is expedient to do so having regard to offences which have been, or are reasonably suspected to have been, committed.

An inspector who has given an authorisation must, as soon as it is practicable to do so, inform a superintendent or above.

Any authority given must be in writing and signed by the officer giving it, specifying the grounds on which it was given, the locality in which it is exercisable, and the period of validity.

A person will commit an offence if he fails to remove an item worn by him when required to do so by a constable exercising this power.

Crossbows

CROSSBOWS ACT 1987

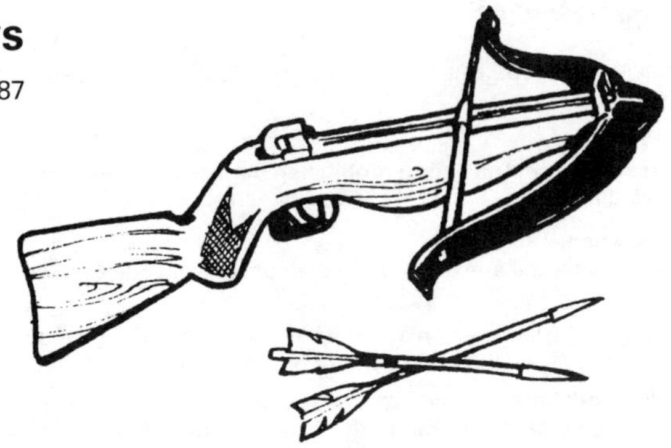

OFFENCES

Sale To sell or hire a crossbow or part of a crossbow to a person under the age of 17 years, unless he believes and has reasonable grounds to believe him to be 17 years.

Purchase For a person under 17 years to buy or hire a crossbow or part of a crossbow

Possession For a person under 17 years to have with him a crossbow (whether assembled or not) capable of discharging a missile unless under the supervision of a person of 21 years or older.

The Act does not apply to crossbows with a draw weight of less than 1.4 kg.

POLICE POWERS

Search Where a constable suspects with reasonable cause, that a person is committing, or has committed an offence of unlawful possession, he may search that person or vehicle, and may detain the person or vehicle for that purpose.

Seizure A constable may seize and retain for the purpose of proceedings any crossbow or part of a crossbow discovered in the course of the search.

Entry For the purpose of exercising the above powers a constable may enter any land **other than a dwelling house**.

Fireworks

FIREWORKS ACT 2003. FIREWORKS REGULATIONS 2004 (AS AMENDED)

Any person who contravenes a prohibition imposed by these Regulations commits an offence (S 11)

Possession under 18
No person under the age of 18 years shall possess an adult firework in a public place. (Reg. 4).

"Public Place" includes any place to which at the material time the public has or is permitted access, whether on payment or otherwise. (Reg. 4).

"Adult firework" means any firework (except for a cap, cracker snap, novelty match, party popper, serpent, sparkler or throwdown) which does not comply with BS 7114. (Reg. 3).

Possession of Category 4 firework
No person shall possess a category 4 firework. (Reg. 5). This does not apply to a person transporting fireworks in the course of employment in, or trade or business of, transporting fireworks. (Reg. 6).

"**Category 4 firework**" means classified as such by B.S. 7114.

Exceptions to Regs. 4 & 5
(a) Professional operator or organiser of firework displays;
(b) Manufacturer of fireworks or assemblies;
(c) Supplier of fireworks or assemblies;
(d) Local authority employee for a firework display, national public celebration or national commemorative event;
(e) Special effects in theatre, film or TV;
(f) A body having enforcement powers;
(g) Government department for firework display, national public celebration, national commemorative event, or research or investigation;
(h) Supplier of goods used for fireworks or assemblies, for testing purposes; or
(i) Navy, military or air force employees for firework display, national public celebration or national commemorative event. (Reg. 6).

Use of fireworks at night
No person shall use an adult firework during night hours (11 pm to 7 am) except:
(a) during a permitted fireworks night; or
(b) a person employed by a local authority putting on a firework display, national public celebration or national commemorative event. (Reg. 7).

"**Permitted fireworks night**" means a period:
(a) beginning at 11 pm on the first day of the Chinese New Year and ending at 1 am the following day;
(b) beginning at 11 pm and ending at midnight on 5th November;
(c) beginning at 11 pm on the day of Diwali and ending at 1 am the following day; or
(d) beginning at 11 pm on 31st December and ending at 1 am the following day.

Enforcement
The above offences concerning possession and use are enforced by the police. (Reg. 12). A power to stop, search and seize prohibited fireworks was inserted into S1 PACE by the Serious Organised Crime and Police Act 2005 (see later).

Racially or Religiously Aggravated Offences

Ss 28–32 CRIME AND DISORDER ACT 1998

Where any of the following offences are committed and there exists 'racial or religious aggravation', the severity of the maximum liability is increased.

OFFENCE	LIABILITY ON INDICTMENT
Assaults	
S 20 Offences against the Person Act 1861 (malicious wounding or GBH)	7 years
S 47 of that Act (actual bodily harm)	7 years
Common Assault	2 years
Criminal Damage	
S 1(1) Criminal Damage Act 1971 (destroying or damaging property belonging to another)	14 years
Public Order Offences	
S 4 Public Order Act 1986 (fear or provocation of violence)	2 years
S 4A of that Act (intentional harassment, alarm or distress)	2 years
S 5 of that Act (harassment, alarm or distress)	Level 4 fine
Harassment etc	
S 2 Protection from Harassment Act 1997 (harassment)	2 years
S 4 of that Act (putting people in fear of violence)	7 years

Racially or religiously aggravated means:

(a) at the time or immediately before or after doing so the offender demonstrates hostility based on the victim's racial or religious group; or

(b) the offence is wholly or partly motivated by hostility towards members of a racial or religious group.

Racial Hatred

Ss 17–23 PUBLIC ORDER ACT 1986

A person is guilty of an offence if he

Uses **WORDS OR BEHAVIOUR** or displays written material, which is (S 18)

PUBLISHES or distributes written material which is (S 19)

POSSESSES written material or a recording of visual images or sounds which is (S 23)

PROVIDES, USES WORDS OR BEHAVIOUR IN, OR PRODUCES OR DIRECTS a programme of visual images or sounds which is (S 22)

DISTRIBUTES, SHOWS OR PLAYS a recording of visual images or sounds which are (S 21)

PRESENTS OR DIRECTS a public performance of a play which involves words or behaviour which are (S 20)

THREATENING, ABUSIVE OR INSULTING

If he intends thereby to stir up **RACIAL HATRED** or, having regard to all the circumstances racial hatred is likely to be stirred up thereby

Hatred against a group of persons in Great Britain defined by reference to colour, race, nationality (including citizenship) or ethnic or national origins (S 17)

Trespassers on Land

Ss 61, 62, 62A, 62B & 62C CRIMINAL JUSTICE AND PUBLIC ORDER ACT 1994

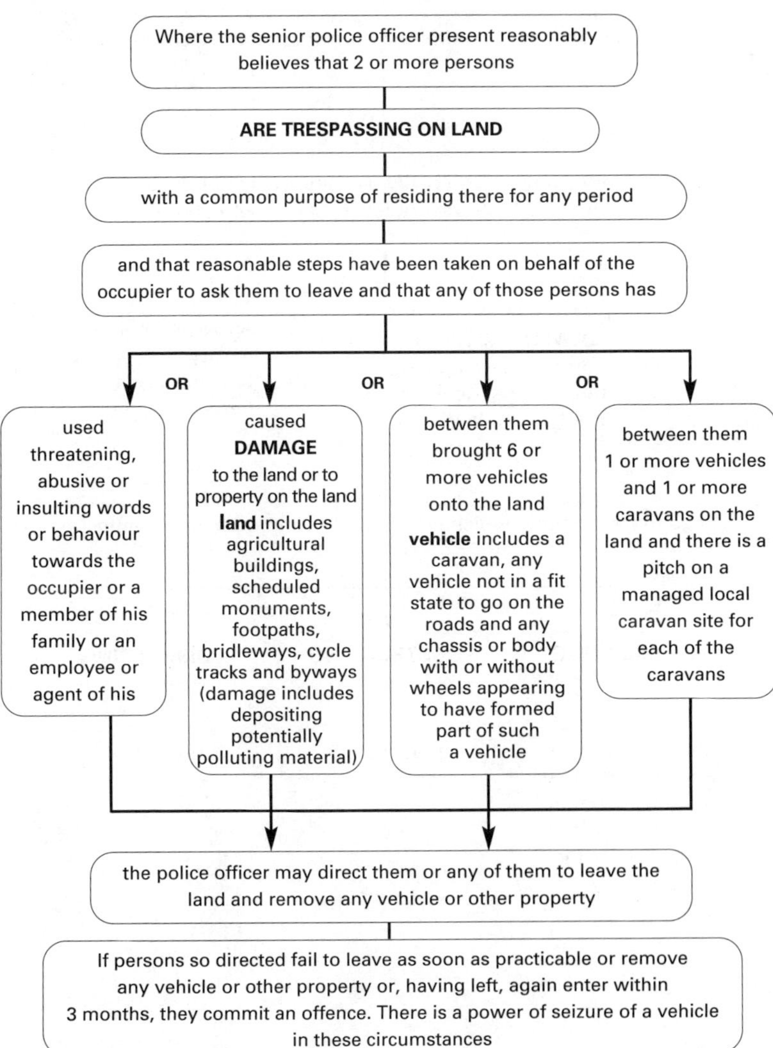

Aggravated Trespass

S 68 CRIMINAL JUSTICE AND PUBLIC ORDER ACT 1994

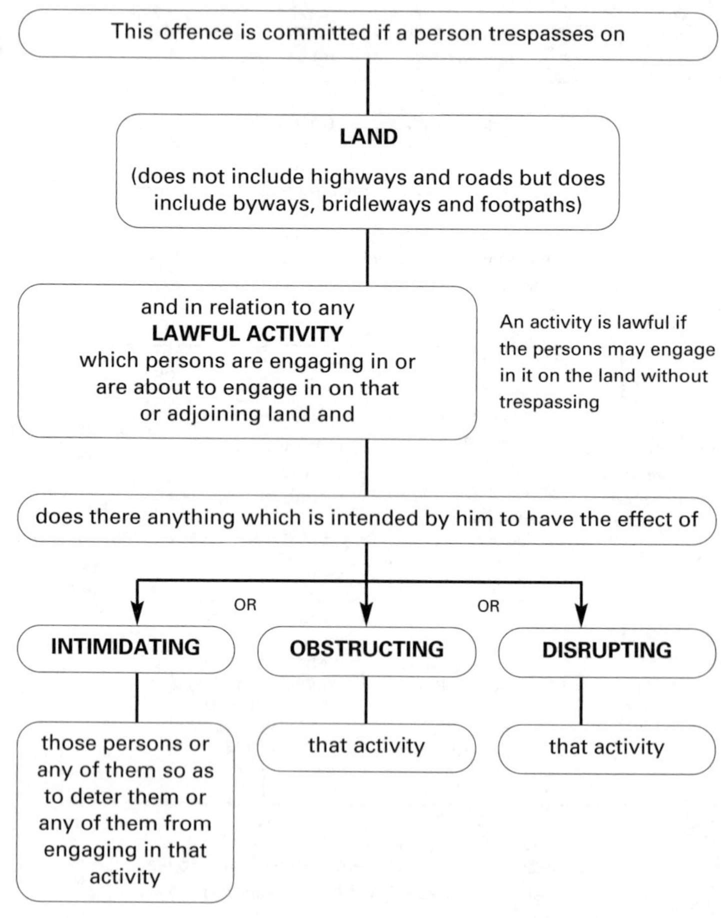

Aggravated Trespass – Removal of Persons

S 69 CRIMINAL JUSTICE AND PUBLIC ORDER ACT 1994

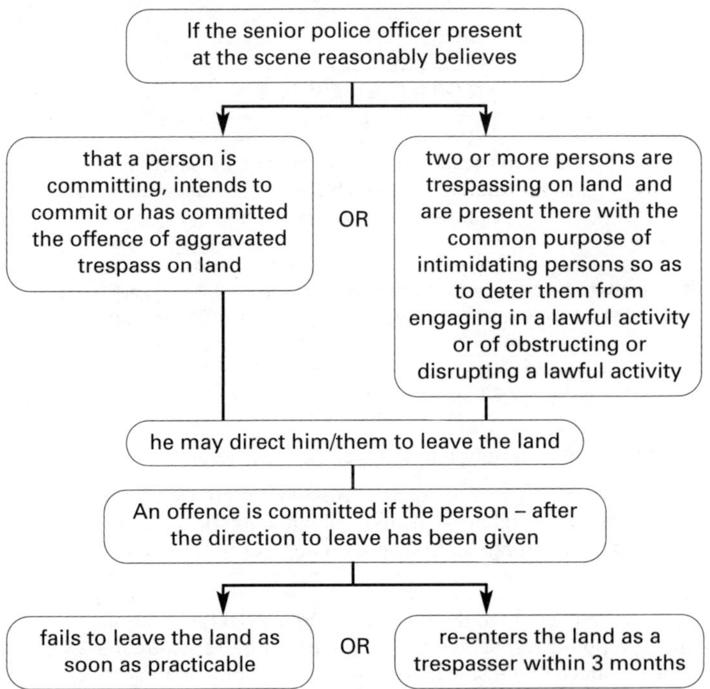

The direction to leave may be communicated by a constable at the scene.

Defence
If a person shows he was not trespassing or that he had a reasonable excuse for not leaving or for re-entering.

Trespassory Assemblies

S 14A PUBLIC ORDER ACT 1986, INSERTED BY S 70 CRIMINAL JUSTICE AND PUBLIC ORDER ACT 1994

If the chief officer of police (or the Commissioner of Police for the City of London or Metropolis) reasonably believes that an

ASSEMBLY OF 2 OR MORE PERSONS

is intended to be held in any district at a place on land (in the open air) to which the public has no (or limited) right of access and

it is likely to be held without the permission of the occupier of the land or to conduct itself in such a way as to exceed the limits of any permission or right of access

and may result:

(i) in a serious disruption to the life of the community, or

(ii) where the land or a building or monument on it is of historic, architectural, archaeological or scientific importance, in significant damage to the land, building or monument

he may apply to the council of the district for an order prohibiting for a specified period the holding of such trespassory assemblies in the specified district or part of it. In the City of London and the Metropolitan area the relevant commissioner may, with the consent of the Home Secretary, make such an order

The order may only be made for a period not exceeding 4 days and for an area not exceeding 5 miles radius from the specified centre

Trespassory Assemblies – Powers

Ss 14B & 14C PUBLIC ORDER ACT 1986,
INSERTED BY Ss 70–71 CRIMINAL JUSTICE AND PUBLIC ORDER ACT 1994

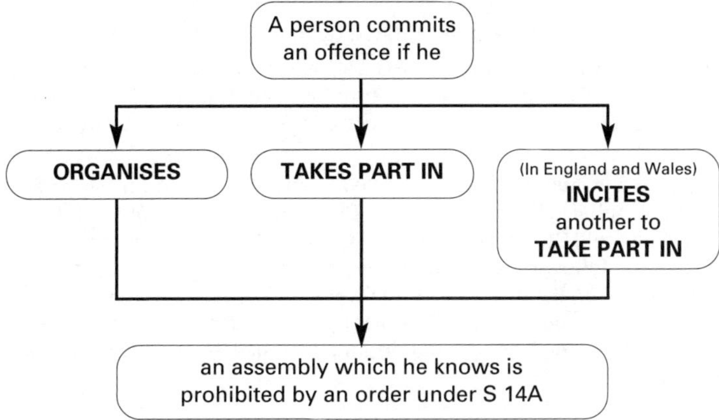

STOPPING PERSONS FROM PROCEEDING TO TRESPASSORY ASSEMBLIES

If a constable in uniform reasonably believes that a person is on his way to an assembly within the area to which an order under S 14A applies, which the constable reasonably believes to be an assembly prohibited by that order he may **stop** that person and direct him not to proceed towards the assembly (**but** the power may only be exercised within the area to which the order applies)

Failure to comply is an offence

Trespassing on Protected Site

S 128 SERIOUS ORGANISED CRIME AND POLICE ACT 2005, S 12 TERRORISM ACT 2006 & SERIOUS ORGANISED CRIME AND POLICE ACT 2005 (DESIGNATED SITES) ORDERS 2005 & 2007

A person commits an offence if he enters, or is on, any protected site in England and Wales or Northern Ireland as a trespasser. A 'protected site' means a nuclear site or a designated site.

Trespassing on Protected Site – Cont.

S 128 SERIOUS ORGANISED CRIME AND POLICE ACT 2005, S 12 TERRORISM ACT 2006 & SERIOUS ORGANISED CRIME AND POLICE ACT 2005 (DESIGNATED SITES) ORDERS 2005 & 2007

The following sites have been designated by the above order:

H.M. Naval Base Clyde, Northwood HQ, RAF bases- Brize Norton, Croughton, Fairford, Feltwell, Fylingdales, Lakenheath, Menwith Hill, Mildenhall, and Welford, R.N. Armaments Depot Coulport, and Sea Mounting Centre Marchwood.

The following sites were added by the 2007 Order- 85 Albert Embankment, London; Buckingham Palace; MoD Main Building, Whitehall; Old War Office Building, Whitehall; St. James's Palace, London; Thames House, London; and parts of the following sites as designated on maps included in the Order- Chequers Estate, Buckinghamshire; 10 Downing Street, London; GCHQs at Cheltenham(2), Scarborough & Bude; Highgrove House, Gloucestershire; Palace of Westminster, London; Sandringham House, Norfolk; and Windsor Castle, Berkshire.

Demonstrating without authorisation in Designated Area

S 132 SERIOUS ORGANISED CRIME AND POLICE ACT 2005, SERIOUS ORGANISED CRIME AND POLICE ACT 2005 (DESIGNATED AREA) ORDER 2005

Any person who, in a public place in the designated area, organises a demonstration, takes part in a demonstration, or carries on a demonstration by himself, is guilty of an offence if, when the demonstration starts, authorisation has not been given by the Commissioner of Police. The above order designated the area bounded by streets in the vicinity of Parliament.

Power to Direct a Person to Leave a Place

S 112 SERIOUS ORGANISED CRIME AND POLICE ACT 2005

A constable may direct a person to leave a place if he believes, on reasonable grounds, that the person is in the place at a time when he would be prohibited from entering it by virtue of:

(a) an order made, by virtue of any enactment, following the person's conviction for an offence, and which prohibits the person from entering the place or from doing so during a period specified in the order; or

(b) a condition which was imposed, by virtue of any enactment, as a condition of the person's release from a prison in which he was serving a sentence following his conviction for an offence, and which prohibits the person from entering the place or from doing so during a period specified in the condition.

Such a direction may be given orally.

Any person who knowingly contravenes such a direction is guilty of an offence

Raves

S 63 CRIMINAL JUSTICE AND PUBLIC ORDER ACT 1994
(AS AMENDED BY THE ANTI-SOCIAL BEHAVIOUR ACT 2003)

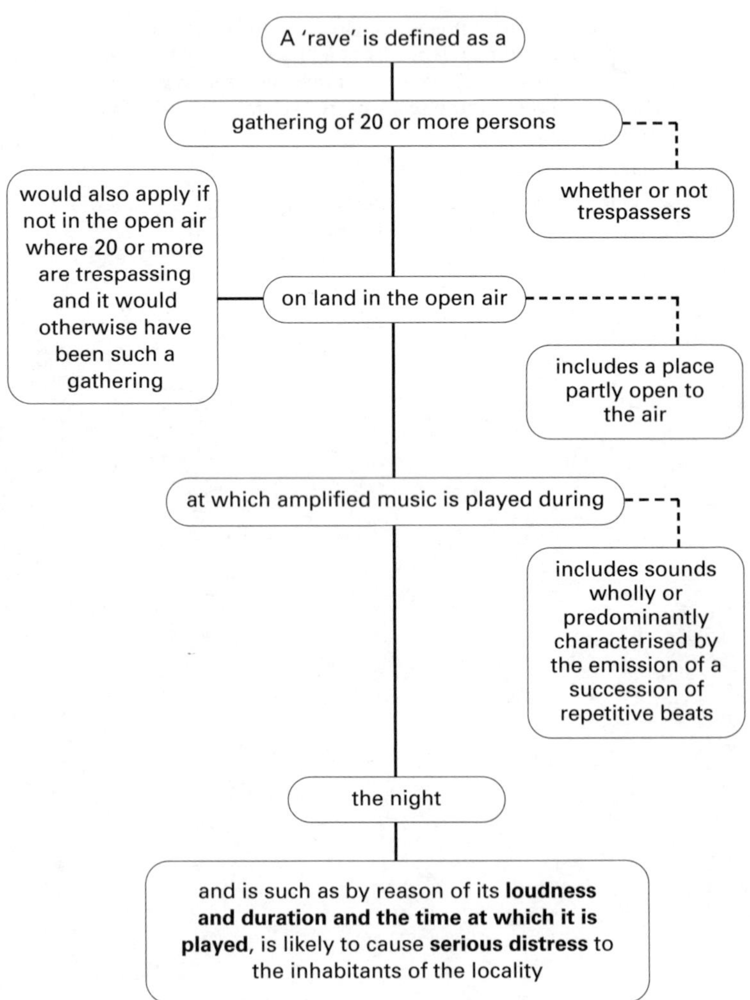

Raves – Powers

Ss 63–65 CRIMINAL JUSTICE AND PUBLIC ORDER ACT 1994

Removal of Persons S 63

A police officer of at least the rank of superintendent who reasonably believes that:

(a) 2 or more persons are making preparations for a rave;
(b) 10 or more persons are waiting for it to begin; or
(c) 10 or more persons are attending a rave in progress;

may **direct** those persons and any other persons who arrive, to leave the land and remove any vehicles or other property that they have with them. The direction may be communicated by any constable at the scene. It will be treated as having been communicated if reasonable steps have been taken to bring it to their attention. Failure to leave or re-entry within 7 days is an offence. A person also commits an offence if a direction has been given which he knows applies to him, and he makes preparations for or attends such a gathering within 24 hours of the direction being given.

Entry and Seizure S 64

A superintendent or above who believes the above direction would be justified in the circumstances, may authorise any constable to enter the land for the purposes of ascertaining whether such circumstances exist and to exercise any of the above powers and to seize and remove a vehicle or sound equipment which the person to whom a direction has been given has failed to remove and which appears to the constable to belong to him or to be in his possession or control. Also applies where a person has re-entered the land with a vehicle and/or sound equipment within 7 days.

Stopping Persons from Attending S 65

If a constable in uniform reasonably believes that a person is on his way to a gathering to which S 63 applies and in respect of which a direction is in force, he may stop that person and direct him not to proceed in the direction of that gathering. This power may be exercised within 5 miles of the boundary of the site of the gathering. Failure to comply is an offence.

Violent Entry to Premises

S 6 CRIMINAL LAW ACT 1977 AS AMENDED BY S 72 CRIMINAL JUSTICE AND PUBLIC ORDER ACT 1994

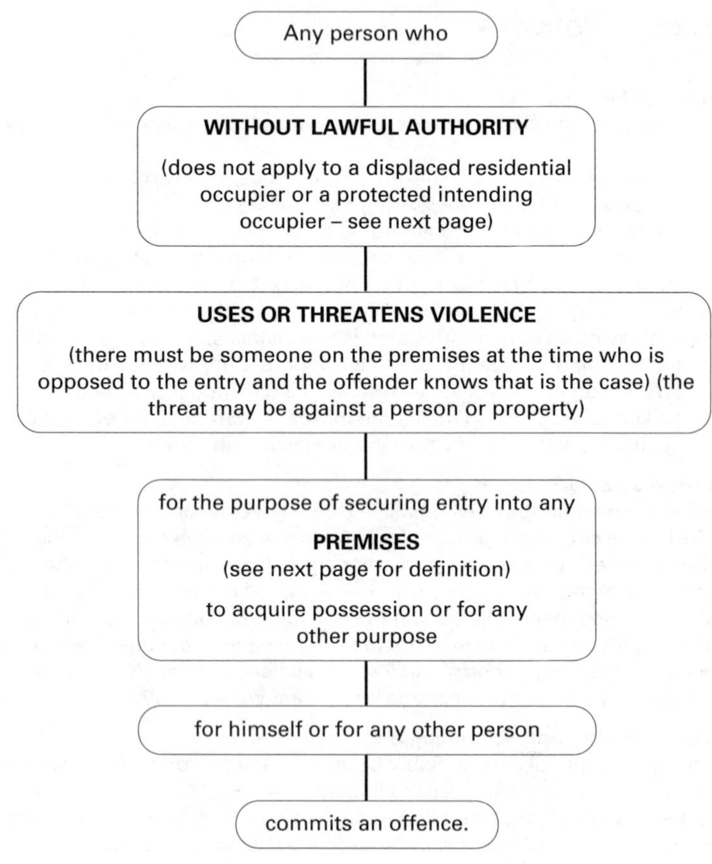

Squatters

S 7 CRIMINAL LAW ACT 1977, AS SUBSTITUTED BY S 73 CRIMINAL JUSTICE AND PUBLIC ORDER ACT 1994

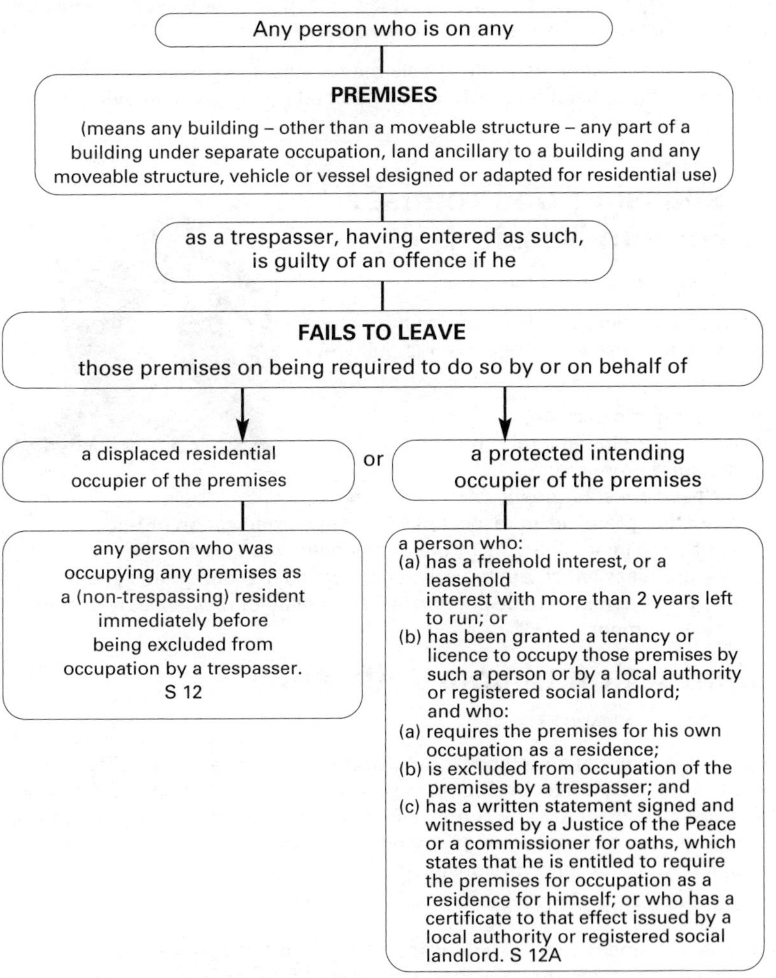

Defences: The premises were used mainly for non-residential purposes and offender was not on a residential part. Belief that person requiring him to leave was not a displaced residential occupier or protected intending occupier.

Trespassing With an Offensive Weapon

S 8 CRIMINAL LAW ACT 1977

A person who is on any premises as a trespasser, after having entered as such, is guilty of an offence if, without lawful authority or reasonable excuse, he has with him on the premises any weapon of offence.

'Weapon of offence' means any article made or adapted for use for causing injury to or incapacitating a person, or intended by the person having it with him for such use.

Trespassing on Premises of Foreign Missions etc

S 9 CRIMINAL LAW ACT 1977

A person who enters or is on any of the following premises as a trespasser is guilty of an offence:

(a) a diplomatic mission;
(b) a closed diplomatic mission;
(c) consular premises;
(d) a closed consular post;
(e) any other premises in respect of which any organisation or body is entitled to inviolability by or under any enactment; and
(f) any premises which are the private residence of a diplomatic agent or of any other person who is entitled to inviolability of residence by or under any enactment.

Obstruction of court officers

S 10 CRIMINAL LAW ACT 1977

A person is guilty of an offence if he resists or intentionally obstructs any person who is an officer of a court engaged in executing any process issued by the High Court or by any county court for the recovery of any premises or for the delivery of possession of any premises which have been entered or occupied without licence or consent.

'Officer of a court' means:

- any sheriff, under sheriff, deputy sheriff, bailiff or officer of a sheriff; and
- any bailiff or other person who is an officer of a county court

Affray

S 3 PUBLIC ORDER ACT 1986

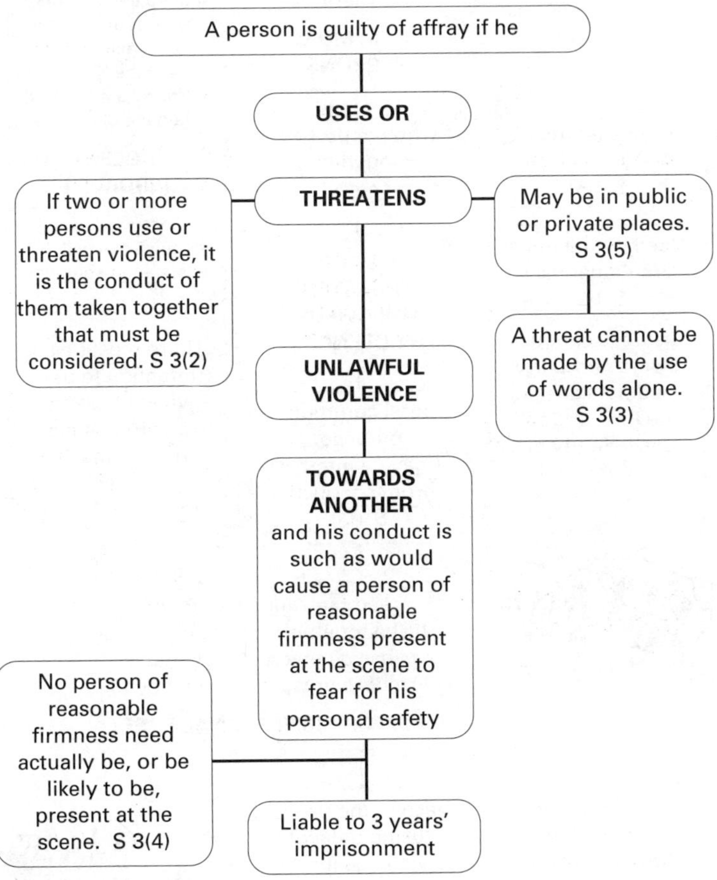

Riot / Violent Disorder

S 1 & 2 PUBLIC ORDER ACT 1986

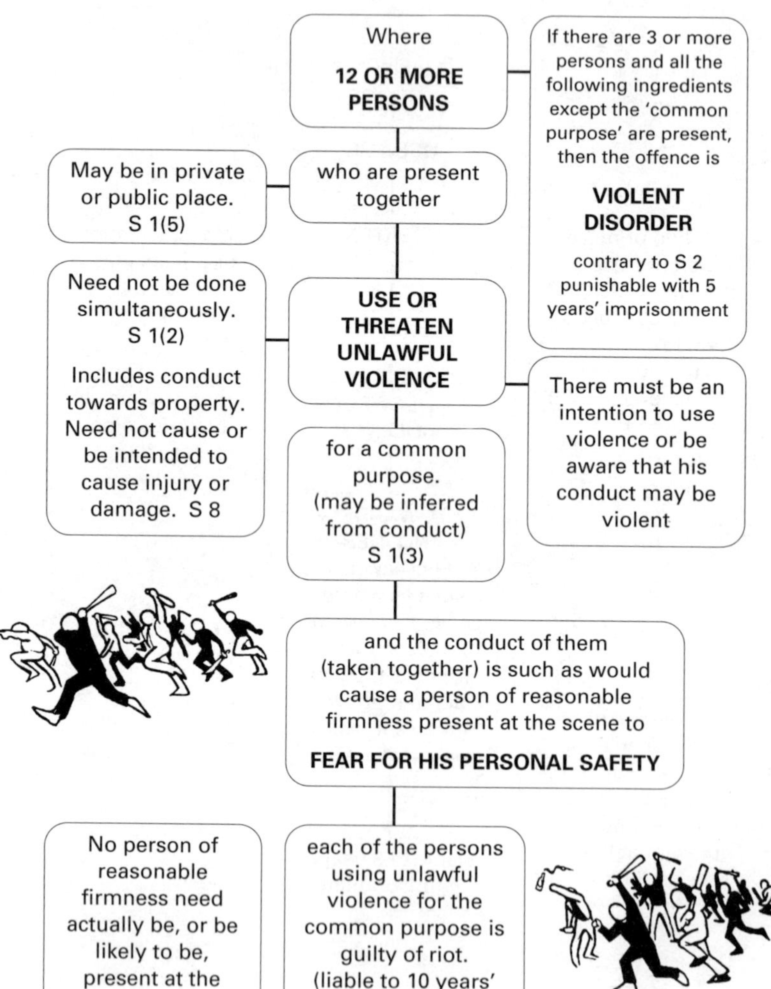

Public Meetings

S 1 PUBLIC MEETING ACT 1908

Any person who at a lawful

PUBLIC MEETING

acts in a disorderly manner for the purpose of preventing the transaction of the business of the meeting shall be guilty of an offence

It is the duty of the police to prevent any action likely to result in a breach of the peace. Refusing to desist is an obstruction of the police in the execution of their duty

POWER OF ENTRY

The police have a right to enter premises at which the public have been invited to attend if they reasonably apprehend a **breach of the peace**

Any person who incites a person to commit such an offence shall be guilty of a like offence

If a constable reasonably suspects a person to be committing such an offence he may, if requested by the chairman of the meeting, request the offender to give his name and address. If he fails or refuses or gives a false name and address he shall be guilty of an offence

Uniforms

S 1 PUBLIC ORDER ACT 1936

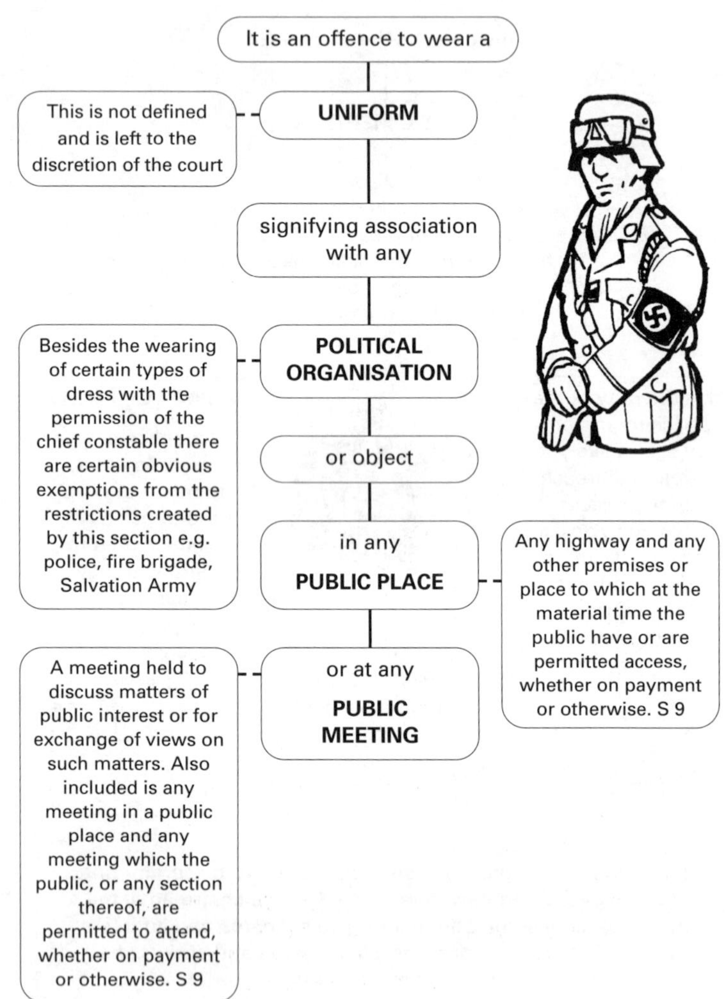

Organisations

S 2 PUBLIC ORDER ACT 1936

It is an offence to be involved in

CONTROLLING, MANAGING, ORGANISING, TRAINING OR EQUIPPING

any association of persons for the purpose of enabling them to be employed for

usurping the functions of the

POLICE OR ARMED FORCES

promoting any

POLITICAL OBJECT

by force, or arousing a fear that they are to be used for such a purpose

But this section does not prevent the employment of a reasonable number of stewards to assist in the preservation of order at any public meeting held on private premises, or giving them instruction in their duties, or giving them badges, etc.

Chemical Weapons

CHEMICAL WEAPONS ACT 1996

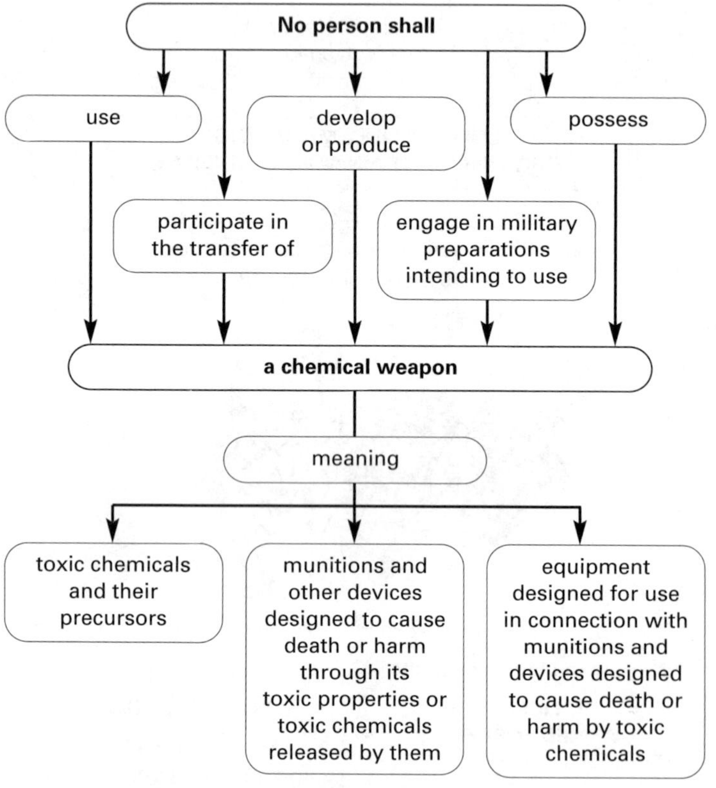

The Act describes various 'permitted purposes' i.e. peaceful purposes; purposes related to protection against toxic chemicals; legitimate military purposes; and purposes of enforcing the law.

Biological Weapons

S 1 BIOLOGICAL WEAPONS ACT 1974

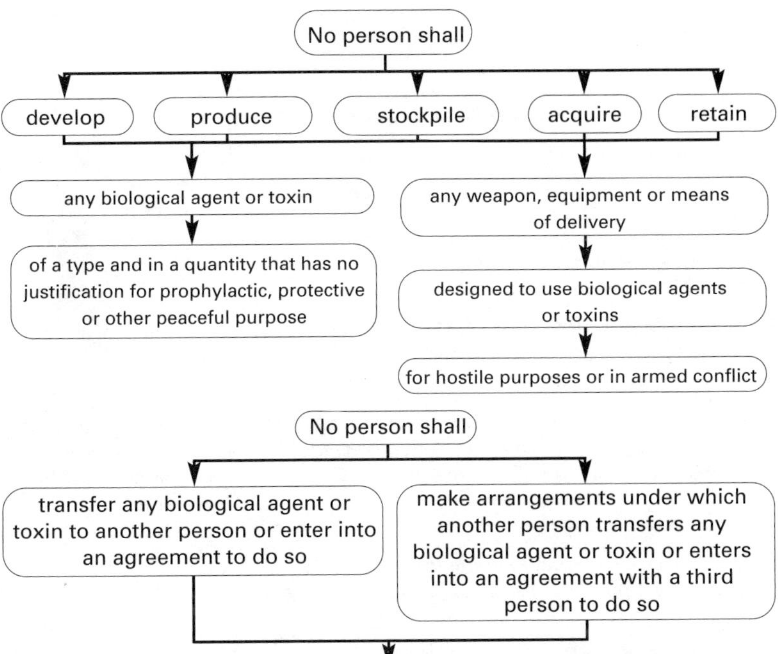

if the biological agent or toxin is likely to be kept or used (whether by the transferee or any other person) otherwise than for prophylactic, protective or other peaceful purposes and he knows or has reason to believe that that is the case.

'biological agent' means any microbial or other biological agent.

'toxin' means any toxin, whatever its origin or method of production.

Extraterritorial application section 1
Section 1 applies to acts done outside the UK, but only if done by a UK national, a Scottish partnership or a body incorporated under a law of part of the UK.

Terrorism – Interpretation

S 1 TERRORISM ACT 2000

Terrorism means the use or threat of action which

1. involves serious violence against a person,
2. involves serious damage to property,
3. endangers a person's life, other than that of the person committing the action,
4. creates a serious risk to the health or safety of the public or a section of the public, or
5. is designed seriously to interfere with or seriously to disrupt an electronic system

and the use or threat is designed to influence the government or an international government organisation or to intimidate the public, or a section of the public

But the use or threat of action which involves the use of firearms or explosives is 'terrorism' whether or not this part is satisfied

and the use or threat is made for the purpose of advancing a political, religious or ideological cause

'action' includes action outside the United Kingdom

the reference to any person or property means wherever situated

'public' includes the public of a country other than the United Kingdom

'government' means the government of the UK, or a part of the UK or of a country other than the UK

Terrorism – Offences

Ss 11–12 TERRORISM ACT 2000

Offences are committed in the following circumstances:

MEMBERSHIP (S 11): Belonging to or professing to belong to a proscribed organisation.

It is a **defence** to prove:
(a) that the organisation was not proscribed on the last occasion he became a member or began to profess to be a member, and
(b) that he has not taken part in the activities of the organisation at any time while it was proscribed.

SUPPORT (S 12(1)): Inviting support for a proscribed organisation, and the support is not, or is not restricted to, the provision of money or other property.

ARRANGING MEETINGS (S 12(2)): Arranging, managing or assisting in arranging or managing a meeting which he knows is:

(a) to support a proscribed organisation,
(b) to further the activities of a proscribed organisation, or
(c) to be addressed by a person who belongs or professes to belong to a proscribed organisation (but it would be a defence at a private meeting to prove that he had no reasonable cause to believe that the address would support a proscribed organisation or further its activities).

ADDRESSING MEETINGS (S 12(3)): Addressing a meeting and the purpose of the address is to encourage support for a proscribed organisation or to further its activities.

'Meeting' means a meeting of 3 or more persons, whether or not the public are admitted. A meeting is *private* if the public are not admitted.

For list of organisations which are **'proscribed'** see later.

Terrorism – Offences – Cont.

Ss 13 & 15 Terrorism Act 2000

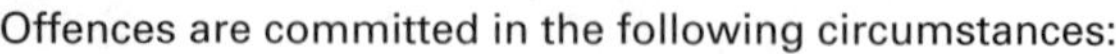

Offences are committed in the following circumstances:

UNIFORM (S 13)

In a public place if a person:

(a) wears an item of clothing, or
(b) wears, carries or displays an article,

in such a way or in such circumstances as to arouse reasonable suspicion that he is a member or supporter of a proscribed organisation.

A constable in Scotland may arrest a person if he has reasonable grounds to suspect the person to be guilty of this offence.

FUND-RAISING (S 15(1))

Inviting another to provide money or other property, intending that it should be used, or having reasonable cause to suspect that it may be used, for the purposes of terrorism.

RECEIVING MONEY OR OTHER PROPERTY (S 15(2))

Receiving money or other property intending that it should be used, or having reasonable cause to suspect that it may be used, for the purposes of terrorism.

PROVIDING MONEY OR OTHER PROPERTY (S 15(3))

Providing money or other property, knowing or having reasonable cause to suspect that it will or may be used for the purposes of terrorism.

Provision of money or other property means being given, lent or otherwise made available, whether or not for consideration.
Purposes of terrorism includes for the benefit of a proscribed organisation (see later).

The offence will be committed even if the act is done outside the UK (S 63)

For list of organisations which are **'proscribed'** see later.

(CONTINUED ON NEXT PA

Terrorism – Offences – Cont.

Ss 16–18 & 21 TERRORISM ACT 2000

Offences are committed in the following circumstances:

USE AND POSSESSION (S 16)

(a) Using money or other property for the purposes of terrorism.
(b) Possessing money or other property, intending that it should be used, or having reasonable cause to suspect that it may be used, for the purposes of terrorism.

FUNDING ARRANGEMENTS (S 17)

Entering into or becoming concerned in an arrangement as a result of which money or other property is made available or is to be made available to another, knowing or having reasonable cause to suspect that that it will or may be used for the purposes of terrorism.

The offence will be committed even if the act is done outside the UK (S 63)

MONEY LAUNDERING (S 18)

Entering into or becoming concerned in an arrangement which facilitates the retention or control by or on behalf of another person of terrorist property:
(a) by concealment,
(b) by removal from the jurisdiction,
(c) by transfer to nominees, or
(d) in any other way.
It is a defence to prove that he did not know and had no reasonable cause to suspect that the arrangement related to terrorist property.

'TERRORIST PROPERTY' MEANS:

(a) money or other property which is likely to be used for the purposes of terrorism (including any resources of a proscribed organisation),
(b) proceeds of the commission of acts of terrorism, and
(c) proceeds of the acts carried out for the purposes of terrorism (S 14).

CO-OPERATION WITH THE POLICE (S 21)

A person does not commit an offence under Ss 15 to 18 if he is acting with the express consent of a constable. Neither does he commit an offence under those sections by involvement in a transaction or arrangement relating to money or other property if he discloses to a constable:
(a) his suspicion or belief that the money or other property is terrorist property, and
(b) the information on which his suspicion or belief is based.

But the above only applies where he makes the disclosure:
(a) after he becomes concerned in the transaction,
(b) on his own initiative, and
(c) as soon as reasonably practicable.

Terrorism – Offences – Cont.

S 54 TERRORISM ACT 2000

Offences are committed in the following circumstances:

WEAPONS TRAINING (S 54)

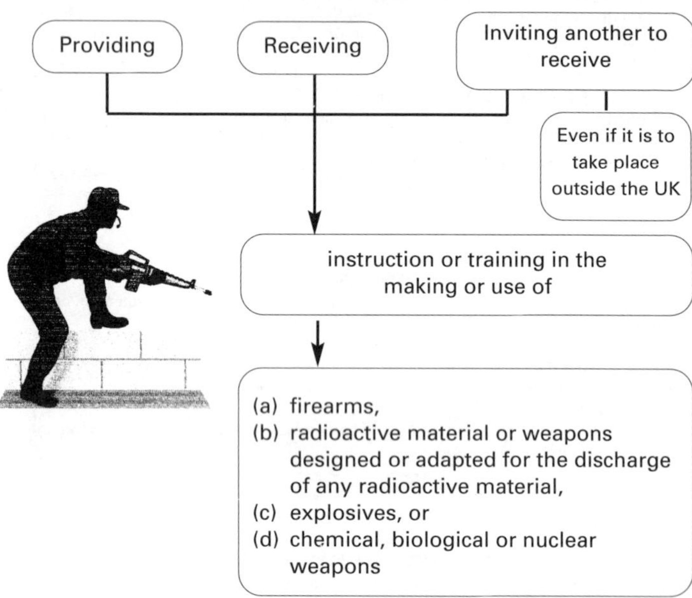

(a) firearms,
(b) radioactive material or weapons designed or adapted for the discharge of any radioactive material,
(c) explosives, or
(d) chemical, biological or nuclear weapons

'Providing instruction' and 'inviting' includes making it available either generally or to one or more specific persons.

It will be a defence to prove that his action or involvement was for a purpose other than terrorism.

(CONTINUED ON NEXT PAGE)

Terrorism – Offences – Cont.

Ss 56–58 TERRORISM ACT 2000

Offences are committed in the following circumstances:

DIRECTING ORGANISATIONS (S 56)
Directing, at any level, the activities of a terrorist organisation.

POSSESSION OF ARTICLES (S 57)
Possessing an article in circumstances which gave rise to a reasonable suspicion that it was connected with the commission, preparation or instigation of an act of terrorism.

It is a defence to prove that it was not for a terrorist purpose.
It will be assumed that the person *possessed* the article if it was:
(a) on any premises at the same time as that person, or
(b) on premises which the person occupied or habitually used other than as a member of the public,
unless he proves that he did not know of its presence or that he had no control over it.

'Article' includes substance and any other thing (S 121)

COLLECTION OF INFORMATION (S 58)

Collecting or making a record of

Possessing a document or record containing

information likely to be useful to a person committing or preparing an act of terrorism

'record' includes a photographic or electronic record

It is a defence to prove that he had a reasonable excuse for his action or possession.

Terrorism – Offences – Cont.

Ss 59–63 TERRORISM ACT 2000

Offences are committed in the following circumstances:

INCITING TERRORISM OVERSEAS (S 59)
Inciting a person to commit an act of terrorism wholly or partly outside the UK, and the act would, if committed in England and Wales, constitute one of the following offences:
(a) murder,
(b) wounding with intent (S 18 Offences Against the Person Act 1861),
(c) poisoning (S 23 or 24 of the above Act),
(d) explosions (S 28 or 29 of the above Act), or
(e) endangering life by damaging property (S 1 Criminal Damage Act 1971).

It is immaterial whether or not the person incited is in the UK at the time of the incitement.

ACTS OF TERRORISM OUTSIDE THE UK
By S 62 of the 2000 Act a person commits an offence if he does anything outside the UK as an act of terrorism or for the purposes of terrorism, and the action would, if done in the UK, constitute one of the following offences:

(a) causing explosions, etc (S 2, 3 or 5 Explosive Substances Act 1883)
(b) biological weapons (S 1 Biological Weapons Act 1974)
(c) chemical weapons (S 2 Chemical Weapons Act 1996)

By S 17 of the 2006 Act if a person does anything outside the UK, and his action, if done in a part of the UK, would constitute one of the below offences, he will be guilty in that part of the UK of the offence, irrespective of whether the person is a British Citizen or, in the case of a company, a company incorporated in a part of the UK. Proceedings may be taken in any part of the UK.The offences are-

Ss 1 – 6 of the 2006 Act relating to a Convention offence (encouragement, dissemination of publications, internet activities, preparatory acts, and training).

Ss 8 – 11 of the 2006 Act (attendance at place of training, making and possession of devices, etc, and threats).

S 11(1) of the 2000 Act (membership of proscribed organisations).

S 54 of the 2000 Act (weapons training).

Conspiracy, inciting, attempting, or aiding abetting counselling or procuring any of the above.

Terrorism – Offences – Cont.

S 1–3 TERRORISM ACT 2006

Offences are committed in the following circumstances:

ENCOURAGEMENT OF TERRORISM (S 1)

Publishing a statement or causing another to publish a statement, and at that time:

(a) intending members of the public to be directly or indirectly encouraged or otherwise induced by the statement to commit, prepare or instigate acts of terrorism or Convention offences*; or
(b) being reckless as to whether members of the public will be so encouraged or induced.

Such statements must be understood by members of the public as a direct or indirect encouragement or inducement to commit, prepare or instigate acts of terrorism or Convention offences*. 'Indirect' statements include those which:

(a) glorify the commission or preparation (whether in the past, in the future or generally) of such acts or offences; and
(b) from which members of the public could reasonably be expected to infer that what is being glorified is conduct which should be emulated by them in existing circumstances.

*For meaning see later under 'Convention offences'.

'Glorify' includes any form of praise or celebration, and cognate expressions are to be construed accordingly. (S 20)

Terrorism – Offences – Cont.

S 1–3 TERRORISM ACT 2006

DISSEMINATION OF TERRORIST PUBLICATIONS (S 2)

Intending that (or being reckless as to whether) his conduct will be a direct or indirect encouragement or other inducement to, or the provision of assistance in, the commission, preparation or instigation of acts of terrorism:

(a) distributes or circulates a terrorist publication;
(b) gives, sells or lends such a publication;
(c) offers such a publication for sale or loan;
(d) provides a service to others that enables them to obtain, read, listen to or look at such a publication, or to acquire it by means of a gift, sale or loan;
(e) transmits the contents of such a publication electronically; or
(f) has such a publication in his possession with a view to its becoming the subject of conduct falling within (a) to (e).

It will be a 'terrorist publication' if matter contained in it is likely:

(a) to be understood, by some or all of the persons to whom it is or may become available, as a direct or indirect encouragement or other inducement to them to the commission, preparation or instigation of acts of terrorism; or
(b) to be useful in the commission or preparation of such acts and to be understood, by some or all of those persons, as being wholly or mainly for such use.

For the meaning of 'indirect' see explanation under S 1 above.

Where the statement or record mentioned above involves a service provided electronically, a constable may serve a notice on the person providing the service declaring that the statement or record is terrorist related and requiring it not to be available to the public within two working days of the notice being served. Failure to comply will result in the statement or record being regarded as having the endorsement of that person. (S 3)

Terrorism – Offences – Cont.

S 5 & 6 TERRORISM ACT 2006

Offences are committed in the following circumstances

PREPARATION OF TERRORIST ACTS (S 5)

With the intention of committing acts of terrorism or assisting another to do so, engaging in any conduct in preparation for giving effect to his intention, whether relating to one or more particular acts of terrorism, acts of terrorism of a particular description or acts of terrorism generally.

TRAINING FOR TERRORISM (S 6)

Providing instruction or training in any of the skills mentioned below, and at the time knowing that a person receiving it intends to use the skills:

(a) for or in connection with the commission or preparation of acts of terrorism or Convention offences*; or
(b) for assisting the commission or preparation by others of such acts or offences.

It is also an offence to receive training in the above circumstances.

The skills mentioned above are:

(a) the making, handling or use of a noxious substance, or of substances of a description of such substances;
(b) the use of any method or technique for doing anything else that is capable of being done for the purposes of terrorism, in connection with the commission or preparation of an act of terrorism or Convention offence* or in connection with assisting the commission or preparation by another of such an act or offence; and
(c) the design or adaptation for the purposes of terrorism, or in connection with the commission or preparation of an act of terrorism or Convention offence*, of any method or technique for doing anything.

It is irrelevant for the purposes of the above offences whether:

(a) any instruction or training is provided to one or more persons or generally;
(b) the acts or offences consist of one or more particular acts of terrorism or Convention offences*, acts of terrorism or Convention offences* of a particular description or acts of terrorism or Convention offences* generally; and
(c) assistance that the person intends to provide to others is intended to be provided to one or more particular persons or to one or more persons whose identities are not yet known.

*For meaning see later under 'Convention offences'.

Terrorism – Offences – Cont.

S 8 & 9 TERRORISM ACT 2006

Offences are committed in the following circumstances:

ATTENDANCE AT A PLACE FOR TERRORIST TRAINING (S 8)

(a) attending at any place, whether in the UK or elsewhere;
(b) whilst there, instruction or training of the type mentioned in S 6 of this Act, or weapons training under S 54 of the 2000 Act (see earlier) is provided;
(c) instruction or training is provided there wholly or partly for purposes connected with the commission or preparation of acts of terrorism or Convention offences*; and
(d) either (i) he knows or believes that instruction or training is being provided wholly or partly for purposes connected with the commission or preparation of acts of terrorism or Convention offences*, or (ii) a person attending at that place throughout the period of that person's attendance could not reasonably have failed to understand that instruction or training was being provided for such purposes.

It is immaterial whether:

(a) the person concerned receives the instruction or training himself; and
(b) the instruction or training is provided for purposes connected with one or more particular acts of terrorism or Convention offences*, acts of terrorism or Convention offences* of a particular description or acts of terrorism or Convention offences* generally.

*For meaning see later under 'Convention offences'.

MAKING AND POSSESSION OF DEVICES OR MATERIALS (S 9)

(a) makes or has in his possession a radioactive device, or
(b) has in his possession radioactive material,

with the intention of using the device or material in the course of or in connection with the commission or preparation of an act of terrorism or for the purposes of terrorism, or of making it available to be so used.

It is irrelevant whether the act of terrorism to which an intention relates is a particular act of terrorism, an act of terrorism of a particular description or an act of terrorism generally.

Terrorism – Offences – Cont.

S 10 & 11 TERRORISM ACT 2006

Misuse of devices or material, misuse and damage of facilities (S 10) and terrorist threats relating to devices, materials or facilities (S 11)

Offences are committed in the following circumstances:

In the course of or in connection with the commission of an act of terrorism or for the purposes of terrorism

→ using a radioactive device or radioactive material (S 10); or

using or damaging a nuclear facility in a manner which causes a release of radioactive material, or creates or increases a risk that such material will be released (S 10); or

→ making a demand:

(a) for the supply to himself or to another of a radioactive device or of radioactive material;
(b) for a nuclear facility to be made available to himself or to another; or
(c) for access to such a facility to be given to himself or to another

and (i) he supports the demand with a threat that he or another will take action if the demand is not met, and (ii) the circumstances and manner of the threat are such that it is reasonable for the person to whom it is made to assume there is a real risk that the threat will be carried out if the demand is not met (S 10); or

→ making a threat:

(a) to use radioactive material;
(b) to use a radioactive device; or
(c) to use or damage a nuclear facility in a manner that releases radioactive material or creates or increases a risk that such material will be released

and the circumstances and manner of the threat are such that it is reasonable for the person to whom it is made to assume there is a real risk that the threat will be carried out if the demand is not met (S 11).

Nuclear facility means:

(a) a nuclear reactor, including a reactor installed in or on any transportation device for use as an energy source in order to propel it or for any other purpose; or
(b) a plant or conveyance being used for the production, storage, processing or transport of radioactive material.

Terrorism – Offences – Cont.

S 20 & SCHED. 1 TERRORISM ACT 2006

CONVENTION OFFENCE

This means an offence listed below or an equivalent offence under the law of a country or territory outside the UK.

Act	Section	Description
Offences against the Person Act 1861*	28–30	Causing injury by explosions and handling or placing explosives.
Explosive Substances Act 1883*	2	Causing an explosion likely to endanger life.
	3	Preparation of explosions.
	5	Ancillary offences.
Biological Weapons Act 1974	1	Development etc. of biological weapons.
Internationally Protected Persons Act 1978*	1(1)(a)	Attacks against protected persons.
	1(1)(b)	Attacks on relevant premises or vehicle.
	1(3)	Threats in relation to protected persons.
Taking of Hostages Act 1982	1	Hostage-taking.
Aviation Security Act 1982	1	Hijacking.
	2	Destroying, damaging or endangering safety of aircraft.
	3	Other acts endangering safety of aircraft.
	6(2)	Ancillary offences.
Nuclear Material (Offences) Act 1983	1(1)	Offences relating to nuclear material.
	2	Preparatory acts and threats relating to nuclear material.

(CONTINUED ON NEXT PAGE)

Terrorism – Offences – Cont.

S 20 & SCHED. 1 TERRORISM ACT 2006

Act	Section	Description
Aviation and Maritime Security Act 1990	1	Endangering safety at aerodromes.
	9	Hijacking of ships.
	10	Seizing or exercising control of fixed platforms.
	11	Destroying ships or fixed platforms or endangering their safety.
	12	Other acts endangering or likely to endanger safe navigation.
	13	Threats relating to ships or fixed platforms.
	14	Ancillary offences.
Chemical Weapons Act 1996	2	Development etc. of chemical weapons.
Terrorism Act 2000	15	Terrorist fund-raising.
	16	Use or possession of terrorist funds.
	17	Funding arrangements for terrorism.
	18	Money laundering of terrorist funds.
	56	Directing a terrorist organisation.
Anti-terrorism, Crime and Security Act 2001	47	Use, development etc. of nuclear weapons.
Conspiracy, incitement, attempts, and aiding, abetting, counselling or procuring any Convention offence.		

* In Scotland it will only be a Convention offence if it is an act of terrorism, or done for the purposes of terrorism.

Terrorism – Disclosure of Information

Ss 19 & 20, TERRORISM ACT 2000

Where a person :

(a) believes or suspects that another person has committed an offence under sections 15 to 18 (see earlier), and
(b) bases his belief or suspicion on information which comes to his attention in the course of a trade, profession, business or employment

the person commits an offence if he does not disclose to a constable as soon as reasonably practicable:

(a) his belief or suspicion, and
(b) the information on which it is based.

This does not require disclosure by a professional legal adviser of
(a) information which he obtains in privileged circumstances, or
(b) a belief or suspicion based on information which he obtains in privileged circumstances.

This does not apply if the information came to the person in the course of a business in the regulated sector. (Sched 3A lists the types of business which are 'regulated'. These include national savings, credit unions, banking, building societies, investments, life insurance, etc.) However, a similar offence of failure to disclose in the regulated sector is provided by section 21 A.

but it is a defence to prove that he had a reasonable excuse for not making the disclosure.
It is also a defence where:
(a) a person is in employment,
(b) his employer has established a procedure for the making of disclosures of such matters, and
(c) he is charged with such an offence,
to prove that he disclosed the matters in accordance with the procedure.

A person may make such disclosures to a constable notwithstanding any restriction on disclosing it imposed by statute or otherwise (S 20).

Terrorism – Investigations

Ss 33–39 TERRORISM ACT 2000

CORDONED AREAS (Ss 33–36)

If considered expedient for the purposes of a terrorist investigation, a superintendent (or lower rank in the case of urgency) may designate an area to be cordoned.

A constable in uniform may:

(a) order a person in a cordoned area to leave it immediately;
(b) order a person immediately to leave premises which are wholly or partly in or adjacent to a cordoned area;
(c) order the driver or person in charge of a vehicle in a cordoned area to move it from the area immediately;
(d) arrange for the removal of a vehicle from a cordoned area;
(e) arrange for the movement of a vehicle within a cordoned area;
(f) prohibit or restrict access to a cordoned area by pedestrians or vehicles.

A person commits an offence if he fails to comply with an order, prohibition or restriction imposed as above. But it is a defence to prove that he had a reasonable excuse for his failure.

FAILURE TO DISCLOSE INFORMATION (S 38B)

Where a person has information which he knows or believes might be of material assistance:

(a) in preventing an act of terrorism, or
(b) in securing the apprehension, prosecution or conviction of another person in the UK, for an offence of terrorism,

he commits an offence if he does not disclose the information as soon as reasonably practicable to a constable or (in Northern Ireland) a member of HM Forces.

It is a defence to prove that he had a reasonable excuse for not making the disclosure.

DISCLOSURE OF INFORMATION (S 39)

Where a person knows or has reasonable cause to suspect that a constable is conducting or proposes to conduct a terrorist investigation, he commits an offence if he:

(a) discloses to another anything which is likely to prejudice an investigation, or
(b) interferes with material which is likely to be relevant to the investigation.

He would also commit an offence by a similar disclosure or interference where a disclosure had been or was to be made under the aforementioned sections 19, 21 or 38B.

It would be a defence to prove that:

(a) he did not know and had no reasonable cause to suspect that the disclosure or interference was likely to affect a terrorist investigation, or
(b) that he had a reasonable excuse for the disclosure or interference.

An offence would not be committed in the case of a professional legal adviser.

Terrorism – Police Powers

Ss 40–43 TERRORISM ACT 2000, S 28 TERRORISM ACT 2006

ARREST WITHOUT WARRANT (S 41)
A constable may arrest without warrant anyone he reasonably suspects to be a terrorist.
'Terrorist' is defined as a person who:
(a) has committed any offence under any of sections 11 (membership), 12 (support), 15 (fund raising), 16 (use and possession), 17 (funding), 18 (money laundering), 54 (weapon training), 56 (directing organisations), 57 (possession of articles), 58 (collection of information), 59 (inciting overseas), 60 (Northern Ireland), 61 (Scotland), 62 (bombing outside UK) or 63 (finance outside UK), or
(b) is or has been concerned in the commission, preparation or instigation of acts of terrorism.

SEARCH OF PREMISES
A justice of the peace may issue a warrant for a constable to search specified premises if he is satisfied that there are reasonable grounds to suspect that a person to whom para (b) in the above definition applies is to be found there. (S 42 2000 Act).

A warrant may also be issued to enter and search premises and seize anything found there which is believed to be a terrorist publication subject to S 2 of the 2006 Act. Such force as is necessary may be used in exercising the power. (S 28 2006 Act)

SEARCH OF PERSONS (S 43)
A constable may stop and search a person whom he reasonably suspects to be a terrorist (see above definition) or a person arrested under S 41 above to discover whether he has in his possession anything which may constitute evidence that he is a terrorist.
The search must be carried out by a person of the same sex.
A constable may seize and retain anything discovered in the course of the search which he reasonably suspects may constitute evidence that the person is a terrorist.

GENERAL (S 114)
Any power conferred by this Act is additional to any other powers at common law or other enactment, and will not affect those powers. A constable may use reasonable force if necessary in exercising the powers under this Act.

Terrorism – Stop and Search

Ss 44–45 TERRORISM ACT 2000

A constable in uniform may be authorised to **stop**

a vehicle

and to *search*:

(a) the vehicle;

(b) the driver of the vehicle;

(c) a passenger in the vehicle;

(d) anything in or on the vehicle or carried by the driver or a passenger.

a pedestrian

and to *search*:

(a) the pedestrian;

(b) anything carried by him.

Authorisation may be given:

by an ACC, a commander in London or the metropolitan area, or an ACC in Northern Ireland.

Authorisation may be given by an ACC of the BTP or MOD police but only in relation to BTP or MOD premises respectively.

if he considers it expedient for the prevention of acts of terrorism.

Exercise of Power

The power may be exercised only for the purpose of searching for articles of a kind which could be used in connection with terrorism, whether or not the constable has grounds for suspecting the presence of such articles.

Seizure

Articles which are discovered and which are reasonably suspected to be intended to be used in connection with terrorism may be seized and retained.

Removal of Clothing

A constable may not require a person to remove any clothing in public except headgear, footwear, an outer coat, a jacket or gloves.

Detention

A constable may detain the person or vehicle for such time as is reasonably required to permit the search to be carried out.

Offences

A person will be guilty of an offence if he fails to stop, or if he fails to stop the vehicle, when required to do so, or if he wilfully obstructs the constable.

Terrorism – Restrictions on Parking

Ss 48–52 TERRORISM ACT 2000

A constable in uniform may be authorised to prohibit or restrict the parking of vehicles on a road specified in the authorisation.

Authorisation may be given
by an ACC, a commander in London or the metropolitan area, or an ACC in Northern Ireland, if he considers it expedient for the prevention of acts of terrorism.

Exercise of Power
The power is exercised by placing a traffic sign on the road concerned. A constable may suspend a parking place and this will be treated as a restriction for the purposes of removal of vehicles illegally parked or for the purposes of committing offences (see below).

Duration of Authorisation
The period of authorisation shall not exceed 28 days but it may be renewed.

Offences
A person commits an offence if:

(a) he parks a vehicle in contravention of a prohibition or restriction.

(b) he is the driver or other person in charge of the vehicle which has been permitted to remain at rest in contravention of a prohibition or restriction and he fails to remove the vehicle when ordered to do so by a constable in uniform.

It will be a defence to prove that he had a reasonable excuse for the act or omission. Possession of a disabled person's badge shall not itself constitute a reasonable excuse.

No Parking

Terrorism – Proscribed Organisations

S 3 & SCHED 2 TERRORISM ACT 2000

An organisation is **'proscribed'** if it is mentioned in the list below or operates under the same name as an organisation so mentioned:

Abu Nidal Organisation
Abu Sayyaf Group
Al-Gama'at al-Islamiya
Al-Ghurabaa
Al Ittihad Al Islamia
Al-Qaeda
Ansar Al Islam
Ansar Al Sunna
Armed Islamic Group (GIA)
Asbat Al-Ansar
Babbar Khalsa
Baluchistan Liberation Army.
Basque Homeland and Liberty (ETA)
Cumann na mBan
Egyptian Islamic Jihad
Fianna na hEireann
Groupe Islamique Combattant Marocain
Hamas-Izz al-Din al-Qassem Brigades
Harakat Mujahideen
Harakat-ul-Jihad-ul-Islami
Harakat-ul-Jihad-ul-Islami (Bangladesh)
Harakat-ul-Mujahideen/Almi
Hezb-e Islami Gulbuddin
Hizballah External Security Organisation
International Sikh Youth Federation
Islamic Army of Aden
Islamic Jihad Union
Islamic Movement of Uzbekistan
Jaish e Mohammed
Jamaat ul-Furquan
Jemaah Islamiyah
Jundallah
Khuddam ul-Islam
Kurdistan Worker's Party (PKK)
(also known as 'Kongra Gele Kurdistan' and 'KADEK').
Lashkar-e Jhangvi
Lashkar e Tayyaba
Liberation Tigers of Tamil Eelam (LTTE)
Libyan Islamic Fighting Group
Mujaheddin e Khalq
Palestinian Islamic Jihad – Shaqaqi
Revolutionary Teople's Liberation Party – Front (DHKP-C)
Salafist Group for Call and Combat (GSPC)
Saor Eire
Sipah-e Sahaba Pakistan
Teyrebaz Azadiye Kurdistan
The Continuity Army Council
The Irish National Liberation Army
The Irish People's Liberation Organisation
The Irish Republican Army
The Loyalist Volunteer Force
The Orange Volunteers
The Red Hand Commando
The Red Hand Defenders
The Saved Sect
The Ulster Defence Association
The Ulster Freedom Fighters
The Ulster Volunteer Force
17 November Revolutionary Organisation (N17)

Terrorism – Nuclear Weapons

S 47 ANTI-TERRORISM, CRIME AND SECURITY ACT 2001

A person commits an offence if he:

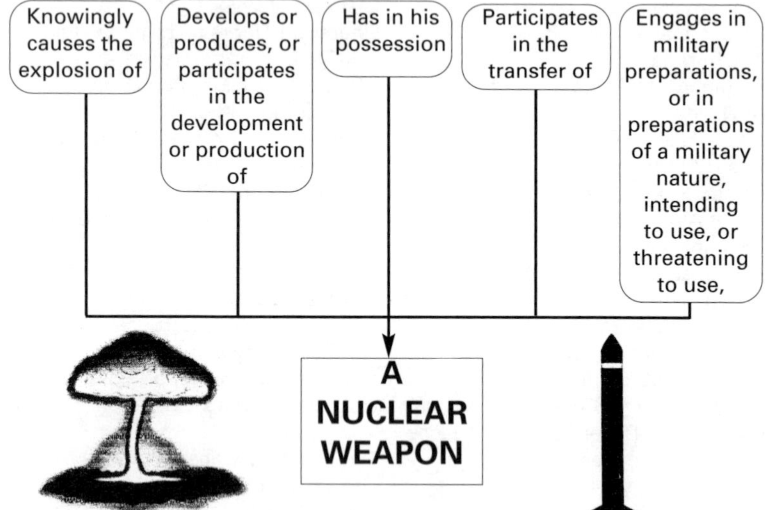

'Participates in the development or production' means doing any act which:
(a) facilitates the development by another of the capability to produce or use, a nuclear weapon; or
(b) facilitates the making by another of a nuclear weapon
knowing or having reason to believe that his act has (or will have) that effect.

'Participates in the transfer' means:
(a) buying or otherwise acquiring it or agreeing with another to do so;
(b) selling or otherwise disposing of it or agreeing with another to do so; or
(c) making arrangements under which another person either acquires or disposes of it or agrees with a third person to do so.

Terrorism – Use of Noxious Substances

S 113 ANTI-TERRORISM, CRIME AND SECURITY ACT 2001

A person commits an offence if he takes any action which:

involves the use of a noxious substance or other noxious thing;

which has or is likely to have the effect of:

(a) causing serious violence against a person anywhere in the world;
(b) causing serious damage to real or personal property anywhere in the world;
(c) endangers human life or creates a serious risk to the health or safety of the public or a section of the public; or
(d) induces in members of the public the fear that the action is likely to endanger their lives or create a serious risk to their health or safety;

but any effect on the person taking the action is to be disregarded; and

is designed to influence a government or an international government organisation or to intimidate the public or a section of the public

An offence will also be committed if a person:

(a) makes a threat that he or another will take any action which constitutes the above offence; and
(b) intends thereby to induce in a person anywhere in the world the fear that the threat is likely to be carried out.

'substance' includes any biological agent and any other natural or artificial substance (whatever its form, origin or method of production).
'government' means the government of the UK, of a part of the UK or of a country other than the UK.
'public' includes the public of a country other than the UK.

Terrorism – Hoaxes Involving Noxious Substances

S 114 ANTI-TERRORISM, CRIME AND SECURITY ACT 2001

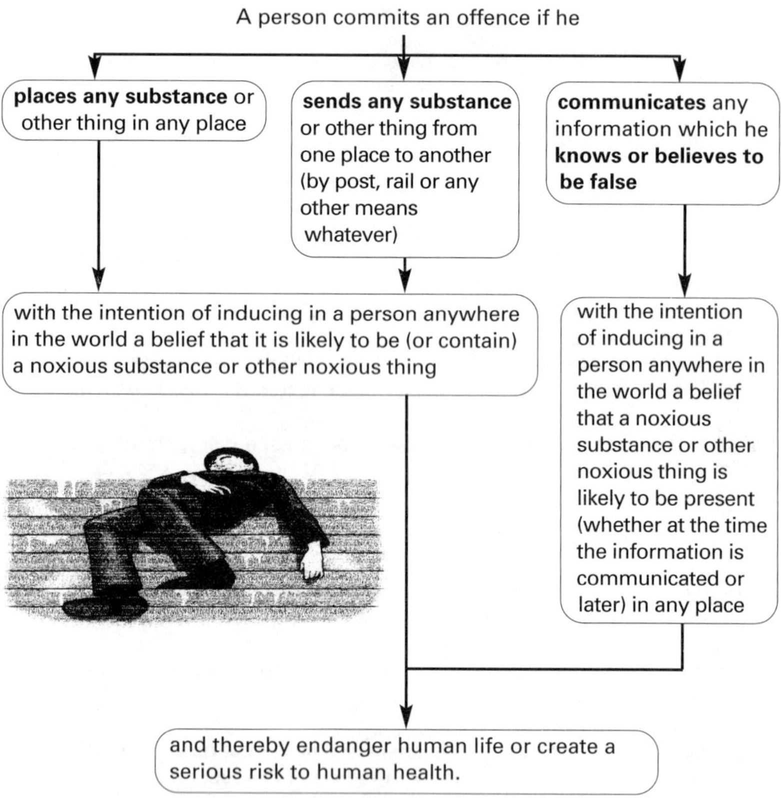

For meaning of **'substance'** see previous page.

Terrorism – Control Orders

PREVENTION OF TERRORISM ACT 2005

S 1. A **Control Order** means an order against an individual that imposes **obligations** on him for purposes connected with protecting members of the public from a risk of terrorism. It may be made by the Secretary of State or a court.

Obligations may include a **prohibition or restriction** on:

(a) possession or use of specified articles or substances;
(b) specified services or specified facilities, or specified activities;
(c) work, occupation or business;
(d) association or communication with other persons;
(e) place of residence, or to whom he gives access;
(f) presence at specified places, areas, times and days;
(g) movement to, from or within the UK;

or the following **requirements**:

(h) to comply with restrictions on other movements for a period not exceeding 24 hours;
(i) to surrender his passport or anything specified in the order;
(j) to give access to specified persons to his residence or other place;
(k) to allow specified persons to search premises to ascertain contravention of obligations;
(l) to allow specified persons to remove anything found in the premises;
(m) to allow himself to be photographed;
(n) to co-operate with specified arrangements to allow his movements, communications or other activities to be monitored by electronic or other means;
(o) to comply with a demand to provide information to a specified person;
(p) to report to a specified person at specified times and places.

S 5. **Arrest and detention pending derogating control order** may be made by a constable if the Secretary of State has made an application to the court for such an order, and the constable believes arrest is necessary to ensure he is available to be given notice of the order. He must be taken to a designated place, where he may be held for not more than 48 hours (extendable by a court for a further 48 hours)

S 9. **Offences:**

(a) contravention of an obligation imposed by a control order;
(b) failing to report to a specified person on his re-entry to the UK after an order has expired;
(c) obstructing a person carrying out a search of premises for a person on whom a notice of a control order is to be served.

Fraudulent Use Of Telecommunications System

Ss 42 TELECOMMUNICATIONS ACT 1984

A person who dishonestly obtains a licensed telecommunications service with intent to avoid payment of any charge shall be guilty of an offence.

Possession of Equipment for Fraudulent Use

S 42A

Where a person has in his custody or under his control anything which may be used to obtain a licensed telecommunications service, he commits an offence if he intends:

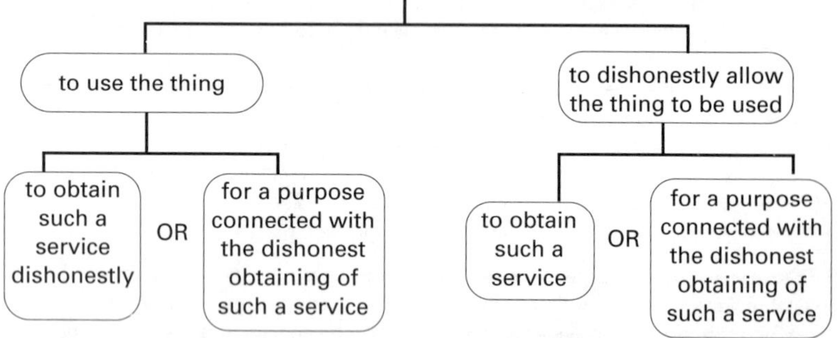

An offence is also committed if a person supplies or offers to supply anything which may be used for the above purposes if he knows or believes the person to whom it is supplied or offered intends to use it for such a purpose.

Re-programming Mobile Telephone

MOBILE TELEPHONES RE-PROGRAMMING ACT 2002
VIOLENT CRIME REDUCTION ACT 2006

Changing or interfering with a unique device identifier (S 1)

A person commits an offence if he-
- (a) changes a unique device identifier;
- (b) interferes with the operation of a unique device identifier;
- (c) offers or agrees to change, or interfere with the operation of, a unique device identifier; or
- (d) offers or agrees to arrange for another person to change, or interfere with the operation of, a unique device identifier.

Possession or supply of equipment, etc (S 2)

A person commits an offence if he-
- (a) has in his custody or under his control anything which may be used for the purpose of changing or interfering with the operation of a unique device identifier; and
- (b) intends to use the thing unlawfully for that purpose or allow it to be used unlawfully for that purpose.

A person commits an offence if he-
- (a) supplies anything which may be used for the purpose of changing or interfering with the operation of a unique device identifier; and
- (b) he knows or believes that the person to whom the thing is supplied intends to use it unlawfully for that purpose or to allow it to be used unlawfully for that purpose.

A person commits an offence if he-
- (a) offers to supply anything which may be used for the purpose of changing or interfering with the operation of a unique device identifier; and
- (b) he knows or believes that the person to whom the thing is offered intends if it is supplied to him to use it unlawfully for that purpose or to allow it to be used unlawfully for that purpose.

'Unique device identifier' means an electronic equipment identifier which is unique to a mobile wireless communications device.
'Unlawfully' means for the purpose of committing an offence under S 1.

Postal Offences

POSTAL SERVICES ACT 2000

Prohibition of Advertisements
(S 86)

A person commits an offence if, without due authority:

- he affixes any advertisement, document, board or thing in or on any universal postal service post office, letter box or other property belonging to, or used by, a universal postal service provider, or
- he paints or in any way disfigures any such office, box or property.

Prohibition on sending certain articles by post (S 85)

A person commits an offence if he sends by post a postal packet:

- which encloses any creature, article or thing of any kind which is likely to injure other postal packets in course of their transmission by post or any person engaged in the business of a postal operator (does not apply to things allowed by the operator); 
- which encloses any indecent or obscene print, painting, photograph, lithograph, engraving, cinematograph film or other record of a picture or pictures, book, card or written communication, or any other indecent or obscene article; or
- which has on the packet, or on the cover of the packet, any words, marks or designs which are of an indecent or obscene character.

Malicious Communications

S 1 MALICIOUS COMMUNICATIONS ACT 1988 (AS AMENDED BY THE CRIMINAL JUSTICE AND POLICE ACT 2001)

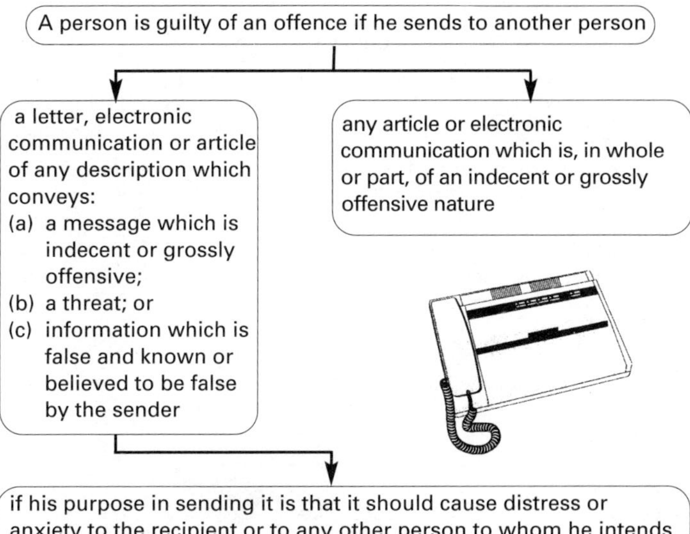

A person is guilty of an offence if he sends to another person

a letter, electronic communication or article of any description which conveys:

(a) a message which is indecent or grossly offensive;
(b) a threat; or
(c) information which is false and known or believed to be false by the sender

any article or electronic communication which is, in whole or part, of an indecent or grossly offensive nature

if his purpose in sending it is that it should cause distress or anxiety to the recipient or to any other person to whom he intends that it should be communicated.

But, in relation to (b) he will not be guilty if he shows:

(a) that the threat was used to reinforce a demand made by him on reasonable grounds; and
(b) that he believed, on reasonable grounds, that the use of the threat was a proper means of reinforcing the demand.

'Electronic communication' includes:

(a) any oral or other communication by means of a telecommunication system; and
(b) any communication (however sent) that is in electronic form.

'Sends' includes delivering or transmitting and causing to be sent, delivered or transmitted.

Improper Use of Public Telecommunication System

S 43 TELECOMMUNICATIONS ACT 1984

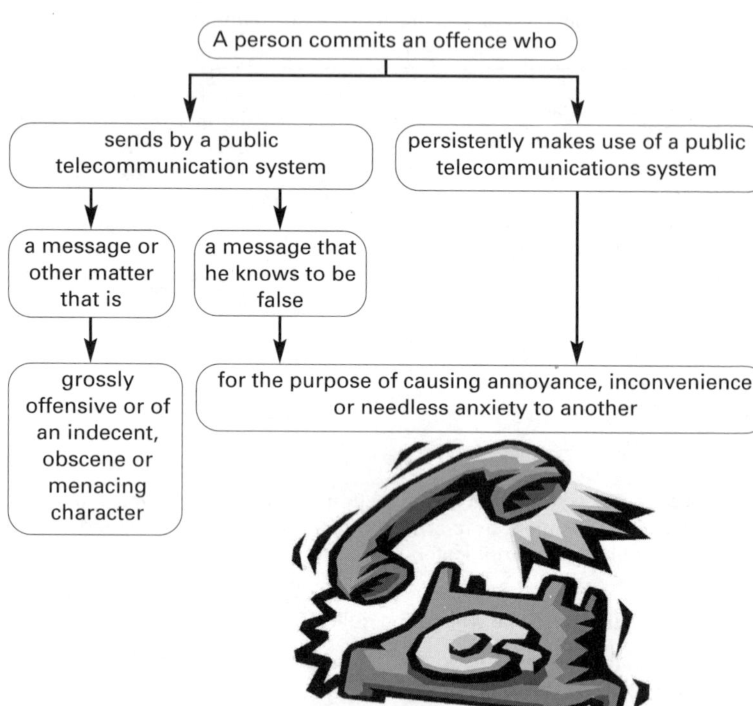

'Telecommunications system' means a system for the conveyance, through the agency of electric, magnetic, electromagnetic, electrochemical or electromechanical energy, of:

(a) speech, music and other sounds;
(b) visual images;
(c) signals serving for the impartation of any matter otherwise than in the form of sounds or visual images; or
(d) signals serving for the actuation or control of machinery or apparatus.

Bomb Hoaxes

S 51 CRIMINAL LAW ACT 1977

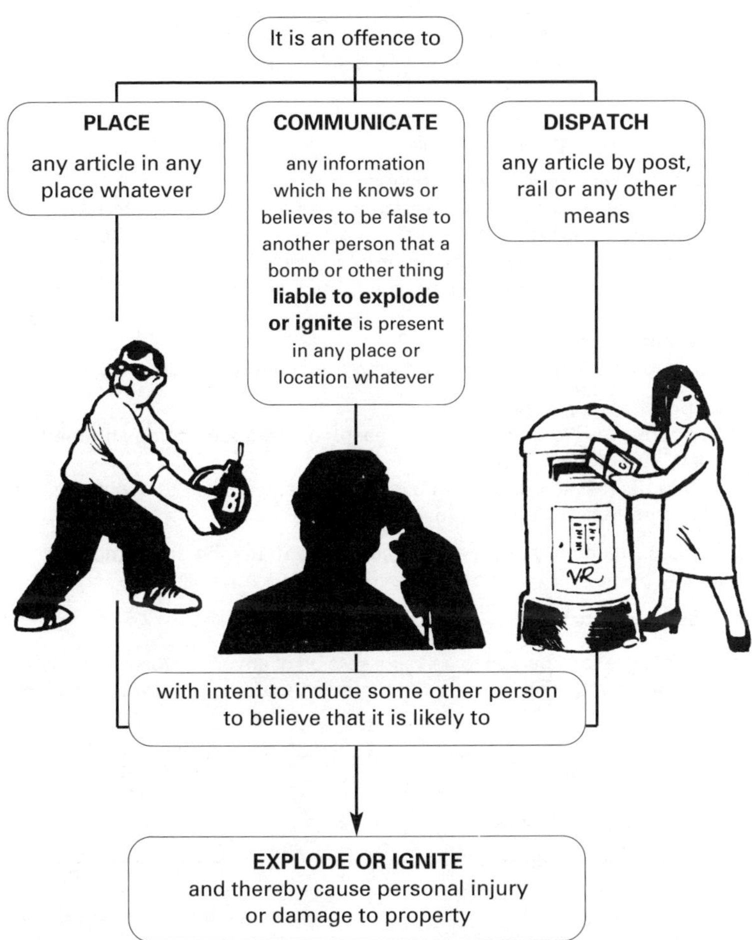

Contamination of Goods

S 38 PUBLIC ORDER ACT 1986

Contamination etc

(1) It is an offence for a person, with the intention of causing:

(a) public alarm or anxiety;
(b) injury to members of the public consuming or using the goods;
(c) economic loss to any person by reason of the goods being shunned by members of the public; or
(d) economic loss to any person by reason of steps taken to avoid any such alarm or anxiety, injury or loss,

- to contaminate or interfere with goods, or
- make it appear that goods have been contaminated or interfered with, or
- to place goods which have been contaminated or interfered with, or which appear to have been contaminated or interfered with, in a place where goods of that description are consumed, used, sold or otherwise supplied.

Threats and claims

(2) It is also an offence for a person with the intention of causing:

(a) public alarm or anxiety;
(b) economic loss to any person by reason of the goods being shunned by members of the public; or
(c) economic loss to any person by reason of steps taken to avoid any such alarm or anxiety, injury or loss,

to threaten that he or another will do, or to claim that he or another has done, any of the acts mentioned above.

Possession of articles

It is an offence for a person to be in possession of any of the following articles with a view to the commission of an offence under subsection (1) above:

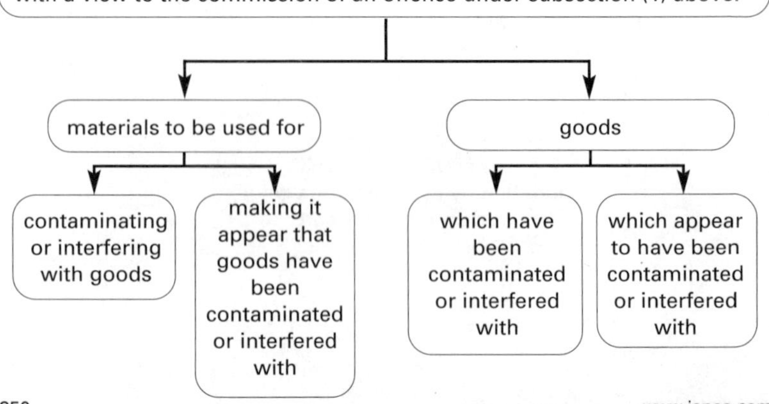

Taxi Touts

S 167 CRIMINAL JUSTICE AND PUBLIC ORDER ACT 1994

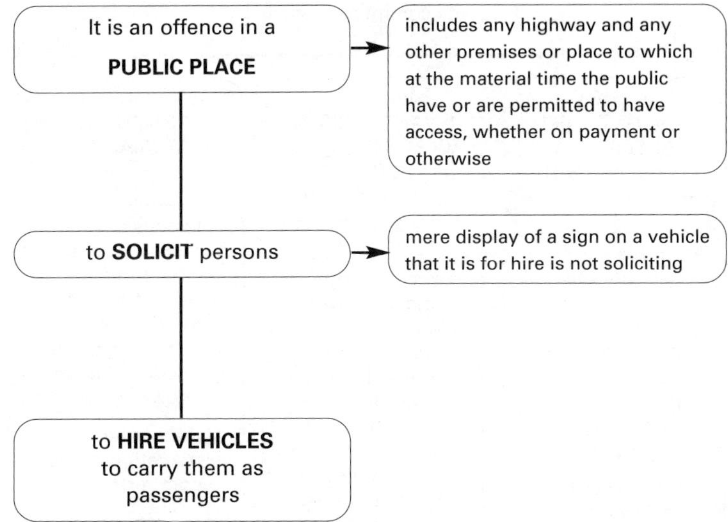

No offence is committed where sharing of taxis is permitted under S 10 of the Transport Act 1985 (schemes for sharing taxis).

It is a defence if soliciting for passengers to be carried at separate fares by public service vehicles on behalf of, and with the authority of, the holder of a PSV operator's licence.

Computer Misuse

COMPUTER MISUSE ACT 1990

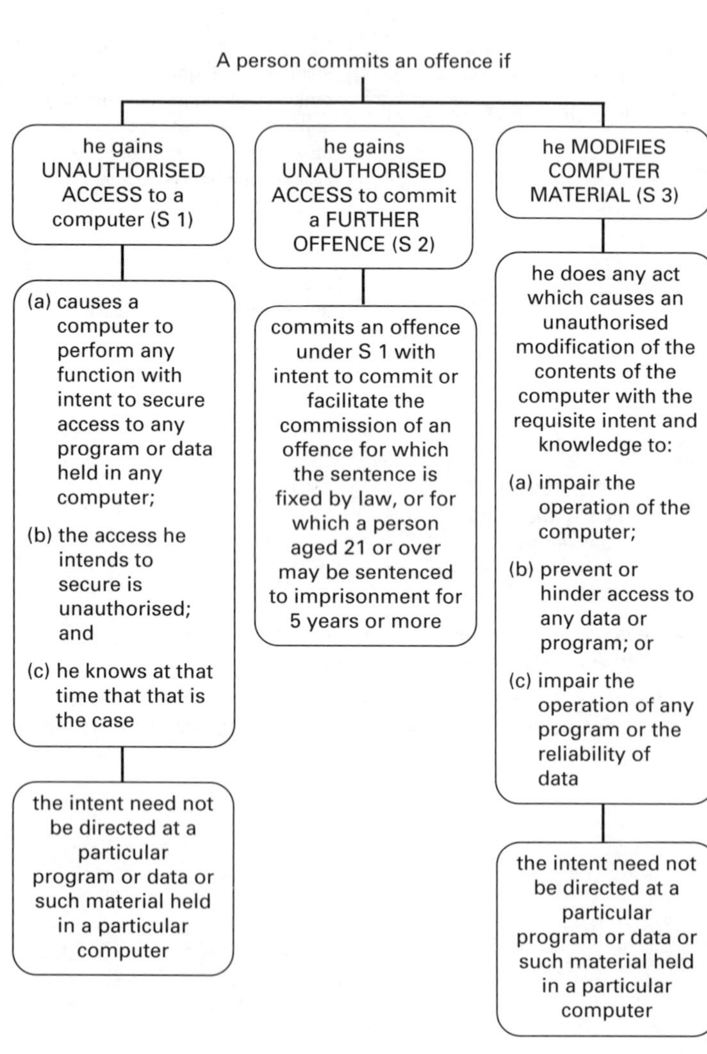

Intimidation of Witnesses, Jurors and Others

S 51 CRIMINAL JUSTICE AND PUBLIC ORDER ACT 1994

Ss 39 & 40 CRIMINAL JUSTICE AND POLICE ACT 2001

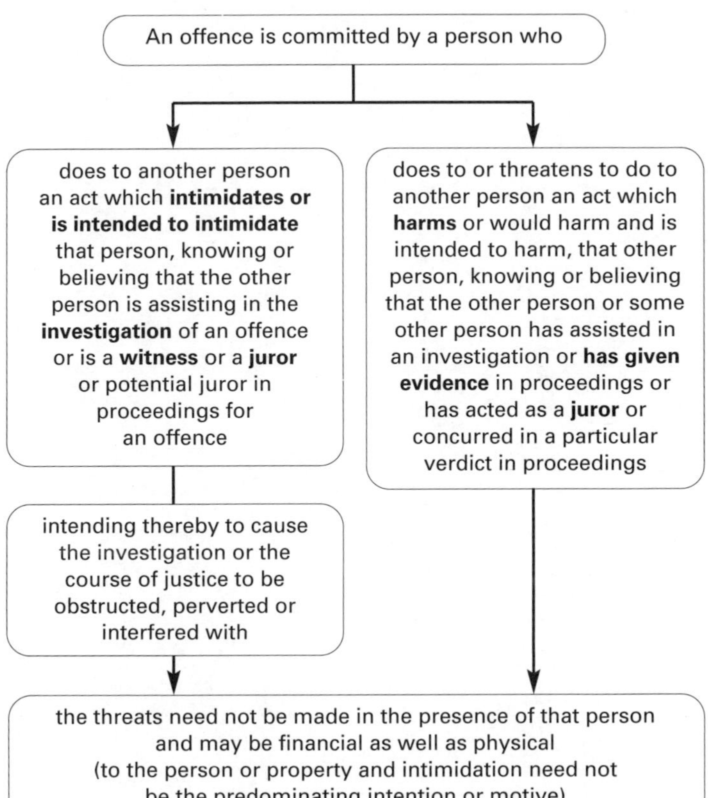

The above offences relate to criminal proceedings. The Criminal Justice and Police Act 2001, extending the provisions to proceedings which are not for an offence, introduced 2 similar offences.

Chapter 8
Procedure

Cautions

CODE OF PRACTICE, CODE C

When a caution must be given

1. **Suspected of an offence.** Where there are grounds to suspect a person of an offence, he must be cautioned before any questions about an offence, or further questions if the answers provide the grounds for suspicion, are put to him. This applies if the person's answers or silence may be given in evidence. But no caution is necessary if questions are for other purposes, e.g. to establish identity or ownership of a vehicle. At the same time as the caution the person must be told that he is not under arrest and is free to leave.
2. **Arrest.** A person who is arrested, or further arrested, must be informed at the time, or as soon as practicable thereafter, that he is under arrest and the grounds for his arrest. He must also be cautioned unless:
   (a) it is impracticable to do so by reason of his condition or behaviour at the time; or
   (b) he has already been cautioned immediately prior to arrest when being questioned.

Terms of the caution

The caution must be in the following terms:

> **"You do not have to say anything. But it may harm your defence if you do not mention when questioned something which you later rely on in court. Anything you do say may be given in evidence."**

Where the restriction on drawing adverse inferences from silence applies (e.g. because he has not been allowed legal advice), the caution will be:

> **"You do not have to say anything, but anything you do say may be given in evidence."**

Minor deviations from the words of any caution do not constitute a breach provided the sense of the caution is preserved.

After any break in questioning under caution, the person must be made aware they remain under caution.

A person who, after being cautioned, fails to co-operate or answer questions which may affect his immediate treatment, must be informed of any relevant consequences, eg failure to give name and address when charged may make him liable to detention.

Juveniles and persons who are mentally disordered or mentally vulnerable. If such persons are cautioned in the absence of the appropriate adult, the caution must be repeated in the adult's presence.

Documentation. When a caution is given a record shall be made, either in the interviewer's pocket book or in the interview record.

Adverse Inferences

Ss 34, 36 & 37 CRIMINAL JUSTICE AND PUBLIC ORDER ACT 1994

Circumstances under which inferences may be drawn (S 34)

If at any time:

(a) before being charged with an offence, on being questioned under caution by a constable investigating the offence; or
(b) on being charged with an offence or informed that he might be prosecuted for it,

the person failed to mention any fact which he could reasonably have been expected to mention, and later relied on it in his defence in any court proceedings, the court may draw such inferences from the failure as appear proper.

Failure to account for objects, substances or marks (S 36)

Where:

(a) a person is arrested by a constable and there is on his person, clothing, footwear, or in his possession, or in any place where he was when arrested, an object, substance or mark, or there is a mark on any object; and
(b) the constable believes that it may be attributable to the person being involved in an offence; and
(c) the constable asks the person to account for the presence of it; and
(d) the person fails or refuses to do so,

the court may draw such inferences from the failure or refusal as appear proper.

Failure to account for presence at a particular place (S 37)

Where:

(a) a person arrested by a constable was found at a place at or about the time of the commission of the offence for which arrested; and
(b) the constable believes that the person's presence at that place and time may be attributable to him being involved in the offence; and
(c) the constable asks him to account for that presence; and
(d) the person fails or refuses to do so,

the court may draw such inferences from the failure or refusal as appear proper.

But where the accused was at an authorised place of detention at the time of the failure under Ss 34, 36 or 37 above inferences may not be drawn if he had not been allowed to consult a solicitor prior to being questioned or the request being made.

Adverse Inferences – Cont.

CODES OF PRACTICE, CODE C

Drawing adverse inferences (CODE C)
For an inference to be drawn when a suspect fails to answer a question, he must first be told in ordinary language:

(a) what offence is being investigated;
(b) what fact they are being asked to account for;
(c) this fact may be due to them taking part in the commission of the offence;
(d) a court may draw an inference if they fail to account for this fact; and
(e) the interview is being recorded and it may be given in evidence.

Restrictions on drawing adverse inferences (CODE C)
The restriction applies:

(a) to a detainee at a police station who, **before being interviewed, charged or informed he may be prosecuted**, has asked for legal advice, has not been allowed to consult a solicitor (unless he declines to ask for the duty solicitor), and has not changed his mind about wanting legal advice; or
(b) to any person **charged** with, or informed he may be prosecuted for an offence who:
    (i) has had brought to his notice a written statement made by another person or the content of an interview with such person, which relates to that offence;
    (ii) is interviewed about the offence; or
    (iii) makes a written statement about the offence.

Terms of the caution when the restriction applies
If a restriction on drawing adverse inferences from silence applies, the caution shall be:

> **"You do not have to say anything, but anything you do say may be given in evidence."**

Where a restriction either begins to apply, or ceases to apply, the person should be told that the caution he was given previously no longer applies, and the reason. The relevant caution should then be given.

Interviews – General

CODES OF PRACTICE, CODE C

Action

Interviews must be carried out under caution. The person must be informed of the nature of the offence. Procedures under S 7 of the Road Traffic Act 1988 do not constitute interviews for this purpose.

If arrested, the interview must take place at a police station or other authorised place of detention, unless the consequent delay would be likely to:

(a) lead to interference with or harm to evidence or people, or serious loss of, or damage to, property;
(b) lead to alerting other people suspected of committing an offence but not yet arrested for it; or
(c) hinder the recovery of property obtained by the commission of an offence.

Interviewing in these circumstances must cease once the risk has been averted, or the necessary questions have been put to attempt to avert it.

Before any interview at a police station or other authorised place of detention, the suspect should be reminded of his entitlement to free legal advice, and that the interview can be delayed to obtain it unless one of the exceptions applies. All reminders should be recorded.

At the beginning of the interview, the suspect shall be asked whether he confirms or denies any significant statement or silence which occurred before the start of the interview.

Answers and statements may not be obtained by oppression. The interviewer may not (unless directly asked) volunteer information on what action will be taken as a result of the suspect answering questions, making a statement or refusing to do either.

Where a person has not been charged, or has not been told they may be prosecuted, the interview must cease when all relevant questions have been put, account has been taken of any other evidence, and there is sufficient evidence for a conviction.

Interview records

Must be kept for every interview stating the place, time it began and ended, breaks, and the names of persons present. It must be made and completed during the interview unless not practicable or would interfere with the conduct of the interview, in which case it must be made as soon as practicable afterwards and the reason recorded. It must be a verbatim record of what has been said or an account which adequately and accurately summarises it. The record must be timed and signed by the maker. Unless impracticable, the suspect (and the appropriate adult or solicitor) should be allowed to read it and sign it as correct. If a person cannot read or refuses to read it the interviewer should read it to the suspect and record what has occurred. Any refusal to sign must be recorded.

(CONTINUED ON NEXT PAGE)

Interviews – General – Cont.

CODES OF PRACTICE, CODE C

Juveniles and mentally disordered or mentally vulnerable people
Such persons should not be interviewed or asked to read or sign statements or records in the absence of the appropriate adult. Juveniles may only be interviewed at school in exceptional circumstances, in which case the parent, person responsible or appropriate adult should be notified and allowed to be present. Unless unavoidable they should not be arrested at school.

Vulnerable suspects
The following persons may not be interviewed unless a superintendent or above considers delay would lead to one of the consequences above, and the interview would not harm the person's physical or mental state:

(a) of a juvenile or mentally disordered or mentally vulnerable person, if the appropriate adult is not present;
(b) of any other person who appears to be unable to appreciate the significance of the questions and answers, or understand what is happening because of drink, drugs or any illness, ailment or condition; or
(c) of a person who has difficulty understanding English or has a hearing disability, if an interpreter is not present.

These interviews may not continue once sufficient information has been gained to avoid the said consequences.

'Appropriate adult' means, in the case of a **juvenile**:
(a) the parent, guardian, or, if in care, the representative of the authority or organisation;
(b) social worker of the local authority social services; or
(c) failing these, a responsible adult over 18 who is not a police officer or police employee;

and in the case of a **mentally disordered or mentally vulnerable** person:

(a) a relative, guardian or other person responsible for his care or custody;
(b) someone experienced in dealing with such persons but not a police officer or police employee; or
(c) failing these, a responsible adult over 18 who is not a police officer or police employee.

Interviews at Police Stations

CODES OF PRACTICE, CODE C

(1) Action

Delivery into interviewer's custody. The custody officer is responsible for deciding whether a detainee may be delivered into an officer's custody to be interviewed.

Period of rest. In any period of 24 hours a detainee must be allowed a continuous period of at least 8 hours for rest, free from questioning, travel, or any interruption in connection with the investigation. This period should normally be at night or other appropriate time which takes account of when he last slept. If a detainee is arrested at a police station after voluntarily attending, the 24 hours starts at the time of arrest. The period of rest may not be interrupted or delayed except:

(a) where not delaying or interrupting would involve (i) a risk of harm to people or serious loss of, or damage to, property; (ii) delaying the person's release from custody; or (iii) otherwise prejudicing the outcome of the investigation;

(b) at the request of the detainee, the appropriate adult or legal representative; or

(c) where it is necessary to (i) comply with the legal obligations and duties regarding reviews of detention, or (ii) take action relating to the detainee's care and treatment or in accordance with medical advice.

If interrupted under (a) above, a fresh period must be allowed.

Fitness to be interviewed. Before interview, the custody officer must assess, in consultation with the investigating officer and the appropriate health care professionals as necessary, whether the detainee is fit enough to be interviewed. An interview should not be allowed if it would cause significant harm to the detainee's physical or mental state. Vulnerable suspects must only be interviewed in accordance with the rules appertaining to such persons.

Heating, lighting and ventilation. As far as practicable interview rooms should be adequately heated, lit and ventilated.

Refusal of interview. If a detainee takes steps to prevent himself being interviewed, e.g. by refusing to leave his cell, he should be advised that his consent for interview is not required, cautioned and informed the interview may take place in the cell, and that fact may be given in evidence. He should then be invited to go to the interview room.

Standing. People being questioned or making statements shall not be required to stand.

Interviews at Police Stations – Cont.

CODES OF PRACTICE, CODE C

Introductions. Before an interview begins, the interviewer shall identify himself and any other persons present (except enquiries linked to terrorism or if such identification might put them in danger, in which case they shall use their warrant or other identification numbers).

Breaks. Breaks from interviewing should be made at recognised meal times, or taking account of when the detainee last had a meal. Short breaks shall be provided at 2-hour intervals unless the interviewer believes it would:

(a) involve a risk of harm to people, or serious loss of, or damage to, property;
(b) delay the detainee's release; or
(c) otherwise prejudice the outcome of the investigation.

Complaints. If during the interview a complaint is made concerning the provisions of this Code, the interviewer should record it on the interview record and inform the custody officer.

(2) Documentation

A record shall be made of the:

(a) time the detainee is not in the custody of the custody officer, and why;
(b) reason for refusal to deliver the detainee out of that custody;
(c) reasons for not using an interview room;
(d) action taken as a result of the detainee's refusal to be interviewed; and
(e) reasons for delaying a break in an interview.

All written statements made at police stations under caution shall be on the forms provided and the interviewee shall be reminded of his right to legal advice.

Written Statements under Caution

CODES OF PRACTICE, CODE C, ANNEX D

1. Written by a person under caution

A person shall always be invited to write down what they say.

Whether or not a person has been charged with, or informed that he may be prosecuted for, an offence to which the statement relates, he shall:

(a) unless a restriction on drawing adverse inferences from silence applies, be asked to write out and sign the following before writing what he wants to say:

> **"I make this statement of my own free will. I understand that I do not have to say anything but that it may harm my defence if I do not mention when questioned something which I later rely on in court. This statement may be given in evidence."**

(b) if a restriction on drawing adverse inferences from silence applies, be asked to write out and sign the following before writing what he wants to say:

> **"I make this statement of my own free will. I understand that I do not have to say anything. This statement may be given in evidence."**

Where the person has already been charged with, or informed they may be prosecuted for any offence, asks to make a statement relating to the offence and wants to write it he shall be asked to write out and sign the following before writing what he says:

> **"I make this statement of my own free will. I understand that I do not have to say anything. This statement may be given in evidence."**

Any person writing his own statement shall be allowed to do so without any prompting except an indication as to which matters are material, or to question any ambiguity in the statement.

Written Statements under Caution – Cont.

CODES OF PRACTICE, CODE C, ANNEX D

2. Written by a police officer or other police staff

If a person says he would like someone to write the statement for him, a police officer or other police staff shall write the statement.

Whether or not a person has been charged with, or informed that he may be prosecuted for, an offence to which the statement relates, he shall, before starting:

(a) unless a restriction on drawing adverse inferences from silence applies, be asked to sign, or make his mark, to the following:

> **"I, ..., wish to make a statement. I want someone to write down what I say. I understand that I do not have to say anything but that it may harm my defence if I do not mention when questioned something which I later rely on in court. This statement may be given in evidence."**

(b) if a restriction on drawing adverse inferences from silence applies, be asked to sign, or make his mark, to the following:

> **"I, ..., wish to make a statement. I want someone to write down what I say. I understand that I do not have to say anything. This statement may be given in evidence."**

Where the person has already been charged with, or informed he may be prosecuted for any offence, asks to make a statement relating to the offence he shall, before starting, be asked to sign, or make his mark, to the following:

> **"I,.................., wish to make a statement. I want someone to write down what I say. I understand that I do not have to say anything. This statement may be given in evidence."**

The person writing the statement must take down the exact words without editing or paraphrasing. Any questions necessary, e.g. to make it more intelligible must be recorded, together with the answers given, on the statement form.

When the statement is finished the person making it shall be asked to read it and to make any corrections, alterations or additions he wants, then asked to write and sign or make his mark on the following:

> **"I have read the above statement, and I have been able to correct, alter or add anything I wish. This statement is true. I have made it of my own free will."**

If the person cannot read, or refuses to read it, or to write the certificate at the end or to sign it, the person taking it shall read it to him and ask him if he would like to correct, alter or add anything and put his signature or mark at the end. The person taking it shall certify on the statement what has occurred.

Interpreters

CODES OF PRACTICE, CODE C

General

Arrangements must be in place for the provision of suitably qualified interpreters for people who are deaf, or do not understand English. Wherever possible, interpreters should be drawn from the National Register of Public Service Interpreters (NRPSI) or The Council for the Advancement of Communication with Deaf People (CACDP) Directory of British Sign Language/English Interpreters.

Foreign languages

A person must not be interviewed in the absence of a person capable of interpreting if:

(a) he has difficulty understanding English;
(b) the interviewer cannot speak the person's own language; and
(c) the person wants an interpreter present.

The interpreter must make a note of the questions and answers in the interview at the time, in the person's own language, and certify its accuracy. The person should be allowed to read the record or have it read to him and sign it as correct.

Where the person makes a written statement other than in English, the interpreter records the statement in the language it is made, the person is invited to sign it, and an official English translation is made.

Deaf people and people with speech difficulties

If a person appears to be deaf or there is doubt about his hearing or speaking ability, he must not be interviewed in the absence of an interpreter unless he agrees in writing to be interviewed without one. The same applies if the parent or appropriate person has such a disability where a juvenile is to be interviewed.

Circumstances where an interpreter will not be required

An interpreter will not be required if one of the following applies:

(1) the consequent delay would be likely to:
   (a) lead to interference with or harm to evidence or people, or serious loss of, or damage to, property;
   (b) lead to alerting other people suspected of committing an offence but not yet arrested for it; or
   (c) hinder the recovery of property obtained by the commission of an offence; or

Interpreters – Cont.

CODES OF PRACTICE, CODE C

(2) a superintendent or above considers delay would lead to one of the consequences above, and the interview would not harm the person's physical or mental state:
  (a) in the case of a juvenile or mentally disordered or mentally vulnerable person, if the appropriate adult is not present;
  (b) in the case of any other person who appears to be unable to appreciate the significance of the questions and answers, or understand what is happening because of drink, drugs or any illness, ailment or condition; or
  (c) in the case of a person who has difficulty understanding English or has a hearing disability, if an interpreter is not present.

Interviewing in these circumstances must cease once the risk has been averted, or the necessary questions have been put to attempt to avert it.

Additional rules

All reasonable attempts should be made to make the detainee understand that interpreters will be provided at public expense.

If the detainee cannot communicate with his solicitor, an interpreter must be called. The interpreter may not be a police officer or other police staff in this case. In other cases a police officer or other police staff may act as interpreter if the detainee and the appropriate adult agree in writing or if the interview is tape-recorded or visually recorded.

Where a custody officer cannot establish effective communication with a detainee, arrangements must be made as soon as possible to have an interpreter explain the offence and any other information.

Persons in transit

If a person has been arrested by one force on behalf of another, the lawful period of detention has not commenced and the person is in transit, no questions may be put about the offence other than to clarify any voluntary statement they make.

Persons in hospital

Where a person is in police detention in a hospital, they may not be questioned without the consent of the responsible doctor.

Powers of Arrest Without Warrant – Constables

S24 POLICE AND CRIMINAL EVIDENCE ACT 1984 (AS AMENDED BY S 110 OF THE SERIOUS ORGANISED CRIME AND POLICE ACT 2005)

1. **A constable** may arrest without warrant:
   (a) anyone who is **about to commit** an offence;
   (b) anyone who is **in the act of committing** an offence;
   (c) anyone whom he has reasonable grounds for suspecting to be about to commit an offence;
   (d) anyone whom he has **reasonable grounds** for suspecting to be **committing** an offence.
2. If a constable has **reasonable grounds for suspecting that an offence has been committed**, he may arrest without a warrant anyone whom he has **reasonable grounds to suspect of being guilty** of it.
3. If an offence **has been committed**, a constable may arrest without a warrant:
   (a) anyone who **is guilty** of the offence;
   (b) anyone whom he has **reasonable grounds for suspecting to be guilty** of it.

Grounds for exercising the powers

The powers of arrest are only exercisable if the constable has reasonable grounds for believing that it is necessary to arrest the person for any of the following reasons:

(a) to enable the name of the person in question to be ascertained (in the case where the constable does not know, and cannot readily ascertain, the person's name, or has reasonable grounds for doubting whether a name given by the person as his name is his real name);
(b) correspondingly as regards the person's address;
(c) to prevent the person in question:
   (i) causing physical injury to himself or any other person;
   (ii) suffering physical injury;
   (iii) causing loss of or damage to property;
   (iv) committing an offence against public decency (but this only applies where members of the public going about their normal business cannot reasonably be expected to avoid the person in question);
   (v) causing an unlawful obstruction of the highway.
(d) to protect a child or other vulnerable person from the person in question;
(e) to allow the prompt and effective investigation of the offence or of the conduct of the person in question;
(f) to prevent any prosecution for the offence from being hindered by the disappearance of the person in question.

These powers have effect in relation to any offence, whenever committed.

The general arrest conditions and the definition of serious arrestable offence cease to have effect. (SOCAP S 110)

Powers of Arrest Without Warrant – Other Persons

S 24A POLICE AND CRIMINAL EVIDENCE ACT 1984 (AS AMENDED BY S 110 OF THE SERIOUS ORGANISED CRIME AND POLICE ACT 2005)

1. **A person other than a constable** may arrest without a warrant:
   (a) anyone who is **in the act of committing** an indictable offence;
   (b) anyone whom he has **reasonable grounds for suspecting to be committing** an indictable offence.
2. **Where an indictable offence has been committed**, a person other than a constable may arrest without a warrant:
   (a) anyone who is guilty of the offence;
   (b) anyone whom he has reasonable grounds for suspecting to be guilty of it.

Grounds for exercising the powers

The powers of arrest are only exercisable if:

(a) the person making the arrest has reasonable grounds for believing that it is necessary to arrest the person in question for any of the following reasons:
   (i) causing physical injury to himself or any other person;
   (ii) suffering physical injury;
   (iii) causing loss of or damage to property; or
   (iv) making off before a constable can assume responsibility for him; and

(b) it appears to the person making the arrest that it is not reasonably practicable for a constable to make it instead.

These powers have effect in relation to any offence, whenever committed.

The general arrest conditions and the definition of serious arrestable offence cease to have effect. (SOCAP S 110)

Repealed and Preserved Powers of Arrest

S 26 & SCHED 2 POLICE AND CRIMINAL EVIDENCE ACT 1984

Repealed powers of arrest

Apart from the powers listed below, those parts of any Act (including a local Act) passed before this Act which enable a constable to:

1. arrest a person for an offence without warrant; or
2. arrest a person otherwise than for an offence without warrant or order of a court, shall cease to have effect.

Preserved powers of arrest

The powers of arrest under the following enactments are preserved:

ENACTMENT	PRESERVED POWER OF ARREST
Military Lands Act 1892, S 17(2)	
Emergency Powers Act 1920, S 2	Contravention of regulations
Prison Act 1952, S 49	Unlawfully at large
Visiting Forces Act 1952, S 13	Deserters and absentees without leave
Army Act 1955, S 186 & 190B	Deserters, absentees without leave and persons unlawfully at large
Air Force Act 1955, S 186 & 190B	Deserters, absentees without leave and persons unlawfully at large
Naval Discipline Act 1957, S 104 & 105	Deserters, absentees without leave and persons unlawfully at large
Children and Young Persons Act 1969, S 32	Absentee from remand home, etc.
Immigration Act 1971, Sched 2 (paras 17, 24 & 33), Sched 3 (para 7)	Persons liable to examination or removal, breaking bail, or contravening restrictions imposed by a court
Bail Act 1976, S 7	Absconding or breaking conditions of bail
Representation of the People Act 1983, Sched 1, rule 36	
Mental Health Act 1983, S 18, 35(10), 36(8), 38(7), 136(1) and 138	Absence from hospital detention, absconding from hospital to which remanded or detained by interim order, mentally disordered person found in public place, or escaping from custody whilst being conveyed
Repatriation of Prisoners Act 1984, S 5(5)	

Powers of Arrest – Cross-border

S 137 CRIMINAL JUSTICE AND PUBLIC ORDER ACT 1994

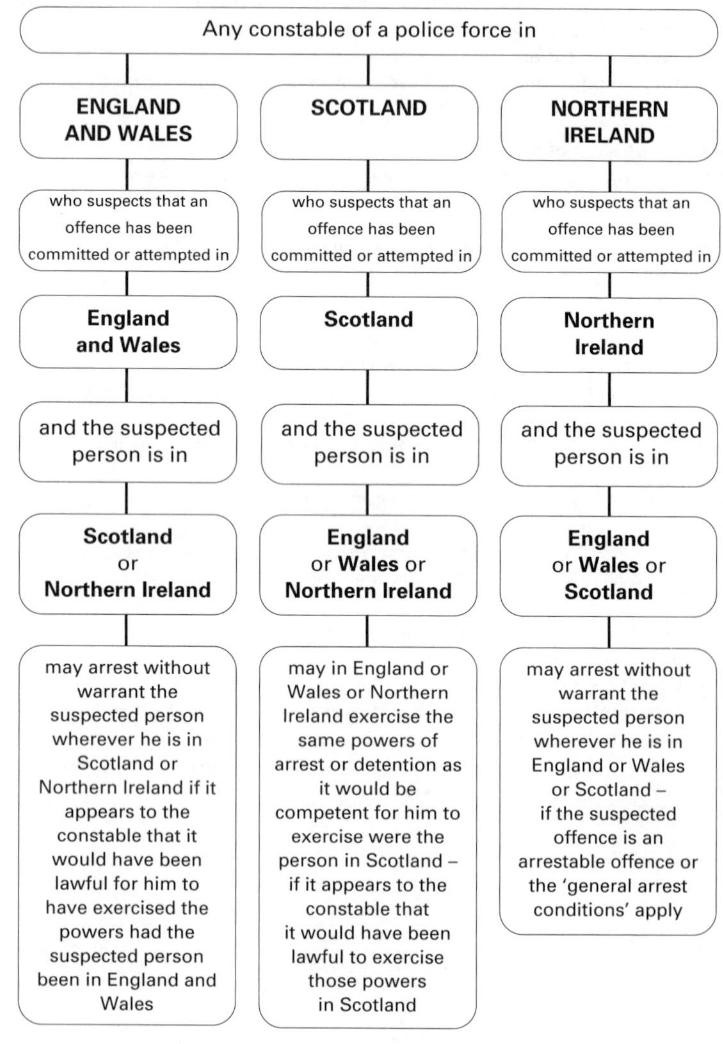

Mode of Arrest

Ss 28 and 30 Police and Criminal Evidence Act 1984

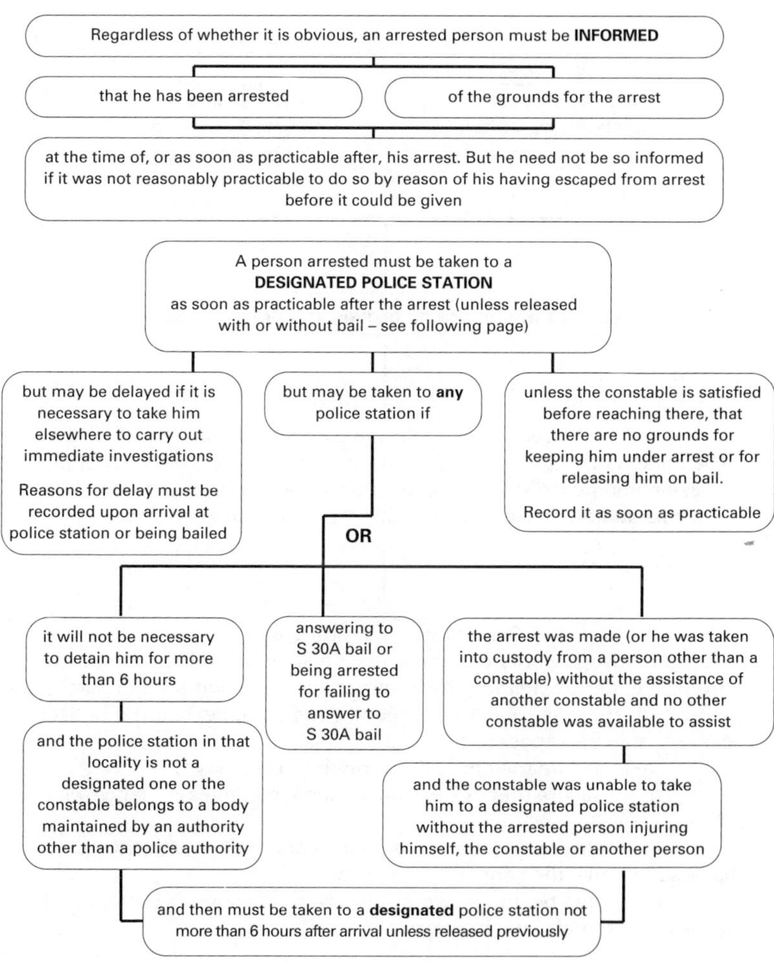

Bail Elsewhere than at a Police Station

Ss 30A, 30B, 30C & 30D POLICE AND CRIMINAL EVIDENCE ACT 1984

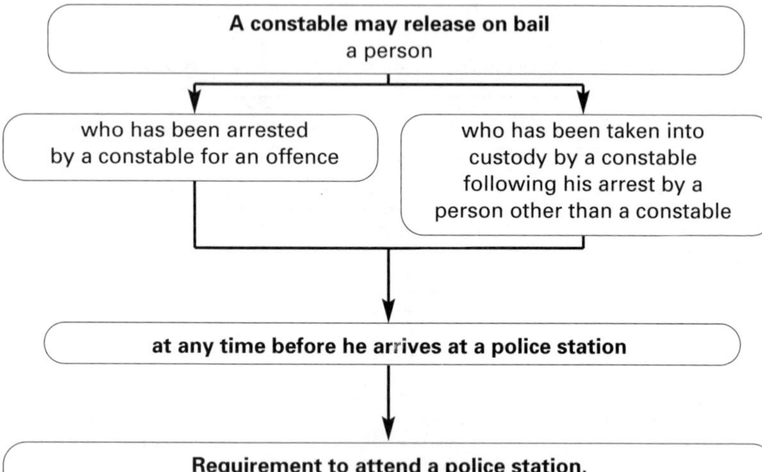

Requirement to attend a police station.
The person must be required to attend any police station (but if not a designated police station, he must be either released or taken to a designated police station within 6 hours of answering bail).

Conditions on granting bail.
No recognizance, security or surety may be attached to the bail in order to secure surrender to custody. No requirement to attend a bail hostel may be imposed. However, such other conditions as appear to the constable necessary may be imposed-

(a) to secure the person's surrender to custody,

(b) to secure that the person does not commit an offence whilst on bail,

(c) to secure that the person does not interfere with witnesses or otherwise obstruct the course of justice, or

(d) for the person's own protection or, if under 17 years, for his own welfare or in his own interests.

Bail Elsewhere than at a Police Station – Cont.

Service of notice.

The constable must serve the person with a notice before he is released stating the offence and grounds for arrest.

The notice may contain the name of the police station to which bailed and the time and date to attend, but if it does not, a separate notice must be served on the person giving that information. The name of the police station and time and date may be changed by serving a written notice of the change, but only one such notice may be served. A notice may also be served to say that attendance is no longer required.

The notice must also specify the requirements of any conditions attached to the bail.

↓

Re-arrest

A person may be re-arrested if new evidence comes to light after his release.

↓

Failure to answer bail.

A person failing to answer bail may be arrested by a constable and taken to a police station.

A person may be arrested if the constable has reasonable grounds to suspect that the person has broken any of the conditions of bail.

Conduct of a Search

S 2 POLICE AND CRIMINAL EVIDENCE ACT 1984

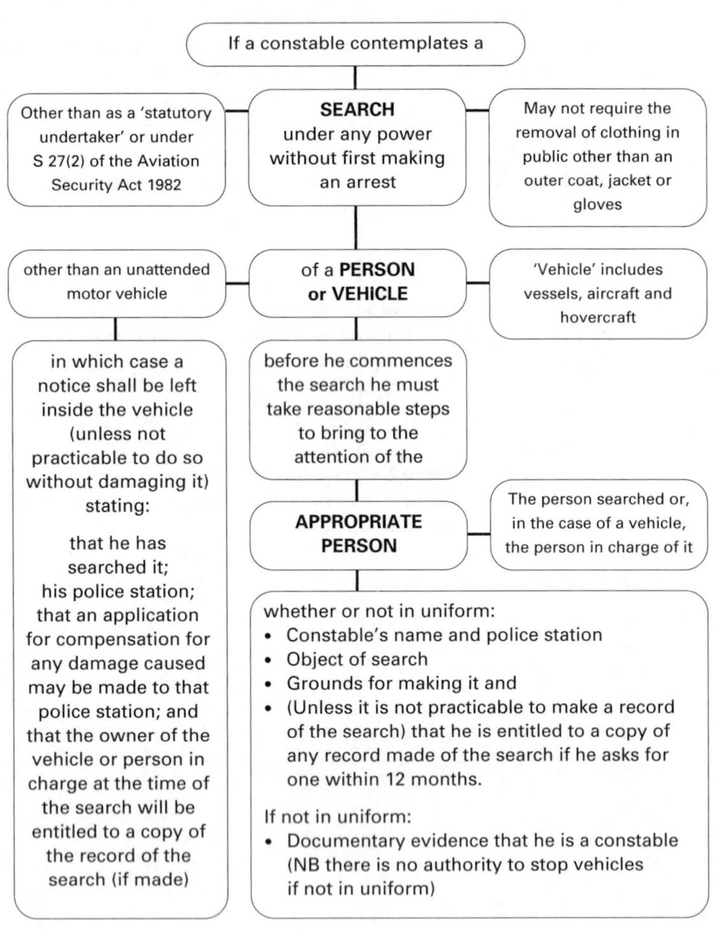

Conduct of a Search – Cont.

CODE OF PRACTICE, CODE A

Principles
Powers to stop and search must be used fairly, responsibly, with respect, and without unlawful discrimination (on the grounds of race, colour, ethnic origin, nationality or national origins).

Detention for the purposes of a search must be brief, and at or near the location of the stop.

A search must not be carried out, even with the person's consent, where no power to search is applicable. The only exception is in relation to persons entering sports grounds or other premises carried out with their consent given as a condition of entry.

Explanation of powers to stop and search.
The code applies to:

(a) **Searches requiring reasonable grounds for suspicion.**There must be an objective basis for the suspicion based on facts, information and/or intelligence which are relevant to the likelihood of finding an article of a certain kind or, in the case of searches under S 43 of the Terrorism Act 2000, to the likelihood that the person is a terrorist. It can never be supported on the basis of personal factors alone, e.g. race, age, appearance, religion or previous convictions. Nor can it be based on generalisations or stereotypical images. An officer who has reasonable grounds for suspicion may detain the person for the purpose of carrying out the search. There is no power to stop or detain persons in order to find grounds for a search. Where grounds for suspicion arise during encounters which do not involve detaining people against their will, the person may be searched even though there was no suspicion before the encounter began. If an officer is detaining someone for the purpose of a search, he should inform the person as soon as the detention begins.

(b) **Searches authorised under S 60 of the Criminal Justice and Public Order Act 1994.** See later under "Search, serious violence". Reasonable suspicion is not a requirement.

(c) **Powers to require removal of face coverings.** See earlier under "Removal of disguises".

(d) **Searches authorised under S 44 of the Terrorism Act 2000.** See earlier under "Terrorism, stop and search". Reasonable suspicion is not a requirement. These powers must not be used to stop and search for

Conduct of a Search – Cont.

CODE OF PRACTICE, CODE A

reasons unconnected with terrorism. Particular care must be taken not to discriminate against members of minority ethnic groups. However, in certain circumstances it may be appropriate to take account of a person's ethnic origin in selecting persons to be stopped in response to a specific terrorist threat.

(e) **Powers to search in the exercise of a power to search premises.** The following powers to search premises also authorise the search of a person, not under arrest, who is found on the premises during the course of the search: (i) S 139B of the Criminal Justice Act 1988 (bladed or pointed articles or offensive weapons on school premises), and (ii) a warrant under S 23(3) of the Misuse of Drugs Act 1971 if the search of persons are specifically authorised in the warrant.

Minimising embarrassment

All stops and searches must be carried out with courtesy, consideration and respect for the person concerned. Embarrassment to the person being searched must be kept to a minimum.

Co-operation

The co-operation of the person searched must be sought in every case, even if the person initially objects.

Use of force

A forcible search may only be made if the person is unwilling or resists. Reasonable force may be used as a last resort to search a person or to detain a person or vehicle for the purposes of a search.

Duration

The length of time a person is detained must be kept to a minimum.

Extent

The extent of the search will depend on the nature of the thing being searched for, eg where an article is seen to be placed into a pocket, the search will be limited to that pocket. If, however, it is a small article which could be concealed anywhere on the person, the search may have to be more extensive.

Conduct of a Search – Cont.

CODE OF PRACTICE, CODE A

Where reasonable suspicion not required

In the case of searches which do not require reasonable grounds of suspicion, a search may still be carried out for items for which the power exists.

Removal of outer clothing

There is no power to require a person to remove any clothing in public other than an outer coat, jacket or gloves (except under S45(3) of the Terrorism Act 2000 where the removal of headgear and footwear may be required, or S66AA of the Criminal Justice and Public Order Act 1994 where items worn to conceal identity may be removed). The search in public of clothing which has not been removed must be restricted to superficial examination of outer garments. This, however, does not prevent searching inside pockets, feeling inside collars, socks or shoes or searching hair.

Removal of other clothing

More thorough searches involving the removal of other clothing must be done out of public view. Any search involving the removal of clothing other than an outer coat, jacket, gloves, headgear or footwear, or any other item concealing identity, may only be done by persons of the same sex as the person being searched, and may not be in the presence of any person of the opposite sex unless the person being searched specifically requests it.

Intimate searches

Searches involving exposure of intimate parts of the body must not be a routine extension of a less thorough search, simply because nothing was found in the initial search. Such searches may only be carried out at a nearby police station or other place (not a police vehicle) out of public view and in accordance with procedures (see later under intimate searches). Intimate searches of body orifices other than the mouth may not be authorised or carried out under any stop and search powers.

Conduct of a Search – Cont.

CODE OF PRACTICE, CODE A

Steps to be taken prior to a search

Provision of information

Before any search of a person or attended vehicle the officer must give to the person to be searched or person in charge of the vehicle the following information:

(a) that they are being detained for the purposes of a search;
(b) the officer's name (except in the case of terrorism or where the officer believes that by giving his name might put him in danger – in which case a warrant or other identification number may be given) and the police station to which he is attached;
(c) the legal search power which is being exercised; and
(d) a clear explanation of:
  (i) the purpose of the search in terms of the articles for which there is a power of search; and
  (ii) in the case of powers requiring reasonable suspicion, the grounds for that suspicion; or
  (iii) in the case of powers which do not require reasonable suspicion, the nature of the power and of any necessary authorisation and the fact that it has been given.

Warrant cards

Officers not in uniform must show their warrant cards.

Requirement to be in uniform

Stops and searches under S 60 Criminal Justice and Public Order Act 1994, or S 44 Terrorism Act 2000, may only be carried out by an officer in uniform.

Conduct of a Search – Cont.

CODE OF PRACTICE, CODE A

Copy of search record

The officer must inform the person (or the owner or person in charge of a vehicle which is to be searched) of his or her entitlement to:

- a copy of the record of the search; or
- if it was not practicable to make a record at the time, a copy of the record if an application is made within 12 months.

Where the copy was not made at the time, the person must be told how he may obtain a copy.

Individual's rights

The person should be given information about police powers to stop and search and the individual's rights.

If the person does not appear to understand what is being said, or there is any doubt about his ability to understand English, reasonable steps must be taken to bring to his attention information about his rights and any relevant provisions of the Code of Practice.

If the person is deaf or cannot understand English and is accompanied by someone, the officer must try to establish whether that person can interpret or otherwise help the officer to give the information.

Records of Searches

S 3 POLICE AND CRIMINAL EVIDENCE ACT 1984

Where a constable has carried out a

SEARCH under any power

Other than as a 'statutory undertaker' or under S 27(2) of the Aviation Security Act 1982

he shall make a **RECORD** of it in writing unless it is **NOT PRACTICABLE** to do so

If it could be made, but not practicable to make it on the spot, he shall make it as soon as practicable afterwards

- Stating the name of the person searched (but he may not be detained to find out his name)
- Including (if name not known by constable) a description of the person
- Including a description of any vehicle searched
- Stating
  - object of the search
  - grounds for making it
  - date and time made
  - place made
  - whether anything found, and if so, what
  - any injury to a person or damage to property which appears to the constable to have resulted from the search
  - identity of constable

The person who was searched, and the owner or person in charge of a vehicle at the time it was searched, are entitled to a **COPY** of any record made if they ask for one within 12 months

'Vehicle' includes vessels, aircraft and hovercraft

Recording of Encounters not Governed by Statutory Powers

CODES OF PRACTICE, CODE A

When a record must be made
Where an officer (includes a community support officer) requests a person in a public place to account for themselves, i.e. their actions, behaviour, presence in an area or possession of anything, a record of the encounter must be completed at the time and a copy given to the person who has been questioned.

Identification of the officer
The record must identify the name of the officer who has made the stop and conducted the encounter (unless linked to the investigation of terrorism or otherwise where there is reasonable belief that by recording the name the officer might be endangered, in which case the officer's identification number and station should be recorded).

When a record need not be made
The requirements do not apply:

1. if there are exceptional circumstances which would make it wholly impracticable;
2. to general conversations such as giving directions or seeking witnesses;
3. when seeking general information or questioning people to establish background to incidents which have required officers to intervene to keep the peace or resolve a dispute;
4. when stopping a person in a vehicle where a HORT/1, VDRS or fixed penalty is issued; or
5. when requiring a specimen of breath under Section 6 of the Road Traffic Act 1988.
6. when stopping a person to issue a penalty notice for an offence.

Entitlement to a copy
Officers must inform the person of their entitlement to a copy of a record of the encounter.

Information to be included in the record
(a) date, time and place of the encounter;
(b) registration number of vehicle (if applicable);
(c) reason why the officer questioned that person;
(d) the person's self-defined ethnic background (see following page); and
(e) the outcome of the encounter.

Requirement to give information
There is no power to require the person to give personal details. If the person refuses to give their self-defined ethnic background, a form must still be completed, including a description of the person's ethnic background.

Requests for records to be made
A record of an encounter must always be made when a person requests it, regardless of whether the officer considers it necessary (in which case this should be recorded on the form). In such cases the officer can refuse to issue the form if it is believed that the purpose is to deliberately frustrate or delay legitimate police activity.

Self-defined Ethnic Classification Categories

CODES OF PRACTICE, CODE A, ANNEX B

WHITE	W
A. White – British	W1
B. White – Irish	W2
C. Any other white background	W9
MIXED	M
D. White and black Caribbean	M1
E. White and black African	M2
F. White and Asian	M3
G. Any other mixed background	M9
ASIAN/ASIAN–BRITISH	A
H. Asian – Indian	A1
I. Asian – Pakistani	A2
J. Asian – Bangladeshi	A3
K. Any other Asian background	A9
BLACK/BLACK – BRITISH	B
L. Black – Caribbean	B1
M. Black – African	B2
N. Any other black background	B9
OTHER	O
O. Chinese	O1
P. Any other	O9
NOT STATED	NS

Summary of Main Stop and Search Powers

CODES OF PRACTICE, CODE A

POWER	OBJECT	EXTENT	WHERE
Public Stores Act 1875, S 6	HM stores	Persons, vehicles, vessels	Anywhere
Firearms Act 1968, S 47	Firearms	Persons & vehicles	Anywhere
Misuse of Drugs Act 1971	Drugs	Persons & vehicles	Anywhere
Customs & Excise Management Act 1979, S 163	Duty not paid; import/export; liable to forfeiture	Vehicles & vessels	Anywhere
Aviation Security Act 1982, S 27(1)	Stolen/unlawfully obtained goods	Airport employees & vehicles, aircraft	Designated airport
Police & Criminal Evidence Act 1984, S 1	Stolen goods, articles used in theft, offensive weapons; including bladed or sharply pointed articles (except folding pocket knives with blade not over 3"); prohibited possession of a grade 4 firework; any person under 18 in possession of an adult firework in a public place; criminal damage: articles made, intended or adapted for use in destroying or damaging property	Persons & vehicles	Public Access
Police & Criminal Evidence Act 1984, S 6(3) (by UKAEA constables).	HM stores (goods and chattels belonging to British Nuclear Fuels plc)	Persons, vehicles, vessels	Anywhere
Sporting Events (Control of Alcohol etc.) Act 1985, S 7	Intoxicating Liquor	Persons, coaches, trains	Designated sports grounds & transport travelling to/from
Crossbows Act 1987, S 4	Crossbows or parts	Persons & vehicles	Anywhere except dwellings
Criminal Justice Act 1988, S 139B	Offensive weapons, bladed or sharply pointed article	Persons	School premises
Poaching Prevention Act 1862, S 2	Game or equipment	Persons & vehicles	Public Place
Deer Act 1991, S 12	Evidence	Persons & vehicles	Anywhere except dwellings
Conservation of Seals Act 1970, S 4	Seals or equipment	Vehicles	Anywhere
Badgers Act 1992, S 11	Evidence	Persons & vehicles	Anywhere
Wildlife & Countryside Act 1981, S 19	Evidence	Persons & vehicles	Anywhere except dwellings
Terrorism Act 2000, S 43	Evidence to arrest under S 14	Persons	Anywhere
Terrorism Act 2000, S 44(1)	Articles for terrorism	Vehicles, drivers & passengers	Anywhere in authorised area
Terrorism Act 2000, S 44(2)	Articles for terrorism	Pedestrians	Anywhere in authorised area
Terrorism Act 2000, sched 7	Anything relevant	Persons, vehicles, vessels, etc.	Ports & airports
Criminal Justice & Public Order Act 1994, S 60	Offensive weapons, bladed or sharply pointed article; dangerous instruments	Persons & vehicles	Anywhere in authorised area

Selector

The subject of searching, etc. is rather involved and the reader may be assisted by selecting the appropriate circumstances below and referring to the relevant section in the following pages. In addition, specific powers relating to Firearms, Drugs, Crossbows, Game and Offensive Weapons may be found in the relevant pages of this book.

HAS AN ARREST BEEN MADE?	REASON FOR SEARCH?	TYPE OF SEARCH		
		PERSON	PREMISES	VEHICLE
YES	Material valuable to the investigation and relevant evidence		F	
	Evidence on premises occupied or controlled by arrested person		C	C
	Offender, potential offender or witness to serious arrestable offence, or person unlawfully at large			G
YES, OTHER THAN AT A POLICE STATION	Anything which might cause injury	E		
	Evidence of offence for which arrested		E	
NO	Arresting a person, saving life or preventing damage		B	B
	Stolen or prohibited articles	A		A
	Securing evidence or seizing anything obtained in commission of an offence		D	D
	Material valuable to the investigation and relevant evidence		F	
	Offender, potential offender or witness to serious arrestable offence, or person unlawfully at large			G
	Prevention of serious violence/offensive weapons	H		H

For conduct and recording of a search see section 'A'

Stop and Search (General)

S 1 POLICE AND CRIMINAL EVIDENCE ACT 1984

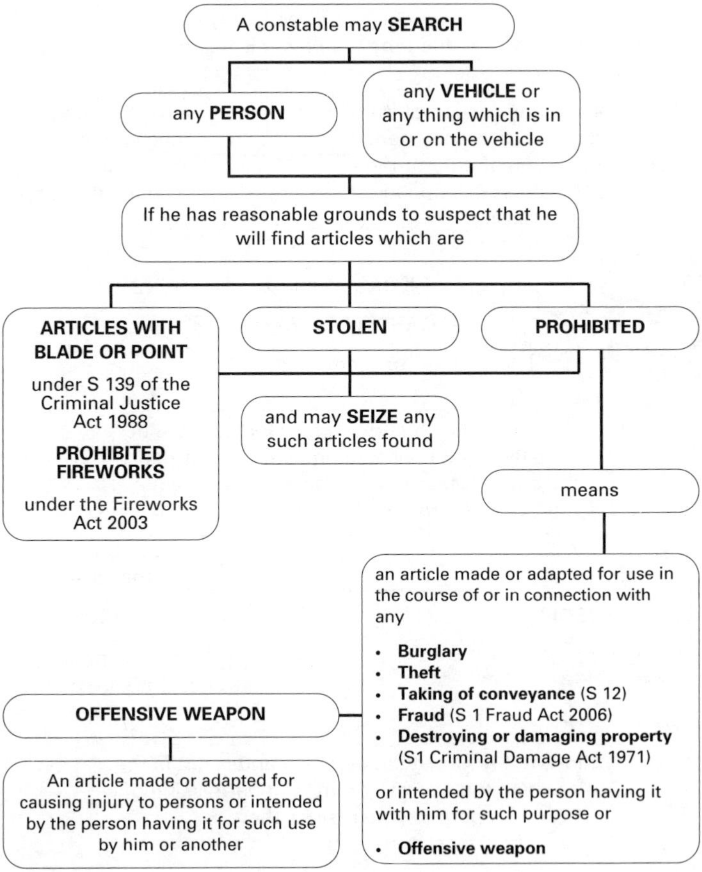

A constable may **SEARCH**

any **PERSON**

any **VEHICLE** or any thing which is in or on the vehicle

If he has reasonable grounds to suspect that he will find articles which are

ARTICLES WITH BLADE OR POINT

under S 139 of the Criminal Justice Act 1988

PROHIBITED FIREWORKS

under the Fireworks Act 2003

STOLEN

PROHIBITED

and may **SEIZE** any such articles found

means

an article made or adapted for use in the course of or in connection with any

- **Burglary**
- **Theft**
- **Taking of conveyance** (S 12)
- **Fraud** (S 1 Fraud Act 2006)
- **Destroying or damaging property** (S1 Criminal Damage Act 1971)

or intended by the person having it with him for such purpose or

- **Offensive weapon**

OFFENSIVE WEAPON

An article made or adapted for causing injury to persons or intended by the person having it for such use by him or another

A constable may detain a person or vehicle for the purposes of such a search and may use reasonable force if necessary.

Stop and Search – Cont.

Ⓐ

S 1 POLICE AND CRIMINAL EVIDENCE ACT 1984

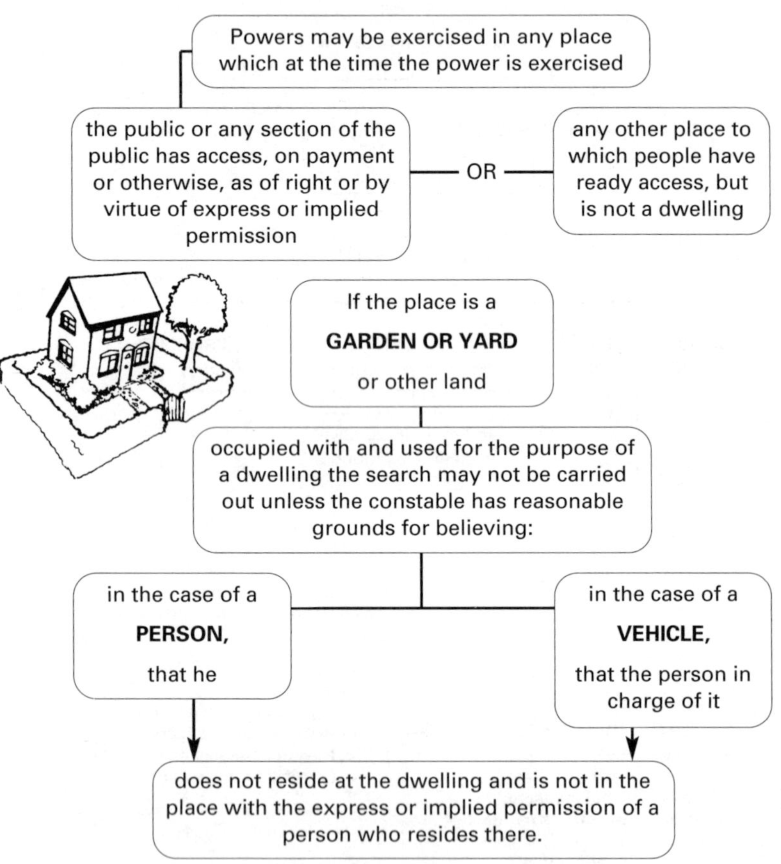

Entry and Search of Premises

S 17 POLICE AND CRIMINAL EVIDENCE ACT 1984

If a person has been arrested, see following page

A constable may

ENTER and **SEARCH**

Power of entry to deal with or prevent a breach of the peace not affected but all other common law powers to enter are abolished

ANY PREMISES

Includes any place and in particular includes any vehicle, vessel, aircraft, hovercraft, offshore installation, tent or moveable structure

for the purpose of

- Executing a warrant of arrest or commitment
- Arresting a person for:
  - an indictable offence
  - an offence under S 1 (political uniforms) of the Public Order Act 1936
  - an offence under S 4 (fear or provocation of violence) of the Public Order Act 1986
  - an offence under S 4 (driving, etc when under the influence of drink or drugs) or S 163 (failure to stop when requested to do so by a constable in uniform) of the Road Traffic Act 1988
  - an offence under Ss 6 to 8 or 10 of the Criminal Law Act 1977 (entering and remaining on property) (but constable must be in uniform)
  - an offence under S 76 of the Criminal Justice and Public Order Act 1994 (failing to comply with an interim possession order) (but constable must be in uniform)
  - an offence under S 61 of the Animal Health Act 1981 (rabies)
- Saving life or limb or preventing serious damage to property
- Arresting a child or young person who has been remanded or committed to local authority accommodation
- Recapturing a person unlawfully at large

If material is sought, a warrant may be required. See later

All of these powers, except the last one, are only exercisable:

if the constable has reasonable grounds for believing the person sought is on the premises, or

where the premises consist of two or more separate dwellings, in those parts in common use and where the constable reasonably suspects the person to be

Entry and Search of Premises (Occupier Arrested)

Ⓒ

S 18 POLICE AND CRIMINAL EVIDENCE ACT 1984
See also S 32 relating to search of arrested person and premises upon arrest

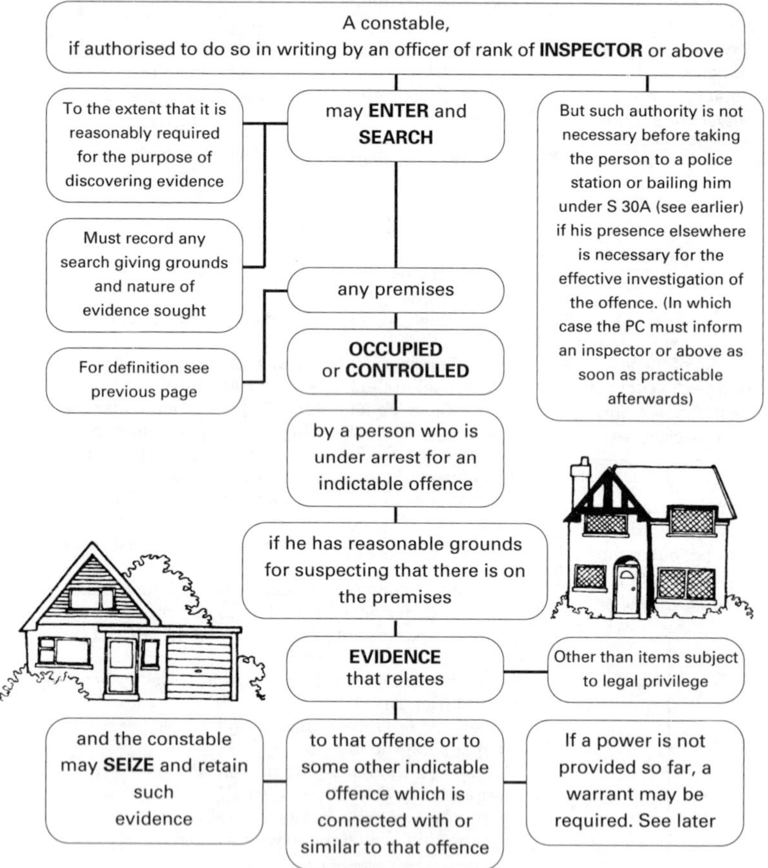

Seizure to Prevent Loss etc

S 19 POLICE AND CRIMINAL EVIDENCE ACT 1984

A constable who is lawfully on any

PREMISES

For definition see under 'entry and search'

may **SEIZE** anything which is on the premises if he has reasonable grounds for believing that it

- has been obtained in consequence of the commission of an offence
  - and it is necessary to seize it to prevent it being concealed, lost, damaged, altered or destroyed
- is evidence relating to an offence which he is investigating or any other offence
  - and it is necessary to seize it to prevent the evidence being concealed, lost, altered or destroyed

may require any **INFORMATION** contained in a computer and accessible from the premises, to be produced in a form in which it can be taken away and read, if he has reasonable grounds for believing that it

- is evidence relating to an offence which he is investigating or any other offence
- has been obtained in consequence of the commission of an offence

and it is necessary to do so to prevent it being concealed, lost, tampered with or destroyed

Items subject to legal privilege may not be seized

These powers are in addition to any other powers

Additional Powers of Seizure from Premises or Person

S 50 & S 51 CRIMINAL JUSTICE AND POLICE ACT 2001

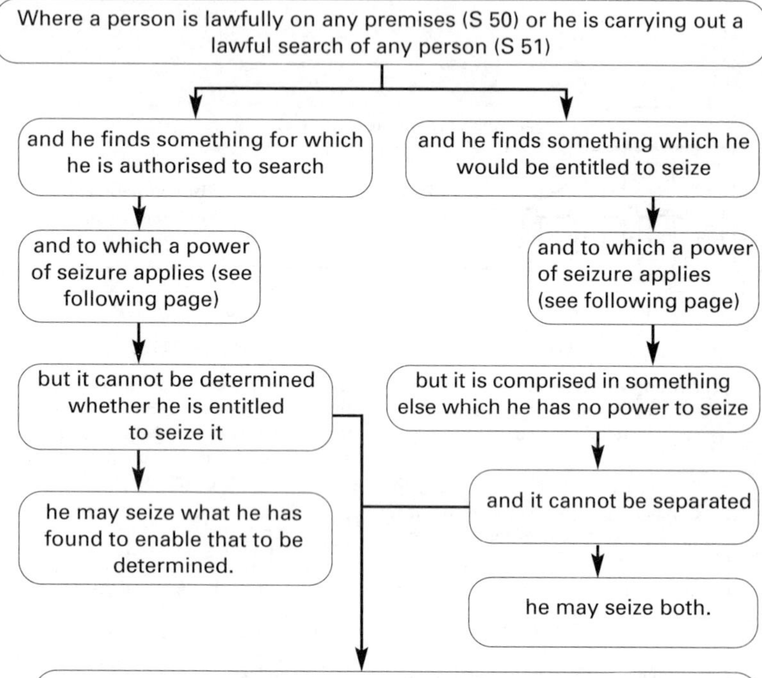

The factors to be taken into account in determining whether he is entitled to seize it, or whether it can be separated, are confined to the following:

(a) how long it would take;
(b) the number of persons that would be required to carry it out within a reasonable time;
(c) whether it would involve damage to property;
(d) the apparatus or equipment needed; and
(e) in the case of separation, whether it would be likely to prejudice the use of the seized property.

Powers to Which S 50 Applies

Ⓓ

CRIMINAL JUSTICE AND POLICE ACT 2001, SCHED 1

The Schedule contains a long list of powers of seizure to which this section applies. The following are the ones most likely to affect operational police work.

SEIZURE FROM PREMISES	
DESCRIPTION	**ENACTMENT**
Betting, gaming and lotteries	Betting, Gaming and Lotteries Act 1963, S 51(1)
Biological weapons	Biological Weapons Act 1974, S 4(1)(b), (c) & (d)
Chemical weapons	Chemical Weapons Act 1996, S 29(2)(c), (d) & (e)
Club documents	Licensing Act 2003, S 94
Drug trafficking	Drug Trafficking Act 1994, S 56(5)
Drugs	Misuse of Drugs Act 1971, S 23(2) & (3)
Firearms	Firearms Act 1968, S 46
Gaming	Gaming Act 1968, S 43(5)
General entry, search and seizure	PACE Act 1984, Parts 2 & 3
Harmful publications	C & YP (Harmful Publications Act 1955, 3(1)
Immigration	Immigration Act 1971, S 28D(3), 28E(5) & 28F(6)
Indecent photographs	Protection of Children Act 1978, S 4(2)
Knives publications	Knives Act 1997, S 5(2)
Lotteries and Amusements	Lotteries and Amusements Act 1976, S 19
Obscene publications	Obscene Publications Act 1959, S 3(1) & (2)
Official secrets	Official Secrets Act 1911, S 9(1)
Stolen goods	Theft Act 1968, S 26(3)
Terrorist investigations	Terrorism Act 2000 Sched 5

SEIZURE FROM THE PERSON	
Arrest	PACE Act 1984, Part 3
Firearms	Firearms Act 1968, S 46
Drugs	Misuse of Drugs Act 1971, S 23(2) & (3)
Immigration	Immigration Act 1971, S 28G(7)
Biological weapons	Biological Weapons Act 1974, S 4(1)(b), (c) & (d)
Arrest under cross border powers	Criminal Justice and Public Order Act 1994, S 139
Terrorist investigations	Terrorism Act 2000 Sched. 5
Terrorist arrest	Terrorism Act 2000, S 43(4)

Notice of Seizure

S 52 CRIMINAL JUSTICE AND POLICE ACT 2001

Where a person exercises a power of seizure from premises under S 50 (or seizure from the person (S 51), he must give to the occupier of the premises (or person from whom the seizure is made) a written notice specifying:

(a) what has been seized;
(b) the grounds for the seizure;
(c) his remedies and safeguards;
(d) to whom he may apply for return of the property; and
(e) to whom he may apply to attend the initial examination of the property.

If the occupier of the premises is not there but some other person in charge of the premises is present, the notice is to be served on that other person. If no one is present, he shall, before leaving the premises, attach the notice in a prominent place on the premises.

Examination and Return of Seized Property

S 53 CRIMINAL JUSTICE AND POLICE ACT 2001

The person in charge of property seized under Ss 50 or 51 must ensure that:

(a) an initial examination is carried out as soon as reasonably practicable after the seizure;
(b) that examination is confined to whatever is necessary to determine how much of the property:
    (i) is property for which there was a power to search (but is not subject to legal privilege);
    (ii) is property which it is necessary to retain to prevent it being concealed, lost, altered, damaged or destroyed, it having been obtained by the commission of an offence, or is evidence relating to an offence; or
    (iii) cannot be separated from property falling within (i) or (ii) above;
(c) anything which is found not to fall within (b) above is returned as soon as reasonably practicable; and
(d) the seized property is kept separate from anything seized under any other power.

Legally Privileged Property

S 50(4) and 51(4) of this Act state that S 19(6) of the Police and Criminal Evidence Act 1984 (power to seize not to include a power to seize anything which is legally privileged) will not apply to the power of seizure in circumstances where it is comprised in something else which cannot be seized, but the two cannot be separated.

'Legally privileged' means communications between a professional legal adviser and his client in connection with legal advice or legal proceedings, and items enclosed with or referred to in such communications. Items held with the intention of furthering a criminal purpose are not legally privileged. (PACE Act 1984, S 10).

Search Upon Arrest

S 32 POLICE AND CRIMINAL EVIDENCE ACT 1984

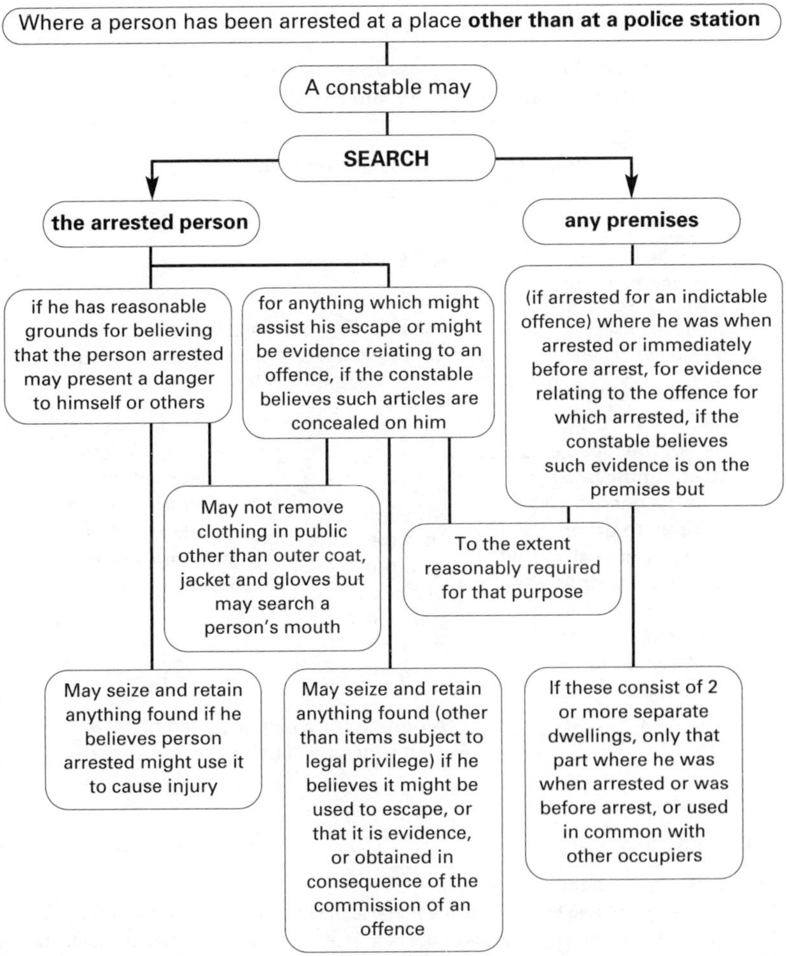

Where a person has been arrested at a place **other than at a police station**

A constable may

SEARCH

the arrested person

if he has reasonable grounds for believing that the person arrested may present a danger to himself or others

for anything which might assist his escape or might be evidence relating to an offence, if the constable believes such articles are concealed on him

May not remove clothing in public other than outer coat, jacket and gloves but may search a person's mouth

To the extent reasonably required for that purpose

May seize and retain anything found if he believes person arrested might use it to cause injury

May seize and retain anything found (other than items subject to legal privilege) if he believes it might be used to escape, or that it is evidence, or obtained in consequence of the commission of an offence

any premises

(if arrested for an indictable offence) where he was when arrested or immediately before arrest, for evidence relating to the offence for which arrested, if the constable believes such evidence is on the premises but

If these consist of 2 or more separate dwellings, only that part where he was when arrested or was before arrest, or used in common with other occupiers

Nothing above will affect the power conferred by S 43 of the Terrorism Act 2000.

Search Warrants

S 8 POLICE AND CRIMINAL EVIDENCE ACT 1984

A justice of the peace may issue a warrant to a constable authorising him to enter and search premises if

an indictable offence has been committed and there is

MATERIAL

other than items subject to legal privilege, excluded material or special procedure material

on the premises which is likely to be of substantial value to the investigation and is relevant evidence, **and**

it is not practicable to **communicate** with a person entitled to grant entry or (if such communication **is** possible) with a person entitled to grant **access** to the evidence

or

entry **will not be granted** without a warrant

or

the purpose of the search will be frustrated or seriously prejudiced unless **immediate entry** can be secured

Anything for which a search has been authorised as above may be seized

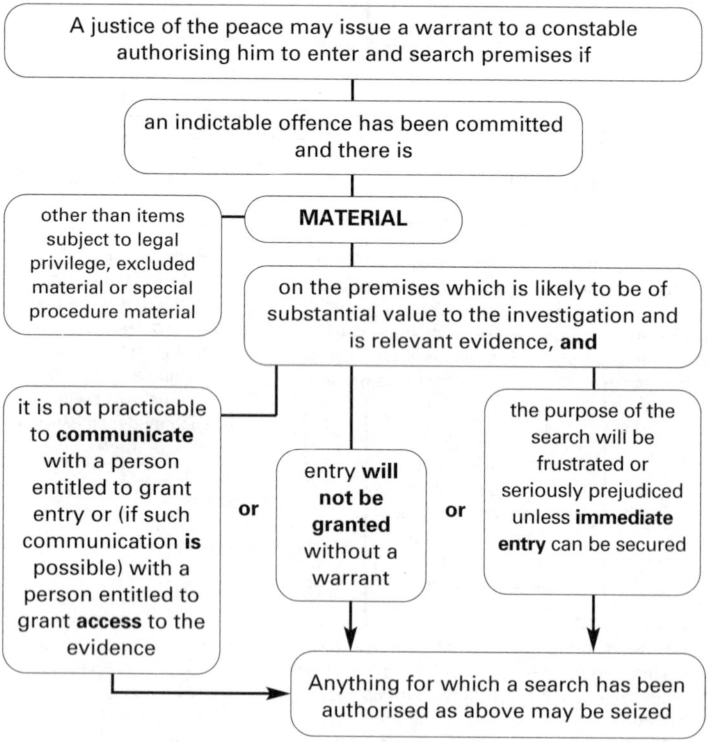

EXECUTION S 16

Must be within **3 months** of issue
Must be at a **reasonable hour** unless the purpose may be frustrated by doing so.
Where occupier or person in charge of the premises is present, constable must **identify himself, produce the warrant** and supply him with a copy. If no such person is present, a copy must be left in a prominent place on the premises.

Road Checks

(G)

S 4 POLICE AND CRIMINAL EVIDENCE ACT 1984

Under certain circumstances, a PC needs authority to carry out a road check

WHAT IS A ROAD CHECK?

The exercise in a locality of the power conferred by s 163 of the Road Traffic Act 1988, to stop either all vehicles or vehicles selected by any criterion

WHAT TYPE OF CHECK NEEDS TO BE AUTHORISED?

Where it is necessary to ascertain whether a vehicle is carrying:

- A person who has committed an indictable offence (other than a traffic or excise offence) and may be in the locality
- A person who is a witness to an indictable offence
- A person who intends to commit an indictable offence and may be in the locality
- A person who is unlawfully at large and may be in the locality

WHO CAN AUTHORISE IT?

Normally a superintendent must authorise it in writing. But it may be authorised by an officer below that rank as a matter of urgency, in which case, as soon as practicable, he must make a written record of the time he gives it and cause a superintendent to be informed

The locality at which the check is to be carried out must be specified

HOW LONG MAY IT LAST?

The superintendent or above (not below) must specify a period, not exceeding seven days, during which it may take place (may be renewed in writing). He may direct whether it shall be continuous or conducted at specified times

Stop and Search (Serious Violence)

S 60 CRIMINAL JUSTICE AND PUBLIC ORDER ACT 1994

Serious Violence/Offensive Weapons

If an inspector or above reasonably believes that incidents involving serious violence may take place in his area and it is expedient to give authorisation to prevent their occurrence, or that persons are carrying dangerous instruments or offensive weapons without good reason, he may authorise (in writing) stopping and searching of persons and vehicles in that locality for a period not exceeding 24 hours for offensive weapons or dangerous instruments. The authorisation may be extended for a further 24 hours by a superintendent having regard to the offences which have, or are reasonably suspected to have, been committed. If an inspector or chief inspector gave the initial authorisation, he must inform a superintendent as soon as practicable. A constable in uniform may stop any person or vehicle and make any search he thinks fit whether or not he has any grounds for suspecting that weapons or articles of that kind are present. Any dangerous instrument or article may be seized.

"Dangerous instrument" means instruments which have a blade or are sharply pointed.

"Vehicle" includes ships, aircraft and hovercraft.

Power to Stop and Search at Aerodromes

S 24B AVIATION SECURITY ACT 1982 (INSERTED BY S 12 POLICE AND JUSTICE ACT 2006)

A constable may, without a warrant, search-

(a) any person, vehicle or aircraft in an aerodrome, or

(b) anything which is in or on such a vehicle or aircraft,

for stolen or prohibited articles, if he has reasonable grounds for suspecting that stolen or prohibited articles will be found.

For the purposes of exercising the power a constable may-

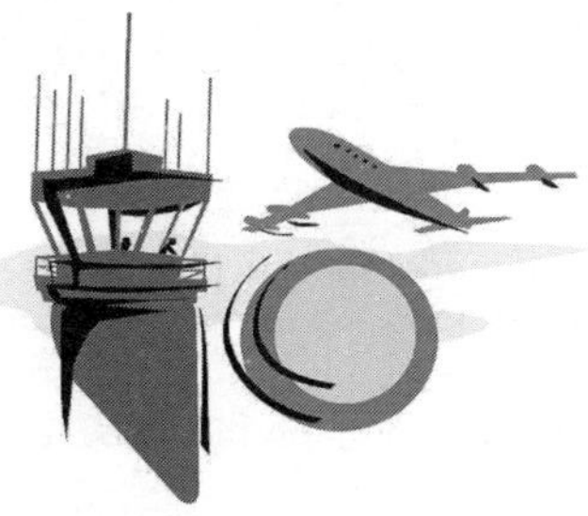

(a) enter any part of the aerodrome;

(b) detain a person, vehicle or aircraft;

(c) board the aircraft.

but he may not enter a dwelling for this purpose.

A constable may seize any article discovered in the course of the search if he has reasonable grounds to suspect it to be stolen or prohibited.

Prohibited article means an article-

(a) made or adapted for use in the course of or in connection with criminal conduct, or

(b) intended by the person having it with him for such use by himself or another person.

Criminal conduct means conduct which (a) constitutes an offence in the UK where the aerodrome is situated, or (b) would constitute an offence in that part of the UK if it occurred there.

The above powers are without prejudice to any other powers exercisable by the constable.

Identification Methods

POLICE AND CRIMINAL EVIDENCE ACT 1984. CODES OF PRACTICE, CODE D

Methods

There are a number of methods of identifying suspects. They may be conveniently grouped as identification by:

1. witnesses,
   - by video,
   - identification parades, (including voice identification where appropriate),
   - group identification,
   - confrontation,
   - photographs,
2. fingerprints,
3. footwear impressions
4. examination, e.g. to find marks such as tattoos or scars
5. body samples and impressions, e.g. blood or hair to generate a DNA profile,

These will be examined in more depth on the following pages.

General

The provisions of Code C relating to

- persons who are mentally disordered or otherwise mentally vulnerable;
- persons appearing to be under the age of 17 years;
- persons who appear to be blind, seriously visually impaired, deaf, unable to read or speak or have difficulty orally because of speech impediment;
- the definitions of 'appropriate adult', and 'solicitor', also apply to this Code.

Identification by Witnesses

POLICE AND CRIMINAL EVIDENCE ACT 1984. CODES OF PRACTICE, CODE D

Record of suspect's description
A record must be made of the suspect's description as first given by a witness, before the witness takes part in any of the procedures applicable to cases where the suspect is known.

(a) When the suspect's identity is not known
A witness may be taken to a neighbourhood or place to see whether they can identify the person. The principles applicable to identification by video, identification parades, or group identification (see below) must be followed as far as practicable, e.g. (i) a record to be kept of the witness's description of the suspect, (ii) the witness's attention is not to be directed to any individual, but this does not prevent him being asked to look towards a group or particular direction to ensure that a possible suspect is not overlooked, (iii) where there is more than 1 witness, they should be kept separate and taken to the area independently, (iv) once there is sufficient information to justify an arrest, the provisions applicable to 'Where a suspect is known and available' (below) shall be followed for any subsequent witness, (v) a record of action taken is to be recorded in the officer's pocket book as soon as possible.

A witness must not be shown photographs, composite likenesses or pictures if the identity of the suspect is known to the police and the suspect is available to take part in video, parade or group identification. If the suspect's identity is not known, the showing of such images must be done in accordance with the procedure for showing photographs (see later).

(b) When the suspect is known and available
If available, the following procedures may be used:

(i) **video** (where a witness is shown moving images of a suspect together with similar images of others who resemble the suspect). Moving images must be used unless (a) the suspect is known but not available, or (b) replication of a physical feature can not be achieved, or it is not possible to conceal the feature – in which case still images may be used;
(ii) **identification parade** (where the witness sees the suspect in a line of others who resemble the suspect); or
(iii) **group identification** (where the witness sees the suspect in an informal group of people).

Specific requirements for carrying out each of the above procedures are contained in the following pages.

Arranging identification procedures
Normally the arrangements for, and the conduct of, identification procedures, and the circumstances in which they are held, are the responsibility of an officer not below the rank of inspector. However, the arranging and conduct of such procedures may, under supervision, be delegated to other officers or civilian staff. No person involved in the investigation of the case against the suspect may take any part in these procedures.

When an identification procedure must be held
Prior to any formal identification procedure taking place, where a witness has identified, is purported to have identified, expresses an ability to identify, or there is a reasonable chance of him being able to identify, a suspect, and the suspect disputes being the person the witness claims to have seen, an identification procedure shall be held (unless it is not practicable to do so or it would serve no useful purpose).

Identification by Witnesses – Cont.

POLICE AND CRIMINAL EVIDENCE ACT 1984. CODES OF PRACTICE, CODE D

Selection of the procedure

If a procedure is to be held, the suspect shall initially be offered **video** identification unless:

- it is not practicable;
- an **identification parade** is both practicable and more suitable than a video identification; or
- the officer in charge of the investigation considers that a **group identification** is more suitable than video identification or an identification parade and the identification officer considers it practicable to arrange.

The identification officer and the investigating officer must consult each other to determine which option is to be offered.

A suspect who refuses the procedure first offered shall be asked to state their reason and this shall be recorded. If appropriate, the identification officer will then arrange for the suspect to be offered an alternative.

Notices to suspect

Before any of the above is arranged, the following shall be explained to the suspect, and a written copy given to him, which he will be asked to sign to indicate his willingness to co-operate:

(a) the purpose of the identification;
(b) entitlement to free legal advice;
(c) procedures, including right to have a solicitor or friend present;
(d) that they do not have to consent and co-operate;
(e) if they do not consent and co-operate, their refusal may be given in evidence, and the police may proceed covertly without their consent, or make other arrangements;
(f) in the case of video identification, whether images have previously been obtained, and that they may provide further images instead;
(g) any special arrangements for juveniles, mentally disordered or otherwise mentally vulnerable people;
(h) that if they significantly alter their appearance between being offered a procedure, and any attempt to hold it, this will be given in evidence and other forms of identification may then be considered;
(i) if they change their appearance before an identification parade, it may not be practicable for another to be arranged, and alternative methods may be considered;
(j) a moving image or photograph may be taken when they attend for any identification;
(k) whether, before their identity became known, the witness was shown photographs, etc;
(l) they or their solicitor will be provided with the description first given by the witness.

(c) When the suspect is known but not available or ceased to be available

In these cases (and in cases involving juveniles when consent of the parent or guardian has been refused or when reasonable efforts to obtain it have failed) **video identification** or, using the same procedures, **still images** may be used. These may be obtained covertly if necessary. Alternatively, group identification may be used. If none of the aforementioned options are practicable, arrangements may be made for the suspect to be **confronted** by the witness in accordance with specific procedures (see later).

Identification by Witnesses – Videos

POLICE AND CRIMINAL EVIDENCE ACT 1984. CODES OF PRACTICE, CODE D

Video identification must be carried out in accordance with the following:

Obtaining the images
Arrangements for obtaining the images is the responsibility of the identification officer, who has no direct involvement in the case.

Composition of images
The images must include the suspect and at least 8 other people who, so far as possible, resemble the suspect in age, height, general appearance and position in life. Only 1 suspect is to appear in any set unless there are two suspects of roughly similar appearance, in which case they may be shown together with at least 12 other people.

If the suspect has an unusual feature, e.g. a facial scar, tattoo, distinctive hair style or hair colour, which does not appear on the images of other people, steps may be taken to conceal the feature, or replicate it on the images of the other people. If the feature has been described by witnesses, it should, if practicable, be replicated. If it has not, it should be concealed. In either case, the reason for replicating or concealing should be recorded. If a witness requests to see an image without such replication or concealment, they should be allowed to do so.

The images shall show the suspect and other people in the same positions or carrying out the same sequence of movements. They must appear under identical conditions unless the identification officer reasonably believes that, (a) because of the suspect's failure or refusal to co-operate or other reasons, it is not practicable, and (b) any difference in the conditions would not direct a witness's attention to any individual image.

Identification of participants
All persons shown must be identified by a number. If police officers are shown, any numerals or identifying badges must be concealed. If prison inmates are shown, then either all or none should be in prison clothing.

Suspect's access to images
The suspect, solicitor or friend must be shown the images before they are shown to a witness, but before this, they must be provided with details of the first description of the suspect provided by the witness.

Conducting the identification
Witnesses must not be able to communicate with each other before they see the images, and they must not be told whether a previous witness has made an identification. Only one witness may see the images at a time. There is no limit to the number of times a witness may see the images or any part of them, but they should not make a decision as to identification until they have seen the whole set at least twice. The witness may then be invited to identify the suspect by number of the image. That image is then again shown to the witness to confirm the identification.

Identification by Witnesses – Identification Parades

POLICE AND CRIMINAL EVIDENCE ACT 1984. CODES OF PRACTICE, CODE D

General. Suspects must be given the opportunity to have a solicitor or friend present. The parade may take place either in a normal room or one equipped with a one-way screen (but a screen may only be used when a solicitor, friend or appropriate adult is present, or the parade is being recorded on video). Before the parade, details of the witness's first description must be provided to the suspect. When the suspect is brought to the place where the parade is to be held he shall be asked if he has any objection to the arrangements or any of the participants on the parade. Steps must be taken to remove the grounds for any reasonable objection.

Conduct of the parade. Immediately before the parade, the suspect must be reminded of the procedures and cautioned. All unauthorised persons must be excluded. Before witnesses attend the parade, appropriate arrangements must be made to ensure that they are not able to-

1. communicate with each other or overhear a witness who has already seen the parade;
2. see any member of the identification parade;
3. see, or be reminded of, any photograph or description of the suspect or be given any other indication of the suspect's identity; or
4. see the suspect before or after the parade.

After the parade has been formed everything must be done in the presence and hearing of the suspect or representative (unless a screen is used in which case any communication with a witness must be done in the presence and hearing of the representative, or be recorded on video). The person conducting a witness to a parade must not discuss the composition of the parade, nor disclose whether a previous witness has made any identification. Witnesses shall be brought in one at a time and before they inspect the parade must be told that the person they saw on a previous occasion may, or may not, be present, and that if they cannot make a positive identification, they should say so. They should also be told that they should not make any positive identification until they have looked at each member at least twice. After the witness has properly looked at each member of the parade, they shall be asked if the person they saw on a previous occasion is on the parade and if so, to indicate the number of the person. The witness may ask to hear any member speak, adopt a posture or move. Where the request is to hear a person speak, the witness should be told that the members were chosen on the basis of physical appearance only.

Composition of the parade. It must consist of at least 8 people in addition to the suspect, who should, as far as possible, resemble the suspect in age, height, general appearance and position in life. Only 1 suspect shall be included in the parade unless two suspects have roughly the same appearance, in which case they may appear together with at least 12 other people. The suspect may select his own position in the line and, where there is more than 1 witness, must be allowed to change his position after each witness has left the room. Each position in the line must be clearly numbered. Where separate parades are held, they must be made up of different people. If the suspect has an unusual feature, e.g. a facial scar, which cannot be replicated on other members of the parade, the location of that feature may be concealed on the suspect and all other members, if the suspect agrees, e.g. by use of a plaster or hat. If police officers in uniform form a parade, any numerals or identifying badges shall be concealed.

Identification by Witnesses – Group Identification

POLICE AND CRIMINAL EVIDENCE ACT 1984. CODES OF PRACTICE, CODE D

General. Group identifications may take place either with the suspect's consent or covertly without consent. The location of the identification should take into account any representations made by the suspect or his representative. However, it should be held where other people are either passing by or waiting around informally, in groups such that the suspect is able to join them and be capable of being seen by the witness at the same time as others in the group. The general appearance and numbers of people likely to be present must be considered. Over the period of observation the witness should be able to see a number of others whose appearance is broadly similar to the suspect. If, because of the unusual appearance of the suspect, none of the practicable locations would satisfy this requirement, a group identification need not be held. Immediately after the identification procedure, a colour photograph or video should be taken of the general scene if practicable. Alternatively, if practicable, the identification may be video recorded. If neither of these is practicable, a photograph or film should be taken later, if practicable. If, at the time of being seen by the witness, the suspect was on his own rather than in a group, this will still be a group identification. Before the identification takes place the suspect or his representative shall be provided with the witness's first description.

Identification with the consent of the suspect. The suspect must be given the opportunity for a representative to be present. Those present may be concealed from the sight of individuals in the group if it is considered that this will assist the conduct of the identification. A person conducting a witness to the scene must not discuss the group identification with the witness, nor disclose whether a previous witness has made any identification. Witnesses must not be able to communicate with each other; overhear a witness who has seen the group; see the suspect; or see or be reminded of any photographs or description of the suspect, or given any other indication of the suspect's identity. Witnesses must be brought to the place one at a time. Before they are asked to look at the group they shall be told that the person they saw may, or may not, be in the group, and that if they cannot make a positive identification, they should say so.

Moving groups. If 2 or more suspects consent to an identification, each should be subject to separate procedures, although they may take place consecutively on the same occasion. Once the witness has been asked to observe the group, the suspect may take whatever position in the group they wish.

Stationary groups. If 2 or more suspects consent to an identification, each should be subject to separate procedures unless they are of broadly similar appearance, when they may appear in the same group. If separate identifications are used, they must be made up of different people. The suspect may take whatever position in the group they wish. The witness shall be asked to pass along, or amongst the group and look at each person at least twice.

Identifications without the suspect's consent. As far as practicable these should follow the rules for identification with consent. The suspect has no right to have a representative present. Any number of suspects may be identified at the same time.

Identification at police stations. These should only take place for reasons of safety, security or because it is not practicable to hold them elsewhere. They may take place either in a room with a screen, or anywhere else considered appropriate.

Identifications involving prison inmates may only take place in prison or a police station. If within a prison, other inmates may take part. If an inmate is the suspect, they do not have to wear prison clothing unless the other participants are wearing the same clothing.

Identification by Witnesses – Confrontation

POLICE AND CRIMINAL EVIDENCE ACT 1984. CODES OF PRACTICE, CODE D

Before the confrontation takes place the witness must be told that the person they saw may, or may not, be the person they are about to confront and that if they are not that person, they should say so. The suspect or solicitor shall be provided with details of the first description given by the witness.

The confrontation. Force may not be used to make the suspect's face visible to the witness. The confrontation must take place in the presence of the suspect's representative, unless this would cause unreasonable delay. The suspect shall be confronted individually by each witness, who shall be asked "Is this the person?". The confrontation should normally take place in the police station, either in a normal room or one with a screen so the witness can not be seen by the suspect. If the room is equipped with a screen the suspect's representative must be present, or the confrontation must be recorded on video.

After the procedure each witness must be asked whether they have seen any broadcast or published films or photographs or any descriptions of suspects relating to the offence – and their reply recorded.

Identification by Witnesses – Photographs

POLICE AND CRIMINAL EVIDENCE ACT 1984. CODES OF PRACTICE, CODE D

Responsibility for proceedings. Although an officer of sergeant or above shall be responsible for the procedure, the actual showing may be done by another officer or civilian support staff. The first description of the suspect given by the witness must be recorded before showing the photographs.

The procedure. Only one witness may be shown the photographs at a time. Each witness shall be given as much privacy as practicable and not allowed to communicate with any other witness. They shall be shown not less than 12 photographs at a time, all of a similar type. When shown the photographs the witness must be told that the person they saw may, or may not, be amongst them and that if they can not make a positive identification, they should say so. They should also be told that they should not make a decision until they have viewed at least 12 photographs. The witness may not be prompted or guided in any way.

After the identification. Once a positive identification is made, whether by photographs, computerised or artist's composite or similar likeness, other witnesses should not be shown photographs or likeness, but both they and the identifying witness should be asked to attend an identification by video, parade or group, unless there is no dispute about the suspect's identification. Where a witness has made a positive identification from photographs or other likeness, the suspect and solicitor must be informed of this fact before any subsequent identification by video, parade or group takes place. The photographs used should not be destroyed. They should be numbered and produced in court if needed.

Identification by Other Methods

POLICE AND CRIMINAL EVIDENCE ACT 1984. CODES OF PRACTICE, CODE D

So far we have dealt with identification by witnesses. Now we will consider other methods which may be used.

Identification by fingerprints

For the provisions of Ss 27 & 61 of The Police and Criminal Evidence Act 1984, see under 'Fingerprinting'. References to 'fingerprints' means any record, produced by any method, of the skin pattern and other physical characteristics or features of a person's fingers or palms.

S 61 of PACE permits the taking of the fingerprints without consent in certain circumstances from any person over the age of 10 years. In such cases reasonable force may be used, if necessary, to take them. Where fingerprints are taken in connection with a 'recordable offence' (see definition under 'recordable offence') they may be subject of a 'speculative search', which means that they may be checked against other fingerprints held by the police or other enforcement authorities. Where the person has not been arrested, charged or reported for such an offence, but is suspected of committing it, the speculative search may only be carried out with the person's consent. Otherwise, consent is not required.

Identification by footwear impressions

Impressions of a person's footwear may be taken in connection with the investigation of an offence only with consent unless S 61A PACE applies (see below). If the person is at a police station consent must be in writing.

S 61A allows for footwear impressions to be taken without consent from a person who is over the age of 10 years who is detained at a police station:

(a) who has been arrested for, charged with, or reported for a recordable offence; and
(b) such impressions have not already been taken (or, if taken, were not complete or of sufficient quality). In such circumstances reasonable force may be used if necessary.

Before any impressions are taken, by consent or otherwise, the person must be informed:

(a) of the reason;
(b) that the impression may be the subject of a speculative search; and
(c) that they may witness their destruction if required to be destroyed.

Identification by Other Methods – Cont.

POLICE AND CRIMINAL EVIDENCE ACT 1984. CODES OF PRACTICE, CODE D

A record must be made as soon as possible of the reason for taking an impression without consent; where force is used, the circumstances and persons present; and, where appropriate, when a person has been informed of a speculative search.

Searching or examination of detainees at police stations

S 54A(1) of PACE allows a detainee at a police station to be searched, or examined, or both to establish:

(a) whether they have any marks, features or injuries that would tend to identify them as a person involved in the commission of an offence, and to photograph any identifying marks; or
(b) their identity.

Such a search/examination may be carried out without the detainee's consent if authorised by an inspector or above. Searches, examinations and photographing may only be done by a police officer of the same sex as the detainee. Reasonable force may be used if necessary. The extent of the search must be no more than necessary to achieve the purpose. An intimate search may not be carried out under this power.

Photographing detainees at police stations and other persons elsewhere than at a police station

Under S 64A of PACE, an officer may photograph:

(a) any person whilst they are detained at a police station; and
(b) any person who is elsewhere than at a police station and who has been:
    (i) arrested by a constable for an offence;
    (ii) taken into custody by a constable after being arrested for an offence by a person other than a constable;
    (iii) subject to a requirement to wait with a community support officer;
    (iv) given a penalty notice under Chapter 1 of the Criminal Justice and Police Act 2001; S 444A of the Education Act 1996; or S 54 of the Road Traffic Offenders Act 1988;
    (v) given a notice in relation to a relevant fixed penalty offence by a community support officer or an accredited person.

The person may be required to remove any item or substance worn on or over their head or face. If they fail to comply the officer may remove it.

Identification by Other Methods – Cont.

POLICE AND CRIMINAL EVIDENCE ACT 1984. CODES OF PRACTICE, CODE D

If the person does not co-operate and it is not practicable to take the photograph covertly, reasonable force may be used. A photograph may be taken of a person without their consent on a camera system installed in a police station.

Information to be given

Except where a photograph is obtained covertly or by a system installed in a police station, before a person is searched, examined or photographed as above, the person must be informed of:

(a) the purpose;
(b) the grounds on which the relevant authority, if applicable, has been given; and
(c) the purpose for which the photograph may be used.

A full record must be made of the process.

Persons at police stations not detained

Where a person is suspected of a criminal offence and is at a police station voluntarily and not detained, the above provisions should apply subject to the following modifications:

(a) force may not be used to:
    (i) search and/or examine the person in order to discover whether they have any marks which might identify them as the person involved; or to establish their identity;
    (ii) take photographs of identifying marks; or
    (iii) take photographs of the person;
(b) photographs must be destroyed if not taken in accordance with PACE S 54A or S 64A, unless the person:
    (i) is charged with, or informed they may be prosecuted for, a recordable offence;
    (ii) is prosecuted for a recordable offence;
    (iii) is cautioned or given a warning or reprimand for a recordable offence; or
    (iv) gives written consent for them to be retained. Where destruction is required the person must be given the opportunity to witness the destruction or to have a certificate confirming the destruction (provided it is applied for within five days of being informed of the requirement).

Identification by Other Methods – Cont.

POLICE AND CRIMINAL EVIDENCE ACT 1984. CODES OF PRACTICE, CODE D

Identification by body samples and impressions

'Intimate' and 'non-intimate' samples are dealt with by Ss 62 & 63 of PACE (see under respective headings). However, whereas S 62 prescribes the circumstances under which intimate samples may be taken, it does not prevent such samples being taken for elimination purposes with the consent of the person concerned. In such circumstances, where applicable, the role of the 'appropriate adult' should be applied (see under 'Identification Methods' earlier). Where hair samples are taken for the purpose of DNA analysis, the suspect should be permitted to choose which part of the body the hairs are taken from. Hairs which are plucked should be plucked individually, and no more should be taken than necessary for a sufficient sample. Before being asked to provide an intimate sample the suspect must be warned that refusal without good cause may harm their case. They must also be reminded of their entitlement to free legal advice.

Chapter 9

Detention and Treatment of Persons

Custody Officers – Qualification

S 36 POLICE AND CRIMINAL EVIDENCE ACT 1984

Are appointed by the chief officer of police or other police officer directed by the chief officer

WHO MAY BE A CUSTODY OFFICER?

Must be at least the rank of sergeant. However, functions may be performed by any rank if a custody officer is not readily available. Where a person is taken to a non-designated police station (or attends there in answer to S 30A bail), and an officer not involved in the investigation of the offence is not available, any officer may perform the functions of the custody officer. If that officer is the officer taking the arrested person to the police station (or the officer who granted S 30A bail), he must inform an inspector or above who is attached to a designated police station, as soon as practicable, that he is to do so.

WHO MAY NOT BE?

None of the functions of a custody officer may be performed by an officer who is involved in the investigation of the offence for which the person is in detention, except:

A custody officer

- Performing a function assigned to him by the Act or a Code of Practice;
- Carrying out duties imposed by S 39 of the Act;
- Doing anything connected with the identification of a suspect; or
- Doing anything under Ss 7 & 8 of the RTA 1988

Custody Records

POLICE AND CRIMINAL EVIDENCE ACT 1984
CODE OF PRACTICE, CODE C

REQUIREMENT	A separate custody record must be opened as soon as practicable for each person who is brought to a police station under arrest or is arrested at the police station having attended there voluntarily or attending a police station in answer to street bail. All information which has to be recorded under this code must be recorded as soon as practicable, in the custody record unless otherwise specified. Such persons must be brought before the custody officer as soon as practicable after their arrival at the station (designated or non-designated) or, if appropriate, following arrest after attending voluntarily. "At the station" means within the boundary of the building or enclosed yard. When a person is answering street bail any documentation relating to the arrest should be linked with the custody record and any further action recorded on the custody record. Where a person is transferred to another police station the record or a copy of it must accompany him. The record shall show the time and reason for the transfer and the time of release from detention.
AUTHORITY	In the case of any action requiring the authority of an officer of a specified rank, his name and rank must be noted in the custody record. All entries must be signed and timed by the maker. The requirement to give a name will not apply in cases linked to terrorism or where it is believed that such disclosure might put them in danger. In such cases a warrant or other identification number may be given, and the name of their police station.
ACCURACY	The custody officer is responsible for the accuracy and completness of the custody record All entries in custody and written interview records must be timed and signed by the maker Any refusal by a person to sign either a custody or an interview record when asked to do so in accordance with the provisions of this code must itself be recorded
SUPPLY OF COPY	When a person leaves police detention he or his legal representative shall be supplied on request with a copy of the custody record as soon as practicable. This entitlement lasts for 12 months after his release

Responsibility for Detained Persons

S 39 POLICE AND CRIMINAL EVIDENCE ACT 1984

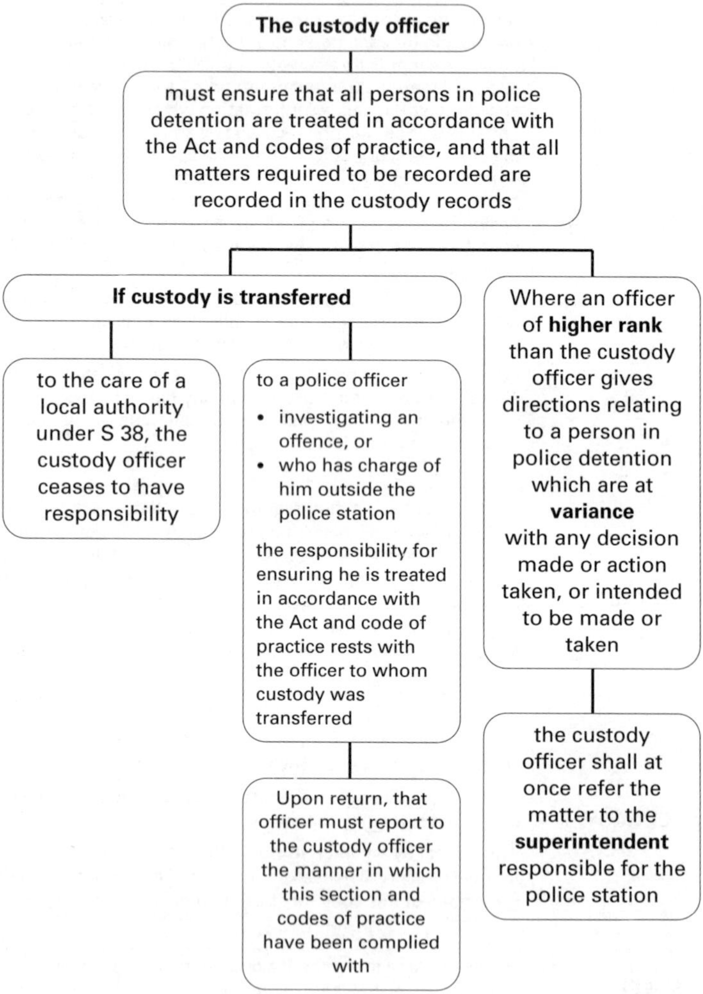

The custody officer

must ensure that all persons in police detention are treated in accordance with the Act and codes of practice, and that all matters required to be recorded are recorded in the custody records

If custody is transferred

to the care of a local authority under S 38, the custody officer ceases to have responsibility

to a police officer

- investigating an offence, or
- who has charge of him outside the police station

the responsibility for ensuring he is treated in accordance with the Act and code of practice rests with the officer to whom custody was transferred

Upon return, that officer must report to the custody officer the manner in which this section and codes of practice have been complied with

Where an officer of **higher rank** than the custody officer gives directions relating to a person in police detention which are at **variance** with any decision made or action taken, or intended to be made or taken

the custody officer shall at once refer the matter to the **superintendent** responsible for the police station

Custody Officers – Initial Action

CODES OF PRACTICE, CODE C

Detained persons – normal procedure

Informing of rights

Where a person is brought to a police station under arrest, or arrested at the police station having gone there voluntarily the custody officer must inform him of the following:
1. the right to have someone informed of his arrest;
2. the right to consult privately with a solicitor and that free independent legal advice is available; and
3. the right to consult the Codes of Practice.

Notices

The detainee must also be given a notice setting out:
1. the above 3 rights;
2. the arrangements for obtaining free legal advice;
3. the right to a copy of the custody record;
4. the caution; and
5. entitlements whilst in custody (this in a separate notice from the rest).

The detainee will be asked to sign for receipt of these notices on the custody record.

Foreign detainees

A citizen of an independent Commonwealth country or national of a foreign country must be informed about his right to consult with the High Commission, Embassy or Consulate.

Questioning and responses

Any comment the detainee makes in relation to the arresting officer's account (but such comment shall not be invited) shall be noted on the custody record. He shall be informed of the grounds for his detention before being questioned about the offence, and any comment in response (but may not be invited) shall be noted. The custody officer shall not question him about the offence, nor about any response as aforementioned. However, any unsolicited comments relevant to the offence should be noted. If the arresting officer is not physically present when the detainee is brought to the police station, the arresting officer's account must be made available to the custody officer remotely or by a 3rd party on his behalf.

Determination of needs

The custody officer shall:
1. ask the detainee whether he would like legal advice or want someone informed of his detention;
2. ask him to sign the custody record in respect to his responses to (1) above;
3. determine whether the detainee needs medical attention, an appropriate adult, help checking documentation, or an interpreter; and
4. record the decision in respect of (3).

Risk assessment

In determining the above needs the custody officer must as soon as practicable carry out a risk assessment which may include consulting others and the PNC. Reasons for delaying the assessment must be recorded. Risk assessment must follow a structured process which clearly defines the categories of risk to be considered, and the results entered on the custody record. The custody officer is responsible for implementing the response to any specific risk, e.g. reducing opportunities for self harm, calling for health care, or increasing levels of monitoring or observation. Risk assessment is an ongoing process subject to review if circumstances change.

Video cameras

If video cameras are installed in the custody area, notices shall be prominently displayed showing cameras are in use. Any request to switch them off shall be refused.

Custody Officers – Initial Action – Cont.

CODE OF PRACTICE, CODE C

Detained persons – special groups

Interpreters

If the detainee appears to be deaf or there is doubt about his hearing or speaking ability, or ability to understand English, and effective communication cannot be established by the custody officer, he must as soon as practicable call an interpreter for assistance in the normal procedure (see previous page).

Juveniles

If practicable the custody officer must identify a person responsible for the welfare of the juvenile:

- the parent or guardian;
- if in care or otherwise being looked after under the Children Act 1989, a person appointed by the authority or organisation; or
- any other person who has, for the time being, assumed responsibility for his welfare.

That person must be informed as soon as practicable of the arrest, the reason for it, and where detained. Juveniles must not be held incommunicado.

If a juvenile is under a court supervision order, the person responsible for the supervision must be informed.

Juveniles and mentally disordered or mentally vulnerable persons

If the detainee is such a person the custody officer must, as soon as practicable, inform the appropriate adult of the grounds for his detention and his whereabouts, and ask the adult to attend the police station to see the detainee. Mentally disordered and mentally vulnerable persons detained under S 136 Mental Health Act 1983 must be assessed as soon as possible by an approved social worker and a registered medical practitioner. Once they have been assessed and arrangements made for treatment and care, they can no longer be detained under S 136. If the medical practitioner concludes that they are not mentally disordered, they must be released from detention.

Compliance with procedure in presence of appropriate adult

If the appropriate adult is at the police station, the normal procedures (see previous page) must be complied with in his presence. If he is not at the police station when they are carried out, they must be repeated when he arrives. The detainee must be advised that the appropriate adult is there to give advice and may be consulted in private. Where either the detainee or appropriate adult request legal advice, the conditions applicable to such provision will apply.

Persons who are blind or unable to read

In these cases (unless the person is not a juvenile, not mentally disordered or not mentally vulnerable) the custody officer shall ensure that a solicitor, relative, appropriate adult, or some other person likely to take an interest in them and not involved in the investigation, is available to help check any documentation. Such person may sign on behalf of the detainee if he prefers.

Persons attending a police station voluntarily

Such persons may leave at will unless arrested, in which case they must be informed at once that they are under arrest and brought before the custody officer who will then treat them in the same way as other detainees. Persons not under arrest but cautioned must be informed of their right to free legal advice and to speak with a solicitor on the telephone.

Legal Advice

S 58 POLICE AND CRIMINAL EVIDENCE ACT 1984 CODES OF PRACTICE, CODE C

Information about rights
Unless a delay has been authorised, all detainees must be informed that they may at any time consult and communicate privately with a solicitor, whether in person, in writing or by telephone, and that free legal advice is available from the duty solicitor. A poster advertising the right to legal advice must be prominently displayed in the charging area.

Dissuading
A detainee may not at any time be dissuaded from obtaining legal advice.

Action to secure legal advice
Unless a delay has been authorised, where legal advice is requested action must be taken to secure it without delay. In any case he must be permitted to consult with a solicitor within 36 hours of the relevant time. If requested the solicitor may be present during the interview.

Access to telephone legal advice
If the right is declined, the detainee must be informed that he may speak with a solicitor on the telephone. The reasons for any continued decline should be recorded on the custody or interview record.

Juveniles
In the case of a juvenile, an appropriate adult should decide whether legal advice from a solicitor is required. If the juvenile indicates they do not want legal advice, the adult may ask for a solicitor to attend if this would be in the best interests of the juvenile.

Interviews not to take place without legal advice
Where legal advice has been requested, an interview may not take place or continue until such advice has been received unless a delay has been authorised.

Delays
A delay may be permitted where:

(a) (S 58 PACE and Code C): a person is in police detention for an indictable offence and an officer of superintendent rank or above has reasonable grounds for believing that the exercise of the right at that time might:
- lead to interference with, or harm to, evidence connected with an indictable offence, or to other persons;
- lead to alerting other people suspected of having committed such an offence but not yet arrested;
- hinder the recovery of property obtained from the commission of such an offence;
- hinder the recovery of proceeds from a drug trafficking offence; or
- hinder the recovery of property obtained, or a pecuniary advantage derived, from an offence under Part VI of the Criminal Justice Act 1988 (confiscation orders);

but once sufficient information has been obtained to avert the risk, the questioning must cease;

(b) (Code C) Annex B applies (see later), when the restriction on drawing of adverse influences will apply because the person has not had the opportunity to consult with a solicitor;

(c) (Code C): a superintendent or above has reasonable cause to believe that
- awaiting the arrival of a solicitor who has been contacted would cause unreasonable delay to the process of investigation; or
- delay might lead to serious loss of, or damage to, property;

(d) (Code C): the selected solicitor:
  (i) cannot be contacted;
  (ii) has previously indicated that they do not wish to be contacted; or
  (iii) having been contacted, has declined to attend, and the detainee has been advised of the duty solicitor scheme but has declined to ask for him, in which case an inspector may authorise the interview to take place;

(e) (Code C): the detainee changes his mind about wanting legal advice, in which case the interview may take place if he agrees and an inspector has authorised it.

Legal Advice – Cont.

CODES OF PRACTICE, CODE C

Solicitor
In this code 'solicitor' means a solicitor who holds a current practising certificate; or an accredited or probationary representative included on the register of representatives maintained by the Legal Services Commission. If the solicitor sends a non-accredited or probationary representative then he shall be admitted to the police station for this purpose unless an officer of the rank of inspector or above considers that such a visit will hinder the investigation of crime and directs otherwise. Once admitted to the police station, the provisions relating to solicitors apply. For matters to be taken into account in reaching this decision, refer to Code of Practice C para 6.13.

If the inspector refuses access to a non-accredited or probationary representative or a decision is taken that such a person should not be permitted to remain at an interview, he must forthwith notify a solicitor on whose behalf the person was to have acted or was acting, and give him an opportunity of making alternative arrangements.

Requirement to Leave
The solicitor may only be required to leave the interview if his conduct is such that the investigating officer is unable properly to put questions to the suspect. If this happens the investigating officer will stop the interview and consult an officer not below the rank of superintendent, if readily available, otherwise an officer not below the rank of inspector, who is not connected with the investigation. That officer will decide, after speaking to the solicitor, whether or not the interview should continue in the presence of that solicitor. If he decides that it should not, the suspect will be given the opportunity to consult another solicitor before the interview continues and that solicitor will be given an opportunity to be present at the interview. The removal of a solicitor from an interview is a serious step and if it occurs, the officer who took the decision will consider whether the incident should be reported to the Law Society. If the decision to remove the solicitor has been taken by an officer below the rank of superintendent, the facts must be reported to an officer of at least superintendent rank who will consider whether a report to the Law Society would be appropriate. In the case of a duty solicitor a report should also be made to the Legal Services Commission.

Records
Any request for legal advice and the action taken on it shall be recorded.

If a person has asked for legal advice and an interview is commenced in the absence of a solicitor or his representative (or the solicitor or his representative has been required to leave an interview) this must be recorded in the interview record.

Notification of Arrest

S 56 POLICE AND CRIMINAL EVIDENCE ACT 1984 CODES OF PRACTICE, CODE C

When a person has been arrested and is held in custody in a police station or other premises, he shall be entitled, if he requests, to have a person told, as soon as practicable (and in any case within 36 hours (48 hours in the case of terrorism acts) from the relevant time) that he has been arrested and is being detained there. If the person can not be contacted, the detainee may choose up to two alternatives. If there is still no success, the officer has discretion whether to allow further attempts. These rights are exercisable whenever he is transferred from one place to another. If a person enquires about a detainee's whereabouts, this information shall be given if the detainee agrees.

Delays

A delay may be permitted where:

(a) (S 56 PACE): a person is in police detention for an indictable offence and an officer of inspector rank or above has reasonable grounds for believing that the consequent delay might:

- (i) lead to interference with, or harm to, evidence connected with an indictable offence, or to other persons;
- (ii) lead to alerting other people suspected of having committed such an offence but not yet arrested;
- (iii) hinder the recovery of property obtained from the commission of such an offence;
- (iv) hinder the recovery of proceeds from a drug trafficking offence; or
- (v) hinder the recovery of property obtained, or a pecuniary advantage derived, from an offence under Part VI of the Criminal Justice Act 1988 (confiscation orders).

(b) (Code): the exercise of the above right in respect of each person nominated may only be delayed in accordance with Annex B (see later).

If a delay is authorised the detained person will, as soon as practicable, be told the reason for it and the reason shall be noted on the custody record.

There may be no further delay once the reason for authorising it ceases to subsist.

The fact that grounds for delaying notification of arrest may be satisfied does not automatically mean that the grounds for delaying access to legal advice will also be satisfied.

Right not to be held incommunicado (Code C)

In addition to the above provisions, a detainee has the following privileges:

Visits

The detainee may receive visits at the custody officer's discretion. These should be allowed whenever possible, subject to being able to supervise a visit or causing hindrance to the investigation.

Writing materials and telephone calls

He shall be given writing materials on request and allowed to telephone one person for a reasonable time (in addition to the telephone call mentioned above). But these privileges may be denied or delayed if an inspector or above considers sending a letter or making a telephone call may result in any of the relevant consequences mentioned in Annex B (see later).

Intercepting contents of communications

Before any letter or message is sent, or telephone call made, the detainee shall be informed that what they say (other than to a solicitor) may be read or listened to and may be given in evidence. A telephone call may be terminated if it is being abused.

Documentation

A record must be kept of any requests made and action taken; letters, messages or telephone calls made or received or visit received; or refusal by the detainee to have information about them given to an enquirer (and the detainee must be asked to countersign).

Delay in Notifying Arrest or Allowing Access to Legal Advice

CODES OF PRACTICE, CODE C, ANNEX B

A person detained under PACE

Delays to either or both rights (although where one is justified, those grounds will not automatically justify the other) may be delayed if a person is in police detention for an indictable offence, has not yet been charged with an offence and a superintendent or above has reasonable cause to believe that their exercise will:

- lead to interference with, or harm to, evidence connected with an indictable offence; or interference with, or physical harm to, other people; or
- lead to the alerting of other people suspected of committing an indictable offence but not yet arrested for it; or
- hinder the recovery of property obtained in consequence of such an offence; or
- hinder the recovery of the value of the property constituting a benefit from the person's criminal conduct (under the Proceeds of Crime Act 2002).

These rights may be delayed only for as long as grounds exist and in no case beyond 36 hours of the relevant time under S 41 of PACE.

General condition for authorising a delay

Authority to delay consultation with a solicitor may only be given if it is believed that the solicitor will, inadvertently or otherwise, pass on a message from the detainee or act in some other way which will have any of the above consequences – in which case the detainee must be allowed to choose another solicitor.

The right may only be delayed as long as necessary but not beyond 48 hours from their arrest or detention.

Adverse inferences

Where a person is interviewed without a solicitor, the court or jury may not draw adverse inferences from their silence.

Treatment of Detained Persons

CODES OF PRACTICE, CODE C

General

If a complaint is made about a detained person's treatment since his arrest, or it comes to the notice of any officer that he may have been treated improperly, a report must be made as soon as practicable to an officer of the rank of inspector or above who is not connected with the investigation. If a possible assault or the possibility of the unnecessary or unreasonable use of force is involved then the appropriate health care professional must also be called as soon as practicable.

Visits

Detainees should be visited at least every hour. If no foreseeable risk has been identified there is no need to wake a person who is asleep. However, if he is suspected of being intoxicated through drink or drugs or having swallowed drugs, or his level of consciousness causes concern he must, subject to any directions given by a health care professional, be visited and roused at least every half hour, have his condition assessed, and clinical treatment arranged as appropriate.

Illness

The custody officer must as soon as practicable ensure the appropriate clinical attention is given (or, in urgent cases, send the person to hospital or call the nearest available medical practitioner) if a person brought to a police station or already detained there appears to be ill (mentally or physically), injured, insensible (other than through drunkenness alone) or appears to need medical attention, whether or not the person requests medical attention. The need for clinical attention must also be considered in relation to those suffering the effects of alcohol or drugs.

Infectious disease

If it appears that a person brought to the police station under arrest may be suffering from a significant infectious disease the custody officer should isolate the person and his property until he has obtained medical directions as to where the person should be taken, whether fumigation should take place and what precautions should be taken by officers.

Clinical examination

If a detained person requests a clinical examination the appropriate health care professional must be called as soon as practicable. He may also be examined by his own doctor at his own expense.

Medication

If a person is required to take or apply any medication in compliance with medical directions prescribed before his detention, the custody officer must consult the

Treatment of Detained Persons – Cont.

appropriate health care professional before the use of the medication. The custody officer is responsible for its safe keeping and for ensuring that he is given the opportunity to take or apply it at the appropriate times. No police officer may administer controlled drugs subject to the Misuse of Drugs Act 1971 for this purpose.

Records

A record must be made of any arrangements made for an examination by a police surgeon, any complaint reported and medical directions to the police.

The custody record shall detail the medicines the person has with him on arrival at the police station and any which he claims to need but does not have.

Conditions of Detention

CODES OF PRACTICE, CODE C

Cells
So far as is practicable, not more than one person shall be detained in each cell. Cells must be adequately heated, cleaned and ventilated. They must be adequately lit, subject to such dimming as is compatible with safety and security, to allow people detained overnight to sleep. No additional restraints should be used within a locked cell unless absolutely necessary, and then only approved restraint equipment which is reasonable and necessary in the circumstances having regard to the detainee's demeanour and to ensure his safety and the safety of others. Particular care must be taken in deciding to use restraints on persons who are deaf, mentally disordered or mentally vulnerable.

Bedding
Bedding should be of a reasonable standard and in a clean and sanitary condition.

Toilets
Access to toilet and washing facilities must be provided.

Clothing
If a person's clothes have to be removed for investigation, hygiene or health reasons or for cleaning, replacement clothing of a reasonable standard of comfort and cleanliness shall be provided. A person may not be interviewed unless adequate clothing has been offered to him.

Meals
At least two light meals and one main meal shall be offered in any period of 24 hours. Drinks should be provided at mealtimes and upon reasonable request between meals. Whenever necessary, advice shall be sought from the appropriate health care professional on medical or dietary matters. Special dietary needs or religious beliefs should be met where practicable. At the custody officer's discretion, meals may be supplied by family or friends at the prisoner's, or their, expense.

Exercise
Brief daily, outdoor exercise shall be provided where practicable.

Juveniles
Should not be put in a cell unless other secure accommodation is not available or is impracticable to supervise or is less comfortable than a cell. A juvenile may not share a cell with an adult.

Force
Reasonable force may be used if necessary:

- to secure compliance with reasonable instructions, or
- to prevent escape, injury, damage to property or the destruction of evidence.

Checks
Detainees should be visited at least every hour. If no reasonably foreseeable risk was identified in risk assessment there is no need to wake a sleeping detainee. Suspects who are intoxicated through drink or drugs or whose level of consciousness causes concern must, subject to any clinical directions given by the appropriate health care professional, be visited and roused at least every half hour, have their condition assessed, and have clinical treatment arranged if appropriate.

Records
Replacement clothing and meals offered must be recorded. If a juvenile is placed in a cell, the reason must be recorded. The use of any restraints, the reason for it and, if appropriate, enhanced supervision whilst restrained, shall be recorded.

Fingerprinting

S 27 & S 61 POLICE AND CRIMINAL EVIDENCE ACT 1984

General principle (S 61)
Fingerprints may only be taken with the appropriate consent, which, if given at a police station, must be in writing.

Taking fingerprints without consent – detained at a police station
Fingerprints of a person detained at a police station may be taken without consent by any constable, or, where a designation applies, by a civilian if:

(a) he is detained following his arrest for a recordable offence, or he has been charged with, or told he will be reported for, such an offence, and
(b) he has not had his fingerprints taken in the course of the investigation by the police (unless they were not a complete set or were not of sufficient quality to allow satisfactory analysis, comparison or matching).

Taking fingerprints without consent – answering bail
The fingerprints of a person who has answered to bail at a court or police station may be taken without consent if the court or an officer of at least the rank of inspector authorises them to be taken. Such authorisation may only be given if the person answering bail:

(a) has done so for a person who has had his fingerprints taken on a previous occasion and there are reasonable grounds for believing that he is not the same person; or
(b) claims to be a different person from a person whose fingerprints were taken on a previous occasion.

Authorisation may be given orally or in writing, but if given orally must be confirmed in writing as soon as practicable.

Taking fingerprints without consent – recordable offence
Any person's fingerprints may be taken without consent if, in relation to a recordable offence, he has been convicted; cautioned (which he admits); or warned or reprimanded under S 65 Crime and Disorder Act 1998.

Information to be given
Where fingerprints are taken without consent the person shall be told the reason before they are taken. The reason shall also be recorded as soon as practicable after they have been taken.
Where fingerprints are taken at a police station, with or without consent, the person shall be told before they are taken that they may be the subject of a speculative search; and the fact that he has been told shall be recorded as soon as practicable after they have been taken.

Custody record
If a person is detained at a police station when his fingerprints are taken, the reason for taking them and, if applicable, the fact that the person has been told of the possibility of a speculative search, shall be recorded on the custody record.

Exclusions
None of the above applies to powers under the Immigration Act 1971, the Terrorism (Temporary Provisions) Act 1989, (except S 15(10) and para. 7(6) Sched. 5), or the Extradition Act 2003 (see later).

Fingerprinting of offenders (S 27)
If a person has been convicted of a recordable offence; has not been in police detention for the offence; and has not had his fingerprints taken in the course of the investigation or since the conviction, any constable or, where a designation applies, a civilian, may within 1 month after the conviction require him to attend a police station to have them taken. The person must be given a period of 7 days during which he must attend, and times between which he must attend may be specified. A constable may arrest without warrant any person who fails to comply.

'**Recordable offence**' means convictions for and cautions, reprimands and warnings in respect of any offence punishable with imprisonment; and any offence specified in the schedule to the National Police Records (Recordable Offences) Regulations 2000.

Photographing of Suspects, etc

S 64A POLICE AND CRIMINAL EVIDENCE ACT 1984

A person who is **detained at a police** station may be photographed:

(a) with the appropriate consent; or
(b) if the appropriate consent is withheld, or it is not practicable to obtain it, without it.

A person may be photographed elsewhere than at a police station either with the appropriate consent, or, if consent is withheld or it is not practicable to obtain it, without it, if the person has been:

(a) arrested by a constable for an offence;
(b) taken into custody by a constable after being arrested for an offence by a person other than a constable;
(c) required to wait with a community support officer;
(d) given a penalty notice or a fixed penalty notice by a constable in uniform; given a notice in relation to a relevant fixed penalty offence by a community support officer or an accredited person.

A person proposing to take a photograph:

(a) may require the removal of any item or substance worn on or over the whole or any part of the head or face; and
(b) if the requirement is not complied with, may remove the item or substance.

The only persons entitled to take a photograph under this section are constables and, where a designtion applies, civilians.

A photograph taken under this section:

(a) may be used by, or disclosed to, any person for any purpose related to the prevention or detection of crime, the investigation of an offence or the conduct of a prosecution or to the enforcement of a sentence; and
(b) after being so used or disclosed, may be retained but may not be used or disclosed except for the above purposes.

Photograph includes any process by means of which a visual image may be produced. It also includes a moving image.

Intimate Searches

S 55 POLICE AND CRIMINAL EVIDENCE ACT 1984

An 'intimate search' consists of the physical examination of a person's body orifices other than the mouth.

Authorisation

If an officer of at least the rank of inspector has reasonable grounds for believing:

(a) that a person who has been arrested and is in police custody may have concealed on him anything which:
   (i) he could use to cause physical injury to himself or others; and
   (ii) he might so use while he is in police detention or in the custody of the court; or

(b) that such a person:
   (i) may have a class A drug concealed on him; and
   (ii) was in possession of it with the appropriate criminal intent (possession with intent to supply, or unlawful export) before his arrest,

he may authorise an intimate search of that person if he has reasonable grounds for believing that it cannot be found without an intimate search. Authorisation may be given orally (later confirmed in writing) or in writing.

Drug offences

A drug offence search shall not be carried out unless the appropriate consent has been given in writing. If consent is refused without good cause, the court may draw such inferences from the refusal as appear proper. Where a search is proposed the person shall be informed of the giving of authorisation for it and the grounds for such authorisation. The giving of the authorisation, the grounds for it, and the fact that the appropriate consent was given shall be stated on the custody record.

Persons authorised to carry out the search

An intimate search for a drug offence may only be carried out by a suitably qualified person (a registered medical practitioner or a registered nurse). A search on any other grounds must be carried out by a suitably qualified person unless an inspector or above considers that this is not practicable, in which case it may be carried out by a constable of the same sex as the person being searched, or, where a designation applies, by a civilian of the same sex.

Intimate Searches – Cont.

S 55 POLICE AND CRIMINAL EVIDENCE ACT 1984

Venue

An intimate search may only be carried out:

(a) at a police station (but not if for a drug offence);
(b) at a hospital;
(c) at a registered medical practitioner's surgery; or
(d) at some other place used for medical purposes.

Custody record

If an intimate search is carried out, as soon as reasonable practicable after its completion, it must be shown on the custody record which parts of the body were searched, and why they were searched.

Seizure of items found

The custody officer may seize and retain anything which is found on an intimate search:

(a) if he believes that the person may use it-
    (i) to cause physical injury to himself or another person;
    (ii) to damage property;
    (iii) to interfere with evidence; or
    (iv) to assist him to escape; or
(b) if he has reasonable grounds for believing that it may be evidence relating to an offence.

Intimate Searches – Cont.

CODES OF PRACTICE, CODE C, ANNEX A

Before the search begins the detainee must be told that the authority to carry out the search has been given, and the grounds for giving the authorisation and for believing that the article cannot be removed without an intimate search. Where the search is for a drug offence, the detainee's consent must be given in writing. Before being asked to give such consent they must be warned that if they refuse without due cause, their refusal may harm their case if it comes to trial.

Juveniles or mentally disordered or mentally vulnerable persons

Intimate searches of such persons may only take place in the presence of an appropriate adult of the same sex, unless the detainee specifically requests a particular adult of the opposite sex who is readily available. In the case of a juvenile the search may take place in the absence of the appropriate adult only if the juvenile signifies in the presence of the appropriate adult they do not want the adult present during the search and the adult agrees. A record shall be made of the juvenile's decision and signed by the adult.

Police officers carrying out searches

Where an intimate search for items which may be used to cause physical injury, is carried out by a police officer, it must be carried out by a person of the same sex as the person being searched. A minimum of two people, besides the detainee, must be present during the search. No person of the opposite sex to the person being searched (other than a medical practitioner or nurse) may be present, nor may anyone whose presence is unnecessary. The search shall be conducted with proper regard to the sensitivity and vulnerability of the detainee.

Documentation

As soon as practicable the custody officer shall record:

- the authorisation to carry out the search;
- the grounds for giving the authorisation;
- the grounds for believing the article could not be removed without an intimate search;
- for drug searches, the giving of the required warning;
- for drug searches, the fact that consent was given or refused and, if refused, any reason given for the refusal.
- which parts of the body were searched;
- who carried out the search;

Intimate Searches – Cont.

CODES OF PRACTICE, CODE C, ANNEX A

- who was present;
- the result; and
- if carried out by a police officer, the reason why it was impracticable for it to be conducted by a registered medical practitioner or registered nurse.

Strip searches (means removal of more than outer clothing)

May take place to remove an article which the detainee would not be allowed to keep, and which he has concealed. They must not be routinely carried out. When strip searches are conducted:

- a police officer must be of the same sex as the person searched;
- must be in an area where it cannot be seen by anyone who does not need to be present, or by the opposite sex (except an appropriate adult);
- if it involves exposing intimate parts of the body, two persons must be present (one must be an appropriate adult in the case of a juvenile or mentally disordered person);
- it must be carried out with due regard to sensitivity and vulnerability and should not involve removal of all clothes at the same time;
- the detainee may be required to hold arms in the air or stand with legs apart and bend forward so a visual examination may be made of genital and anal areas but there must be no physical contact;
- if the detainee refuses to hand over articles found in a body orifice other than the mouth, an intimate search would need to be carried out;
- it must be conducted as quickly as possible and the detainee allowed to dress as soon as the search is completed.

X-rays and Ultrasound Scans for Drugs

S 55 A POLICE AND CRIMINAL EVIDENCE ACT 1984, S 5 DRUGS ACT 2005

Authorisation

If an officer of at least the rank of inspector has reasonable grounds for believing that a person who has been arrested for an offence and is in police detention:

(a) may have swallowed a Class A drug; and
(b) was in possession of it with the appropriate criminal intent before his arrest,

the officer may authorise that an x-ray is taken of the person or an ultrasound scan is carried out on the person (or both).

Consent

An x-ray or ultrasound scan may not be carried out unless the appropriate consent has been given in writing. If consent is refused without good cause, the court may draw such inferences from the refusal as appear proper.

Information to be given

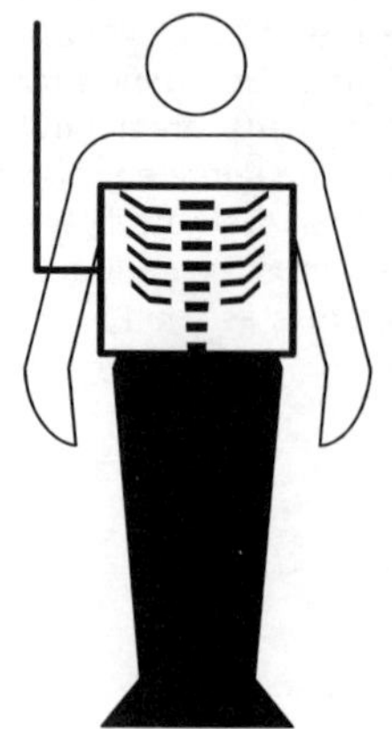

The person must be informed of:

(a) the giving of the authorisation for it; and
(b) the grounds for giving the authorisation.

Venue

An x-ray or ultrasound scan may only be carried out by a suitably qualified person, and only at:

(a) a hospital;
(b) a registered medical practitioner's surgery; or
(c) some other place used for medical purposes.

Custody records

The custody record must state:

(a) the authorisation by virtue of which it was carried out;
(b) the grounds for giving the authorisation; and
(c) the fact that the appropriate consent was given.

Such information must be recorded as soon as practicable afterwards.

Searches to Ascertain Identity

S 54A POLICE AND CRIMINAL EVIDENCE ACT 1984

Authority to search, etc

An officer of at least the rank of inspector may authorise the search or examination, or both, of a person who is detained in a police station:

(a) to ascertain whether he has any mark that would tend to identify him as a person involved in the commission of an offence; or
(b) to facilitate the ascertainment of his identity,

if he has refused to identify himself; or it is suspected that the person is not who he claims to be.

But a search/examination may only be authorised under (a) above if:

(a) the appropriate consent has been withheld; or
(b) it is not practicable to obtain such consent.

An authorisation may be given orally or in writing, but if orally, it shall be confirmed in writing as soon as practicable.

Photographs

Any identifying mark found may be photographed:

(a) with the appropriate consent; or
(b) if consent is withheld or it is not practicable to obtain it, without it.

Conduct of the search, etc

Any search, examination or photograph may only be carried out by constables, or, where a designation applies, by a civilian, and such force as is necessary may be used.

A person may not carry out a search or examination of a person of the opposite sex. Nor may a photograph be taken of any part of the body of a person of the opposite sex.

An intimate search may not be carried out under this section.

Exclusion

None of the above applies to persons arrested under the Extradition Act 2003 (see later).

Intimate Samples

Ss 62, 65 POLICE AND CRIMINAL EVIDENCE ACT 1984

An
INTIMATE SAMPLE

is a sample of blood, semen, any other tissue fluid, urine, pubic hair or a swab taken from any part of a person's genitals (including pubic hair) or from a person's body orifices (other than the mouth) or a dental impression

and may be taken from a **person in police detention**

if authorised by an officer of at least the rank of inspector who has reasonable grounds for suspecting the person's involvement in a recordable offence and for believing that the sample will tend to prove or disprove his involvement

and if the appropriate consent is given in writing

and may be taken from a person **not** in police detention

if in the course of the investigation two or more non-intimate samples suitable for the same means of analysis have been taken, and have proved insufficient and an inspector or above authorises it and the appropriate consent is given

A sample, other than of urine, may only be taken by a registered medical practitioner or registered nurse or registered paramedic; and a dental impression may only be taken by a registered dentist

Non-Intimate Samples

S 63 POLICE AND CRIMINAL EVIDENCE ACT 1984

A **NON-INTIMATE SAMPLE**

is a sample of hair (other than pubic hair), a sample taken from a nail or from under a nail, a swab taken from any part of the body other than a part from which a swab taken would be an intimate sample, saliva, or a skin sample (a record of the skin pattern and other physical characteristics or features of a foot or any other part of the body).

It may not be taken from a person without consent given in writing. But it may be taken without consent by any constable if:

(a) being held in police custody by authority of a court and an inspector or above authorises it (he may only authorise it if he suspects his involvement in a recordable offence, and that the sample will tend to confirm or disprove his involvement),
(b) in police detention for a recordable offence and either (i) he has not had the same type of sample taken from the same part of the body in the course of the investigation, or (ii) he has had such a sample taken but it was insufficient,
(c) whether or not in police detention or held in police custody by authority of a court, he has (i) been charged with, or told he will be reported for, a recordable offence, and (ii) he has not had an intimate sample taken from him (or, if taken, was not suitable for analysis or was insufficient),
(d) convicted of a recordable offence, or
(e) detained following acquittal on grounds of insanity or unfitness to plead.

Exclusion

None of the above applies to persons arrested under the Extradition Act 2003 (see later).

Fingerprints and Samples

Ss 63A, 64 POLICE AND CRIMINAL EVIDENCE ACT 1984

Fingerprints or samples or the information derived from samples taken from a person arrested for a recordable offence or reported for such an offence may be checked against other fingerprints or samples or the information derived from them contained in records held by or on behalf of the police or in connection with the investigation of an offence.

Fingerprints may be taken without consent from a person aged over ten if the conditions set out above exist, and reasonable force may be used.

Destruction: S 64 PACE requires the destruction of fingerprints or samples as soon as is practicable after the conclusion of proceedings except that samples need not be destroyed if they were taken for the purpose of the same investigation of an offence for which a person from whom one was taken has been convicted or he has consented in writing to them not being destroyed.

Testing for Presence of Class A Drugs

S 63B POLICE AND CRIMINAL EVIDENCE ACT 1984. SCHED. 6 CRIMINAL JUSTICE AND COURT SERVICES ACT 2000. S 5 CRIMINAL JUSTICE ACT 2003. S 7 & 9 DRUGS ACT 2005

A sample of urine or a non-intimate sample may be taken from a person in police detention for the purpose of ascertaining whether he has any specified Class A drug in his body if:

(a) either the arrest condition or the charge condition are met;

(b) both the age condition and the request condition are met; and

(c) the notification condition is met in relation to the arrest condition, the charge condition or the age condition (as the case may be).

The arrest condition is that the person has been arrested for an offence but has not been charged with that offence and either:

(a) the offence is a trigger offence; or

(b) an inspector or above has reasonable grounds for suspecting that the misuse by that person of a specified Class A drug caused or contributed to the offence and has authorised the sample to be taken.

The charge condition is that the person has been charged either:

(a) with a **trigger offence**; or

(b) with an offence and a police officer of at least the rank of inspector, who has reasonable grounds for suspecting that the misuse by that person of any specified Class A drug caused or contributed to the offence, has authorised the sample to be taken.

The age condition is:

(a) if the arrest condition is met, that the person concerned has attained the age of 18;

(b) if the charge condition is met, that he has attained the age of 14.

The request condition is that a police officer has requested the person concerned to give the sample.

The notification condition is that the relevant chief officer has been notified by the Secretary of State that appropriate arrangements for the taking of samples have been made for the police area or police station in which the person is detained.

The authorisation mentioned above may be given orally or in writing, but if given orally, it must be confirmed in writing as soon as is practicable. (S 63C).

Testing for Presence of Class A Drugs – Cont.

S 63B POLICE AND CRIMINAL EVIDENCE ACT 1984. SCHED. 6 CRIMINAL JUSTICE AND COURT SERVICES ACT 2000. S 5 CRIMINAL JUSTICE ACT 2003. S 7 & 9 DRUGS ACT 2005

Before requesting the sample the person must be warned that failure to give a sample without good cause may lead to prosecution; and, where authorisation has been given by an inspector or above under 'the arrest condition' or 'the charge condition', informed of the grounds for it. (But if in one of the designated police areas, and the person is under 17, the request, warning and taking of the sample must be in the presence of an appropriate adult (see below)).

Where a sample is taken from as a result of the arrest condition being met, no other sample may be taken during the same period of detention but, if the charge condition is also met, the sample taken must be treated as one taken as a result of the charge condition being met.

Appropriate adult means (a) the parent or guardian (or if in care, a representative of that organisation), (b) a social worker of a local authority social services, or (c) if none of the previous mentioned are available, any responsible person over 18 who is not a police officer or police employee.

Trigger offences. These are the following offences under:

1. the **Theft Act 1968**: S 1 (theft); S8 (robbery); S 9 (burglary); S 10 (aggravated burglary); S 12 (taking vehicle, etc. without authority); S 12A (aggravated vehicle-taking); S 22 (handling stolen goods); S 25 (going equipped for stealing);
2. the **Misuse of Drugs Act 1971**, if committed in respect of a specified Class A drug: S 4 (production and supply); S5(2) (possession); S 5(3) (possession with intent to supply);
3. S 1(1) of the **Criminal Attempts Act 1981,** if committed in respect of one of the following offences under the Theft Act 1968: S 1 (theft); S 8 (robbery); S 9 (burglary); S 15 (obtaining property by deception); S 22 (handling stolen goods);
4. the **Vagrancy Act 1824**: S 3 (begging); S 4 (persistent begging).
5. the **Fraud Act 2006**: S1 (fraud), S6 (possession etc. of articles for use in frauds), S7 (making or supplying articles for use in frauds).

Initial assessment by a suitably qualified person to establish a person's dependence on, or misuse of, a Class A drug may be required if a sample has been taken and analysis reveals such a drug may be present in the body. This is subject to age and notification conditions being met. Failure to attend is an offence.

Testing for Presence of Class A Drugs – Cont.

CODES OF PRACTICE, CODE C

The following requirements of the Codes of Practice (including Notes for Guidance) should be read in conjunction with the previous two pages.

Before making the request an officer must inform the person that the purpose of taking the sample is to test for Class A drugs; warn the person that if he fails to provide a sample he may be liable to prosecution; where authorisation has been given by an inspector, the fact that it has been so given and the grounds for it; and remind the person of his rights to: have someone informed of his arrest; consult privately with a solicitor; free legal advice; and to consult the Codes of Practice.

Persons under 17. The making of the request for a sample, the giving of the warning and information, and the taking of the sample, may not take place except in the presence of an appropriate adult (see previous page).

Detention. Custody officers may authorise continued detention for up to 6 hours from the time of charge to enable a sample to be taken. Where the arrest condition is met, a detainee whom the custody officer has decided to release on bail without charge, may continue to be detained, but not beyond 24 hours from the relevant time, for the purpose of obtaining the sample. The same applies where the arrest condition, but not the charge condition, is met where his release would otherwise be required before a sample could be taken.

Documentation. The Inspector's authorisation (if applicable), the warning, and the time of charge (or arrest where the arrest condition is being relied on) and taking the sample, must all be recorded on the custody record.

Taking the sample. Samples may only be taken by (a) a police officer; (b) a person employed by a police authority or police force for the purpose of taking such samples; and (c) a person employed by a contractor engaged by a police authority or police force for such purposes. (SI 2001/2645). **Force** may not be used to take any sample for the purpose of drug testing.

Use of the sample. May only be used for testing for Class A drugs. Must be retained until the person has made his first appearance before the court.

Form of warning. The following words may be used:

"You do not have to provide a sample, but I must warn you that if you fail or refuse without good cause to do so, you will commit an offence for which you may be imprisoned, or fined, or both".

Sufficiency of sample. It must be sufficient and suitable in quantity and quality to enable drug testing analysis to take place.

Limits on Detention

S 34 POLICE AND CRIMINAL EVIDENCE ACT 1984

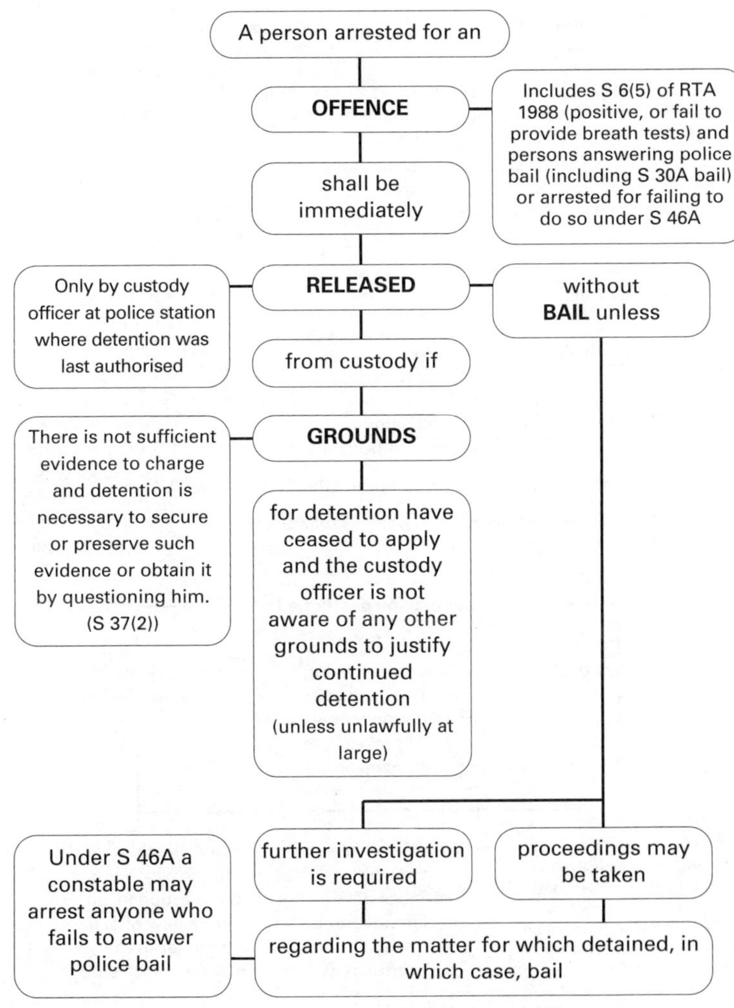

See also S 41 (post)

Reviews of Detention

S 40 POLICE AND CRIMINAL EVIDENCE ACT 1984

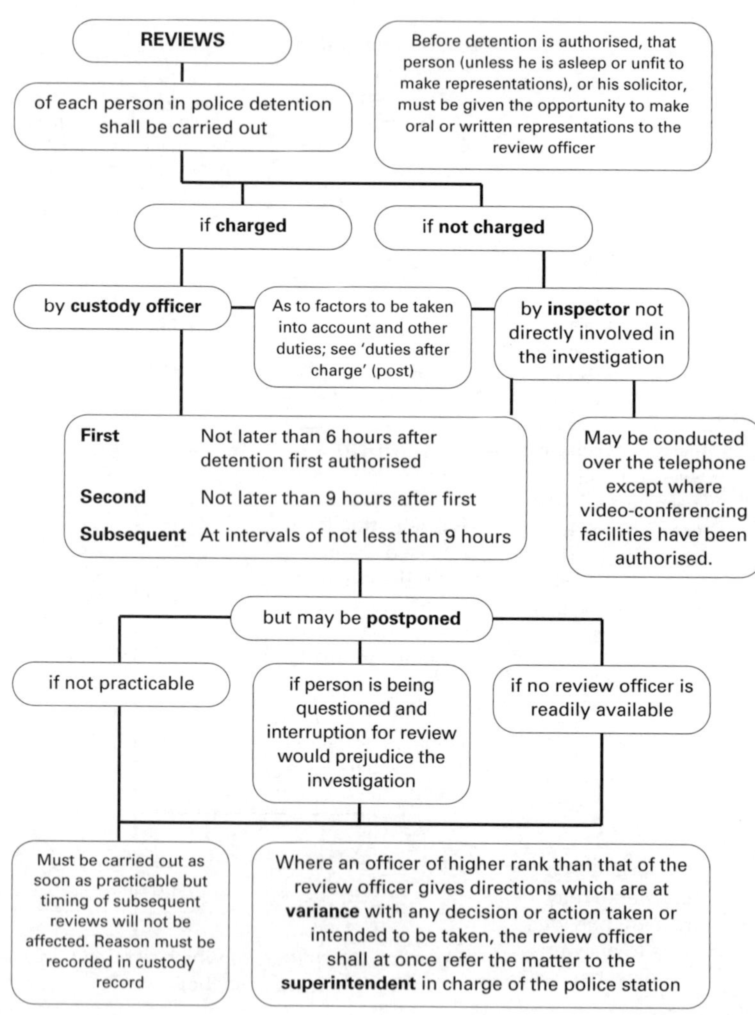

Limits on Periods of Detention Without Charge

S 41 POLICE AND CRIMINAL EVIDENCE ACT 1984

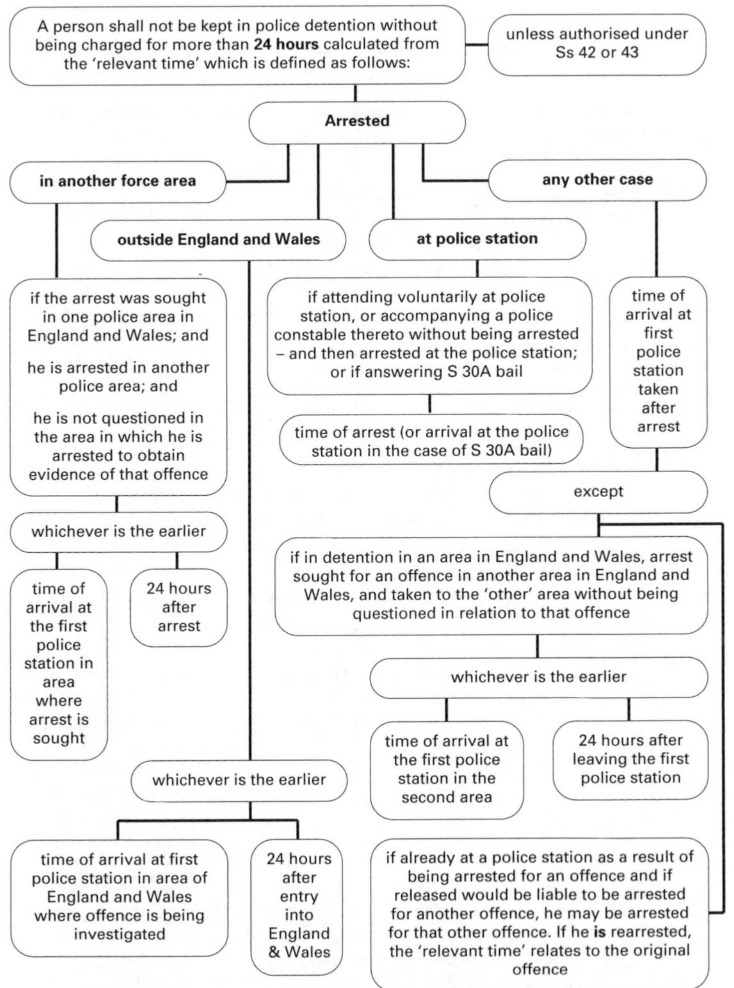

Continued Detention

S 42 POLICE AND CRIMINAL EVIDENCE ACT 1984

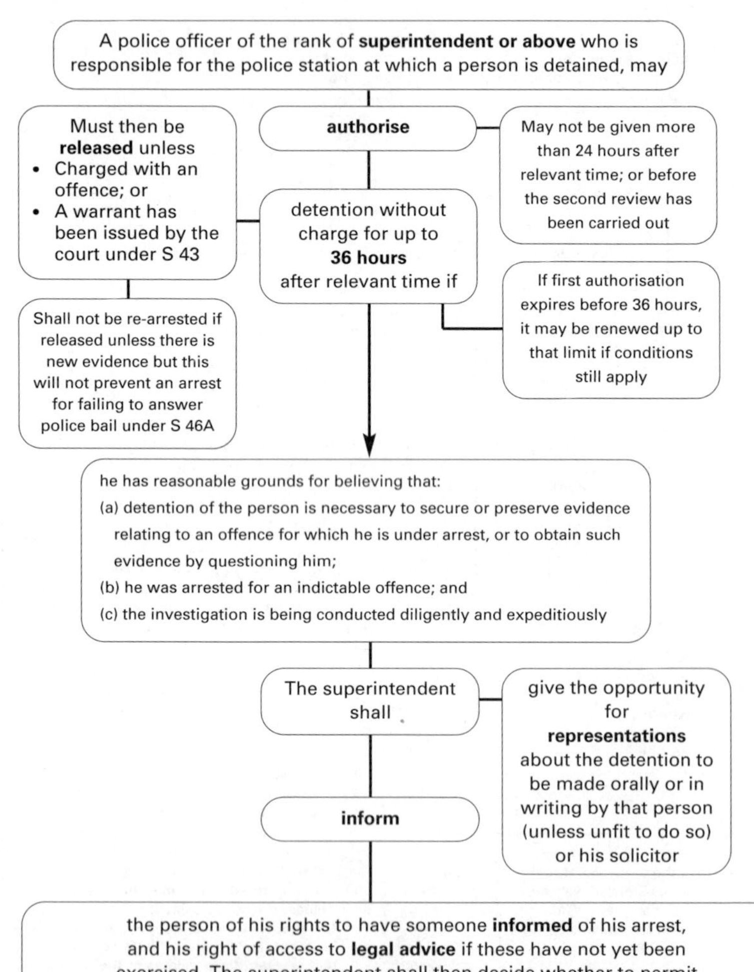

Warrant of Further Detention

S 43 POLICE AND CRIMINAL EVIDENCE ACT 1984

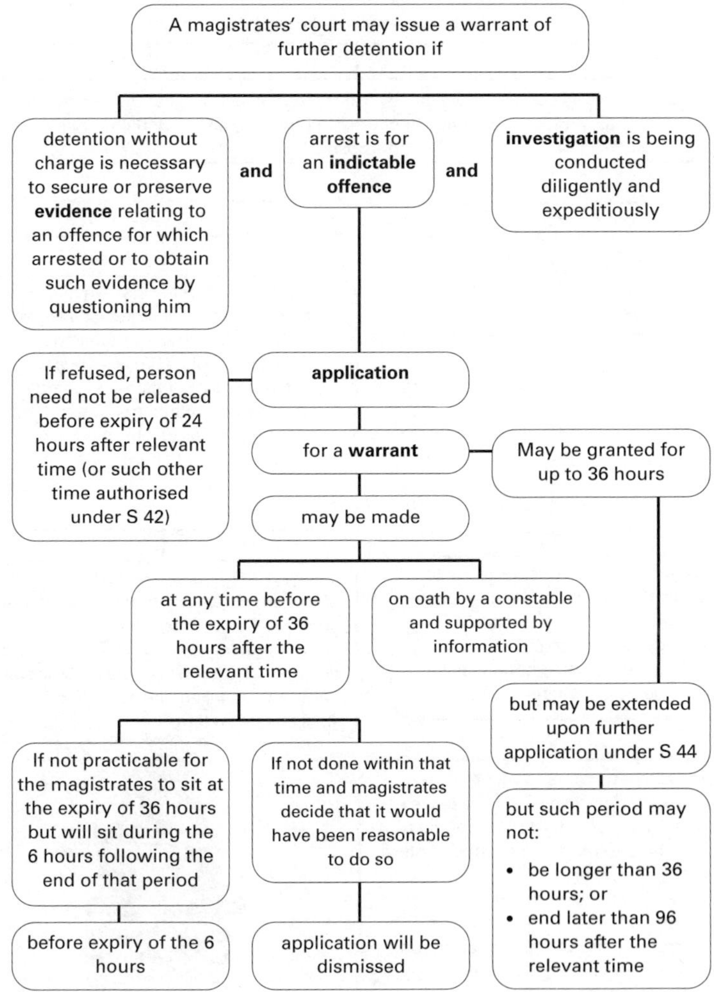

Duties Before Charge

S 37 POLICE AND CRIMINAL EVIDENCE ACT 1984, SCHED. 1 DRUGS ACT 2005

The custody officer at a police station where a person is detained following arrest without warrant, or with a warrant not endorsed for bail (if a juvenile see also following pages)

↓

shall determine, as soon as practicable after the person's arrival at the police station, whether he has sufficient evidence to charge the person (and may detain him for that purpose).

If he does not

↓

the custody officer must release either with or without bail

↓

unless he has reasonable cause to believe that detention without charge is necessary to secure or preserve evidence relating to the offence for which arrested, or to obtain such evidence by questioning him.

↓

He may then detain and record the grounds for doing so in the presence of the detained person. At that time he must inform the person of the grounds unless he is:

(a) incapable of understanding;
(b) violent or likely to become so; or
(c) in urgent need of medical attention.

If he does

↓

the custody officer decides whether to:

(a) release without charge on bail or keep in police detention to enable the Director of Public Prosecutions to make a decision as to whether to charge;
(b) release without charge on bail, but not for the above purpose;
(c) release without charge and without bail; or
(d) charge.

↓

If dealt with under (a) above the custody officer should inform him of the purpose of his release or detention. If released under (b) or (c) above, and at that time a decision whether he should be prosecuted has not been taken, the custody officer shall so inform him

Continued detention to obtain a drug sample under S 63B of PACE may be permitted for up to 24 hours after the relevant time if the offence for which the person has been arrested is one which would enable such a sample to be taken.

Charging

CODES OF PRACTICE, CODE C

Decision to charge

When the officer in charge of the investigation reasonably believes there is sufficient evidence to provide a realistic prospect of the detainee's conviction, he must cease the interview and shall, without delay, inform the custody officer who will consider whether he should be charged. The custody officer must take into account alternatives to prosecution under the Crime and Disorder Act 1988, reprimands and warnings for under 18s, and national guidance on the cautioning of offenders.

Where a person is detained for more than one offence it is permissible to delay informing the custody officer until there is sufficient evidence in relation to all offences. If the detainee is a juvenile, mentally disordered or otherwise mentally vulnerable, any resulting action shall be taken in the presence of the appropriate adult if present.

Cautioning before charge

When a detainee is charged with or informed they may be prosecuted for an offence (but a warning or NIP under the Road Traffic Offenders Act 1988 is not included), he shall be cautioned as follows (unless a restriction on drawing adverse inferences from silence applies):

"You do not have to say anything. But it may harm your defence if you do not mention now something which you later rely on in court. Anything you do say may be given in evidence."

If a restriction on drawing adverse inferences from silence applies the caution shall be as follows:

"You do not have to say anything, but anything you do say may be given in evidence."

Serving of notices

When a detainee is charged he shall be given a written notice showing particulars of the offence in simple terms but also showing the precise offence in law, and the case reference number. The officer's name shall also be shown unless the offence is linked to terrorism or the officer reasonably believes that recording his name might put him in danger. If the detainee is a juvenile, mentally disordered or mentally vulnerable, the notice should be given to the appropriate adult.

Statements of other persons

If, after a detainee has been charged or informed he may be prosecuted for an offence, an officer wants to tell him about any written statement or interview with another person relating to such an offence, the detainee shall either be handed a true copy of the statement or have brought to his attention the content of the interview record. Nothing shall be done to invite a reply or comment except to:

(a) caution the detainee, **"You do not have to say anything, but anything you do say may be given in evidence"**; and
(b) remind the detainee about his right to legal advice.

If the detainee cannot read, the document may be read to him. If he is a juvenile, mentally disordered or mentally vulnerable, the appropriate adult shall also be given a copy, or the interview record brought to his attention.

(CONTINUED ON NEXT PAGE)

Charging–Cont.

CODES OF PRACTICE, CODE C

Interview after charge

A detainee may not be interviewed about an offence after being charged or informed he may be prosecuted for an offence, unless it is necessary:

(a) to prevent or minimise harm or loss to some other person, or the public;

(b) to clear up an ambiguity in a previous answer or statement; or

(c) in the interests of justice to put to the detainee information concerning the offence which has come to light since he was charged or told that he may be prosecuted;

but before any such interview he must be:

(a) cautioned, **"You do not have to say anything, but anything you do say may be given in evidence."**, and

(b) reminded about his right to legal advice.

Presence of the appropriate adult

Where applicable, the above provisions must be complied with in the presence of the appropriate adult if he is present. If he is not, they must be repeated in his presence when he arrives unless the detainee has been released. There is no power to detain a person solely to await the arrival of the appropriate adult.

Juveniles

Where a juvenile is charged with an offence and his continued detention is authorised after charge, the custody officer must try to arrange for the juvenile to be taken into the care of the local authority to be detained pending appearance in court, unless:

(a) he certifies that it is impracticable to do so; or

(b) in the case of a juvenile over 12, no secure accommodation is available, and there is a risk to the public of serious harm from that juvenile (see following page).

Except as above, a juvenile's behaviour, the nature of the offence or the lack of secure accommodation will not be grounds for deciding it is impracticable.

If he is not transferred into the care of the local authority the custody officer must record the reasons and complete a certificate to be produced before the court.

Documentation

A record shall be made of anything a detainee says when charged.

Any questions put and answers given after being charged shall be recorded in full on the forms provided, and signed by the detainee. If he refuses it shall be signed by the interviewer and any third parties present.

Duties After Charge

S 38 POLICE AND CRIMINAL EVIDENCE ACT 1984

Requirement to release on bail
Where a person is charged with an offence the custody officer shall order his release either with or without bail, unless:

(a) **if the person is not a juvenile** and it is believed that his detention is necessary:
  (i) because there is doubt whether the name and address furnished is his real one, or that his name and address cannot be ascertained;
  (ii) because he will fail to appear in court in answer to bail;
  (iii) to prevent him committing an offence, where the offence is punishable with imprisonment;
  (iv) to enable a sample to be taken from him to test for class A drugs under S 63B of this Act (see earlier under "Testing for Class A Drugs");
  (v) to prevent him causing physical injury to any other person or from causing loss of, or damage to, property (but detention not to exceed 6 hours from when charged);
  (vi) to prevent him from interfering with the administration of justice or with the investigation of offences, where the offence is not punishable with imprisonment; or
  (vii) for his own protection,

(b) **if the person is a juvenile** and it is believed that his detention is necessary:
  (i) for any of the above reasons but in relation to the police areas mentioned in the substituted (iv) above, only if the juvenile has attained the age of 14; or
  (ii) in his own interests; or

(c) **if it is one of the following offences,** and he has been previously convicted of any such offence:
  (i) murder;
  (ii) attempted murder;
  (iii) manslaughter;
  (iv) rape; or
  (v) attempted rape

when bail will only be granted in exceptional circumstances.

Factors to be considered in refusing bail
In taking a decision to refuse to grant bail, the custody officer must be satisfied that, if released on bail, the detainee would:

(a) fail to surrender to custody;
(b) commit an offence while on bail; or
(c) interfere with witnesses or otherwise obstruct the course of justice.

Records
Any authorisation for police detention shall, as soon as practicable, be recorded in writing in the presence of the detainee, who shall be informed at that time of the grounds for it (unless the person is incapable of understanding what is being said to him; is violent or likely to become so; or is in urgent need of medical attention).

Juveniles
Where juveniles are to be kept in police detention, they should be removed to local authority accommodation unless the custody officer certifies:

(a) that it is impracticable for him to do so; or
(b) if the juvenile is over 12, that no secure accommodation is available and that keeping him in other local authority accommodation would not be adequate to protect the public from serious harm from him.

Extradition – Treatment of Arrested Persons

EXTRADITION ACT 2003

The following provisions apply where a person has been arrested under an extradition arrest power and is detained at a police station.

Fingerprints and non-intimate samples may be taken by a constable only with written consent (unless an inspector or above authorises it). (S166)

Searches and examination may be carried out by a constable (or person designated by the Chief Constable) if an inspector or above authorises it, to facilitate the identification of the person. An identifying mark so found may be photographed with consent (or without consent if it is withheld or it is not practicable to obtain it). A search, examination or photograph of any part of the body (other than the face) may not be carried out by a person of the opposite sex. This section does not authorise intimate searches. (S167)

Photographs may be taken by a constable (or person designated by the Chief Constable) with consent (or without consent if it is withheld or it is not practicable to obtain it). Any item or substance worn over the head or face may be removed.

Police and Criminal Evidence Act. Sections 54, 55, 56 and 58 apply with modifications as indicated:

(a) S54(4)(b) (searches of detained persons). For "an offence" there is substituted the offence for which extradition is sought.
(b) S55(12)(b) (intimate searches). For "an offence" there is substituted the offence for which extradition is sought.
(c) S56(2)(a) and 56(5)(a) (right to have someone informed when arrested). For "a serious arrestable offence", there is substituted "an offence for which extradition is sought that would be an offence if committed in England and Wales".
(d) S58(6)(a) and 58(8)(a) (access to legal advice). For "an offence", there is substituted "an offence for which extradition is sought that would be an offence if committed in England and Wales".

Terrorism — Detention, Treatment and Questioning of Arrested Persons

CODES OF PRACTICE - CODE H

Many of the sections of Code H are substantially the same as for other forms of police detention under Code C. The substantive changes are set out below.

Custody records

All entries on custody records must be timed and identified by the maker. But the identity of officers or other police staff need not be recorded or disclosed in the case of enquiries linked to the investigation of terrorism. In these cases they shall use their warrant or other identification numbers and the name of their police station.

Initial action in respect of arrested individuals

The record of the arrest will show that the detainee was arrested under S 41 of the Terrorism Act 2000, as opposed to a specific offence. (Para. 3.4).

Risk assessments do not form part of the custody record and should not be shown to the detainee or their legal representative. (Para. 3.8).

Detainees' property

A simplification of circumstances relating to when a custody officer should ascertain what a detainee has in his possession. These are when the detainee comes to the police station either on the first occasion or on any subsequent occasions in connection with that detention. (Para. 4.1).

Right not to be held incommunicado

The right not to be held incommunicado may be delayed only in accordance with Annex B below. (Para. 5.2).

Where the detainee has requested particular visitors or where visitors have identified themselves to the police, the custody officer should liaise closely with the investigation team to allow risk assessments to be made. Where the nature of the investigation means that such requests can not be met consideration should be given to increasing the frequency of visits from independent visitor schemes. Official visitors may include accredited faith representatives, members of either House of Parliament, public officials, other persons visiting with the approval of the chief investigating officer, and consular officials of the detainee's country. (Para. 5.4).

Either or both of the privileges of being given writing materials or making a telephone call may be denied or delayed if an inspector or above considers it may result in one of the consequences contained in Annex B below, particularly in relation to the making of a telephone call in a language which a listening officer does not understand. (Para. 5.6).

Terrorism — Detention, Treatment and Questioning of Arrested Persons — Cont.

Right to legal advice

An officer of the rank of commander or assistant chief constable may give a direction that a detainee may only consult a solicitor within the sight and hearing of a 'qualified officer' if he has reasonable grounds to believe that if it were not given the solicitor may, inadvertently or otherwise, pass on a message from the detainee or act in some other way which will have any of the following consequences:

(a) interference with or harm to evidence of an indictable offence;

(b) interference with or physical injury to any person;

(c) the alerting of persons who are suspected of having committed an indictable offence but have not been arrested for it;

(d) hindering the recovery of property obtained as a result of an indictable offence;

(e) interference with the gathering of information about the commission, preparation or instigation of acts of terrorism;

(f) the alerting of a person and thereby making it more difficult to prevent an act of terrorism;

(g) the alerting of a person and thereby making it more difficult to secure a person's apprehension, prosecution or conviction in connection with an act of terrorism; and

(h) by informing the named person of the detention the recovery of the value of the proceeds of the offence. (Para. 6.5).

A 'qualified officer' means-

(a) is at least the rank of inspector,

(b) is of the uniformed branch of the same force as the officer giving the direction, and

(c) in the opinion of the officer giving the direction, has no connection with the detained person's case.

Conditions of detention

If facilities exist indoor exercise should be offered if outside conditions are not suitable (for example because of weather), or if requested by the detainee, or for reasons of security. (Para. 8.7).

Terrorism — Detention, Treatment and Questioning of Arrested Persons — Cont.

Where practicable, provision should be made for detainees to practice religious observance, including the provision of a separate room for praying, the supply of appropriate food and clothing, and religious books. (Para. 8.8).

Reading material including religious texts are to be made available where practicable. (Para. 8.10).

Representatives of the main religious communities should be consulted to ensure the provision of religious observance is adequate, or to seek advice on the appropriate storage and handling of religious texts, etc. (note for guidance 8D).

Care and treatment of detained persons

Detainees who are held for more than 96 hours must be visited by a healthcare professional at least once every 24 hours. (Para. 9.1).

Interviews in police stations

During extended periods where no interviews take place, because of the need to gather or analyse evidence, detainees and their legal representative must be informed that the investigation remains ongoing and, if practicable, made aware of reasons for long gaps. (Para. 12.9).

Terrorism — Detention, Treatment and Questioning of Arrested Persons — Cont.

Reviews and extensions of detention

A review officer may authorise continued detention up to 48 hours from the time of arrest under S 41 (or from the commencement of the examination if detained under Sched. 7) if it is necessary-

(a) to obtain relevant evidence whether by questioning him or otherwise,

(b) to preserve relevant evidence,

(c) while awaiting the result of an examination or analysis of relevant evidence,

(d) for the examination or analysis of anything with a view to obtaining relevant evidence,

(e) pending a decision to apply to the Secretary of State for a deportation notice to be served on the detainee, the making of such an application, or the consideration of it,

(f) pending a decision to charge the detainee with an offence.
(S 24(1) Terrorism Act 2006 and note for guidance 14B).

If detention is necessary for longer than 48 hours, a superintendent or above (or a Crown Prosecutor) may apply for warrants of further detention. (Para. 14.3).

Where such an application is made, the detainee and their representative must be informed of their rights which include a written or oral notice of the warrant, the right to make oral or written representations to the judicial authority, the right to be present and legally represented at the hearing (unless specifically excluded by the judicial authority) and the right to free legal advice. (Para. 14.4).

Annex B

The right not to be held incommunicado and the right to legal advice may be delayed if the person is detained under S 41 of the Terrorism Act 2000, has not yet been charged with an offence and an officer of superintendent or above has reasonable grounds for believing that the exercise of either right will have one of the following consequences-

(a) interference with or harm to evidence of a serious offence,

(b) interference with or physical injury to any person,

Terrorism — Detention, Treatment and Questioning of Arrested Persons — Cont.

(c) the alerting of persons who are suspected of having committed a serious offence but who have not been arrested for it,

(d) the hindering of the recovery of property obtained as a result of a serious offence or in respect of which a forfeiture order could be made under S 23,

(e) interference with the gathering of information about the commission, preparation or instigation of acts of terrorism,

(f) the alerting of a person and thereby making it more difficult to prevent an act of terrorism, or

(g) the alerting of a person and thereby making it more difficult to secure a person's apprehension, prosecution or conviction in connection with the commission, preparation or instigation of an act of terrorism.

These rights may also be delayed if the officer has reasonable grounds for believing that-

(a) the detained person has benefited from his criminal conduct (to be decided in accordance with Part 2 of the Proceeds of Crime Act 2002) and

(b) the recovery of the value of the property constituting the benefit will be hindered by informing the named person of the detained person's detention, or by the exercise of the right.

CHRONOLOGICAL TABLE OF LEGISLATION

Legislation	Page
Vagrancy Act 1824	266
S 3	267
S 4	266, 267
Night Poaching Act 1828	
S 1	221
S 2	222
S 9	222
Game Act 1831	
S 3	219
S 24	219
S 30	220
S 31	220, 223
S 31A	223
S 32	220
S 35	220
Hares Act 1848	218
Game Licences Act 1860	218
Poaching Prevention Act 1862	223
Dogs Act 1871	206
Pedlars Act 1871	263
Licensing Act 1872	181
Town Police Clauses Act 1847	
S 28	114
Offences Against the Person Act 1861	
S 5	48
S 18	45
S 20	44
S 38	46
S 47	42
S 60	48
Licensing Act 1872	
S 12	114, 181
Ground Game Act 1880	218
Uniforms Act 1894	257
Licensing Act 1902	181

Legislation	Page
Public Meeting Act 1908	315
Police, Factories etc. (Miscellaneous Provisions) Act 1916	184
Official Secrets Act 1920	257
Infant Life (Preservation) Act 1929	48
Children and Young Persons Act 1933	
S 1	249
S 3	255
S 4	253
S 5	251
S 7	251
S 11	254
S 17	249
S 18	250
S 107	248
Public Order Act 1936	
S 2	317
Infanticide Act 1938	48
House to House Collections Act 1939	184
House to House Collections Regulations 1947	184
Visiting Forces Act 1952	257
Dogs (Protection of Livestock) Act 1953	205
Air Force Act 1955	257, 258
Army Act 1955	257, 258
Children and Young Persons (Harmful Publications) Act 1955	82
Sexual Offences Act 1956	
S 33	86
S 34	87
S 35	87
S 36	87
Naval Discipline Act 1957	257
Obscene Publications Act 1959	81
Street Offences Act 1959	
S 1	83
Game Laws (Amendment) Act 1960	223
Indecency with Children Act 1960	
S 1	95
British Transport Commission Act 1962	257
Children and Young Persons Act 1963	250

Legislation	Page
Obscene Publications Act 1964	81
Scrap Metal Dealers Act 1964	264
Education Act 1966	253
Criminal Justice Act 1967	181
Firearms Act 1968	
S 1	106
S 2	109
S 3	112
S 4	114
S 5(1)	103
S 5(1A)	104
S 5A	104, 105
S 7	107
S 9	107
S 10	107
S 11	107, 108
S 12	108
S 13	108
S 14	107
S 15	107
S 16	110
S 16A	110
S 17	110, 111
S 18	110
S 19	113
S 20	113
S 21	113
S 22	115
S 24	115
S 25	114
S 47	116
S 48	116
S 54	108
S 57	102
S 58	108, 109
Theft Act 1968	
S 1	15
S 2	16
S 3	16
S 4	17

Legislation	Page
S 5	18
S 6	18
S 8	23
S 9	24
S 10	24
S 11	19
S 12	20
S 12A	20
S 13	22
S 17	34
S 18	35
S 19	35
S 20	37
S 21	36
S 22	39
S 23	15
S 24A	33
S 25	40
S 32	238
Sched. 1	238
Tattooing of Minors Act 1969	251
Conservation of Seals Act 1970	242
Criminal Damage Act 1971	
S 1(1)	50
S 1(2)	51
S 1(3)	51
S 2	52
S 3	52
Misuse of Drugs Act 1971	
S 3	54
S 4(1)	56
S 4(2)	54
S 4(3)	56, 161
S 4A	56
S 5(2)	57
S 5(3)	58
S 5(4)	57
S 6(2)	58
S 8	59
S 9	60

Legislation	Page
S 9A	55
S 23	61, 376
S 28	53, 56
Guard Dogs Act 1971	210
Immigration Act 1971	
S 1	259
S 2	259
S 3	259
S 24	260
S 24A	260
S 25	260
Children Act 1972	250
Immigration (Hotel Records) Order 1972	261
Biological Weapons Act 1974	319
Control of Pollution Act 1974	272
Rabies (Importation of Dogs, Cats and other Mammals) Order 1974	216
Salmon and Freshwater Fisheries Act 1975	
S 1	239
S 2	239
S 3	239
S 4	239
S 5	239
S 7	239
S 19	241
S 25	240
S 27	240
S 35	240
Sched. 1	241
Dangerous Wild Animals Act 1976	211
Criminal Law Act 1977	
S 6	310
S 7	311
S 8	312
S 9	212
S 10	212
S 12	311
S 12A	311
S 51	349

Legislation	Page
Protection of Children Act 1978	
S 1	79, 99
Refuse Disposal (Amenity) Act 1978	271
Theft Act 1978	
S 3	38
Customs and Excise Management Act 1979	
S 50	54
S 170	99
Highways Act 1980	
S 155	212
S 161	114
S 185	270
Animal Health Act 1981	
S 15	213, 215
S 60	213
S 61	215
S 62	215
Criminal Attempts Act 1981	
S 1	14
S 9	21
Indecent Displays (Control) Act 1981	
S 1	80
Wildlife and Countryside Act 1981	
S 1	232
S 2	233
S 4	233
S 5	234
S 6	235
S 7	236
S 8	236
S 13	202
S 19	202, 237
Sched. 1	231
Sched. 2	231
Sched. 3	231
Sched. 4	231
Sched. 5	200
Aviation Security Act 1982	
S 24A	397

Legislation	Page
Firearms Act 1982	106
Litter Act 1983	270
Mental Health Act 1983	262
Police and Criminal Evidence Act 1984	
S 1	385, 386
S 2	374
S 3	380
S 4	395
S 8	394
S 10	392
S 16	394
S 17	197, 215, 387
S 18	388
S 19	389
S 24	367
S 24A	368
S 26	369
S 27	422
S 28	371
S 30	371
S 30A	372
S 30B	372
S 30C	372
S 30D	372
S 32	393
S 34	435
S 36	410
S 37	440
S 38	443
S 39	412
S 40	436
S 41	437
S 42	438
S 43	439
S 54A	429
S 55	424, 425
S 55A	428
S 56	417
S 58	415

Legislation	Page
S 61	422
S 61A	405
S 62	408, 430
S 63	431
S 63A	431
S 63B	432, 433
S 64	431
S 64A	406, 423
S 65	430
Sched. 2	369
Telecommunications Act 1984	
S 42	344
S 43	348
Sexual Offences Act 1985	
S 1	84
Sporting Events (Control of Alcohol Etc.) Act 1985	
S 1	287
S 1A	287
S 2	287
S 2A	288
S 7	288
Public Order Act 1986	
S 1	314
S 2	275, 276, 314
S 3	313
S 4	275
S 4A	277
S 5	276
S 8	275
S 14A	304
S 14B	305
S 14C	305
S 17 – 23	300
S 38	350
Crossbows Act 1987	297
Criminal Justice Act 1988	
S 39	42
S 139	290
S 139B	376
S 141	291

Legislation	Page
S 141A	292
S 160	99
Criminal Justice Act 1988 (Offensive Weapons) Order 1988	291
Firearms (Amendment) Act 1988	
S 5	112
S 16	108
S 17	108
Malicious Communications Act 1988	347
Road Traffic Act 1988	
S 25	21
Children Act 1989	249
S 46	256
Football Spectators Act 1989	286
Computer Misuse Act 1990	352
Environmental Protection Act 1990	270
Dangerous Dogs Act 1991	
S 1	207
S 2	209
S 3	208
S 5	209
S 6	208
S 7	207
S 10	208
Deer Act 1991	
S 1	224
S 2	225
S 3	225
S 4	226
S 5	225
S 10	227
S 12	228
Sched. 1	225
Football (Offences) Act 1991	285
Aggravated Vehicle-taking Act 1992	20
Charities Act 1992	183
Control of Dogs Order 1992	204
Protection of Badgers Act 1992	
S 1	229
S 2	229
S 4	229

Legislation	Page
S 5	229
S 6	230
S 10	230
Trade Union and Labour Relations (Consolidation) Act 1992	
S 220	274
S 241	273
Criminal Justice and Public Order Act 1994	
S 34	357
S 36	357
S 37	357
S 51	353
S 60	295, 293, 396
S 60AA	296
S 61	301
S 62	301
S 62A	301
S 62B	301
S 62C	301
S 63	308, 309
S 64	309
S 65	309
S 66AA	343
S 68	302
S 69	303
S 70	304
S 71	305
S 72	310
S 73	311
S 84	79
S 137	370
S 154	277
S 166	289
S 167	351
Merchant Shipping Act 1995	257
Chemical Weapons Act 1996	318
Police Act 1996	
S 89	46, 268
S 90	257, 268

Legislation	Page
Sexual Offences (Conspiracy and Incitement) Act 1996	95
Wild Mammals (Protection) Act 1996	199
Knives Act 1997	293, 295
Protection from Harassment Act 1997	278
Crime and Disorder Act 1998	
S 16	252
S 28–32	299
Breeding and Sale of Dogs (Welfare) Act 1999	203
Criminal Justice and Court Services Act 2000	432
Football (Disorder) Act 2000	286
Postal Services Act 2000	346
Terrorism Act 2000	
S 1	320
S 3	327
S 11	321
S 12	321
S 13	322
S 15	322
S 16	323
S 17	323
S 18	323
S 19	334
S 20	334
S 21	323
S 33	335
S 34	335
S 35	335
S 36	335
S 37	335
S 38	335
S 39	335
S 40	336
S 41	336
S 42	336
S 43	336
S 44	337
S 45	337
S 48	338
S 49	338

Legislation	Page
S 50	338
S 51	338
S 52	338
S 54	324
S 56	325
S 57	325
S 58	325
S 59	326
S 60	326
S 61	326
S 62	326
S 63	326
Sched. 2	339
Anti-terrorism, Crime and Security Act 2001	
S 47	340
S 113	341
S 114	342
Criminal Justice and Police Act 2001	
Ss 12–15	182
S 40	353
S 42	279
S 42A	280
S 46	85
S 50	390
S 51	390
S 52	392
S 53	392
Sched. 1	391
Misuse of Drugs Act 2001	49, 51
Vehicle (Crime) Act 2001	265
Police Reform Act 2002	284
Police (Retention and Disposal of Vehicles) Act 2002	284
Anti-social Behaviour Act 2003	
Ss 1–11	62
S 30	283
S 54	52
Criminal Justice Act 2003	432
Extradition Act 2003	444
Fireworks Act 2003	298

Legislation	Page
Licensing Act 2003	
S 1	157, 158
S 2	157, 158
S 11	159
S 12	159
S 14	159
S 15	159
S 17	159
S 18	159
S 19	159
S 24	159
S 26	159
S 33	159
S 57	159
S 60	161
S 94	161
S 97	161
S 98	163
S 100	163
S 101	163
S 104	163
S 107–109	163
S 111	165
S 115	165
S 120	165
S 125	165
S 127–129	165
S 132	165
S 135	165
S 136–139	167
S 140–144	168
S 145	170
S 147–149	172
S 149, 150 & 159	173
S 150 & 151	174
S 152–153	175
S 159	173
S 161–162	177, 178
S 162, 163, 169	178
S 170	178
S 172	179

Legislation	Page
S 173	179
S 174	179
S 175	179
S 179	180
S 180	180
S 191	180
Sched. 1	157
Sched. 2	158
Sexual Offences Act 2003	
S 1	64
S 2	65
S 3	66
S 4	67
Ss 5–8	68
Ss 9–12	69
Ss 14–15	70
Ss 16–19	71
S 21	72
Ss 25–26	73
S 27	74
Ss 30–33	75
Ss 34–37	76
Ss 38–44	77
S 45	79
Ss 47–51	78
Ss 52–54	88
Ss 57–59	89
Ss 61–63	90
Ss 64–65	91
S 66	67
S 67	92
S 69	93
S 70	94
S 71	94, 97
S 72	94
S 74	65, 97
S 75	65, 66, 67 96
S 76	65, 66, 67 96
S 78	97

Legislation	Page
S 79	65, 97
Ss 80–91	98
Sched. 3	99
Female Genital Mutilation Act 2003	47
Domestic Violence, Crime and Victims Act 2004	
S 5	49
Fireworks Regulations 2004	298
Football Spectators (Prescription) Order 2004	286
Hunting Act 2004	
S 1	243
S 2	243
S 3	245
S 4	246
S 5	246
S 8	246
S 11	246
Sched. 1	243
Non Commercial Movement of Pet Animals (England) Regulations 2004	217
Drugs Act 2005	
S 5	428
S 7	432
S 9	432
Sched. 1	62, 440
Gambling Act 2005	
S 3	118
S 4	118
S 5	119
S 6	125
S 7	125
S 8	125
S 9	128
S 10	128
S 11	133
S 12	134
S 13	134
S 14	135
S 15	130
S 16	138

Legislation	Page
S 17	138
S 18	138
S 37	122
S 41	123
S 42	144
S 43	144
S 44	144
S 46	145
S 47	145
S 48	146
S 49	146
S 50	146
S 51	147
S 52	147
S 53	147
S 54	147
S 55	147
S 56	148
S 57	148
S 65	120
S 66	121
S 67	121
S 68	120
S 68	120
S 80	124
S 108	121
S 127	124
S 134	124
S 150	122
S 172	140
S 214	122
S 227	143
S 229	143
S 235	139
S 240	141
S 242	127
S 252	136
S 258	136
S 259	137
S 260	137

Legislation	Page
S 261	137
S 262	137
S 269	126
S 271	141
S 272	126
S 273	127
S 275	127
S 275	126
S 279	128
S 282	128
S 283	129
S 287	129
S 288	129
S 289	123
S 290	130
S 291	123
S 292	123
S 296	131
S 297	131
S 298	132
S 299	132
S 300	132
S 301	132
S 302	131
S 305	149
S 306	149
S 307	150
S 308	150
S 309	150
S 310	150
S 311	150
S 312	150
S 313	150
S 315	149
S 316	149
S 317	151
S 318	152
S 323	152
S 326	152
S 335	135
Sched. 11	136

Legislation	Page
Sched. 12	127
Sched. 13	129
Sched. 15	130
Gaming Machines (Maximum Prizes) Regulations 2005	123
Prevention of Terrorism Act 2005	343
Serious Organised Crime and Police Act 2005	
S 110	367, 368
S 112	306
S 128	305
S 132	306
S 145	281
S 146	282
Serious Organised Crime and Police Act 2005 (Designated Sites) Order 2005	305
Serious Organised Crime and Police Act 2005 (Designated Area) Order 2005	306
Sports Grounds and Sporting Events (Designation) Order 2005	287
Football Spectators (Prescription) (Amendment) Order 2006	286
Terrorism Act 2006	
Ss 1–3	327
Ss 5 & 6	329
Ss 8 & 9	330
Ss 10 & 11	331
S 12	305
S 17	326
S 20	332
S 28	336
Sched. 1	332
Gambling Act 2005 (Definition of Small-scale Operator) Regulations 2006	124
Fraud Act 2006	
S2	25, 26
S3	28
S4	29
S5	25
S6	30

Legislation	Page
S7	30
S9	31
S11	32
Police and Justice Act 2006	
S12	397
Violent Crime Reduction Act 2006	
S24	176
S35	114
Welfare of Animals Act 2006	
S1	186
S2	186
S3	186
S4	187
S5	188
S6	189
S7	190
S8	191
S9	193
S11	194
S18	195
S19	197
S22	197
S24	197
S54	198
S62	187
Docking of Working Dogs' Tails (England) Order 2007	189
Gambling Act 2005 (Inspection) (Provision of Information) Regs. 2007	153
Children and Young Persons (Sale of Tobacco, etc.) Order 2007	251
Sexual Offences Act 2003 (Amendment of Schedules 3 and 5) Order 2007	99
Ticket Touting (Designation of Football Matches) Order 2007	289
Serious Organised Crime and Police Act 2005 (Designated Sites under Section 128) Order 2007	305, 306
Gambling Act, 2005 (Mandatory and Default Conditions) (England and Wales) Regulations 2007	154

Index

Abandoning vehicles 271
Abstracting electricity 22
Abuse of position of trust 71
Abusive words/conduct 275
Accounting, false 34
Actual bodily harm, assault occasioning 42
Administration of poisons, animals 190
Adverse inferences 357
Code of practice 358
Advertising prostitution 85
Advertising rewards 15
Aerodromes, stop and search 397
Aerosols
Sale to Children 52
Affray, definition 313
Aggravated
Burglary 24
Trespass 302
Trespass, removal of persons 303
Air weapon
Ages 115
Prohibited weapon 103
Specially dangerous 106
Aircraft, power to search 397
Alarm
Causing 277
Intentional, causing 276
Vehicle causing 284
Alcohol
Allowing children on premises 170
Allowing consumption by children 173
Allowing delivery to children 174
Allowing sale to children 171
Allowing unsupervised sale by children 175
Consumed in public places 182
Consumption by children 173, 251
Control of, sporting events 288
Delivering to children 174
Exposed for unauthorised sale 167
Kept on premises for unauthorised sale 167
Meaning of 180
Obtaining for drunk person 168
On coaches 287
On trains 287
Public places 181
Purchase by children 172
Purchase on behalf of children 172
Sale to children 171
Sale to drunk person 168
Sending children to obtain 175
Special Occasion order 179
Sporting events 287
Supply of, meaning 160
Ammunition, definition 102
Animal Research Organisations,
Intimidation 282
Protection 281
Animals
Dangerous, wild 211
destruction of 195
Diseases of 213
fights 191
in distress 195
Importation of 216
meaning 186
mutilation of 188
needs, not met 193
On highways 212
Pet travel scheme 217
police powers 197
powers of entry to premises 197
prizes as 194
prohibited procedure 188
protected, meaning 186
responsibility for 186
sale to under 16s 194
seizure of 197
suffering, alleviation 195
unnecessary suffering 187
Annoyance, vehicle causing 284
Antique firearms 109
Anti-social behaviour
Closure orders 62
Dispersal of groups 283
Armed forces
Absentees and deserters 257
Uniforms, wearing illegally 257
Arrest, mode of 361
Cross Border 370
Informing prisoner of 361
Arrest, powers of,
constables 367
other persons 368
Arrest, power to
enter and search premises 215
Arson 51

Index

Articles, removal from places open to the public 19
Assault 41
- Common 42
- Defences 43
- Definition 41
- Occasioning actual bodily harm 42
- On police 46, 268

Attempts, criminal 14
Badgers 229
- Exceptions 230
- Police powers 230

Bail, before arrival at police station 372
Banning orders, football spectators 286
Begging
- Children 253
- Vagrants 267

Betting
- definition 133
- non-commercial, definition 131
- non-commercial, exemption 132
- pool 134
- private, definition 130
- spread bets 133

Betting intermediary 134
Bingo halls, gaming 130
Biological weapons 319
Birds
- Categories 231
- Close season 233
- Confining 236
- Disturbing 232
- Disturbing nests 232
- Eggs, offences 219
- Exceptions 233
- Offences 232
- Prohibited methods of killing, etc. 234
- Registration of captive 236
- Restriction on sale 235
- Shooting events 236

Birth, concealment of 48
Blackmail 36
Bomb hoaxes 349
Brothels 86
- Children frequenting 255
- Landlord Letting premises 87
- Managing 86
- Tenant permitting permises to be used as 87

Burglary 24
- Aggravated 24

Burning, exposing children to risk of 254
Businesses, fraudulent 31
Cannabis, cultivating 58
Carriage, drunk in charge of 181
Casino premises licence 142
Casino, definition 125
Caution
- When given 356
- Wording 356

Charging
- Caution, wording of 441
- Duties after 443
- Duties before 440
- General 441
- Interview after 442
- Juveniles 442
- Records 442
- Relevant time 437
- Sufficient evidence to justify 443

Charitable collections 183
Chemical weapons 318
Child
- causing death of 49
- definition 248
- destruction 49

Children
- Allowing consumption of alcohol by 169
- Allowing delivery alcohol to 167
- Allowing on licensed premises 167
- Allowing sale of alcohol to 171
- Allowing to consume alcohol 251
- And young persons 248
- Begging 253
- Consumption of alcohol by 173
- Cruelty to 249
- Delivering alcohol to 174
- Drunk in charge of 181
- Employment 250
- Exposing to risk of burning 254
- Frequenting brothels 255
- Police protection 256
- Purchase of alcohol by 172
- Purchase of alcohol on behalf of 172
- Sale of alcohol to 171
- Sale of liqueur confectionary to 172
- Sale of tobacco to 251
- Sending to obtain alcohol 175

Index

Tattoos 251
To receive education 253
Tobacco 251
Truancy 252
Unsupervised sale of alcohol by 175
Close season
Birds 232
Fish 241
Game 219
Closure order
Licensed premises 169
Premises used for drugs 62
Club gaming permit 126
Club machine permit 127
Club premises
Allowing children on 161
Certificate 161
Police power to enter 163
Coaches, control of alcohol 287
Collars, dogs 204
Collections 183
Fraudulent, vagrants 267
House to house 184
Street 184
Common assault 42
Communications, malicious 347
Company directors, false statements 35
Company officers, liability of 35
Complex lottery, definition 135
Computer
Misuse 352
Modifying material 352
Unauthorised access 352
Concealment of birth 48
Contamination of goods 350
Continued detention 438
Control of alcohol, sporting events 287
Control of dogs 208
Control orders 343
Controlled drugs 53
Convention offences 327
Conveyance, taking without authority 20
Court officers, obstructing 312
Credit, wrongfully retaining 33
Crime 13
Criminal
Attempts 14
Damage 20
Use of firearms 110
Cross-category activities, gambling 138
Cross border arrests 370
Crossbows
Offences 297
Police powers 297
Cruelty
To children 249
To wild mammals 199
Cultivating cannabis 58
Custody officers, who may be 410
Custody records 411
Damage 50
Intent to endanger life by 51
Possession with intent to 52
Threats to 52
Dangerous dogs, orders for controlling 206
Dangerous wild animals 211
Dealer, firearms 112
Death
causing death of child 49
causing death of vulnerable adult 49
Decorations and Badges 258
Deer 224
Close season 225
Poaching 224
Prohibited weapons, etc. 225
Taking at night 225
Use of weapons, etc. 226
Venison, sale of 227
Demonstrations in designated area 306
Depositing litter 270
Designated area, demonstrating in 306
Designated premises supervisor 160
Designated site, trespassing on 305
Designated sporting areas 287
Designated sports grounds 287
Detained persons
Conditions of detention 421
For extradition treatment 444
Illness 419
Infectious diseases 419
Legal advice 415
Medication 419
Normal procedure 413
Notification of arrest, delays 417
Responsibility for 412
Special groups 414

Index

Detention
- Continued 438
- Continued, to obtain drug sample 440
- Extension 448
- Limits 435
- Relevant time 437
- Reviews 436
- Warrant of further 439
- Without charge, limit of period 437

Diseases
- Of animals 213
- Of animals, definitions 214
- Rabies 215

Disguises, removal of 296
Dishonestly obtaining services 32
Disorderly conduct, allowing 168
Dispersal of groups 283
Displays, indecent 80
Distress
- Causing 276
- Intentional, causing 277
- Vehicle causing 284

Distress, animal in 195
Docking of dogs' tails 189
Dogs' tails, docking 189
Documents, suppression of 37
Dogs
- Collars 204
- Control of 208
- Dangerous 207
- Fouling land 212
- Guard 210
- Orders for controlling dangerous 206
- Sale of 203
- To be kept on lead 212
- Worrying livestock 205

Drugs 53
- Closure of premises, used for 62
- Controlled 53
- Import/export 54
- Police powers 61
- Possession of 57
- Possession with intent to supply 58
- Production 54
- Supply of articles 55
- Supplying 56
- Supplying, aggravated offence 56
- Testing for 432
- Testing for, Code of Practice 434
- Ultrasound scans for 428
- Use of premises 59
- X-rays for 428

Drunk
- And disorderly 168, 169
- In charge of an animal 181
- In charge of a carriage 181
- In charge of children 181
- In charge of firearm 114, 181

Drunkenness 168, 169
Drunk person
- Obtaining alcohol for 169
- Sale of alcohol to 168

Drunks in public places 181
Duties before charging 440
Education, children to receive 253
Electricity, abstracting 22
Electronic communications, malicious 347
Employment of children 250
Enclosed premises, found on 267
Encounters, recording of 381
Endangering life, by damage 51
Entertainment centres, gaming 130
Equal chance gaming
- definition 125
- non-commercial 132

Ethnic classification categories 382
Export and import of drugs 54
Exposing wounds, vagrants 267
Extradition, treatment of arrested persons 444
Failure to leave licensed premises 168
False accounting 34
False statements, company directors 35
Fear or provocation of violence 275
Female gential mutilation 47
Fingerprints 422
Fights, animal 191
Firearms
- Ages 115
- Antique 109
- Certificates 106
- Certificates, exemptions 107
- Converting 114
- Criminal use of 110
- Dealers 112
- Definition 102
- Disqualified by imprisonment, etc. 113
- Drunk in charge of 114, 181
- Firearms Act, Schedule 1 offences 111

Index

Imitation, definition 102
primers, buying or selling 105
Possession 113
Repair of 112
Sale to persons under 17 115
Shortening barrels 114
Supply to drunk or insane persons 114

Fireworks
possession 298
sporting events, at 287

Fish
Close season 241
Offences 239
Unlawful taking 238

Fishing licences 240

Flick knives, offences 290

Football matches, regulated 286

Football offences
Chanting 285
Entering playing area 285
Throwing missiles 285
Ticket touts 289

Football pools, children, invitation to participate in 148

Football spectators, banning orders 286

Footwear impressions 405

Fraudulent collections, vagrants 267

Fraud
abuse of position, by 29
failing to disclose information, by 28
false representation, by 25
false representation, elements of offence 26
fraudulent businesses 31
gain and loss, definition 25
general offence 25
making or supplying articles for 30
possession of articles for use in 30

Fund-raising, proscribed organisations 322

Gain and loss, definition 25

Gambling
assessing compliance 149
chain-gift schemes 144
cheating 144
children, by 145
children, employment of 147
children, invitation to enter premises 145
children, invitation to gamble 145
children, provision for gambling, by 146
cross-category activities 138
definition 118
entering premises, offence suspected 149
entry to premises, use of force 152
facilities, definition 119
justice's warrant to enter premises 149
licence 119
objectives 118
obstructing exercise of powers 153
powers to gather evidence 151
principles 118
remote, definition 118
software 123
specific powers of entry 150
unlawful activities abroad 144

Gambling Act
conditions 154
mandatory conditions 154
default conditions 154

Game
Definition 218
Licences 218
Seasons 219

Game of chance, definition 125

Gaming centres, gaming 130

Gaming machine/s
alcohol licence 128
definition 139
making available for use 141
manufacture, supply, etc. 141
number 140
offences 141
permit, club 129
permit, licensed premises 129
travelling fairs 129

Gaming
alcohol licence 128
bingo halls 130
definition 125
exempt 126
Intermediary, betting 134
non-commercial, definition 131
non-commercial, exemption 132
private, definition 130
prize 129
travelling fairs 130

Genital mutilation 47

Going equipped 40

Gravity knives, offences 290

Index

Grievous bodily harm
- Inflicting 44
- Inflicting with intent 45

Groups, dispersal of 283
Guard dogs 210
Guardian, definition 248
Handling stolen goods 39
Harassment
- Causing 276
- In the home, offence 280
- In the home, prevention 279
- Intentional, causing 277
- Police powers 279
- Protection from 276
- To prevent activities 276

Harmful publications 82
Highways, animals on 212
Hoax, terrorism 342
Homicide 48
House to house collections 184
Hunting
- Hare coursing 246
- Police powers 246
- Wild mammals, assistance 245
- Wild mammals, defence 245
- Wild mammals, exemptions 243
- Wild mammal, meaning 245
- Wild mammals, offence 243

Identification
- Body samples and impressions 408
- By examination 405
- Code of Practice 398
- Confrontation 404
- Fingerprints 405
- Footwear impressions 405
- Groups 403
- Methods 398
- Parades 402
- Photographs 404
- Video 401
- Witnesses 399

Imitation firearm
- Definition 102
- Firearm as 106

Immigration
- Leave to enter country 259
- Offences 260

Import and Export of drugs 54
Importation of animals 216
Incitement, to commit sexual offences outside UK 95
Indecent
- Communications 347
- Displays 80
- Photographs 79

Infanticide 48
Insulting words/conduct 276
Interpreters
- Deaf persons 365
- Foreign languages 365
- When required 365

Interviews
- 'Appropriate adult' 360
- At police station 361
- General 359
- Juveniles 360
- Mentally disordered persons 360
- Records 359
- Statements under caution 363
- Vulnerable suspects 361

Intimate samples 431
Intimate searches 424
- Code of practice 426

Intimidation, witnesses, etc 353
Jurors, intimidation 353
Keeping smuggled goods 168
Kerb-crawling 84
Knives
- Flick, offences 290
- Gravity, offences 290
- Marketing of 293
- Power to search 295
- Sale to persons under 16 292

Late night refreshment 157
Legal advice
- Delays 417
- Detained persons 412

Letter box, prohibited advertisements 346
Liability of company officers 35
License
- operating 120
- personal, gambling 124

Licensable activities 157
- Closure order 177
- Exemptions 157, 179
- Police power to enter premises 180
- Raffle not to constitute 179
- Temporary 163

Index

Tombola not to constitute 179
Unauthorised 167
Licences, gambling 119
Licensed premises, gaming machine permit 129
Licensed premises, failure to leave 168
Licensing qualification 165
Limits on detention 435
Liqueur confectionary
Sale to children 171
Litter, depositing 270
Livestock, dogs worrying 205
Lodging in outhouses, etc. 266
Lottery
children, invitation to participate in 148
complex, definition 135
definition 135
exempt 136
facilitating, offence 137
misusing profits 137
national, exemption 135
prize 135
promoting 136
promoting, offence 136
simple, definition 135
small society 137
Loudspeakers, noise 272
Making off without paying 38
Malicious communications 347
Mammals, wild, cruelty to 199
Manslaughter 48
Mental disorder 262
Mental health 262
Microchip, docking of dogs' tails 189
Military decorations, illegally wearing 258
Mobile telephone, re-programming 345
Mode of arrest 371
Motor salvage operators 265
Murder 48
Mutilation, animal, of 188
National lottery, exemption 135
Needs, animal, not met 193
Noise, loudspeakers 272
Non-commercial betting
definition 131
exemption 132
Non-commercial equal chance gaming 132
Non-commercial gaming
definition 131
exemption 132
Non-commercial prize gaming 132
profits misuse 132
Non-intimate samples 431
Notification of arrest 417
Delays 418
Nuclear weapons, terrorism 340
Obscene publications 81
Obstructing
Court officers 312
Police officer 268
Obtaining services dishonestly 32
Offensive communications 347
Offensive weapon
Definition 290
Sale or supply 291
Sale to persons under 16 292
Types 291
Operating licence
gambling 120
production 121
production of authorisation 149
Opium 60
Frequenting places used for 60
Possession of 60
Using 60
Organisations, illegal political 317
Paint aerosols, sale to children 52
Pawnbrokers, not to take firearms 112
Peaceful picketing 274
Pedlars 263
Permitted temporary activities 163
Personal licence 124
gambling 124
production 124
Pet travel scheme 217
Photographs
Detainees at police stations 406
Indecent 79
Suspects 423
Photographs, at police station, person not detained 406
Photographs, persons elsewhere than at police station 406
Photographing suspects 423
Picketing, peaceful 274
Plants, protection of 202
Poaching
Day 220
Deer 224

Index

Night 221
Night, while armed 222
Poisons, administration of, animals 190
Police
Assault on 46, 268
Impersonating 268
Obstructing 268
Wearing uniform, illegally 268
Police power to enter
Club premises 171
gambling premises 149
Licensed premises 171
Police powers
aerodromes 397
animals 197
Badgers 229
Birds 231
Children 256
Crossbows 297
Deer 224
Diseases of animals 213
Dogs 204
Firearms 115
Fish 238
Harassment 279
Immigration 260
Indecent Displays 80
Knives 294
Mental health 262
Poaching 220
Public meetings 315
Rabies 215
Raves 309
Seals 242
Squatters 311
Stop and search, knives/weapons 295
Terrorism 336
Trespass 301
Trespassory assemblies 305
Police protection, children 256
Political organisations, illegal 317
Pool betting 134
Possession of drugs 57
Intent to supply 58
Possession of opium 60
Possession with intent to damage 52
Post boxes, prohibited advertisements 346
Post, prohibited articles 346
Postal offences 346
Power to direct a person to leave 306
Powers of arrest
Constables 367
Cross border 370
Other persons 368
Repealed and preserved 369
Without warrant 369
Premises
entry to, welfare of animals 197
Landlord letting premises as brothel 87
licence, alcohol 159
licence, gambling 122
Premises used for drugs, closure order 62
Premises used for sex 87
Search to arrest 215
Tenant permitting use as brothel 87
Use of for drugs 59
Violent entry 310
Prevention of harassment in the home 279
Primers, buying or selling 114
Private betting
definition 130
exemption 131
Private gaming
definition 130
exemption 131
Prize competitions 133
Prize gaming 129
permit 129
Prizes, animal as 194
Production of drugs 54
Programme Service,
video recordings, animal fights 191
Prohibited ammunition, exemptions 105
Prohibited procedure,
animals, meaning 188
Prohibited weapons 103
Exemptions 104
Offences 103
Prohibition from entering a place 305
Proscribed organisations
Addressing meetings 321
Arranging meetings 321
List of 339
Membership of 321
Support for 321
Protected animal, meaning 186
Power to direct a person
to leave a place 306

Index

Prostitution, loitering or soliciting 83
Advertising 85
Protected site, trespassing on 305
Protection of plants 202
Protection of wild animals 200
Public collections 183
Public meetings 315
Police powers 315
Wearing uniform 316
Public place
Consuming alcohol in 182
Drunks in 181
Publications, harmful 82
Publications, obscene 81
Qualifying club, meaning 161
Questioning offenders 356
Rabies 215
Racial offences, threatening, abusive or insulting 300
Racially aggravated offences 299
Raffle not to be licensable activity 179
Raves 308
Police powers 309
Recordable offence 422
Refugees 260
Regulated entertainment 157
Regulated football matches 286
Relevant time 437
Removal of articles from places open to the public 19
Removal of disguises 296
Remote gambling, definition 118
Remote operating licence 121
Re-programming mobile telephone 345
Retaining a wrongful credit 33
Reviews of detention 436
Rewards, advertising 15
Riot 314
Road checks 395
Robbery 23
Sale of paint aerosols to children 52
Sale of animals, under 16s 194
Salvage operators, motor 265
Samples
Intimate 430
Non-intimate 431
Taken without consent 432
Scrap metal dealers 264
Seals, offences 242
Search
Articles used for crime 385
Articles with blade or point 385
Conduct of 374
Conduct of, code of practice, executing 375
Conduct of, code of practice principles 375
Detainee at police station 406
Drugs 61
Intimate 424
Intimate, drugs offences 424
Offensive weapon 385
Offensive weapons 396
On dwelling land 386
Premises 387
Prior action to, code of practice 378
Record of 380
Serious violence 396
Stolen articles 385
Summary of main powers 383
To ascertain identity 429
Type selector 384
Upon arrest 393
Warrant 394
Search, on aerodromes 397
Seizure
From premises, occupier under arrest 388
From premises, to prevent loss 389
Of vehicles 284
Seizure, additional powers 390
Legally privileged 392
List of powers 391
Notice of seizure 392
Return of seized property 392
Seizure of animals 197
Self-defined ethnic classification categories 382
Services, obtained dishonestly 32
Sexual offences
Abuse of position of trust 71
Administering substance to engage in sex 90
Animal, intercourse with 93
Assault by penetration 65
Assault by penetration, child under 13 68
Assault, sexual 66
Assault, sexual, child under 13 68
Care workers, sexual activity, mental disorder 77

Index

Child pornography 78
Child prostitution 78
Child sex offence, arranging or facilitating 70
Child sex offence, familial 73
Child sex offences 69
Child, paying for sexual services of 78
Committed outside UK 95
Consent, meaning 97
Consent, presumptions about 96
Corpse, sexual penetration of 94
Engaging in sexual activity with a child 69
Engaging in sexual activity without consent 67
Engaging in sexual activity, child under 13 68
Engaging in sexual activity, position of trust 71
Exploitation of prostitution 88
Exploitation, trafficking for sexual 89
Exposure 67
Familial child sex offences 73
Family relationships, meaning 74
Image, meaning 97
Intercourse with animal 97
Meeting child following sexual grooming 70
Mental disorder, meaning, sexual offences 97
Mentally disordered, sex by inducement 76
Mentally disordered, sex offence against 75
Mentally disordered, sex with care worker 77
Notification requirements, Schedule 3 offences 99
Notification requirements, sex offenders 98
Observation, meaning, sexual offences 97
Outside UK, incitement 95
Part of the body, meaning 97
Penetration, meaning 97
Pornography, child 78
Position of trust, abuse of 71
Position of trust, meaning 72
Preparatory offences, sexual 90
Presumptions about consent 96
Prostitution, causing, inciting or controlling 88
Prostitution, child 78
Prostitution, exploitation of 88
Public lavatory, sexual activity in 94
Rape 64
Rape, child under 13 68
Relative, sex with adult 91
Sex, administering substance to engage in 90
Sex by inducement, mentally disordered person 76
Sex in presence of a child 69
Sex in presence of child, position of trust 71
Sex in presence of person with mental disorder 75
Sex offence against person with mental disorder 75
Sex offence, familial 73
Sex Offenders, notification, offences involved 99
Sex Offenders, notification requirements 98
Sex with adult relative 91
Sexual act, causing child to watch 69
Sexual act, causing to watch, mentally disordered 75
Sexual act, causing to watch, position of trust 71
Sexual activity in public lavatory 94
Sexual activity with child 69
Sexual activity without consent 67
Sexual activity, child family member 73
Sexual activity, child under 13 68
Sexual activity, mental disorder 75
Sexual activity, mental disorder, care workers 77
Sexual activity, position of trust 71
Sexual assault 66
Sexual assault, child under 13 68
Sexual exploitation, trafficking for 89
Sexual grooming, meeting child following 70
Sexual, meaning 97
Sexual offence, committing offence to commit 90
Sexual offence, trespass with intent to commit 90
Sexual offences against child under 13 68
Sexual offences outside U.K. 94
Sexual offences, consent, presumptions about 96

Index

Sexual offences, interpretation 97
Sexual offences, preparatory 90
Sexual penetration of corpse 94
Sexual services of child, paying for 78
Touching, meaning, sexual offences 97
Trafficking for sexual exploitation 89
Trespass with intent to commit sexual offence 90
Vagina, meaning 97
Voyeurism 92

Shotguns
Ages 115
Certificate 109

Silence, adverse inferences from 357
Simple lottery, definition 135
Small society lottery 137
Smuggled goods, keeping 168
Soliciting a prostitute 84
Soliciting, for purpose of prostitution 83
Solicitors, conduct of 416

Sporting events
Alcohol 287
Control of alcohol 287
Designated 287
Designated, definition 287
Fireworks 288

Sports ground
Control of alcohol 287
Designated 287
Designated, definition 287

Squatters 311

Statements
Written by police 364
Written by suspect 363

Statements of other persons shown 441
Stolen goods, handling 39
Stop and search, on aerodromes 397
Street collections 184
Supply of articles for drug use 55
Supplying drugs 56
Suppression of documents 37
Table meal, meaning 173
Tail, dog's, docking of 189
Taking conveyance without authority 20
Tattoos, children 251
Taxi touts 351

Telecommunications
Equipment, fraudulent possession 344
Improper use 348
System, fraudulent use 344

Telephone calls
False 348
Offensive 348

Telephone, mobile, re-programming 345

Temporary
Event notice 163
Licensable activity 163
Police powers of entry 163

Temporary use of premises, gaming 143

Terrorism
Acts outside UK 326
Arrest without warrant 336
Attendance at place for 330
Code of Practice 'H' 445
Collection of information 325
Control orders 343
Convention offences 332
Co-operation with police 323
Cordoned areas 335
Definition 320
Directing organisations 325
Disclosure of information, duty 334
Disclosure of information, failure 335
Disclosure of information, investigations 335
Electronic services, service of notice 328
Encouragement of 327
Fund-raising for 322
Funding 323
Interpretation 320
Investigation, disclosure of information 335
Investigations 335
Money laundering 323
Noxious substances 341
Noxious substances, hoaxes involving 342
Nuclear facility, radioactive release 331
Nuclear facility, threats 331
Nuclear weapons 340
Offences 321
Overseas, inciting 326
Parking of vehicles 338
Police powers 336
Possessing money etc for 323
Possession of articles 325

Index

Preparation of acts 329
Proscribed organisations, addressing meetings 321
Proscribed organisations, arranging meetings 321
Proscribed organisations, list of 321
Proscribed organisations, membership of 321
Proscribed organisations, support for 321
Proscribed organisations, uniforms 322
Providing money etc for 322
Publications, dissemination of 328
Radioactive material, threats 331
Radioactive material/device, demanding 331
Radioactive material/device, making 330
Radioactive material/device, using 331
Receiving money etc for 322
Restrictions on parking 338
Search, persons 336
Search, premises 336
Stop and search, pedestrians 337
Stop and search, vehicles 337
Training for 329
Using money etc for 323
Weapons training 324

Theft
Appropriates 16
Belonging to another 18
Definition 15
Dishonestly 16
Intention to permanently deprive 18
Property 17

Threatening
Communications 347
Words/conduct 275

Threats
To damage 52

Ticket touts 289
Tobacco, sale to children 251
Tombola, not to constitute licensable activity 179
Touts, taxi 351
Trade disputes 273
Trains, control of alcohol 287

Travelling fairs
gaming 130
gaming machines 129

Trespassing
Aggravated 302
Designated site 306
Foreign missions 312
Offensive weapon 312
On land 301

Trespassory assemblies 304
Police powers 306

Trigger Offences, testing for drugs 433
Truancy 252
Ultrasound scans for drugs 428
Unauthorised licensable activities 167
Uniform, police, wearing illegally 268

Uniforms
Armed forces, illegally wearing 257
Proscribed organisations 322
Public order offences 316

Unnecessary suffering, animal 187
Vagrancy 266
Vehicle, power to stop, welfare of animals 198

Vehicles
Abandoning 271
Annoyance 284
Interference 21

Venison, sale of 227
Video recording, animal fights 191

Violence
Fear of, protection from 278
Fear or, provocation of 275

Violent disorder 314
Violent entry to premises 310
Virtual gaming 142
Vulnerable adult, causing death of 49
Warrant of further detention 439

Weapons
Biological 319
Chemical 318
Nuclear 340
Prohibited 103
Prohibited, offences 104
Training, terrorism 324

Welfare of animals 186

Wild animals
Dangerous 211
Protection of 200

Wild mammals, cruelty to 199
Witness intimidation 353
Wounding 44
With intent 45

Young person, definition 248
X-rays for drugs 428

Notes

Notes

Notes

Notes

Notes

Notes